Palgrave Studies in the Enlightenment, Romanticism and Cultures of Print

General Editors: **Professor Anne K. Mellor** and **Professor Clifford Siskin**

Editorial Board: **Isobel Armstrong**, Birkbeck; **John Bender**, Stanford; **Alan Bewell**, Toronto; **Peter de Bolla**, Cambridge; **Robert Miles**, Stirling; **Claudia L. Johnson**, Princeton; **Saree Makdisi**, UCLA; **Felicity Nussbaum**, UCLA; **Mary Poovey**, NYU; **Janet Todd**, Glasgow

Palgrave Studies in the Enlightenment, Romanticism and Cultures of Print will feature work that does not fit comfortably within established boundaries—whether between periods or between disciplines. Uniquely, it will combine efforts to engage the power and materiality of print with explorations of gender, race, and class. By attending as well to intersections of literature with the visual arts, medicine, law, and science, the series will enable a large-scale rethinking of the origins of modernity.

Titles include:

Scott Black
OF ESSAYS AND READING IN EARLY MODERN BRITAIN

Claire Brock
THE FEMINIZATION OF FAME, 1750–1830

Brycchan Carey
BRITISH ABOLITIONISM AND THE RHETORIC OF SENSIBILITY
Writing, sentiment, and slavery, 1760–1807

E. J. Clery
THE FEMINIZATION DEBATE IN 18TH-CENTURY ENGLAND
Literature, Commerce and Luxury

Adriana Craciun
BRITISH WOMEN WRITERS AND THE FRENCH REVOLUTION
Citizens of the World

Peter de Bolla, Nigel Leask and David Simpson *(editors)*
LAND, NATION AND CULTURE, 1740–1840
Thinking the Republic of Taste

Ina Ferris and Paul Keen *(editors)*
BOOKISH HISTORIES
Books, Literature, and Commercial Modernity, 1700–1900

Ian Haywood
BLOODY ROMANTICISM
Spectacular Violence and the Politics of Representation, 1776–1832

Anthony S. Jarrells
BRITAIN'S BLOODLESS REVOLUTIONS
1688 and the Romantic Reform of Literature

Michelle Levy
FAMILY AUTHORSHIP AND ROMANTIC PRINT CULTURE

Robert Miles
ROMANTIC MISFITS

Tom Mole
BYRON'S ROMANTIC CELEBRITY
Industrial Culture and the Hermeneutic of Intimacy

Nicola Parsons
READING GOSSIP IN EARLY EIGHTEENTH-CENTURY ENGLAND

Erik Simpson
LITERARY MINSTRELSY, 1770–1830
Minstrels and Improvisers in British, Irish and American Literature

Mary Waters
BRITISH WOMEN WRITERS AND THE PROFESSION OF LITERARY CRITICISM,
1789–1832

Esther Wohlgemut
ROMANTIC COSMOPOLITANISM

David Worrall
THE POLITICS OF ROMANTIC THEATRICALITY, 1787–1832
The Road to the Stage

Palgrave Studies in the Enlightenment, Romanticism and Cultures of Print
Series Standing Order ISBN 978-1-4039-3408-6   hardback   978-1-4039-3409-3
paperback
(*outside North America only*)

You can receive future titles in this series as they are published by placing a
standing order. Please contact your bookseller or, in case of difficulty, write to us
at the address below with your name and address, the title of the series and the
ISBN quoted above.

Customer Services Department, Macmillan Distribution Ltd, Houndmills,
Basingstoke, Hampshire RG21 6XS, England

Bookish Histories

Books, Literature, and Commercial Modernity, 1700–1900

Edited by

Ina Ferris and Paul Keen

First published 2009 by
PALGRAVE MACMILLAN

Palgrave Macmillan in the UK is an imprint of Macmillan Publishers
Limited, registered in England, company number 785998, of Houndmills,
Basingstoke, Hampshire RG21 6XS.

Palgrave Macmillan in the US is a division of St Martin's Press LLC,
175 Fifth Avenue, New York, NY 10010.

Palgrave Macmillan is the global academic imprint of the above companies
and has companies and representatives throughout the world.

Palgrave® and Macmillan® are registered trademarks in the United States,
the United Kingdom, Europe and other countries.

ISBN-13: 978-0-230-22231-1   hardback
ISBN-10: 0-230-22231-5   hardback

This book is printed on paper suitable for recycling and made from fully
managed and sustained forest sources. Logging, pulping and manufacturing
processes are expected to conform to the environmental regulations of
the country of origin.

A catalogue record for this book is available from the British Library.

A catalog record for this book is available from the Library of Congress.

10 9 8 7 6 5 4 3 2 1
18 17 16 15 14 13 12 11 10 09

Printed and bound in Great Britain by
CPI Antony Rowe, Chippenham and Eastbourne

Contents

Acknowledgements

This collection has a bookish history of its own. It began as a plan for a special session on Bibliomania at an American Society of Eighteenth-Century Studies conference in Montreal, which quickly became a double session as it attracted a growing number of people working on related topics. Almost every participant in this collection either gave a paper at that double session or was in the audience, but we finished the morning with a strong and widely shared sense that we were beginning a discussion rather than ending it. In the two years that followed we found different ways of continuing to share ideas and, inevitably, accumulated a growing list of debts. We are especially grateful to various people within our universities for funding different aspects of this process. At Carleton University, we would like to thank the Dean of the Faculty of Arts and Social Sciences, the Dean of Graduate Studies and Research, the VP (Research), and the Department of English; at the University of Ottawa we would like to acknowledge the support of the Faculty of Arts. We have also been fortunate in our anonymous press reader whose valuable suggestions greatly facilitated the development of this volume.

Our thanks to the University of Chicago Press for permission to reproduce material from Chapter 4 of Andrew Piper's *Dreaming in Books* (University of Chicago, 2009) and to the University of Minnesota Press for permission to use Leah Price's essay from *Repetition*, edited by Michael Moon (University of Minnesota Press, forthcoming).

Notes on Contributors

Barbara M. Benedict is the Charles A. Dana Professor of English Literature at Trinity College. She has written on eighteenth-century book history, popular culture, and literature, and is the author of *Framing Feeling: Sentiment and Style in English Prose Fiction, 1745–1800* (1994), *Making the Modern Reader: Cultural Mediation in Restoration and Eighteenth-Century Literary Anthologies* (1996), and *Curiosity: A Cultural History of Early Modern Inquiry* (2001). She has also edited *Eighteenth-Century English Erotica, 1700–1800*, vol. 4, *Wilkes and the Late Eighteenth Century* (2002), and, with Deidre LeFaye, Jane Austen's *Northanger Abbey* for Cambridge University Press (2006). She is working on the representation of the book in eighteenth-century literature and empiricism and literature.

Simon During is Professor of English at Johns Hopkins University. His books include *Foucault and Literature* (1993), *Patrick White* (1996) and *Modern Enchantments: the cultural power of secular magic* (2002). He is currently completing a manuscript entitled 'Culture's Interests: Literary Institutions in the Secular State'.

Ina Ferris is a Professor of English at the University of Ottawa. Her publications include a critical edition of Charlotte Smith's *The Old Manor House* for the Pickering and Chatto *Works of Charlotte Smith* (2006), a special issue on 'Romantic Libraries' for *Romantic Circles Praxis* (2004), *The Romantic National Tale and the Question of Ireland* (2002), and *The Achievement of Literary Authority: Gender, History and the Waverley Novels* (1991).

Paul Keen is Professor of English at Carleton University. He is the author of *The Crisis of Literature in the 1790s: Print Culture and the Public Sphere* (Cambridge, 1999) and editor of *The Radical Popular Press in Britain, 1817-1821* (Pickering and Chatto, 2003) and *Revolutions in Romantic Literature: An Anthology of Print Culture* (Broadview, 2004).

Thomas Keymer is a Chancellor Jackman Professor at the University of Toronto and a Supernumerary Fellow of St. Anne's College, Oxford. His books include *Sterne, the Moderns, and the Novel* (Oxford, 2002); *Pamela in the Marketplace: Literary Controversy and Print Culture in Eighteenth-Century Britain and Ireland* (with Peter Sabor; Cambridge, 2005); and the

Oxford World's Classics editions of *Robinson Crusoe* (2007) and *Rasselas* (2009). He is also an editor of *Review of English Studies*.

Jon Klancher teaches Romantic and Victorian literature, the sociology of culture, and the history of print at Carnegie Mellon University. He has written widely on Romantic and nineteenth-century British literary and cultural history and the history of reading. Author of *The Making of English Reading Audiences, 1790–1832* (1987), he is currently completing a book, 'Transfiguring "Arts & Sciences": Knowledge and Cultural Institutions in the Romantic Age'. He is also editor of the forthcoming *Concise Companion to the Romantic Age* from Wiley-Blackwell (2009).

Deidre Lynch is a Chancellor Jackman Professor at the University of Toronto, where she teaches in the Department of English and in the Collaborative Program in Book History and Print Culture. She is the author of *The Economy of Character: Novels, Market Culture, and the Business of Inner Meaning* (1998) and the editor, most recently, of a new Norton Critical Edition of Mary Wollstonecraft's *A Vindication of the Rights of Woman* (2008). Her essay in this volume is derived from her current book project, which has the working title 'At Home in English: A Cultural History of the Love of Literature'.

Michael Macovski teaches Textual Theory, English Literature, and Book History at Georgetown University. He has published two books, *Dialogue and Literature: Apostrophe, Auditors, and the Collapse of Romantic Discourse* and *Dialogue and Critical Discourse: Language, Culture, Critical Theory*, both from Oxford University Press. He is also the editor of *Jane Eyre: A Cultural Edition*, forthcoming from Longman, and has edited two special journal issues: 'Placing Romanticism: Sites, Borders, Forms', in *European Romantic Review* (with Sarah Zimmerman); and 'Romanticism and the Law', on the *Romantic Circles* website.

William R. McKelvy is Associate Professor of English at Washington University in Saint Louis. He is the author of *The English Cult of Literature: Devoted Readers, 1774–1880* (2007).

Andrew Piper is Assistant Professor in the Department of German Studies and an associate member in the Department of Art History and Communication Studies at McGill University. He is the author of *Dreaming in Books: The Making of the Bibliographic Imagination in the Romantic Age* (Chicago UP, 2009) and the article, 'Rethinking the Print

Object: Goethe and the Book of Everything', which appeared in the PMLA special issue devoted to 'The History of the Book and the Idea of Literature'. He is also the co-founder of the research group, *Interacting with Print: Cultural Practices of Intermediality, 1700–1830*, which is funded by the Fonds québécois de la recherche sur la société et la culture.

Leah Price is Professor of English at Harvard. Her books include *The Anthology and the Rise of the Novel* (2000) and *Literary Secretaries/Secretarial Culture* (co-ed. 2005); she has also co-edited a special issue of PMLA on *The History of the Book and the Idea of Literature* (2006) and written on old and new media for the *New York Times*, the *London Review of Books*, and the *Boston Globe*. Her chapter in this volume is excerpted from *Victorian Bibliophobia* (Princeton University Press, 2010).

Betty A. Schellenberg is Professor of English at Simon Fraser University. Her recent publications include *Reconsidering the Bluestockings*, co-edited with Nicole Pohl (2003) and *The Professionalization of Women Writers in Eighteenth-Century Britain* (2005). She is currently editing a volume of *The Cambridge Edition of the Correspondence of Samuel Richardson* and writing a book on mid-eighteenth-century literary cultures and media.

Introduction: Towards a Bookish Literary History

Ina Ferris and Paul Keen

'The invention of paper in the eleventh, and of printing in the fifteenth century, are as cheering to the lovers of humanity, as the sea-birds and sea-weeds, signs of approaching land, are to the wearied and despairing navigator.'[1] So wrote the *Retrospective Review* in 1820, as it launched its inaugural issue, its metaphoric flourish animating what had already become a familiar narrative of books and the printing press. At the same time – and more intriguingly – it also announced the emergence of a new field of study: a specialized form of scholarship rooted in the material book that we know today as book history. Europe's arrival on the shores of modern print culture, it turns out, was soon troubled by a crisis of overproduction, as the 'fertile and luxurious crop' of modern literature multiplied to such an extent that (in a kind of bibliographic sublime) literary output spiralled to levels not simply counterproductive but potentially catastrophic. What now threatened was an imminent 'inundation of paper and print'. Warming to the metaphor of inundation, the review informed its readers that 'various dykes or mud-banks have been established and supported, for the purpose of being interposed between the public and the threatened danger' (i). These 'dykes or mud-banks' proved to be the literary reviews, which 'had sprung up ... to stand in the gap in the hour of need', screening the reading public from a rising torrent of publications they could never possibly get through, and which they probably shouldn't want to, were it even possible to do so. For all its drama this is a conventional history of books, the kind often encountered in the period, governed by a tension between competing narratives of progress and corruption. But it was doubled by the *Retrospective*'s reference to a cultural phenomenon whose emergence (like that of the reviews themselves) was also rooted in this 'inundation of paper and print': a bibliographic focus on the physical characteristics of books. 'The knowledge of their external qualities, and the adventitious circumstances attending their formation or history', the review reported, 'has become a science – professors devote their lives to it, with an enthusiasm not unworthy of a higher calling – they have earned the name of *bibliomaniacs*' (vii). To the extent that these professors were involved in something that could be described as a science, it was to be welcomed in critical circles as a companionate activity, an intellectually superior alternative to the preoccupations of those other bibliomaniacs who prized books as objects of conspicuous consumption rather than critical erudition. At the same time, however, the review implied, the effort to reduce their age's textual inundation to some sort of coherence by zooming in on the material qualities of individual books had itself become so obsessive that it doubled rather than corrected the lack of perspective the new field of book history was intended to remedy. Into the critical space thus left open stepped literary history. The *Retrospective Review* was the first British journal devoted to what we now call literary history, and its positioning of itself in this way underlines an ongoing breach between book history and literary history the essays in this volume seek to bridge.

Two centuries later, confronted by conditions at once strikingly similar and very different, literary scholars encounter a robust book history that has come into its own in the academy even as it continues to sit uneasily within most literature departments. Robert Darnton's landmark 1982 essay, 'What is the History of Books?', charts a spontaneous process in which academics from a variety of backgrounds 'decided to constitute a field of their own and to invite in historians, literary scholars, sociologists, librarians, and anyone else who wanted to understand the book as a force in history'.[2] As in the early nineteenth century, this latest version of book history is once again steeped in a sense of cultural inundation. However, it now answers not only to a broad sense of information overload (which makes appealing the focus on concrete particularities of book production) but also to the vast expansion of the field itself. While Darnton's own essay has become something of a manifesto for scholars in the area, its primary motive was to bring order to what appeared to him already in 1982 as 'less like a field than a tropical rainforest'. Overwhelmed by 'interdisciplinarity run riot', Darnton complained that 'the explorer can hardly make his way across it. At every step he becomes entangled in a luxuriant undergrowth of journal articles and disoriented by the crisscrossing of disciplines' (110). Like the bibliomania evoked in the *Retrospective*, then, book history in Darnton signals an excess that threatens critical perspective, and he proposes a 'general model' of the communications circuit to organize chaotic particulars into a coherent view of 'the subject as a whole' (110).

The immense success of book history, however, continues to owe a great deal to a sweeping ambition that allows for a proliferation of methodologies and a heterogeneity of objects. When *Book History* began publication in 1998, for example, it defined its 'new kind of history' as 'the entire history of written communication: the creation, dissemination, and uses of script in any medium'. Having declared its intention to 'freely disregard disciplinary and professional boundaries', the journal opened its pages to 'academics and nonacademics, to scholars of history, literature, sociology, economics, art, education, the classics, communications, journalism, religion, and anthropology, as well as to publishing professionals, book collectors, and librarians'.[3] History of the Book now boasts endless international conferences, a major academic association, research awards and scholarships, highly successful university departments and doctoral programs, numerous job postings, and – a sure sign of academic arrival – a special issue of *PMLA* (Jan 2006). The expansiveness of this intellectual field has been reinforced by a corresponding sense that scholarship in this area matters because its subject has always mattered so much: the printed word 'as a force in history' to borrow Darnton's description of the shared interest defining the various approaches that converge in the field of Book History.[4] As a historical 'force', print has typically been understood in progressive terms, part of a compelling narrative of modernity that found landmark expression in Elizabeth Eisenstein's *The Printing Press as an Agent of Change: Communications and Cultural Transformations in Modern Europe* (1979). Even in more recent studies such as Adrian Johns's *The Nature of the Book: Print and Knowledge in the Making* (1998), which align themselves more fully with the enterprise of cultural history and challenge the technological determinism of Eisenstein's printing history, the question of the historical power of print remains the governing rubric of the inquiry. Moreover, reinforced by deeply rooted narratives about the link between a liberating Protestant reformation and the printing press, this perspective on print has directly shaped historical action not only in periods like the late eighteenth century when the printing press was routinely hailed as a bulwark against tyranny but well into our own time.

And all of this is true. But it is not all true, or at least it is not the whole story. The printed word has always been about much more and often much less than this tale would have it, invoked as often in terms of disease as enlightenment – 'archive fever' is only the most recent and fashionable instance of a well-established tradition – and rooted in a history of wayward private affect as much as emancipatory social effects. As the debate generated by Eisenstein's groundbreaking work has demonstrated, history unfolds in ways that are more complicated and generate more unintended consequences than progressivist narratives of the power of print can accommodate. All the same, our sense of ourselves and our modernity, as Christian Thorne has pointed out, remains bound up in this story, now become 'so familiar it nearly tells itself': 'Europe was once full of imbeciles; then came the printing press, and there were imbeciles no more; for with print came mass literacy, and with literacy came learning, and with learning – it is here that the story gets hazy – came democratic self-fulfillment in some guise or another'.[5] Jurgen Habermas's celebrated if much contested account of the bourgeois public sphere offers the most compelling recent theoretical formulation of this story. In defining the eighteenth-century public sphere as the sphere where 'private people, come together to form a public, readied themselves to compel public authority to legitimate itself before public opinion', he articulates what many of those in the period who involved themselves in debates over literacy, the public, and politics clearly believed to be the stakes in which they engaged.[6] On the eve of the French Revolution the *Analytical Review* gave expression to a widespread view, one not restricted to radicals and reformers, when it declared that 'Literature, by enlightening the understanding, and uniting the sentiments and views of men and nations, forms a concert of wills, and a concurrence of action too powerful for the armies of tyrants'.[7] In the aftermath of the Revolution, William Hazlitt may have appeared somewhat too sanguine in likening the spread of print to a battering ram, knocking down the castle door of the feudal lord whose power depended on his subjects' ignorance, but it was this kind of conviction that underlay the successful push for cheap print in the early 1830s.[8]

The problems with Habermas's model have been well-rehearsed by now: not only does its claim that the public sphere is open to all rational individuals committed to polite debate belie the extent to which the actual public sphere continued to exclude whole sectors of the population but the utopian zeal it encodes played an active role in nudging society's moral centre towards an idealized self-image of the middle class in ways that were crucial to this exclusionary process.[9] More to the point of the essays in our volume, the Habermasian public sphere flattens out the complex and intersecting dimensions of the literary field itself, as well as circumventing the 'untidy and disorderly world of eighteenth-century social practice'.[10] As Robert Jones has argued, the heroic tone adopted by advocates of the bourgeois public sphere (both then and since) evades the sorts of 'conflicts and anxieties' that its reliance on the private commercial activities of its participants would have entailed in the eighteenth century, not least because of the ways it hybridized (or just confused) inherited vocabularies of public and private authority.[11] Like most current approaches, the essays gathered in *Bookish Histories* do not align themselves uncritically with Habermas's emancipatory vision, but they remain alert to the way it draws on (and draws out) powerful elements of belief that exerted their own historical force in shaping key practices and discourses in the period.

They are equally alert to the new awareness of the 'presence' of books and printed matter which took increasing hold in the culture as the eighteenth century ran its course, especially after the explosion of publication following the House of Lords' landmark decision in Donaldson *vs* Becket repealing perpetual copyright in 1774.[12] The 1774 decision marked the final chapter in a series of lawsuits which turned on the question of whether copyright ought to be perpetual or for a fixed term. As publishing historians like William St Clair and James Raven have emphasized, the decision in favour of a fourteen-year term (to be renewed if the author was still living) led to a flood of new versions of older texts which could now be republished without any copyright costs, either as independent (often inexpensive) editions or as part of anthologies, a genre which enjoyed a related boom during these years. In the latter decades of the eighteenth century, the book industry grew rapidly, vastly expanding both the broader 'literate nation' and the narrower 'reading nation' in Great Britain. For the first time the printed word became widely available, incorporated into everyday life as it had not been before.[13] But if print now became entrenched in the culture, it was not yet fully assimilated. It remained visible as a medium, palpable; the physical book (its format, paper, type, etc.) became the subject of commentary in both public and private discourse, far beyond the specialized realm of bibliographers and other bibliomaniacs. Books were not the taken-for-granted objects they would soon become, so that in an important sense this historical moment, when Britain established itself as a book-centred culture, reverberates with our own when for very different reasons books can no longer be taken for granted either.

It has become a critical truism that the advent of digital technology has intensified awareness in intellectual circles of the complex interplay of commercial, technological, legal, and political factors that go into the making of any communications revolution, but for literary critics more specifically the defamiliarization of print technology has fostered a more self-conscious wrestling with the stubborn physical reality of books themselves. What this means, among other things, is that books have begun to appear more clearly within literary studies as what they always were: a historically specific phenomenon that owed its emergence and extraordinary success (as well as its problems) to varying and immensely complicated networks of particular circumstances in particular cultures. Where book historians have typically responded to the challenge of such historical complexity by advocating immersion in the empiricism of precise, technical particularities, turning away from 'theory' (as *Book History* recommended to the 'young professors' it targeted as its readers), literary critics have notoriously theorized away material particulars to posit abstract models of 'form' and 'text' allowing for the concrete 'readings' they themselves like to do. In their different ways both often forget what Roger Chartier identifies as 'the space between text and object, which is precisely the space in which meaning is constructed'.[14] To attend to this 'space' neither a focus on the material 'means' of cultural production nor a focus on its theoretical 'forms' is sufficient precisely because the space wherein meaning is constructed is so thoroughly mediated. Books signify in a variety of dimensions, from their traditional role as vehicles for the signifiers we call writing (a writing itself stratified into a hierarchy of genres) to their function as social signifiers in themselves (e.g. signs of status, gender, taste, etc.) to their overarching symbolic power as 'an expression of a cultural ideal' that, as Carla Hesse puts it, 'has had very little to do with the technology that has produced it'.[15]

The questions of cultural value operating in the space of books' meaning thus cannot be reduced to the material realities of publication and distribution; there is always more to the making and reading of books than attention to the printing shop or bookshop would attest. Even a naive reader like Jane Austen's Catherine Morland proves to have internalized much of the complexity of books' signification, explaining her assumption that Henry Tilney would not have read *The Mysteries of Udolpho* by simply saying, 'gentlemen read better books'.[16] At the same time, the material realities often passed over by literary scholars profoundly condition how books enter into the space of meaning. As D. F. Mackenzie demonstrated in his influential lectures on the 'new' bibliography, *Bibliography and the Sociology of Texts* (1986), typographical details are often central to identifying changes in the meaning of the same text in different contexts. More recently, Richard Sher's massive study of Enlightenment authors and their booksellers documents the care with which both parties decided on matters like publication formats and intervals of publication.[17] Moreover, typography itself will often carry a curious charge in certain historical situations, as evidenced in T. J. Mathias's outburst (amidst the endless stream of bitter political broadsides that fill his *Pursuits of Literature*) against 'the present rage of printing on fine, *creamy* wire-woven, *vellum*, hot-pressed paper': '*No new work whatsoever* should be published in *this* manner, or Literature will destroy itself'.[18] Mathias may have been extreme but he wasn't alone in the period in seeing typography as a bearer of cultural values. A 1794 letter to the *Gentleman's Magazine*, for instance, warns in similar terms that 'among the many luxuries of the present day, none appears to me more hostile to the general welfare of society than that which begins so extensively to prevail in the useful art of printing, and the other branches of the bookselling business. Science now seldom makes her appearance without the expensive foppery of gilding, lettering, and unnecessary engravings, hot-pressing, and an extent of margin as extravagant as a court-lady's train'.[19] This sort of visceral recoil from (as well as fascination with) typographical extravagance underscores Mackenzie's insistence that typography can never be encountered (or studied) in any unmediated way; processes of book production are inscribed within and shaped by cultural attitudes.

How, then, to begin to make sense of so diffuse and complex a phenomenon? At the core of the different approaches to the study of books is an increasingly strong commitment to relational analytic models (i.e. those allowing us to grasp formative links between matters like typography and cultural formation, authors and readers, authors and the market) rather than to the polarities of the more binary models that tended to pertain in the past. The most ambitious and sophisticated of these is Pierre Bourdieu's notion of the literary field, most fully articulated in his *The Field of Cultural Production* (1993). Bourdieu posits the literary field as a semi-autonomous realm of cultural production characterized by a densely mediated network of relations between producers (authors, editors, translators), consumers (buyers, borrowers, readers, collectors), and agents in the book trade (publishers, printers, distributors), all of whom operate in a highly structured but constantly shifting system. The relevance of Bourdieu's model for Book History specifically has been laid out by Peter McDonald, who argues for 'literary field' as a more fruitful analytic concept than Darnton's well-known 'communications circuit'. McDonald makes two main claims: first, Bourdieu's literary field, while relatively autonomous, is embedded within the larger cultural field with which it interacts (thereby restoring a political-historical context absent in Darnton's model); second, Bourdieu adds another crucial dimension when he incorporates the idea of symbolic production, where Darnton concentrates on the level of strictly material production.[20] Agents in Bourdieu are related not only horizontally in terms of their function in the material circuit of production but also vertically in terms of status and legitimacy; hence agents who may never have any direct contact nonetheless affect one another. For Bourdieu, what motivates the field as a whole is the struggle for cultural capital. As new entrants come into the field, they attempt to displace established figures and forms, and this means that notions of literary value are always under contention (therefore the system is in some sense open); at the same time, at the structural level, the field itself retains a formal identity with a set number of available positions (in this sense it is a closed system). The essays in this volume by no means follow in Bourdieu's footsteps – indeed they operate from a variety of critical assumptions and perspectives – but he provides a useful frame for the project in which all are engaged. The notion of the literary field offers a way of thinking about literary production as at once a materially embedded activity, caught up in a thick network of concrete material relations, and an intensely symbolic activity, engaged in the less easily defined pursuit of authority and legitimacy in a competitive artistic and professional (as well as commercial) arena.

If the contributors to *Bookish Histories* trace out these relations in very different ways, they converge in situating the enterprise of literary history at the intersection of book history, cultural history, and literary studies. The essays in the first section, 'Reconfiguring Literary History', set out the volume's central themes and questions. Reconsidering broad issues of and in literary history through a 'bookish' lens, they expand the conventional range of literary agents, genres, and sites by spotlighting overlooked regions of literary activity. In so doing, they allow us to rethink some of the objects of literary history – in particular the category of literary periods – by paying as much attention to what may not have 'taken' in a particular historical moment as to what eventually did 'take'. In this approach, our volume overlaps with other off-centred literary histories like the 'peripheral' readings of Romanticism that have followed in the wake of Katie Trumpener's groundbreaking *Bardic Nationalism: The Romantic Novel and the British Empire* (1997).[21] Its goal, however, is more self-reflexive: we seek to reflect both on literary history as a specific historical practice and, more broadly, on how the history to which literary history attends continues to shape the pressures and imperatives that define our own interpretive communities.

Jon Klancher's 'Wild Bibliography: The Rise and Fall of Book History in Nineteenth-Century Britain' sets the tone, recovering a forgotten moment in early book history to pose a question about today's book history. The essay takes its cue from the conjunction of two intertwined phenomena in the early nineteenth century: the emergence of a 'history of books' and the sudden fashion for collecting rare early modern editions, both of which were gathered under the rubric of 'bibliomania'. Both then quickly disappeared from the historical narrative. In the Romantic period, he argues, bibliography assumed a more theoretical shape, understanding itself precisely as a literary history and taking its place among other intellectual enterprises intent on re-forming and stabilizing the orders of knowledge in a modern commercial society. This new book history, however, remained shadowed by its irreverent cousin, the flamboyant book-collecting bibliomania, whose activities, by contrast, destabilized modern authorship and the modern book. Contaminated by such association, this early form of book history was quickly discredited and forgotten (Klancher's central example is the much ridiculed Thomas Frognall Dibdin), so that when bibliography returned to the intellectual scene later in the century, it reconstituted itself as a more severe 'science', erasing the historical experiments and ambitions that had defined its intervention in the struggle over the meaning of books in the Romantic period. Today's bibliography has recovered that lost historical dimension, transformed into the new book history, which (Klancher suggests) remains as much behind as ahead of its Romantic avatar.

The pressures of a burgeoning print market, which underpin Klancher's account of the encounter of learning, literature and commerce in the early nineteenth century, move more explicitly into the foreground in Paul Keen's '"Uncommon Animals": Making Virtue of Necessity in the Age of Authors'. Taking as his focus the category of the author, Keen traces the complex debate over authorship in the later eighteenth century generated by literature's new immersion in the workaday world of commercial print activity. He draws on Bourdieu's dynamics of the literary field to argue that the modern idea of authorship emerged not out of an agonistic struggle between patrician and commercial definitions but out of the 'friction' between competing definitions of literary professionalism within the commercial order. If the literary market (and writers themselves) promoted 'microcosmopolitan' forms of writing suited to a mobile commercial order in favouring the piecemeal and the quotidian, where did this leave the authority of authors themselves? One version of professionalism responded to this question by synthesizing gentry and bourgeois models to posit a public-spirited commercial humanism, but Keen focuses on a competing version adopted by writers like Samuel Johnson, who rejected commercial humanism's elevated rhetoric (sharply at odds with the realities of writers' actual lives and status) in favour of a transactional model of authorship grounded in its immersion within the distractions of modern life.

Turning to a key later moment in print's history – the advent of cheap print – William McKelvy (like Klancher) returns us to an obscured thread within nineteenth-century literary history in order to rethink the historical origins of our own literary-historical practices. '"This Enormous Contagion of Paper and Print": Making Literary History in the Age of Steam' brings into view a work that has a claim to be 'the first explicit consolidation of our dominant notion of literary history': Robert Chambers's now little-known *History of English Language and Literature* (1835). Concentrating on the intellectual and technological matrix of its genesis, McKelvy argues that the *History* evolved out of Chambers's experience with steam-press publication as writer/publisher of the enormously successful cheap print periodical, *Chambers's Edinburgh Journal*, which was targeted at the new readership brought into being by political and technological innovations after the Reform Bill. Equally central to his project, however, was the example of the fierce opponent of Reform, Sir Walter Scott (at once mentor and warning to Chambers), whose uncanny ability to fuse commercial initiatives, cultural nostalgia, and progressive thinking allowed Chambers to formulate 'a new historiography of literary tradition' rooted in consumption. A literary history reoriented in this way converged with the popularizing effects Chambers pursued more broadly throughout his long career as publisher to the 'people'. His *History* thus provides a particularly compelling instance of the kind of effort to consolidate new forms of cultural and professional legitimacy in the face of changing social, commercial, and technological relations that interests the contributors to *Bookish Histories*.

The essays collected in Part Two, 'Books in the Everyday', rethink some of the stories we have told about 'literature' and its uses by looking more closely at overlooked ramifications of the new familiarization of books and printed material in nineteenth-century culture. Deidre Lynch's wide-ranging 'Canons' Clockwork: Novels for Everyday Use' reconsiders the importance of re-reading – reading as a 'habit' – in order to challenge the centrality we have typically assigned to novelty in our literary histories, mounting an important argument that the novel's ascendancy in this period was bound up with the time-frame and pleasures of routine. Looking at how books became objects of 'everyday love' in the period, she moves into the critical foreground arguments for literature's everydayness in 'the age of Hunt', which accompanied and contested the age's more familiar arguments for literature's exceptionality (its sublimity). As books became personal companions, reading increasingly underwrote a reassuring ('unruffled') experience of time as iteration that redefined literature as a 'steadying influence', thereby aligning reading with the habit widely canvassed in medical writings as the key to health. Ina Ferris's 'Book-Love and the Remaking of Literary Culture in the Romantic Periodical' builds on Lynch's notion of books as objects of 'everyday love' to argue that book-love represents a dimension of bookishness not to be conflated with either the love of reading or the love of literature even as it may underpin both. Stressing the early nineteenth century's fascination with actual personal contact with books, her essay focuses on the articulation in bibliophilic writing of a concrete 'book-sense', something distinct from the more abstract 'book-consciousness' more commonly the subject of reader-based literary histories. Drawing in particular on Leigh Hunt, she shows how the Romantic familiar essayists blurred the distinctions between public and private experience to privilege the intimacy of book-love as the basis of an expanded literary public sphere rooted as much in the quasi-bodily pleasure of books as in the aesthetic pleasures of imagination.

The final two essays in this section pursue the matter of everyday interactions with print by resituating the history of nineteenth-century reading in terms of what Andrew Piper calls a 'logic of sharing'. 'The Art of Sharing: Reading the Romantic Miscellany' brings this overlooked logic to bear on the heterogeneous form of the miscellany. An old genre (arguably coincident with the emergence of the codex itself), the miscellany became newly important in the Romantic period with the emergence of popular literary formats such as the giftbook or annual, formats whose 'mixedness' scrambled distinctions of ownership, authorship, writing, print, and reading. For Piper the romantic miscellany functions as 'a particularly acute space' wherein the mutual relationship of sharing ('common right') and owning ('copyright') could be worked out in the first half of the nineteenth century. As he points out, while literary studies have had a lot to say in recent years about copyright, they know much less about common right, and his essay draws on American, English and German examples to argue that sharing was crucial not just to literary dissemination but to literary and technical innovation in ways that resonate for our own 'file-sharing' age. Locating the history of reading in a rather different site, Leah Price's 'Getting the Reading Out of It: Paper Recycling in Mayhew's London' pursues a history of unintended consequences as it considers how printed text becomes transformed into pages of paper for wrapping things in. Taking as her starting point Henry Mayhew's encyclopedic account of the uses to which paper is put in *London Labour and the London Poor* (1851) – part of his interest in the resale trade – she situates books within a world where virtually everything is reissued in one way or another. Recalling Ferris's emphasis on the leveling impulse behind Leigh Hunt's celebration of bookish interiority, Price argues that Mayhew locates a democratic ethos in the social connectivity implied by this economy of books' afterlives. Where many reformers sought to refashion the working classes in their own idealized middle-class self-image, Mayhew reminded his middle-class readers of their bodies even as he paid tribute to the cultural impulses of those members of the lower orders who remained intent on reading the pages they had bought to put to other uses, or, scrambling matters of priority and precedence even further, who chose the food they bought partially by the reading its wrapping would afford them.

Part Three, 'Remapping the Literary Field', reconsiders some of the literary 'maps' we have constructed to chart our way through the literary fields of the eighteenth and nineteenth centuries with their fierce and changing battles and rivalries. It opens with Barbara Benedict's survey of the status of collection in the eighteenth century in 'Reading Collections: The Literary Discourse of Eighteenth-Century Libraries'. As an ancient institution of book collection, the library was typically linked to learning and social order, drawing its legitimacy from its ancient (often religious) roots. Over the course of the eighteenth century, however, libraries became less elite and found themselves entangled in a consumer culture, taking on privatized new forms that sparked questions and commentary (who was collecting? for whom?). Benedict's essay traces how the different kinds of books and types of libraries assumed distinct and diverse kinds of status as the library turned into an 'ambiguous symbol' of social change, and collection itself came to represent 'the threat and liberation of unmonitored private knowledge'. Pursuing the question of collection in relation to theories of genre, Michael Macovski's 'Imagining Hegel: Bookish Forms and the Romantic Synopticon' looks at how the problem of a burgeoning archive led to the proliferation of various forms of compilation in the early nineteenth century (e.g. anthologies, compendiums, almanacs, keepsakes, and so on). Behind these forms of publication, he suggests, lay the model of the encyclopedia. Given the encyclopedia's strong historical and philosophical association with Diderot's celebrated Enlightenment project, the genre has generally been assimilated to Enlightenment's taxonomic logic, but Macovski finds a more telling philosophical analogue for its early nineteenth-century spinoffs in Hegel's post-Enlightenment model of a 'totalizing knowledge'. Paradoxically, however, as his examples indicate, the forms of compilation (such as the keepsake) produced by the market in the context of Hegel's centripetal model of knowledge tended to exert a centrifugal force, decentralizing and particularizing the knowledge they sought to centralize and universalize.

Turning to another dimension of our literary-historical mappings, Betty Schellenberg's '"The Society of Agreeable and Worthy Companions": Bookishness and Manuscript Culture after 1750' reconsiders the relationship between scribal and print cultures in the later eighteenth century. While the persistence of scribal culture in this period is now acknowledged (displacing earlier models of the history of technology as set of clearly demarcated and progressively linked epochs), its persistence is generally seen as anachronistic and aberrant. By contrast, Schellenberg argues that scribal culture persisted as a 'still-intact, though increasing finespun web', and her essay poses the question of the extent to which (and in what ways) the norms of manuscript circulation may have continued to remain in play in the culture. She considers three sites of ongoing coterie practice in the 1770s – the Shenstone network of manuscript circulation, the evolution of Lake District tour writing, and the discussion of coterie writing following the *Donaldson vs. Becket* decision in 1774 – to show that scribal culture not only retained vitality but forced the printed book to learn how to offer its consumers 'the insider access, approved taste, and elegance-by-association' of manuscript publications.

Our last two essays spotlight the relationship between commercial modernity and the category of the literary – the subject of much recent attention – to focus in on the period when both the book trade and literature began to assume their modern contours but were not yet fully in place. Their interest lies in how the instabilities, crossovers, and sheer irrationalities characteristic of markets in periods of transition brought 'legitimate' and 'illegitimate' cultural forms into an uncomfortably close proximity that cuts against some of our ready critical distinctions. Thomas Keymer's 'The Practice and Poetics of Curlism: Print, Obscenity, and the *Merryland* Pamphlets in the Career of Edmund Curll' approaches the career of the notorious bookseller (best known today for his feud with Alexander Pope) as a self-conscious exercise in the 'art of effrontery', one that aroused so much fierce controversy among contemporaries because the shameless Curll did not in fact operate in opposition to but in 'uneasy symbiosis' with the respectable branches of the trade. Keymer's point is not to rehabilitate Curll (not least because Curll himself typically embraced denunciation as an

ironic badge of honour) but to argue that restoring to view the soon
forgotten 'Curlism' opens up a fruitful perspective on questions about
commercial ethics and literary property central to the formation of the
eighteenth-century literary field; at the same time, it allows for a more
nuanced understanding of that field by underlining that the 'tenuously
regulated' world of eighteenth-century publishing was 'marked by differences of degree more than kind'. Simon During's 'Charlatanism and
Resentment in London's Mid-Eighteenth Century Literary Marketplace'
makes a similar case for the proximity rather than demarcation of reputable practices and their supposedly fraudulent antitheses. His focus is
the period of 1750–80, a 'moment of relative disorganization' (much
like that of Curll), which saw the emergence of two seemingly distinct
phenomena: a 'charlatanized literary scene' on the one hand (it is no
accident that the book trade and the patent medicine trade were often
conducted on the same premises) and, on the other, the emergence on
the part of writers of what would come to be called *ressentiment*. In this
period literary value, commercial value, and social value began to pull
apart, reflecting literature's own struggle to come to terms with a new
commercial order. The tensions so generated produced the resentment
we find in writers like Oliver Goldsmith and Christopher Smart whom
During finds representative of an oddly hollowed out yet vital literary
scene from which Romanticism and *ressentiment* would emerge. Thus
pointing back to the early nineteenth-century moment with which the
volume opened, this concluding essay underlines the way the volume
as a whole offers less a definitive story about than a series of ways into
literary history both as a subject (a 'then') and as a critical discipline (a
'now'). The essays collected here approach literary history in the mode
of reflection, probing but seeking to keep open the question posed by
Jon Klancher at the outset: 'What is the history of books, print and
reading *for*?'

Notes

1. *The Retrospective Review* 1 (London, 1820) vii.
2. Darnton, *The Kiss of Lamourette: Reflections in Cultural History* (New York and London: Norton, 1990), p. 108.
3. *Book History* 1 (1998) ix.
4. This has remained a central phrase in Darnton's ongoing accounts of Book History; see, most recently, 'Interview with Robert Darnton', *Eurozine*, http://www.eurozine.com/articles/2004-06-21-darnton-en.html (21 June 2006), and 'The Library in the New Age', *New York Review of Books* 55.10 (12 June 2008), 72.

5. Thorne, 'Thumbing Our Nose at the Public Sphere: Satire, the Market, and the Invention of Literature', *PMLA* 116 (May 2001) 531.

6. Habermas, *The Printing Press as an Agent of Change: Communications and Cultural Transformations in Modern Europe*, 2 vols. (Cambridge: Cambridge University Press, 1979), pp. 25–6.

7. *Analytical Review* 2 (1788) 324–5.

8. William Hazlitt, *The Complete Works of William Hazlitt*, ed. P. P. Howe. Vol. 17 (London: Dent, 1930–4), pp. 325–7.

9. For political critiques of Habermas' account, see the influential collection, *Habermas and the Public Sphere*, ed. and intro. Craig Calhoun (Cambridge, MA: MIT Press, 1992).

10. John Brewer, '"The Most Polite Age and the Most Vicious": Attitudes Towards Culture as a Commodity, 1660–1800', *The Consumption of Culture 1600–1800: Image, Object, Text*, ed. Ann Bermingham and John Brewer (London: Routledge, 1995), p. 345.

11. Jones, *Gender and the Formation of Taste in Eighteenth-Century Britain: The Analysis of Beauty* (Cambridge: Cambridge University Press, 1998).

12. On the 1774 decision, see William St Clair, *The Reading Nation in the Romantic Period* (Cambridge: Cambridge University Press, 2004), chap. 6.

13. St Clair, chap 1; James Raven, *The Business of Books: Booksellers and the English Book Trade 1450–1850* (New Haven and London: Yale University Press, 2007). Also see Heather Jackson, *Romantic Readers: The Evidence of the Marginalia* (New Haven and London: Yale University Press, 2005), chap. 1.

14. Chartier, *The Order of Books: Readers, Authors, and Libraries in Europe between the Fourteenth and Eighteenth Centuries*, trans. Lydia G. Cochrane (Cambridge: Polity Press, 1994), p. 10.

15. Hesse, 'Books in Time', *The Future of the Book*, ed. Geoffrey Nunberg (Belgium: Brepols, 1996), p. 23.

16. Austen, *Northanger Abbey*, ed. Claire Grogan (Peterborough, Ontario: Broadview Press, 2002), p. 120.

17. Mackenzie, *Bibliography and the Sociology of Texts* (Cambridge: Cambridge University Press, 1999); Richard B. Sher, *The Enlightenment & the Book: Scottish Authors & Their Publishers in Eighteenth-Century Britain, Ireland, & America* (Chicago and London: University of Chicago Press, 2006).

18. Thomas James Mathias, *The Pursuits of Literature: A Satirical Poem in Dialogue*, revised 2nd edn (London, 1797), p. 40.

19. *Gentleman's Magazine* 64 (1794) 47.

20. McDonald, 'Implicit Structures and Explicit Interactions: Pierre Bourdieu and the History of the Book', *The Library* 6th series, 19 (June 1997) 105–21.

21. See, for example, the notion of periods governing Murray Pittock's recent *Scottish and Irish Romanticism* (Oxford: Oxford University Press, 2008).

Part I: Reconfiguring Literary History

1
Wild Bibliography: The Rise and Fall of Book History in Nineteenth-Century Britain

Jon Klancher

This essay is about a new field of study that arose in Britain around 1800 which called itself the 'history of books'—a bibliographical field that was soon to become entwined with, if not indistinguishable from, the more notorious and volatile Bibliomania of the Romantic age. This book history was, of course, not the same history of print that we associate today with the names of Robert Darnton, Elizabeth Eisenstein, or Roger Chartier, which is of much more recent origin and which remains, to judge by a recent special issue of *PMLA*, not fully at ease with what its editors call 'the idea of literature' or literary history.[1] Advocates of a new book history in the early nineteenth century believed it *was* literary history, and they construed that history as a wide array of codex histories— those of writing, printing, typography, bookmaking and binding, the formation of private libraries and public archives, as well as categories of modern knowledges and imaginative works. From 1797, when the word *bibliographia* first appeared in a British encyclopedia of arts and sciences, to 1814, when Thomas Hartwell Horne published the two-volume *Introduction to the Study of Bibliography*, such efforts amounted to a then-unprecedented effort to reveal to British readers what Jerome McGann, with reference to the digital, has called the 'bibliographical codes' of the printed word.[2] Thomas Frognall Dibdin, the bibliographical writer who was also becoming the major publicist of the Bibliomania, was so confident of this kind of history-writing that he told his readers, 'The History of Books *is* the history of human knowledge.'[3] Despite their familiar sound now, those were new words for British readers to contemplate in the first decade of the nineteenth century.

Yet this emerging field of material and intellectual knowledge was hotly contested almost as soon as it began. Dibdin would have to reassure his readers that there was nothing in the new field of bibliography

that would 'offend the grave, disgust the wise, or shock the good.'[4]
There were, in fact, some bibliographical shockers in store for those who
picked up the latest news about the new attention to books as material
forms, and there was enough offense or disgust—along with more calculated efforts to diminish its impact—to eventually ruin Dibdin's own
reputation by the mid-1820s, and to discredit the book-history itself by
the end of the nineteenth century. Recollection of this early episode had
so largely disappeared from literary and cultural history by the 1950s
that today's historiography of print, books, and reading would essentially have to be built all over again.

I want to begin understanding what was at stake in the simultaneous rise of bibliohistory and Bibliomania in Britain by raising two sorts
of questions. First, why would an explosion of interest in antiquarian,
early-modern printed books create such a violent commotion for those
living in a modernizing print culture around 1800 that was becoming—
to adopt the terms used by Adrian Johns in his debate with Elizabeth
Eisenstein—increasingly stabilized, credible to its public, and trusted as
the essential medium of the modern discourses of knowledge?[5] I will
want to keep in mind in what follows that around 1800, at least five key
features of the modern book's growing stability or 'fixity' had recently
come into place: the principle of copyright or intellectual property;
the growing authority and professionalizing of authorship; the rise of
a lucrative book-trade industry in anthologies and reprints that owed
its existence to the 1774 copyright decision; the power of reviewing
journals; and the modernizing of the printed page. By these measures,
we would expect that the stability or fixity being gradually achieved by
print around 1800 should have been making the bibliographical codes
of the book *less* visible then, not more so.

That the opposite happened—the 'wild bibliography' of the Romantic
age, as I will call it—needs explaining. British attempts to come to
grips with the nature, history, and materiality of the book in the early
nineteenth century have been long obscured in literary history by early
bibliography's garish twin, the Bibliomania. To pursue some answers
to these questions will mean to take the Bibliomaniacs more seriously
than usual as the Romantic period's most aggressive and unwished-for
specialists in the instability of the modern book.[6] Thus another, more
sociological kind of question needs asking: to whom, exactly, did the
'biblio' in the broadest sense become a 'mania' in the first decades
of the nineteenth century? Whose interests were most at stake in the
modern history of print, not only commercially but institutionally?
Whose cultural visions were being advanced, and whose at risk? And

what would such interests or visions have to do with the state of book history and textual controversies now?

Civilizing, or bibliography and the 'Arts & Sciences'

Few would doubt that the practices of bibliography have been somehow critical to establishing the modern domain and authority of the category 'Arts & Sciences'—but just *how* and *when* is less easy to say. Eighteenth-century encyclopedias using the phrase 'Arts & Sciences' did not always agree about what kind of knowledge or practice belonged to what, as Richard Yeo's work on the classification of early-modern knowledges has persuasively shown. Long before 1800, Europe's antiquarian book collectors had been making an incalculable impact on the long-term formation of the very archives on which we now so heavily depend to reconstruct and grasp what we call 'modernity' itself. Between 1600 and 1800, it has been said, 'the private collector was supporting scholarship at its very foundations.'[7]

The earliest bibliographies on the Continent had been faltering, discontinuous efforts to account for these private collections. But as a first approach to the public controversies about bibliography and the Bibliomania in early nineteenth-century Britain, we should see what it meant for an enormous number of long-sequestered early-modern printed books, confined since the fifteenth, sixteenth, and seventeenth centuries to private libraries, to suddenly go *public* when the French Revolution confiscated the nation's aristocratic and clerical estates. An estimated 12 million volumes of early-modern print—confined since the fifteenth, sixteenth, and seventeenth centuries to private libraries— cascaded into a public realm hardly prepared to receive them. Throughout the 1790s, the new republican state faced this deluge of print by insti- tuting, all across Paris, government warehouses to domicile the books and courses of public instruction to teach rudimentary and unfamiliar bibliographical methods. Librarians were rapidly professionalized, men of letters were expected to catch up on their knowledge of the material history of printing, and what before had been the specialized province and knowledge of only the keenest booksellers or collectors was being reshaped as a subject any educated print citizen could be expected to know at least something about. By 1802, the French bibliographer Gustave Peignot coined an ambitious word, *bibliologie*, to embrace the scope of this project. For him *bibliologie* meant not merely the listing and classifying of books but also what he called 'the *theory* of bibliogra- phy, including the totality of human knowledge.'[8]

As Peignot's then-unfamiliar expression 'theory of bibliography' may suggest, however, a key emphasis on words like *study, philosophy, theory,* or *science* would differentiate the newer bibliographical attention from the older book catalog or bibliographical compilations going back to Gabriel Naude's *Bibliographica Politica* in 1633. This was to be a second-order level of observing the older first-order practices of bibliographic listing, classifying, or describing. As British readers began hearing much more, in their very different and counterrevolutionary context of 1800, about title pages, editions, publication dates, or lurid tales of violent Bibliomaniacal collecting passions in weekly or monthly magazines,[9] they were also being encouraged to *study* the bibliographical realm as a mode of public and, despite the old age of the books, of *modern* knowledge. If they opened one of the earliest British bibliographical research studies, such as Adam Clarke's 8-part *Bibliographical Dictionary* (1802–6), they would discover a wide-ranging, cosmopolitan account of over 25,000 books in a reference work of global reach—citing Arabic, Persian, Armenian, and Syrian publications as well as those of European nations and even China.[10] And if they reached volumes 7 and 8 of that sprawling work, readers would find more—theories and mappings of modern knowledge that Clarke had mostly translated from French works, but that were decidedly of a bibliographical rather than an encyclopedic type. Here there was no single Tree of Knowledge, as in the encyclopedic projects from Chambers to Diderot, but a forest of 'grand trunks' (knowledge as a stand of Sequoias) that were irreducibly multiple and, in their tangled branchings, strikingly complex. Clarke compared four of these 'systems' in 1806, finally preferring the one elaborated in the later eighteenth century by Guillaume de Bure, which largely owed itself, not to Enlightenment encyclopedism, but to the Jesuit-trained Jean Marnier, a scholar, bookseller, and library-maker of the mid-seventeenth century. As Clarke updated Marnier's and De Bure's schema, 'typography' moved from a mechanical art to one of the 'liberal arts,' while 'literary and bibliographical history' now became a prominent category of historiography and included branches called the 'history of the sciences' and the 'history of arts' in its wake.[11] My point—leaving many fascinating details out of Clarke's rendering of these earlier bibliographical systems—is that the new bibliographical book history in Britain was proposing a decidedly theoretical turn on the older descriptive or enumerative bibliographies, and not one predictable from the earlier Enlightenment dictionaries of the arts and sciences.

Around 1800 in Britain there was a fundamentally new metropolitan and intellectual framework to welcome such ways of rethinking the orders of knowledge. It was in the midst of what science historians have called England's 'second scientific revolution' of the early nineteenth century that the field of bibliography found itself increasingly in demand—for instance, at the dazzlingly successful scientific, literary, and fine-arts lecturing institutions that spread through London from the Royal Institution to the Surrey, the Russell, the London, the British and other such institutions, all established between 1800 and 1810. Although mainly known to students of Romanticism for the way they launched the scientific careers of Davy or Faraday or the literary lectures of Coleridge and Hazlitt, historians of science and of the fine arts have been more acutely aware that such institutions may have profoundly transformed the physiognomy of British 'arts and sciences' in the early nineteenth century by reshaping the public conditions for the making of emerging fields of both scientific and aesthetic practices.[12]

A key part of this project was to build commanding libraries and thereby better to establish the legitimacy of the sciences' claim to the legacy of *all* modern knowledge since the fifteenth-century printing revolution. This effort had been made before: since the 1660s, the Royal Society had repeatedly tried and largely failed to build an internationally-recognized library to demonstrate England's scientific leadership by showing natural philosophy's place in the entire printed archive of modernity. This need was to be better answered by the founding collections of the British Museum in 1753; but as its critics were still complaining nearly a century later, the British Library remained chaotic, a jumble of book and natural-history collections jostling for space, nowhere near as clearly differentiated and thereby soundly defined as in the great Continental libraries and museums, as Charles Lyell was still complaining in his *Quarterly Review* essays for 1826.[13]

For the Royal Institution a significant print library would materialize in 1804 at the death of Thomas Astle, author of the influential *Origin and Progress of Writing* (1784), whose 30,000-volume library would offer the Royal Institution a firm archival grounding in print culture assembled by a working historian of writing and publishing—and thus impressively representative of the range of modern knowledges that had been committed to the form of the book. Though its number of 'scientific' books was not noticeably larger than the categories of history, classics, moral philosophy, or fine arts, the library's catalog depicts the newly reshaped category of bibliography standing prominently among the major forms of emerging knowledge.[14]

These public scientific and literary institutions made a special point of hiring the new bibliographical writers. Adam Clarke and William

Beloe (author of *Anecdotes of Literature and Scarce Books*) were made chief librarians at the Surrey and Russell Institutions. The cutting-edge Royal Institution hired Thomas Frognall Dibdin, not as its archivist but as its chief lecturer on the topics of 'The Art of Printing' and then the more ambitious 28-lecture series called 'History of English Literature.' Set in London's most fashion-conscious venue of higher learning alongside star performers like Davy and Sydney Smith, the Dibdin lectures aimed to link the early-modern nation's production of books and the impressive powers of the new London scientific world now reaching out to public acclaim. Nevertheless, his lectures had to be strange. To judge by what little survives of them, these antiquarian public performances must have been the most non-narrative talks about literary history ever given. With little attention to authors, periods, or phases of national development, Dibdin focused his roughly 500 listeners every week on a lengthy chronology of rare or unique editions, publication-dates, hot-blooded book auctions, or reasons why they should not fear the book collector's mania for the 'black-letter.'[15] Just before beginning his own lectures at the Royal Institution in early 1808, Samuel Coleridge attended the last of Dibdin's. No two versions of English literary history could have been less alike. Coleridge would fashion his own lectures, sometimes reportedly with sublime effect, on the power and originality of the poets who gave English literature the voice of a dawning national spirit. There could have been little feeling of transport in Dibdin's antiquarian literary history, which depicted modern authors as indentured to previous books and writers, collectors as the shapers of a national literary heritage, and English books as rarities in the vast universe of time, as densely material as planets in a Copernican sky.

Hence did the arrival of bibliographical self-consciousness on British shores contribute its own share to a burgeoning scientific print culture, and—considering the sciences' own powers to redefine the scope of the arts in these decades—to a wider transformation of how the 'arts & sciences' in modernity were to be grasped as well. The unlikely courtship of the modernizing sciences with antiquarian bibliohistory was to prove volatile in the long run, but in the short term, immensely productive. Besides lecturing and teaching, the new scientific and arts institutions generated their own formats of print to herald the changes underway. To link the scientifically-focused Royal Institution with the British Institution for the Promotion of the Fine Arts, for a key instance, Dibdin and his patron Thomas Bernard launched the journal *The Director* in 1807, where Dibdin made his first and possibly most ambitious case for the new field of bibliographical history. Running a brief six months from January to July, this weekly journal was also probably the first in England to begin articulating the new shape of the 'Arts & Sciences' as the institution-builders and reformers were remaking it.[16] Dibdin's weekly articles titled 'Bibliographiana' made his arguments for bibliography's promise while pushing against the more extreme practices of the British antiquarian book collectors, urging them to transform their private pursuit of book wealth into a national public good—and thus drafting much of what would appear in 1809 as the first and briefest edition of *The Bibliomania; or Book-Madness*. That first version of his argument was straightforward, even earnest, by contrast to the fanciful, baroque dialogues among aristocratic collectors featured in the enlarged 1811 rewriting of the book (with the subtitle 'A Bibliographical Romance') that has since bewildered, amused, or irritated countless readers in five different editions through 1903.

Later on, after Dibdin had became famous, notorious, and then dead broke from his involvement in the Bibliomania controversy, he would credit this moment in 1807 for germinating a career that would turn out to be as contradictory a vocation as any in the Romantic age: the bibliographical author. The disappearance of collector culture from twentieth-century bibliography has obscured the tensions in Dibdin's Bibliomania writings between the collector's private acquisitive obsessions and the effort to make book-history a pivotal field among the 'Arts & Sciences.' 'It is much to be wished,' he wrote in the 1811 edition of *The Bibliomania* that is usually cited to portray his fealty to the aristocratic collector, that

> whatever may be the whims of desperate book-collectors ... we had a more clear and satisfactory account of the rise and progress of the arts and sciences ... Over what a dark and troublesome ocean must we sail, before we get even a glimpse at the progressive improvement of our ancestors in civilized life. Oh, that some judicious and faithful reporter had lived three hundred and odd years ago!—we might then have had a more satisfactory account of the *origin of printing with metal types* (emphasis in original).[17]

This is a rather different Dibdin than the public figure splashed with glitter from the gaudy Roxburghe sale of 1812. It helps explain the persistence of arguments for book history amid the more garish episodes of the 'romances' in peculiar literary inventions like the *Bibliographical Decameron* of 1817, and why he could think his bibliographical book history was on the way to becoming a pivotal field of study within the broader restructuring of scientific, literary, and fine-arts knowledges being accomplished by these new cultural institutions.[18]

Dibdin's other serious project from 1807 to 1810 was re-editing the only undisputed classic of British bibliographical scrutiny before this time, Joseph Ames's four-volume *Typographical Antiquities* (first published in 1749). It was with regard to this large undertaking that Dibdin would claim in *The Director* that

> Typography has given keys to science; and by pointing out where these keys are lodged, we shall be enabled to unlock those treasures of genius and instruction, which for ages have been accumulating, and of which a considerable part has yet escaped the researches of man.[19]

As Adam Clarke had pointed out in 1806, the history and intelligibility of typography were still 'amazingly obscure.'[20] Dibdin's high-flown promise that it would offer 'keys to science' may have signaled an effort to put his own bookish activity into roughly the same discursive and experimental space as Humphry Davy's chemical and electrical breakthroughs at the Royal Institution. But he was not alone in using the term *typography* in a strangely exalted sense around 1800. Several years earlier, Coleridge had used it in an analogous way while writing to urge his publisher, Joseph Cottle, to think more innovatively about the design, format, and typeface of their new and forthcoming book, *Lyrical Ballads*. Finding it difficult to persuade Cottle to adopt a very black ink, a streamlined title page, or expensively wide margins, Coleridge remarked, 'I meant to have written you an Essay on the Metaphysics of Typography.'[21] Cottle must have been impressed enough at Coleridge's threat to let the authors have their way, as he largely did, until his mysterious decision to sell off the book's copyright to another publisher just before the book's public appearance in September 1798. As to what Coleridge's never-written essay on what a typographical metaphysics might have looked like, we can't tell, and the problem partly lies in the way we today define that term. A recent, credible study on typography and interpretation defines it, as almost everyone now does, as 'the selection and arrangement of type, and other visual elements on a page.'[22] Yet to the late eighteenth and early nineteenth century, it entailed significantly more—beyond the visual look of the page, 'typography' extended to the physical form of the book, the history of printing, the accrediting of its invention, its development and dispersion. If type*faces* had some privileged place among those bibliographical codes and histories, it had partly to do with a sensitive reception of printed words and visible letters that modern readers, according to the antiquarian bibliographers, were already beginning to lose.

Barbarism, or the bibliographical shockers

Thus far, I have been pointing to how the various proponents of book history in Britain shortly after 1800 hoped their work would become a new force for the stabilization of British print culture—and the domain of 'arts and sciences' it appeared to support—by providing it with a history and a method of organized study. Instead it provoked a range of controversies that would eventually bring the field into discredit.

To begin with the more bookish side of these struggles over the nature of the book, I turn to the well-nigh gothic, visually provocative, and biblioclastic practices of rare-book collectors that both supported and threatened the project of gaining modern knowledge by way of bibliographical book history.

According to Thomas Dibdin, the 'violent desire for the black-letter' elicited more aggression and expense than any other bibliographical feature of the Bibliomania.[23] Black-letter texts were not only the incunables that mimicked the manuscript book in the last half of the fifteenth century; they had also appeared in popular street literature, the black-letter ballads, and of course the 1611 King James Bible. In the King James printed page, the black-letter spoke the sacred writ while the Roman typeface of commentaries, cross-referencing, and chapter summaries designated human invention.[24] By 1800 use of this typeface in Britain dwindled largely to decorative status in commercial printing. But the bibliomaniacs were now promoting the hyperexpensive blackletter books and ballads as the *ne plus ultra* of aristocratic print possession. Tory classicists like Thomas James Mathias professed to be repelled by the ugly, repulsive, broken-faced type that now brought back to the public eye Britain's most plebeian media of reading (the typeface of balladry and bawdy). Black-letter mania would confuse what the mainstream commercial print world had been increasingly successful at sorting out, as if the pedants and the peasants, monks and pagans, the haunted castle and the popish plot, all bubbled up at once on the printed page, now in quantities and at levels of prestige that seemed to mock the achieved hierarchies of the modernized page.

There seemed to be a special shudder when speaking of the 'black-letter mania' became talk of 'black-letter *reading*.' That phrase referred not only to the sheer difficulty of making legible the crabbed letters of this now alien family of types, but more controversially to a kind of literacy and a practice of interpretation, to what Dibdin called reading deeply into the 'slender and subtle materials of others, on which later poets and writers have built up a precarious reputation.'[25] Put simply, black-letter-reading plunged the reputedly original modern author back into the dense thicket of print and production from which he had begun. In this proto-historicist mode, John Ferriar's *Illustrations of Sterne* (1798) and Francis Douce's *Illustrations of Shakespeare* (1807) took pains to embed the works for which the most radically original claims of authorship were currently being made in their textual materials and sources. Egerton Brydges, though sometimes professing 'disgust' at the new bibliographical obsessions, himself became a vigorous advocate of a black-letter reading that gives us 'a new delight in the contrast with modern modes of communicating our thoughts' and in which 'forms of phrase which have lost all force from their triteness are relieved by new combinations, and the operations of the mind seem to derive an infusion of vigour from the new light in which they are clothed.' Pulling aside the familiar veil of the modern printed page, Brydges adds, the blackletter also affords us an unexpected way to converse with the dead, 'opening the grave, and bidding the dead to speak' by 'creeping back to converse with our ancestors, in their own idiom.'[26] I would accentuate that last phrase. Defamiliarizing the modern book by way of historicizing its idioms of production, practices, and provenance, Brydges' 'black-letter reading' perplexed the choice between old and new media that the contemporary print industry was anxious to assert. Thus it would be tempting to argue that in its black-letter mode, the early nineteenth century's wild bibliography could stimulate some of the most vigorously 'close' readings to be seen anywhere in the age.

The other outlandish Bibliomaniac practice was related to the black-letter mania in one key way: it combined collecting with reconstruction, this time not in the mode of historical black-letter-reading, but in the workshop of creative destruction that was the collector's own private library. This longest-lasting of all Bibliomaniacal outrages against the book—well into the twentieth century, in fact—was a practice of biblioclasty, when collectors tore old books down to their foundations in order to produce a single, one-of-a-kind, massively larger and often expensively recomposed 'extra-illustrated' book of grandiose proportions.[27] Most often this Grangerizing occurred at the relatively polite scale of adding tens or hundreds of engravings to the original book. But the more extreme cases appeared in the nineteenth century to be dismantling the codex form itself—hopelessly damaging a great many valuable antiquarian books along the way—when collectors performed extraordinary acts of authorship in their own right. What resulted were effectively multi-authored, multimedia concoctions, as when a 3-volume folio of Lord Clarendon's *History of the Rebellion*, the most authoritative account of the English Revolution, could be transformed by extra-illustration into 61 volumes of elephant folio. The new production cost some 10,000 pounds to produce and had uploaded some 19,000 engravings, portraits, or author heads. Posing as a traveler to London, Robert Southey commented in 1807 that 'you rarely or never meet an old book here with the author's head in it; all are mutilated by the collectors.'[28] The ritual beheading of authors by collectors may have belonged to one of the stranger cults of authorship—no collector snipped off the heads of authors in less valued books without reinstalling them in large numbers to adorn the new one. The migration of authors' heads from codex to codex—like some great guillotine in the library, rolling heads from one pile of old books only to be reanimated in some fantastic new one—also tore loose perhaps the most fundamental mooring of the nineteenth century book, the principle of authorship itself.

It was Dibdin's *Bibliomania* that first warned in 1809 against the biblioclasts' apparent disregard for any and all orders of knowledge that could be constructed out of a study of old books by recklessly chewing or cutting them up in the manic collector's form of authorship in the private library. We need again to distinguish between the bibliographical project and the instructively, if also destructively different practices of the Bibliomania in order to see their intimacy, and to understand why Dibdin's career was poised so intriguingly and (to his cost) so unstably across the divide between them. Take it one way, and we have new orders of book-knowledge which carve out histories and futures for the humanities that situate themselves between the 'arts & sciences'; take it another way, and we have the cut-ups of the crazed bibliophiles, who tell a truth unintelligible to the same orders of emerging knowledge.

John Hill Burton, a polite bibliophile unusually sensitive to these possibilities, would call extreme extra-illustrators the 'Ishmaelites of collectors' whose bloody work eats away at the codex foundations of civilized history.[29] No version of this practice might impress students of the Romantic period more than the outlandish 5-volume Grangerized version of Thomas Mathias's *The Pursuits of Literature* held at the Houghton Library. Page after page of this vitriolic work are here faced with stunningly detailed engraved portraits of his victims—in one chapter, photograph-intensity portraits of Godwin, Paine, Horne Tooke,

Mary Robinson, Inchbald, Hannah More, Joanna Baillie, Wollstonecraft and hundreds of less known cultural producers who had faced the scorpion's tail of Mathias's discursive rage. If this collector-producer ('W. B.' from Bath) had meant to celebrate Mathias's famous work this way, it's hard to read today without the opposite effect—the startling detail and clarity of their engraved expressions staring back, as if in embodied form, to reply to the shrill assassin of their public figures. It also was a perhaps unintentionally brilliant means of refuting Mathias's tireless prosecution of anyone who was putting undue emphasis on the material construction of the modern book.

At a time when the overall stabilization of the printed book had reached its definitive plateau in the century of the steam press and the stereotype plate, the extreme extra-illustrators were running the history of print in reverse. Rather than thousands or millions of identical printed copies issuing from a single plate of type, they ran the tape backward by disrupting many books to fashion one scarcely plausible, unsellable, unportable, certainly unduplicable, but unfailingly spectacular printed book. And they might have met their Ishmaelite deaths by the early twentieth century had not a significant new context given them further power to disturb. Even while deploring their literary mayhem, Holbrook Jackson, writing in 1930, could appreciate what to make of these bibliographical shockers in the age of visual mass culture:

> The extra-illustrator viewed the printed word solely as the raw material for his graphic interpretation ... In this way madness lies, not alone in hectic research and <u>wild</u> pursuit of materials, but in the character of the passion which seeks to substitute pictures for thoughts and the written word, in itself a notable relapse into barbarism ... as they who promote picture-theatres and picture-papers well know.[30]

Threats to civilization? This is a rather different role for the nineteenth-century Bibliomaniacs than their better-known reputation as gluttonous aristocrats hoarding costly leather usually suggests. We might say that black-letter-readers and manically-productive extra-illustrators reached alternately far behind and far ahead of their own modernizing moment, gleefully exposing the contingent makeup and built-in hierarchies constituting the modern codex form. The New Bibliography would have to sever all ties between the modern 'science of bibliography' and the collector culture that had long produced both the archives themselves and the extreme detours from modernity's making of the book as its most stable and authoritative medium of knowledge.

Wild bibliography and the 'Religion of the Book'

There was no popular opposition to the bibliographer's work, to my knowledge, nor did William Cobbett take a Rural Ride through the antiquarian library. On the contrary, the radical publisher William Hone joined the bibliographical defense of 'black-letter reading' in 1823 with his book *Ancient Mysteries Described; especially the English Miracle Plays*. Like Hone's *Mysteries*, black-letter readers turned their intensive attention not to the old Quarrel between Ancients and Moderns, but rather, in an often emotional way, to the *early* modern and its still-obscure relation to the appearances of modernity at the start of the nineteenth century. This is why it would be inadequate to identify the wild bibliography of the Romantic age, as Philip Connell does, with an aristocratic or Burkean conservatism alone.[31] The new struggle over books was more often occurring intramurally among Tory conservatives, particularly among Anglican, Methodist, and Evangelical versions of what to make of print and print-history in the modern age. In this sense, the bibliographical controversies of the Romantic age may help us grasp some of the deeper divisions within what Linda Colley has termed, perhaps too homogenously, the 'patrician renaissance.'[32]

One of those divisions requires special emphasis. Bibliographical study in Britain seems to have been intensifying a dispute over what it might mean for Protestantism to be a 'religion of the book.' Though well-regarded for his *Bibliographical Dictionary*, Adam Clarke was far more famous in his time as a 'raving Methodist preacher,' the controversial author of the imposing 8-volume *Commentary on the Bible*. That lifelong project, Clarke wrote to a friend, 'contains a history of the world, and of the church, for upwards of two thousand four hundred years,' using its scope and bibliographic detail to criticize orthodox Methodism for sustaining the dogma of the Eternal Sonship of Christ, while deploying considerable knowledge of natural philosophy and book history to press its case.[33] The ensuing theological debate pivoted on the question of whether the Son of God issued from the same substance as God himself or was produced, as it were, from earthly materials ready to the divine Hand. It could be read in bibliographical terms as an allegory for the problem of authorship as well. Clarke's *Commentary* gained a small army of subscribing Dissenters even as he denied his writings supported any 'sects or parties.' Only his considerable scholarly and bibliographical reputation kept Clarke himself from being expelled by Calvinist critics from the Wesleyan Methodist Conference during this heated pamphlet war of the 1810s. Bibliographical history-writing seemed to be pressing too hard on legacies of the old Calvinist and Arminian struggles that helped fuel civil war in seventeenth-century England. (Even today, Adam Clarke retains a star presence on fundamentalist websites, battling or being refuted by the variously 'neo-,' 'hyper-,' or 'crypto-' Calvinist sects that descend from such Romantic-period controversies.)

To be sure, Dissenters came in all religious and political stripes, including Tory, and it still remains difficult to situate the finer strands of Dissent among the era's complex political alignments.[34] But bookishness made for some strange affinities. Among the many ordained ministers who pursued some form of bibliographical research or compilation in the nineteenth century, Clarke and Dibdin had more in common than their relatively left and right wing, Methodist and Anglican commitments might suggest. Both, in fact, were animated by Evangelical visions of what an emerging modernity should begin to look like. Dibdin seems, at least early in his career, to have shared the cultural ambitions of Anglican Evangelical reformers like Thomas Bernard, whose alliance with William Wilberforce had led to a career of building conservative welfare institutions throughout London (most famously the Society for Bettering the Condition of the Poor in 1796). One strong sign of Dibdin's otherwise rarely visible affiliation with such Evangelical projects is the peculiar 'dream vision' that interrupts every version of his Bibliomania books and first appeared while he was collaborating with Bernard on *The Director* in 1807. Here is the focal point of that dream:

> [In] all the metropolitan cities of Europe—London, Paris, Vienna, Berlin, and Petersburg ... I seemed to be perfect master of every event going on in them—but particularly of the transactions of *Bodies Corporate.* I saw Presidents in their Chairs, with Secretaries and Treasurers by their sides .... Here, an eloquent Lecturer was declaiming upon the beauty of morality ... there, a scientific Professor was unlocking the hidden treasures of nature .... Again I turned my eyes, And ... viewed the proceedings of two learned sister Societies, distinguished for their labours in *Philosophy* and *Antiquity* .... 'These institutions,' observed my guide, 'form the basis of rational knowledge and are the course of innumerable comforts; for the *many* are benefited by the researches and experiments of the *few.*'[35]

This dream-vision of a coming order of the 'Arts & Sciences,' governed by modern professions and bodies of learning, is decidedly hierarchical, and moreover projects an *administrative* view of that world ('perfect master of every event going on in them') that Dibdin no doubt was learning from his association with Bernard, who was perhaps the Romantic period's most active founder and administrator of emerging cultural institutions in London. This dream-passage goes on to promote an Anglican Evangelical program of social reform in the early 1800s—welfare provision, including 'Asylums and Institutions for the ignorant and helpless'; the abolition of slavery, long an Evangelical project; religious toleration for all sects of Christianity, along with a more frightened vision of the '*eastern* empires' that are 'yet ignorant and unsettled.' While his later, on-and-off-again ecclesiastical career seems to have moved him much closer to high-church Anglicans in their dispute with evangelicals by the 1830s, this earlier posture strongly suggests that Dibdin's campaign for a public historical bibliography was grounded in the same religious but essentially modernizing vision of knowledge-diffusion, welfare-provision, anti-slavery campaign, and Evangelical politics that descended, in this case, from the Clapham sect and the labors of Hannah More.[36]

Why did British Evangelicalism, in either its Dissenting or Anglican modes, become so deeply invested in the new British concern with book history? The paradox is telling. Anti-institutional in one important sense (by rejecting the absolute authority of the Church in any of its Protestant or Catholic modes), Evangelicals were—whether Tory or Dissenting, Anglican or Methodist—powerful and effective institution-builders in another way. By the mid-Victorian age it could be hard to tell one kind of Dissenting lineage or Evangelical commitment from another as they had smoothly meshed into a wider institutional order: at least 'society,' by Carlyle's or Arnold's measure, if yet fully as 'culture.'[37] Thomas Bernard's two most important projects, the Royal Institution (for the sciences and other emerging disciplines) and the British Institution for the Promotion of the Fine Arts, would meld almost seamlessly into the Royal Society and the National Gallery by 1850. Both were incubators of Dibdin's bibliographical project as well.

Meanwhile, what partly seem to have separated Adam Clarke from his opponent Richard Watson, and Dibdin from the fierce T. J. Mathias, were bibliographical convictions about the complexity and instability of printed as well as authored texts and lineages of cultural transmission. Watson and Mathias (in their separate orthodox-Methodist and Anglican domains) demanded the firm outlines and readerly accessibility of modern print media as well as doctrinal orthodoxy. The *Anti-Jacobin Review* went further, linking Clarke's public posture as bibliographer at the Dissenting Surrey Institution with notorious Methodist rituals called 'love feasts,' 'band meetings,' where 'three or four persons, always of the same sex, confess their faults to one another'; or 'watch-nights,' which produced 'at least three acts of adultery on the eve of every new-year's day.'[38] By all other reports a mild-mannered bibliographer and cautious scholar, Clarke appears in *The Anti-Jacobin Review* to be 'a fiery specimen of true *covenanting piety*' who mounted the stage of the Surrey Institution to steep the brains of a 'heathenish assembly of philosophers' (247–8) in a bewitching brew of old revolutionary poisons.

Such attacks were hardly indiscriminate: the *Quarterly Review, Anti-Jacobin Review,* William Gifford (who edited both), T. J. Mathias and others made varied but sustained attacks against the bibliographical as well as bibliomaniacal way with a book from 1798 to 1825—that is, throughout the Romantic age in Britain. More than accounts of modern nationalism like Colley's would suggest, Britain's counterrevolutionary establishment after 1800 was far from united on matters concerning the nature of the book in relation to haunting legacies from the political, religious, and (English) revolutionary past.

Undoing romantic-age book history

In one sense, the part Thomas Frognall Dibdin played in disturbing the nineteenth century's sense of security about the modern printed book cast its shadow over the whole Victorian age. *The Bibliomania, or Book-Madness* was reprinted four more times after 1811 (1842, 1856, 1876, 1903, each time more elaborately than in the past). But as we also know, nineteenth-century British culture would come to normalize Dibdin's 1807 dream vision with its proliferation of societies, institutions, and other organizations devoted to differentiating and specializing the fine arts, humanities, and sciences (including bibliophile societies), even as Dibdin himself became a figure of ridicule, the fool of literary history, after his final drubbing by the *Quarterly Review* in 1825.[39] Early British book history would become a vanishing mediator of modernity's histories of knowledge. Adam Clarke's progressive Methodism would similarly blend into a more orthodox Nonconformist Protestant majority by the High Victorian age, while his volatile bibliographical role in the period disappeared from the maps of intellectual history.[40]

As for the Bibliomaniacs' role in the age of wild bibliography, the black-letter mania subsided after 1825 while furnishing the materials for the later systematic study of incunabula by Henry Bradshaw, Williams Blades and others, an accomplishment that would require a simultaneous forgetting of the 'pre-scientific' era of wild bibliography (in the fullest sense, a 'historical bibliography' of an especially volatile kind). Disavowing Romantic bibliography's multiplicity of codex histories, the New Bibliographers peeled off the histories of the library, of printing, of book production and of any intelligible relation to cultural history by refocusing the bibliographical project on author, meaning, and ownership. When today's book history polemically accentuates the difference between editing 'books' and editing 'texts,' particularly in the work of Donald McKenzie and Jerome McGann, their argument for editing a 'social text' effectively makes a more disciplined return to the Bibliomaniacs' long-misunderstood insights into nature and historical mutability of the book.[41] We might also contrast the ways collector culture had exploited ownership of the book with these later nineteenth-century and early twentieth century attempts to exploit authorial ownership of the text on the conviction that 'textual integrity and regulated intellectual property are somehow mutually entailed.'[42] The property-secured stature of authorship left bibliographical labor without legitimate intellectual property and feminized it at the same time. The bibliographer is 'a handmaiden to literature,' as *The Cambridge History of English Literature* put it in 1915; [her] work 'cannot be identified with literature any more than the bibliographer (as such) can be regarded as an author.'[43]

On the whole, the New Bibliographers of the twentieth century professionalized earlier British bibliographical study by expunging the memory of its origins in the historical fascinations or ethical visions that often animated it—often doing so in the name of science, making analogies between their new methods and natural history, botany, entomology or Mendelian genetic evolution.[44] Portraying Romantic-age bibliographical book history as prescientific, as I hope to have suggested, has a rich irony. Today's book history, although in many ways it has advanced well beyond its precursor, is in other ways still trying to catch up with it. Such matters as the meaning of 'literary history,' or genealogies of the library and of discipline-organizing, are currently among its most urgent topics. In trajectory, book history may become the new matrix of the humanities, the larger field of which 'literary history' becomes only a subset, or the archaeology of the new communicative media and systems that still require its knowledge to make their own way—just as early-modern printing required the look and feel of the manuscript book to launch its own more definitive futures. Current print history has many forms—from the most focused and matter-of-fact, to the most ambitious ways of rethinking the book's place in modernity—but it is not yet fully clear what visions or ambitions drive it. What contemporary book history still needs to answer more clearly is the question it first had to confront in the early nineteenth century:

What is the history of books, print and reading *for*?

Notes

1. Leah Price, 'Introduction: Reading Matter,' *The History of the Book and the Idea of Literature*, special issue of *PMLA*, ed. Leah Price and Seth Lehrer (January 2006): 9–16. For valuable readings of this essay at various stages, I want to thank Thora Brylowe, Jerome McGann, and Leah Price.
2. 'Bibliographia,' *Encyclopedia Britannica*, third edition (Edinburgh, 1791–7) Edinburgh; Thomas Hartwell Horne, *An Introduction to the Study of Bibliography* (London: Cadell, Davies, 1814) 2 vols. On the importance and scope of the phrase 'bibliographical codes,' see McGann, *The Textual Condition* (Princeton: Princeton University Press, 1991). Recent work on Romantic-age bibliophilic writing and bibliomania has been especially useful in my thinking through such questions: Paul Keen, chapter 2 of *The Crisis of Literature in the 1790s* (New York: Cambridge University Press, 1999); Ina Ferris, 'Bibliographical Romance: Bibliophilia and the Book-Object' and Deidre Lynch, ''Wedded to Books': Bibliomania and the Romantic Essayists,' both in 'Romantic Libraries,' *Romantic Circles*, http://romantic.arhu.umd.edu/praxis/libraries.
3. Dibdin, 'Preface' to Joseph Ames, *Typographical Antiquities; or the History of Printing in England, Scotland, and Ireland* [1749] (London: William Miller, 1812) II: 3.
4. Dibdin, 'Bibliographiana,' *The Director*, no. 3 (January 1824): I: 84.
5. See Adrian Johns, *The Nature of the Book: Print and Knowledge in the Making* (Chicago: University of Chicago Press, 1998), and his debate with Eisenstein in 'How to Acknowledge a Revolution,' *American Historical Review* 107 (2002): 106–25.
6. Philip Connell accentuates their power to disturb when he points to the 'vertiginous sense of the arbitrariness of economic value' they helped induce that 'threatened to destabilize the more legitimate criteria of textual appreciation implied by the notions of learning and taste.' [Philip Connell, 'Bibliomania: Book Collecting, Cultural Politics, and the Rise of Literary Heritage in Romantic Britain,' *Representations* 71 (Summer 2000): 25, 28.] For reservations about other aspects of Connell's argument, see below.
7. David McKitterick, 'Bibliography, Bibliophily, and the Organization of Knowledge' in *The Foundations of Scholarship: Libraries and Collecting 1650–1750* (Los Angeles: William Andrews Clark Memorial Library, 1992), p. 48; Yeo, Richard. *Encyclopaedic Visions: Scientific Dictionaries and Enlightenment Culture* (Cambridge: Cambridge University Press, 2001).
8. Gustave Peignot, *Dictionnaire raisonee bibliographie* [1802], qu. in Luigi Balsamo, *Bibliography: History of a Tradition* (Berkeley: Bernard Rosenthal, 1990), p. 147.
9. Between 1800 and 1810, essays, reviews, or brief notices of the new inter-est in bibliography appeared in the *Monthly Review*, the *Monthly Magazine*,

the *Anti-Jacobin Review*, the *Quarterly Review*, the *British Critic*, and especially the essays and books cited below: *A Bibliographical Dictionary, The Director, Censuria Bibliographica, Typographical Antiquities, The Bibliomania: or Book-Madness.*

10. Adam Clarke, *A Bibliographical Dictionary: In All Departments of Literature* (London: W. Baynes, 1802–6).

11. Clarke published these last two volumes separately as *The Bibliographical Miscellany* (London: W. Baynes, 1806). See his comparison of bibliographical systems, II: 146–218.

12. For recent work on literary lecturing, see Peter Manning, 'Manufacturing the Romantic Image: Coleridge and Hazlitt Lecturing,' in *Romantic Metropolis: The Urban Scene of British Culture 1780–1840* (New York: Cambridge Univ. Press, 2005), pp. 227–45; Gillian Russell, 'Spouters or Washerwomen: The Sociability of Romantic Lecturing,' in *Romantic Sociability: Social Networks and Literary Culture in Britain 1770–1840*, ed. Gillian Russell and Clara Tuite (Cambridge University Press, 2002), pp. 123–44; and my own 'Transmission Failure: From the London Lecturing Empire to the *Collected Coleridge*,' in *Theoretical Issues in Literary History*, ed. David Perkins (Cambridge: Harvard University Press, 1991), pp. 77–95.

13. McKitterick, 58–61; Charles Lyell, 'Scientific Institutions,' *Quarterly Review* 34 (1826): 154–9.

14. Thomas Astle, *The Origins and Progress of Writing* (1784), second edn (London: White, 1803); Charles Burney, ed., *A Catalogue of the Library of the Royal Institution of Great Britain*, second edn (London: Payne and Foss, 1821). And since the public lectures attracted notably large audiences of women in the early 1800s, the institutions' libraries were conceived as ingenious correctives to what Dibdin called 'the irremediable mischief' of the circulating libraries and their notorious effects on young women readers. (Dibdin, *The Bibliomania*, 1876, p. 551).

15. For the substance of these lectures, see Dibdin, *Reminiscences of a Literary Life* (London: John Major, 1836), I: 233–45; and reports in *The Director*, passim.

16. Throughout this essay I will refer typographically to the 'Arts & Sciences' when I mean the printed discourse articulating this relationship—as it appeared in encyclopedias, dictionaries, or bibliographical writings—and more generically to 'arts and sciences' as a broad affiliation.

17. Thomas Frognall Dibdin, *Bibliomania, or Book-Madness: A Bibliographical Romance* (London: Chatto & Windus, 1876), pp. 539–40. This 'new and improved edition' is now the most widely available in a contemporary reprint (Bristol: Thoemmes Press, 1997); like the 1842 and 1856 editions before it, the 1876 edition combines the early 1809 text with the expanded, arch dialogues of the 1811 revision that is referred to in most scholarship on Dibdin, along with the subtitle 'A Bibliographical Romance' (which did not appear in 1809).

18. It is also clear that Dibdin's lectures and *Director* essays were having impact on new publishing projects by publishers like Longmans and men of letters like Robert Southey. Corresponding with Longman's in August 1807, Southey considers the scope of Longman's proposed *Bibliotheca Britannica*, then defers to Dibdin: 'There is a sort of title-page and colophon knowledge—in one word, bibliology—which is exactly what is wanted for

this purpose, and in which he is very much my superior.' (Robert Southey, letter to Longmans, 20 September 1807, in *The Life and Correspondence of Robert Southey*, ed. Charles Cuthbert Southey [New York: Harper & Brothers, 1855], p. 225.)

19. Dibdin, *The Director*, I: 84.

20. Clarke, Bibliographical Miscellany I: v.

21. Coleridge, *Collected Letters* I: 412, cited in Albert Boehm, 'The 1798 *Lyrical Ballads* and the Poetics of Late Eighteenth-Century Book Production,' *ELH* 63 (1996): 457.

22. Paul Gutjahr and Megan L. Benton, 'Introduction' to *Illuminating Letters: Typography and Literary Interpretation* (Amherst: University of Massachusetts Press, 2001) p. 1.

23. [Thomas James Matthias], *The Pursuits of Literature*, 8th edn (London: T. Becket, 1806); Dibdin extensively quotes his reply to Mathias in an 1807 lecture in *Reminiscences* [1836], vol. 1, pp. 230–37.

24. For good treatments of the black letter's cultural impact, see Sarah A. Kellen, '*Peirs Plouhman* [*sic*] and the 'Formidable Array of Blacketter' in the Early Nineteenth Century,' and Paul Gutjahr, 'The Letter(s) of the Law: four Centuries of Typography in the King James Bible,' in Paul Gutjahr and Megan Benton, pp. 17–43.

25. Dibdin, *Reminiscences* I: 236.

26. Samuel Egerton Brydges, *Censura Literaria* (London: Longman, 180), IX: 1–3.

27. For the following discussion, I have learned much from Robert Shaddy, 'Grangerizing; 'One of the Unfortunate Stages of Bibliomania,'' *The Book Collector 49* (2000): 536–46; Marcia Pointon, 'Illustrious Heads' in *Hanging the Head: Portraiture and Social Formation in Eighteenth-Century England* (New Haven: Yale University Press, 1993); and Lucy Peltz, 'The Extra-Illustration of London: The Gendered Spaces and Practices of Antiquarianism in the Late Eighteenth Century' in *Producing the Past: Aspects of Antiquarian Culture and Practice, 1770–1850*, eds. Martin Myrone and Lucy Peltz (Aldershot: Ashgate, 1999).

28. Robert Southey, *Letters from England* [1807] quoted in Lucy Peltz, 'Facing the Text: The Amateur and Commercial Histories of Extra-Illustration ca. 1770–1840' in *Owners, Annotators, and the Signs of Reading*, ed. Robin Myers et al. (New Castle DE: Oak Knoll, 2006), p. 94.

29. John Hill Burton, *The Book Hunter*, qu. in Shaddy, p. 543.

30. Holbrook Jackson, *The Anatomy of Bibliomania* [1930] (Urbana: Univ. of Illinois Press, 2001), p. 579.

31. Following Linda Colley's account of British nation-building, Connell makes a compelling case for the national impact of the Bibliomania as a cultural display of empire's cultural wealth after its fame crested with the Roxburghe auction of 1812: 'the bibliomania symbolized an attempt to promote the participation of distinctively aristocratic cultural practices within a broader emergent idea of the literary past as a collective national heritage' (p. 28). But he misses the battle among Tories themselves about the politics of the bibliomania and its relation to the wider bibliographical project.

32. Linda Colley, *Britons* (New Haven: Yale Univ. Press, 1993).

33. Adam Clarke and Mrs. Richard Smith, *An Account of the Religious and Literary Life of Adam Clarke* (London: Weslayan Methodist Conference, 1839), pp. 395–400; n.a., *The Life and Labours of Adam Clarke, to Which Is Added an Historical Sketch of the Controversy Concerning the Sonship of Christ* (London: John Stephens, 1834), pp. 462–6. The multivolume work commonly called Clarke's *Commentary on the Bible* was first published as Adam Clarke, *The New Testament of Our Lord and Saviour Jesus Christ* (London: A. Paul, 1825) and republished in many British and American editions since then, most recently in electronic format as 'Adam Clarke's Bible Commentary,'http://www.godrules.net/library/clarke/clarke.htm.

34. For useful distinctions among them, see Daniel White, *Early Romanticism and Religious Dissent* (Cambridge: Cambridge University Press, 2006), and Robert Maniquis, 'Transfiguring God: Religion, Romanticism, Revolution' in *The Blackwell Concise Companion to Romanticism*, ed. Jon Klancher (Oxford: Wiley-Blackwell, 2009).

35. First published in the last number of *The Director* in 1807, this curious dream-passage reappears in all later editions of *The Bibliomania, or Book Madness* from 1811 to 1903; it was almost certainly the result of Dibdin's being deeply impressed with the Evangelical social vision of Thomas Bernard, since it appears otherwise at odds with the book-warrior ethos of the swaggering aristocratic collectors Dibdin was cultivating at the same time—or with his later apparent siding with high-church Anglicans against the Evangelical movements (Dibdin, *Bibliomania*, pp. 473–9.)

36. On Hannah More's version of modernizing Evangelicalism, see especially Kevin Gilmartin, *Writing against Revolution* (Cambridge: Cambridge University Press, 2006), chapter 2.

37. I refer, of course, to Raymond Williams' distinction in *Culture and Society, 1780–1950* (New York: Harper & Row, 1958).

38. 'Nightingale's *Portraiture of Methodism*,' *The Anti-Jacobin Review* 33 (1809): 236–47.

39. 'Mr. Dibdin's Library Companion,' *Quarterly Review* 32 (June 1825): 152–60.

40. For the only attempt to assess his work in twentieth-century bibliohistory, see Francesco Cordasco's brief article 'Adam Clarke's *Bibliographical Dictionary* (1802–1806),' *Studies in Bibliography* 4 (1951–2): 189–92.

41. On the 'social text' and the relationship between editing texts and books, see Jerome McGann, 'From Text to Work: Digital Tools and the Emergence of the Social Text' *Romanticism on the Net* 41–42 (February–May 2006), http://www.erudit.org/revue/RON/2006/v/n41-42/013153ar.html; and D. F. McKenzie, *Bibliography and the Sociology of Texts* [1984] (Cambridge: Cambridge University Press, 1999).

42. Joseph Lowenstein, *The Author's Due: Printing and the Prehistory of Copyright.* (Chicago: University of Chicago Press, 2002), p. 252.

43. *The Cambridge History of English literature* (Cambridge: Cambridge Univ. Press, 1907–1921), p. 15. While dashing Thomas Dibdin's old dream to become respected as a 'bibliographical author,' the *Cambridge History* granted him a compromise destiny. 'Sometimes,' it allowed, 'a bibliographer *may* produce a work which may rank as literature. A Dibdin may write a romance on bibliomania.' At the same time, having established this 'law of selection'

that decisively separates the author from the bibliographer, the *Cambridge History* featured a more thorough account of 'Scholars, Antiquaries and Bibliographers' as situated in the early nineteenth century than any account of bibliographical history since then.

44. For a relatively skeptical view of the claim to science from later advocate of the New Bibliography, see Thomas Tanselle, 'Bibliography and Science,' *Studies in Bibliography* 27 (1974): 55–89; and 'Bibliographical History as a Field of Study' 41 (1988): 33–58.

2
'Uncommon Animals': Making Virtue of Necessity in the Age of Authors

Paul Keen

The vitriolic splendour of eighteenth-century quarrels between the advocates of a patrician model of the man of letters and their more commercially oriented antagonists has at times distracted us from the complexity and force of the tensions which structured debates *within* the latter category. This oversight is crucial because the emergence of modern ideals of authorship was less a matter of the victory of one of these definitions over the rest than the product of the friction between competing versions of literary professionalism. One of the lessons of more sociological approaches to book history has been the productive influence of the logic of resentment which structured relations between different positions within the literary field; new definitions of any of the constituent elements of the field (the author, the reading public, literature itself, the book trade, and so on) did not emerge in some pristine form out of a field of vanquished choices (this rather than that idea of what a writer should be) but, more dialectically, out of the play between these alternatives.

I want to complicate our understanding of some of these dynamics by exploring a version of literary professionalism which circulated in the second half of the eighteenth century and which was rooted in a tension between a case that authors were making about the sorts of writing and knowledge that were best adapted to a modern nation and the terms which this obliged them to adopt in descriptions of themselves. Faced with what Samuel Johnson called the 'miscellaneous and unconnected' nature of a commercial society, many writers responded by celebrating the virtues of a form of literature which was itself miscellaneous and unconnected.[1] Its central features were epitomized by what one periodical, *The Microcosm*, described as a 'microcosmopolitan' style: writing as a form of social and textual affiliation, whose epistemological commitments favoured the particular and the discontinuous, and the resolutely quotidian.[2] To be microcosmopolitan was to appreciate the revelatory power of the fragment ahead of the sorts of general knowledge favoured by advocates of civic humanism – the 'equal wide survey' of the landed aristocrat – but it was also to recognize the primacy of what the *Microcosm* called the 'little world' of day-to-day life.[3] This extended to an emphasis on what Sir John Hawkins, in his biography of Johnson, called 'that lower kind of literature' which prized 'vernacular erudition', or those forms of writing which, as Johnson himself put it, were 'leveled with the surface of daily life'.[4] By aligning itself with those who, in Isaac D'Israeli's words, 'were doomed to have no historian' instead of offering 'a dull chronicle of the reigns of monarchs', microcosmopolitan writing concentrated its focus on the 'minute springs and wheels' which, D'Israeli insisted, were central to the workings of a polite commercial nation.[5]

But it is possible to valorize particular forms of writing in ways that create problems for the case that one might try to make for the stature of the people who produce them. It is one thing to sanctify the commonplace, to insist on the primacy of what Johnson called a 'diminutive' focus, and to embrace the ironic authority of what the periodical *The World* called the 'ignoble state of a fugitive sheet and a half'.[6] It is another thing to convert these literary priorities into a new basis for the social distinction of the authors themselves. The two processes are obviously bound up with one another, but they are not quite the same thing. Flattening established cultural hierarchies in the name of an aesthetic which was 'levelled with the general surface of life' (Johnson's phrase) and which privileged the dignity of 'those who are doomed to have no historian' (D'Israeli) may have made for compelling literature, but without the benefit of a Romantic emphasis on agonized genius it begged the question of how one might define the importance of these writers in ways that distinguished them from this thriving everyday world within which (they insisted again and again) their leveling efforts were immersed.[7]

These sorts of questions were intensified by authors' nervous awareness of what Johnson called the 'very uncertain tenure ... of literary fame' in their own day and the cruel reduction of posterity to a 'magnificent obscurity' epitomized by 'a public library ... crowded on every side by mighty volumes ... now scarcely known but by the catalogue'.[8] It was, at least on one level, a basic problem of supply-and-demand. In an essay in *The Adventurer*, Johnson dubbed 'the present age ... The Age of Authours; for, perhaps, there never was a time in which men of all degrees of ability, of every kind of education, of every profession and employment, were posting with ardour so general to the press'.[9] In his own analysis of the reasons why 'the LITERARY CHARACTER has, in the present day, singularly degenerated in the public mind', D'Israeli refined Johnson's assessment. 'De Foe called the last age, the age of Projectors, and Johnson has called the present, the age of Authors. But there is this difference between them; the epidemical folly of projecting in time cures itself, for men become weary with ruination; but writing is an interminable pursuit, and the raptures of publication have a great chance of becoming a permanent fashion'.[10] The problem, as many critics were quick to point out, was not limited to the self-sustaining inflation of print; more worrying still was the difficulty of separating one person's version of literary self-promotion from another person's more damning sense of the world of projectors: showmen and charlatans devoid of any redeeming virtues.

Addressing the theoretical question of the limited and provisional agency implied by writers' attempts to adapt themselves to the changing nature of their habitus in this age of authors, Nick Jardine proposes the idea of the 'un-dead author', neither about to die another theoretical death nor gloriously resurrected, not quite on life support but still thoroughly divorced from Romantic models of creative autonomy. These un-dead writers may well have tried to make their own history but they did not make it just as they pleased. They were forced by the commercial, legal, technological, and discursive pressures of their age to do so by accommodating the resources of history to their own ends. Accommodation should not, however, be too hastily equated with the negation of agency. Aligning himself with Roger Chartier's description of the 'dependent and constrained' author – 'dependent in that he is not the unique master of the meaning of the text, and ... constrained in that he undergoes the multiple determinations that organize the social space of literary production' – Jardine sides with Mark Twain ahead of Foucault and Barthes, warning 'that the report of the death of the author was an exaggeration'.[11]

The one thing that no one doubted was the popularity of the *idea* of the author as a focus of critical debate. Our historical accounts of the status of authors in a modern commercial society are confronted by the palimpsestic nature of the venture: what we find, along with endless carefully narrated examples of authorship as a practice, are instances of authors posing the same questions and engaging in the same genealogical tasks as us, and by the late eighteenth century, they generally did so in terms of an overtly commercial framework. 'Sense and genius are as proper commodities to traffic in, as courage', the *Connoisseur* insisted, 'and an Author is no more to be condemned as an hackney scribbler, though he writes at the rate of so much *per* sheet, than a Colonel should be despised as a mercenary and a bravo, for exposing himself to be slashed, struck, and shot at for so much *per* day'.[12] Bristling at the idea 'that it should be held reproachful in a man to live by his talent of writing', the *Critical Review* took exception to James Grainer's 'heavy charge' that Tobias Smollett 'depends on writing by the hour-glass for his daily bread'.[13] The *Critical* adopted the same position in its objection to the fact 'that Sir John Hawkins takes every occasion to lessen the merit of those authors who have written for money' in his *Life of Samuel Johnson*. 'He does not surely think it a crime to be rewarded for mental talents? The lawyer, the physician, and the clergyman, will oppose it; and we must look in vain for the distinction'.[14]

Hawkins had certainly emphasized his surprise at the vehemence of Johnson's insistence 'that he knew of no genuine motive for writing, other than necessity', with its denial of any distinction between 'those writings which are the effect of a natural impulse of genius, and those other that owe their existence to interested motives', but not as disapprovingly as the *Critical* suggested.[15] Whatever 'the astonishment of myself who have heard him, and many others' at 'the boldness of this assertion ... that the only true and genuine motive of writing books was the assurance of pecuniary profit', Hawkins offered Johnson himself and a pantheon of illustrious authors such as Hume and Dryden as the 'best apology' for Johnson's insistence on payment as a valid motivation.[16] In his most explicit discussion of the 'evils of an author's profession', Hawkins had objected to the likely 'indigence' rather than the indignity of writing for one's livelihood: the problem was not that writers were paid but that they were not paid enough.[17]

None of these concerns prevented authors from insisting on their unrivalled social importance. 'The chief glory of every people arises from its authors', Johnson had insisted in the Preface to his *Dictionary*.[18] Accounts of authors' influence embraced their role as unacknowledged legislators in terms that ranged from the prosaic to evocations that bordered on Shelley's tribute to the prophetic imagination. Citing Sophocles' claim that 'opinion is the sovereign of man', D'Israeli insisted that

an eloquent author, who writes in the immutable language of truth, will one day be superior to every power in the state. His influence is active, though hidden; every truth is an acorn which is laid in the earth, and which often the longer it takes to rise, the more vigorous and magnificent will be it's maturity. What has been long meditated

in the silence of the study, will one day resound in the aweful voice
of public opinion.[19]

'An author may be considered as a merciful substitute to the legislature',
Goldsmith declared. 'He acts not by punishing crimes, but preventing
them'.[20] 'I consider you as supplemental to the law of the land', a letter
in *The World* agreed. 'I take your authority to begin, where the power
of the law ends'.[21]

Idealistic accounts of the importance of authors were reinforced by a
more fundamental emphasis on the idea of 'the author' as a cherished
and knowable social role, and with it, by a tightening of the connections between text and author that Foucault associates with the late-
eighteenth and early-nineteenth centuries 'when a system of ownership
and strict copyright rules were established'.[22] 'Every reader is possessed
with an inclination to become acquainted with, at least, the name of
an author, whose production he peruses with approbation', the *Critical*
insisted. 'We are desirous of attaching esteem to the person of an
ingenious writer; we love to compare the lineaments of his mind with
the features of his face'.[23] 'There are few books on which more time is
spent by young students, than on treatises which deliver the characters
of authors', Johnson agreed.[24] The canonizing effects of editions such
as Johnson's own *Life of Mr. Richard Savage* (1769) and *Lives of the Poets*
(1779–81), and of editions such as Andrew Millar's *The Works of Henry
Fielding, Esq; With the Life of the Author* (1763) – an 'elegant monument
erected to his memory' which was 'embellished ... by a masterly print
of that author' by Hogarth – were complemented by more modest but
equally reverential accounts of particular authors in literary magazines
such as the *European Magazine*.[25]

These sorts of publications were reinforced by a series of encyclopedic
works such as William Rider's relatively modest *Historical and Critical
Account of the Lives and Writings of the Living Authors of Great-Britain*
(1762), a *Catalogue of Five Hundred Celebrated Authors of Great Britain,
Now Living* (1788), David Rivers' two-volume *Literary Memoirs of Living
Authors of Great Britain* (1798), and the year after, the unfinished *A
New Catalogue of Living English Authors: with Complete Lists of Their
Publications, and Biographical and Critical Memoirs* (only the first volume,
which ended part way through 'C', ever appeared). The breadth of
these encyclopedic accounts actively resisted the canonizing effects of
more exclusively focused works, but they shared the latter's tendency
to encourage readers to value literature primarily as a manifestation of
the inventive power of its creator: an outward sign of the inner genius

of the author.[26] Regardless of the particulars of these various lists and tributes, their sheer force of repetition ensured that readers understood the idea of 'the author' in newly intimate and rarified ways.

But ironically, this cult of 'the author' as a knowable and revered figure only compounded real authors' problems. In a world dominated by the excesses of fashion, writers complained that they had been degraded to the level of a favourite spectacle. 'Men of the world are curious to have a glance at a celebrated Author, as they would be at some uncommon animal', D'Israeli complained. 'He is therefore sometimes exhibited, and spectators are invited. A croud of frivolists gaze at a Man of Letters, and catch the sounds of his ideas, as children regard the reflections of a magic lanthorn'.[27] 'People who are not apt to write themselves, have a strange curiosity to see a LIVE AUTHOR', The World agreed in a favourite set piece in which an author flounders miserably, having been introduced into fashionable society.[28] Worse still, if, as Johnson acknowledged, authors tended to be 'diffident and bashful', having spent 'that season of life in which the manners are to be softened into ease, and polished into elegance ... in the privacies of study', it was the charlatans, the unqualified opportunists and superficial thinkers who tended to shine most successfully outside of the literary world.[29] 'The man of real genius' will inevitably be overshadowed, D'Israeli agreed, left sitting 'awkwardly and silently on his chair' while attention is lavished on 'the intriguing and fashionable author, whose heart is more corrupt than his head, [and who] is admired because he has discovered the art of admiring. ... The frivolist author will be the evening favourite'.[30]

Others were even more pessimistic. James Ralph's The Case of Authors by Profession or Trade, Stated (1758) struck a familiar note in its insistence that 'if Heroes and Patriots constitute the first Column of National Glory, Authors of Genius constitute the second', but, Ralph insisted, this glory only added to the insulting double-edge of the stigmas which plagued an author: 'he is laugh'd at if poor; if to avoid that Curse, he endeavours to turn his Wit to Profit, he is branded as a Mercenary'.[31] 'All know that an author is a thing only to be laughed at', Goldsmith agreed. 'His person, not his jest, becomes the mirth of the company. At his approach, the most fat unthinking face, brightens into malicious meaning. Even aldermen laugh, and revenge on him, the ridicule which was lavished on their forefathers'.[32] This, then, was the cultural predicament of modern authors: to be mocked for their poverty and derided for their wealth, to sit 'awkwardly and silently' while the 'fashionable author ... is admired', to be 'the chief glory of every people' but laughed at by aldermen. Any account of modern authorship would need to resolve these tensions if it was going to be both attractive and convincing.

The ocean of ink

As David Solkin has argued, these tensions could be contained through a rhetoric of commercial humanism which gained its persuasive force by synthesizing the claims of civic humanism and bourgeois liberalism as dominant but competing accounts of virtue.[33] If these two perspectives (marked by their alternative emphases on leisure and industry) could never be reconciled, they could be hybridized in the service of an ideology of professionalism. In his essay, 'On Adorning Life by Some Laudable Exertion', Vicesimus Knox warned that a refined society diminished the 'scope for public spirit' in the older, purely disinterested terms favoured by civic humanists: 'Moral and political knight-errantry would appear in scarcely a less ludicrous light than the extravagancies of chivalry'.[34] But, he argued, this diminution of the opportunity for selfless commitment to the public good ought not to be interpreted as eradicating the possibility of a moral imperative altogether. Quite the contrary, it had produced a paradigm shift that had ultimately renewed rather than undermined the idea of public service but in strikingly new terms by highlighting the need 'to do good in an effectual and extensive manner within the limits of professional influence and by performing the business of a station, whatever it may be, not only with regular fidelity, but with warm and active diligence'.[35] These sorts of people might write for pay, it was true, but also (and perhaps ultimately) out of a love of the work itself, and because they recognized its potential importance to others. The mistake would be to conceive of these commitments as though they were mutually exclusive. 'The Writer who serves himself and the Public together, has as good a Right to the Product in Money of his Abilities, as the Landholder to his rent, or the Money-Jobber to his Interest', Ralph suggested. This model had the double benefit of outflanking both of its most obvious alternatives. Not to expect payment was to risk being dismissed as a trifler, one of the 'Voluntier-Writers' ridiculed by Ralph as mere 'Holiday-Writers' from whom no one could expect anything substantial.[36] But to write only for pay was to be oblivious to the reasons why doing good work mattered, to one's self and to all of those who benefited.

Addressing the same question in his essay, 'On Literary Industry', D'Israeli insisted on the centrality of work to an author's life, even as he sought to cleanse the idea of industry of the sort of 'mean' associations that would be 'more appropriate to mechanical labours' by celebrating a more dignified form of industry which amounted to 'a continued exercise of the noblest faculties'.[37] Doing so enabled D'Israeli to articulate a model of labour that was clearly distinct from 'mechanical assiduity' on the one hand, and from a misguided faith in 'genius ... as inspiration', on the other. The problem with talk about 'genius' was that it tended to overlook the crucial role of hard work in literary productivity.[38] Dismissing the vogue for 'original geniuses' as little more than a symptom of his age's fashionable love of easy distractions, D'Israeli insisted that *'inspired* geniuses have never survived the transient season of popular wonder'.[39] 'None but mad Bards dream of inspiration', he argued in an attack on the 'romance of original powers'.[40] Not that D'Israeli was rejecting the idea of 'the operations of genius' or of 'work[s] of genius' or the excellence of 'a real genius' altogether.[41] But real genius, he insisted, must be understood in terms of the value of hard work rather than 'original powers': not a 'mean' or 'mechanical' form of labour, it was true, but the 'slow and gradual renovations of industry' all the same.[42] If the moral authority of civic humanism was predicated on a particular type of leisure (that which was afforded by landed wealth), commercial humanism legitimated itself by privileging a correspondingly narrow version of labour: all successful authors were necessarily industrious, but not all forms of industry were equally dignified. 'To write is mechanical; but to be an Author is no easy matter', Samuel Paterson agreed.[43]

This is, of course, a fairly standard version of literary professionalism. The problem with it, however, was the gap which many accounts exposed between its morally lofty rhetoric of 'disinterested' service and the workaday realities of 'that unprosperous race of men commonly called men of letters', as Adam Smith described them in *Wealth of Nations*.[44] Knox's celebration of this 'professional' commitment to virtue as part of 'the business of a station' had, for instance, quickly escalated into terms which seemed, by the end of his account, to be little less heroic than the 'extravagancies of chivalry' he had rejected as outmoded. Acknowledging the 'thousand pleasures and advantages we have received from the disinterested efforts of those who have gone before', Knox insisted that 'it is incumbent on us to do something in our generation, both for the benefit of contemporaries and of those who are to follow'.[45] D'Israeli's stress on 'industry' may have represented a significant challenge to loftier approaches to cultural production as a purely abstract phenomenon but as his description gained momentum it began to sound far more like a rarified account of 'genius' than it did the workaday efforts of actual writers.

Johnson's very different account of the 'several thousands' of writers currently working in London, who 'live unrewarded and die unpitied, and who have long been exposed to insult without a defender, and to censure without an apologist', was animated by a realism which exposed the irrelevance of the rarified sensibility of these elevated portraits of literary labour.[46] Far from obeying some 'impulse of genius', he insisted, the usual reason these 'manufacturers of literature' had chosen writing as a trade was simply 'that they have tried some other without success'. Few of them could be said 'to produce, or to endeavour to produce new ideas, to extend any principle of science, or gratify the imagination with an uncommon train of images or contexture of events'. Their 'summons to composition' was determined, not by the unpredictable sway of poetic inspiration or by some noble concern for future generations, but 'by the sound of the clock'. Nor were they deluded about any of these shortcomings. These 'drudges of the pen' made up for their weaknesses as authors with a kind of hard won self-knowledge.[47] Far from dreaming of creating a 'monument of learning, which neither time nor envy shall be able to destroy. ... their productions are seldom intended to remain in the world longer than a week'.[48] They 'have been too long *hackneyed in the ways of men* to indulge the chimerical ambition of immortality'.[49]

Confronted by this gap between the elevated rhetoric which distinguished so many descriptions of modern authors' professional calling and the drudgery of their lived reality, some writers made a virtue out of necessity, or in the language of eighteenth-century discussions of moral authority, made their necessity (in the modern commercial sense) into the cornerstone of a new paradigm of virtue by embracing their 'dependent and constrained' state as the true basis of distinction in ways that these loftier accounts of commercial humanism never could. If the author was 'dependent in that he is not the unique master of the meaning of the text', this reliance on others' interpretations was nothing less than a metonym of the ideal of polite sociability itself: a recognition of the paramount importance of cultivating mutually accommodating forms of behaviour in a transactional world which aligned virtue with appropriate forms of commerce (social and intellectual as much as economic) rather than with subjective autonomy. As Smith had warned in *The Wealth of Nations*, '[i]n civilized society [the individual] stands at all times in need of the co-operation and assistance of great multitudes'.[50] If the author was 'constrained in that he undergoes the multiple determinations that organize the social space of literary production', this was nothing more than admitting that authors were immersed in the division of labour, with all of its pressures and limitations, the same as nearly everyone else.

Authors' virtue resided not in some modified form of transcendence; rather, it arose from the fact they were subject to the same kinds of constraints as the vast bulk of their readers with whom, after all, they were bound up in relations of mutual dependence both as collaborative interpreters of texts and, far more fundamentally, as participants in a much broader process of collective self-fashioning. As J. G. A. Pocock has argued about the nature of commercial subjectivity, 'the individual could exist, even in his own sight, only at the fluctuating value imposed upon him by his fellows, and these evaluations, though constant and public, were too irrationally performed to be seen as acts of political decision or virtue'.[51] In such a relentlessly transactional world, mediation mattered more than abstraction, or what William Cowper had described as the 'secure and more than mortal height' from which authors 'behold/ The tumult'.[52] Authors mattered, not because they were different but because they were relevant; they were able to speak to others' concerns (and were therefore worth listening to) because they shared those concerns as the very basis of their work.

However focussed individual writers may have been on their own short-term, monetary pursuits, they were engaged (albeit in often unconscious ways) in a far broader process of reimagining the evaluative frameworks within which the worth of their efforts might be judged. The impact of this struggle was as lasting as their own focus may have been immediate, and as collective as their personal motivations may have been selfish. Too unintended and multifarious to be called a project, this process helped to establish both the values and the tensions that informed Britain's modernity by adapting its various forms of cultural production and consumption to 'the business of life' in contemporary society. Schemes such as the *Microcosm*'s plan to establish 'A LICENSED WAREHOUSE FOR WIT' with a 'Patent' for selling '*Jokes, Jests, Witticisms, Morceaus,* and *Bon-Mots* every kind', as well as a full range of 'names and titles' for novels in 'the most fashionable and approved patterns', or the proposal in *The Connoisseur,* to convert 'the now useless theatre in *Lincolns Inn Fields*' into 'a LITERARY REGISTER-OFFICE ... a mart for the staple commodities of the literary commonwealth', which would be staffed by authors 'who will be employed from time to time in supplying the public with the requisite manufactures', were animated by a tone of ironic celebration rather than satirical denunciation.[53]

If these sorts of mock proposals revelled in modern literature's immersion in the carnivalesque world of a commercial society attuned to the changing dictates of fashion, dream reveries helped to naturalize the cultural impact of Britain's consumer revolution by deploying its most unsettling aspects in dreamscapes where the jarring novelty of recent changes could be read as part of a stylized world in which the surreal was reassuringly and even comically conventional. Goldsmith's preface to his *Citizen of the World* featured a dream about 'the capriciousness of public taste, or the mutability of fortune' in which the reluctant narrator watches several authors heading out over a frozen Thames to sell their wares at a set of booths or 'FASHION FAIR' which had been erected on the ice.[54] Emboldened by their success, the narrator determined to try his own 'small cargo of Chinese morality' only to have the ice crack under him, 'and wheel-barrow and all went to the bottom'.[55] The third number of the *Connoisseur* employed a similar conceit. Having 'doze[d] over some modern performance', the author found himself 'transported in an instant to the shore of an immense sea, covered with innumerable vessels', which turns out to have been 'the OCEAN OF INK'.[56] While 'he stood contemplating this amazing scene', he was introduced to 'one of those good-natured GENII, who never fail making their appearance to extricate dreamers from their difficulties', but who, in this case, smacked of the more earthly realities of the book trade. 'His complexion was of the darkest hue, not unlike that of the *Daemons* of a printing-house; his jetty beard shone like the bristles of a blacking-brush; on his head he wore a turban of imperial paper; and *There hung a calf-skin on his reverend limbs* which was gilt on the back, and faced with robings of *Morocco*, lettered (like a rubric-post) with the names of the most eminent authors. In his left hand he bore a printed scroll, which from the marginal corrections I imagined to be a proof-sheet; and in his right he waved the quill of a goose'.[57] The dream's increasingly nuanced vision of the different positions which structured the modern literary field (or ocean) is underscored by a dark awareness of the book trade's more invidious realities, from the 'pirates' who had 'infested ... the whole ocean' and who were themselves making for the COAST OF GAIN 'by hanging out false colours, or by forging their pass-ports, and pretending to be freighted by the most reputable traders', to 'several gallies ... rowed by slaves', all of them 'fitted out by very oppressive owners' who force these 'miserable wretches ... to tug without the least respite', and with 'little or no share in the profits'.[58]

Having been steered through this complex topography, the dreamer is finally directed towards 'a spacious channel' first discovered by '"one *Bickerstaff*, in the good ship called THE TATLER, and who afterwards embarked in THE SPECTATOR and GUARDIAN. These have been followed since by a number of little sloops, skiffs, hoys, and cock-boats, which have been most of them wrecked in the attempt. Thither also must your course be directed"'. But proper guidance leads to something more like drowning than a safe arrival. 'At this instant the GENIUS suddenly snatched me up in his arms, and plunged me head-long into the inky flood. While I lay gasping and struggling beneath the waves, methought I heard a familiar voice calling me by my name; which awaking me, I with pleasure recollected the features of the GENIUS in those of my publisher, who was standing by my bed-side, and had called upon me for copy'.[59] Exploring the uncertain fate of authors in a modern commercial society in terms that acknowledged their own complicity with the problems they complained of, these writers repeatedly staged their ambivalence in ways that insistently tied their literary achievements to a sophisticated understanding of the complexity of these issues.

The crowd of life

Authors embraced this vision of necessity as virtue by insisting on their immersion within the 'tumult' as the only basis of a knowledge which was appropriate to the kinds of intersubjectivity which characterized a modern commercial society. If the meaning of texts, like the idea of value itself, had become the product of interpretive communities that spilled over beyond the bounds of easy demarcation, then the only sort of knowledge that could possibly be worth communicating would need to develop out of a practise of social engagement which reflected this sense of mutuality. 'It is universally confessed that learning is an invalu-able acquisition', a letter to the *Gentleman's Magazine* acknowledged, but, it warned,

> a continual intercourse with books, without the possession of a dis-tinct knowledge of mankind, is at best but an incomplete endowment.
> ... so enchanting is the knowledge of humanity, and so prevailing is its influence, that the wise man, without it, is encumbered and fastidious.

It was not enough, the correspondent insisted, to be 'taught to pen-etrate ... into the bosom of antiquity, or through a profundity of sciences'; the 'wise man' must be 'humanized by the world'.[60] 'An extensive communication with the world is as necessary to the truth of reflexions on mankind, as a variety of experiments is to the knowledge of natural philosophy', the *Monthly Review* agreed.[61]

Luckily, 'an extensive communication with the world' was not only the best source of knowledge but of personal fulfilment as well. 'Men were born to live in society; and from society only can happiness be derived', *The Lounger* counselled. 'Let not one disappointment, nor even a series of disappointments, induce them to abandon the common road of life'.[62] 'Man is not born to continue merely an individual separate from the rest of his species, but should look upon himself as the member of one common body', an essay in the *Gentleman's Magazine* insisted in almost identical terms.[63] Objecting to scholars' tendency 'to look on the common business of the world' with 'disdain', and to their 'unwillingness' to 'condescend to learn what is not to be found in any system of philosophy', Johnson agreed that whatever reverence 'abstruse researches and remote discoveries' might excite in some minds,

> yet pleasure is not given, nor affection conciliated, but by softer accomplishments, and qualities more easily communicable to those about us. He that can only converse upon questions, about which only a small part of mankind has knowledge sufficient to make them curious, must lose his days in unsocial silence, and live in the crowd of life without a companion.... No degree of knowledge attainable by man is able to set him above the want of hourly assistance.[64]

Not only were there more kinds of knowledge than the 'abstruse' sort favoured by philosophers, knowledge itself could never compensate for the value of companionship in a world where people were more dependent on each other than ever. However intense some critics' aversion to what Archibald Alison called 'the noise and tumult of vulgar joy' may have been, more judicious authors (so this argument went) understood the importance of not turning their back on 'the crowd of life' if they wanted to enjoy the blessings of social ties or even to have any kinds of insights worth conveying.[65] To 'hover at a distance round the world' was to 'know it only by conjecture and speculation', Johnson warned, and, therefore, not really to know it at all.[66] To resist immersion in favour of the cloistered virtue of college life or the specialist authority of a particular profession was to be a pedant rather than a purist: devoid of the companionable habits that would enable a person to enjoy the fellowship of one's peers, and preoccupied with a form of knowledge that was too arcane or too narrow to interest more than a handful of people anyway.

Recasting the rarified notion of literature's central role in promoting the diffusion of knowledge in a parodic form which refigured Enlightenment priorities in the less intellectual rhythms of daily life, the editor of the *Connoisseur* admitted that 'my vanity has often prompted me to wish, that I could accompany my papers, wheresoever they are circulated ... through all their travels and mutations', from the company of 'the politest men of quality, and ... the closets of our finest ladies' to 'the shame of seeing many of them prostituted to the vilest purposes. If in one place I might be pleased to find them the entertainment of the tea-table, in another I should be no less vexed to see them degraded to the base office of sticking up candles'.[67] The account's proliferating list of the usual 'vile' uses (at the hands of pastry-cooks and trunk makers) culminated in an account of 'an accident, which happened to me the other evening, as I was walking in some field near the town':

> As I went along, my curiosity tempted me to examine the materials, of which several papers kites were made up; from whence I had sufficient room to moralize on the ill fate of authors. On one I discovered several pages of a sermon expanded over the surface; on another the wings fluttered with love-songs; and a satire on the ministry furnished another with ballast for the tail. I at length happened to cast my eye on one taller than the rest, and beheld several of my own darling productions pasted over it.[68]

Having conquered his initial indignation at having 'become the plaything of children', the author managed to convert 'what at first seemed a disgrace into a compliment to my vanity' by recasting the possibility of distinction in terms which reflected the realities of modern fame. 'As the Kite rose into the air, I drew a flattering parallel between the height of it's flight, and the soaring of my own reputation: I imagined myself lifted up on the wings of fame, and like Horace's swan towering above mortality: I fancied myself borne like a blazing star among the clouds, to the admiration of the gazing multitude'.[69] But whatever his momentary susceptibility to the lure of transcendence, even in this modified form, the *Connoisseur*'s account ultimately aligned itself with a version of literature which was firmly 'leveled with the surface of daily life' rather than with William Cowper's vision of the 'secure and more than mortal height' from which authors 'behold/ The tumult'. In his 'fantastic contemplation of my own excellence', he conceded, he had ignored the true lesson afforded by this scene. 'I never considered by how slight a thread my chimerical importance was supported. The twine broke; and the Kite, together with my airy dreams of immortality, dropt to the ground'.[70]

This gravitational pull towards the quotidian world of private affairs and unmemorable routines which distinguished so many of these accounts of modern authors' professional lives manifested itself in a corresponding respect for the radical heterogeneity of the literary field. The ideal of an individual who was distinguished by a form of knowledge which had itself been won through social interaction with endless other people, each with their own limited perspectives, found its natural corollary in critics' emphasis on the composite strengths of a community of this type of knowers, each with their own limitations, and on an equally various sea of readers. In its discussion of *Essays on the Trade, Commerce, Manufactures, and Fisheries of Scotland*, by David Loch, Merchant, the *Monthly Review* insisted that it was 'happy for society, that in every case of great moment, authors of different talents address themselves to the public, each of whom discussing the matter in his own particular manner, adapts his reasoning to the capacities of those who are in the same class with himself'.[71]

This emphasis on adapting literature to the various tastes of the public inverted conventional assessments of literary worth by subordinating the idea of inherent excellence to the social imperative of communication: 'as among mankind at large the class of accurate reasoners is very small in comparison with those who are incapable of investigating any subject with a philosophical precision, it usually happens that, in those disquisitions especially that are intended to engage the attention of the people at large, the best written book is not the most useful, as an inferior performance will more engage the attention of the multitude'. No work, however outstanding, was exempt from this rule. In fact, the more outstanding the work, the more this rule applied, but relations between these different types of writing were better envisioned in terms of reciprocity than contradiction. 'Newton's *Principia* was not in general esteem, even among men of science, till it came to be explained in their own manner by persons of inferior genius', the *Monthly* suggested as evidence of this proposition.[72]

Adopting an ambitious model of ecological balance, the *Monthly* offered the spectre of a world in which the most seemingly trivial and unintentional events were actually part of a broader process of spontaneous regeneration. 'Winds, storms, birds and insects, scatter the seeds of plants upon the surface of this globe, where they spontaneously spring up for the sustenance of those animals which take no care for themselves'. If this biological order was proof of 'the infinite wisdom [with which] the affairs of the universe are directed', the same was equally true of literature: 'the knowledge that is produced by the exertions of men of superior genius is, in like manner, happily differentiated among mankind by the more feeble efforts of those whom nature has adapted to that inferior, though most necessary office'. And crucially, this was true because of (rather than despite) the chaotic and overgrown nature of modern literature with its metaphorical 'winds [and] storms, birds and insects'.[73]

Johnson's description of modern writers as 'manufacturers of literature' might, on first glance, seem to participate in derisive accounts of the manufacture of books as a byword for the degrading effects of the literary marketplace.[74] It was true, he acknowledged, that these manufacturers were not to be confused with those 'heroes of literature' whose 'proper ambition' it was 'to enlarge the boundaries of knowledge by discovering and conquering new regions of the intellectual world' and whose writing was the product of 'the happy minute in which his natural fire is excited, in which his mind is elevated with nobler sentiments, enlightened with clearer views, and invigorated with stronger comprehension'.[75] None of this was the lot of the vast majority of modern writers who, 'like other artificers, have no other care than to deliver their tale of wares at the stated time'.[76] But Johnson's account was actually far closer to this more generous model of ecological balance. Rather than accepting these sorts of apparent limitations at face value, or even making a case for these sorts of writers despite their weaknesses, Johnson's account of the 'manufacturers of literature' inverted this apparent tendency by embracing these limitations as the surest guarantee of relevance and therefore of a particular kind of literary value in a busy, commercial world in which the vast majority of potential readers were similarly preoccupied by their own passing concerns. For these readers, 'the humble author of journals and gazettes must be considered as a liberal dispenser of beneficial knowledge'.[77] Ironically, these writings' limitations made them especially important in an age where people's most pressing cares were often equally immediate. 'These papers of the day, the *Ephemerœ* of learning', he insisted, 'have uses more adequate to the purposes of common life than more pompous and durable volumes'.[78] Readers could appreciate these authors better than that illustrious elite who would be remembered by posterity because, immersed in the pressures and opportunities of their own work-a-day world, readers had more in common with them. And this was true, Johnson suggested, not simply because modern readers were too busy to contemplate anything more taxing than the rushed productions of equally frantic authors, but because they had a natural and laudable need for information which spoke to their most immediate concerns, rather than for more arcane forms of knowledge. 'It is necessary for every man to be more acquainted with his contemporaries than with past generations, and to know rather the events which may immediately affect his fortune or quiet, than the revolutions of ancient kingdoms, in which he has neither possessions nor expectations'.[79]

This celebration of authors' worldliness, with its acceptance of the rich variety of literary 'winds [and] storms, birds and insects' that helped to mediate relations of production and reception was not without its risks or its frustrations. But for many writers, these tensions were more than overshadowed by the greater evil of 'hovering at a distance round the world' in the name of some illusory freedom which turned out to be little more than an 'unsocial silence'. If this spirit of engagement, with its implied determination to situate literature squarely within 'the noise and tumult of vulgar joy', was displaced as notions of literature crystallized into their modern and more narrow emphasis on aesthetic expression (a shift which gave primacy to an equally abstract model of readers as 'the People, philosophically characterized'), it is worth remembering the inventiveness with which some writers articulated their cultural position in ways that made a virtue of necessity.[80]

Notes

1. *The Works of Samuel Johnson, L.L.D.*, ed. Robert Lynam, vol. 5 (London: George Cowie, 1825), pp. 227–8.
2. *The Microcosm* used this phrase repeatedly throughout its first volume. *The Microcosm, a Periodical Work, By Gregory Grifffin, of the College of Eton*, 3rd edn (London: Published by C. Knight, Castle-Street and sold by Mess. Robinsons, Paternaster-Row, and Mr. Debrett, Picadilly, 1786–7).
3. John Barrell, *English Literature in History: An Equal, Wide Survey* (London: Hutchinson, 1983), pp. 51–109; *The Microcosm*, 2: 103.
4. Sir John Hawkins, *The Life of Samuel Johnson, L.L.D.* (London: J. Buckland, J. Rivington and Sons, T. Payne and Sons, et al., 1787), pp. 168–9; Johnson, 2: 630.
5. Isaac D'Israeli, *Literary Miscellanies a New Edition* (London: Murray and Highley, 1801), pp. 105, 27.
6. Johnson 2: 390; *The World. By Adam Fitz-Adam*, vol. 4 (London: R. and J. Dodsley, 1753–7), p. 54.
7. Johnson, 2: 630; D' Israeli, *Literary* 105.
8. Johnson, 1: 103, 1: 495–6.

9. Johnson, 3: 106–7.
10. D'Israeli, *An Essay on the Manners and Genius of the Literary Character* (London: T. Cadell, Jun and W. Davies, 1795; Reprinted: New York: Garland Publishing, Inc, 1970), p. xviii.
11. Nick Jardine, 'Books, Texts, and the Making of Knowledge', *Books and the Sciences in History*, ed. Marina Frasca-Spada and Nick Jardine (Cambridge: Cambridge UP, 2000), pp. 399–400, Roger Chartier, *The Order of Books. Readers, Authors, and Libraries in Europe between the Fourteenth and Eighteenth Centuries*, trans. Lydia G. Cochrane (Stanford: Stanford UP, 1992), p. 28.
12. *The Connoisseur. By Mr. Town, Critic and Censor-General.* 3rd edn, vol. 4 (London: R. Baldwin, 1757), p. 77.
13. *Critical Review* 7 (1759), p. 142.
14. 63 (1785), p. 417.
15. Hawkins, p. 27.
16. Hawkins, pp. 82–4.
17. Hawkins, pp. 158–61.
18. Johnson, 5: 49–50.
19. D'Israeli, *Essay*, pp. 175–6.
20. *The Miscellaneous Works of Oliver Goldsmith*, ed. James Prior, vol. 1 (New York: George P. Putnam, 1850), p. 444.
21. *The World. By Adam Fitz-Adam*, vol. 1 (London: R. and J. Dodsley, 1753–7), p. 106.
22. Michel Foucault, 'What is an Author?' *Language, Counter-Memory, Practice*, ed. and intro. Donald F. Bouchard (Ithaca: Cornell UP, 1977), p. 124.
23. *Critical Review* 8 (1759), p. 341.
24. Johnson, 1: 432.
25. *Critical Review* 14 (1763), p. 1.
26. Mark Rose links this tendency to valorize literature as an expression of the genius of the author to arguments which dominated the copyright trials. See *Authors and Owners: The Invention of Copyright* (Cambridge, MA: Harvard UP, 1993). It is also worth emphasizing the influence of the turn to biography generally, as it manifested itself in projects such as the *Biographia Britannica: Or, the Lives of the Most Eminent Persons Who Have Flourished in Great Britain and Ireland, from the Earliest Ages* (1747–66) and John Aikin's *General Biography; or Lives, Critical and Historical, of the Most Eminent Persons of All Ages, Countries, Conditions, and Professions* (1799–1815). For the growing emphasis on biography within debates about historical writing, see Mark Phillips, *Society and Sentiment: Genres of Historical Writing in Britain, 1740–1820* (Princeton UP, 2000).
27. D'Israeli, *Essay*, p. xvii.
28. *The World*, 3: 182.
29. Johnson, 1: 69.
30. D'Israeli, *Essay*, pp. 88–92.
31. James Ralph, *The Case of Authors by Profession or Trade, Stated. With Regard to Booksellers, the Stage, and the Public. No Matter by Whom* (London: R. Griffiths, 1758), pp. 3, 58.
32. Goldsmith, 1: 440.
33. David Solkin, *Painting for Money: The Visual Arts and the Public Sphere in Eighteenth-Century England* (New Haven: Yale UP, 1992).

34. Vicesimus Knox, *Essays, Moral and Literary*. 2nd edn (London: Charles Dilly, 1779; Reprinted, New York: Garland Publishing, 1972), p. 390.
35. Knox, pp. 390–1.
36. Ralph, 8.
37. D'Israeli, *Literary*, p. 225.
38. D'Israeli, *Literary*, pp. 225–6.
39. D'Israeli, *Literary*, pp. 218–19.
40. D'Israeli, *Literary*, pp. 210–11.
41. D'Israeli, *Literary*, pp. 225, 207, 226.
42. D'Israeli, *Literary*, p. 225.
43. Samuel Paterson, *Joineriana: Or, The Book of Scraps*, vol. 1 (London: Joseph Johnson, 1772), p. 30.
44. Adam Smith, *An Inquiry into the Nature and Causes of the Wealth of Nations*, vol. 1 (London: A. Strahan; and T. Cadell jun. and W. Davies, 1796), p. 205.
45. Knox, p. 391.
46. Johnson, 2: 114.
47. Johnson, 2: 114.
48. Johnson, 2: 114, 115.
49. Johnson, 2: 114.
50. Smith, 1: 21.
51. J. G. A. Pocock, *The Machiavellian Moment: Florentine Political Thought and the Atlantic Republican Tradition* (Princeton: Princeton UP, 1975), p. 464.
52. William Cowper, *The Task, a Poem, in Six Books* (London: J. Johnson, 1785), p. 142.
53. *The Microcosm*, 1: 92, 2: 73; *The Connoisseur*, 3: 188.
54. Goldsmith, 2: 15.
55. Goldsmith, 2: 15–16. Another of Goldsmith's reveries, from the fifth number of *The Bee*, serves as the basis of Frank Donoghue's well-known study, *The Fame Machine: Book Reviewing and Eighteenth-Century Literary Careers* (Stanford: Stanford UP, 1996). See Goldsmith, 1: 94–100. For the history of what were known as frost fairs on the Thames, the most famous of which was held during the winter of 1683–4, see Ian Currie, *Frost, Freezes and Fairs: Chronicles of the Frozen Thames and Harsh Winters in Britain from 1000AD* (Frosted Earth, 1996), and Nicholas Reed, *Frost Fairs on the Frozen Thames* (Folkestone: Lilburne Press, 2002).
56. *The Connoisseur*, 1: 20–1.
57. *The Connoisseur*, 1: 21.
58. *The Connoisseur*, 1: 25–6.
59. *The Connoisseur*, 1: 26.
60. *Gentleman's Magazine and Historical Chronicle* 56 (1786), p. 755.
61. *Monthly Review* 70 (1784), p. 199.
62. *The Lounger. A Periodical Paper* (Edinburgh: William Creech, 1785–6), p. 30.
63. *Gentleman's* 56 (1786), p. 119.
64. Johnson, 2: 75–6.
65. Archibald Alison, *Essays on the Nature and Principles of Taste* (London: J.J.G Robinson & G. Robinson; Edinburgh: Bell & Bradfute, 1790), p. 117.
66. Johnson, 2: 36.
67. *The Connoisseur*, 1: 226.

68. *The Connoisseur*, 1: 228–9.
69. *The Connoisseur*, 1: 229.
70. *The Connoisseur*, 1: 229.
71. *Monthly Review* 63 (1780), p. 172.
72. *Monthly Review* 63 (1780), p. 172.
73. *Monthly Review* 63 (1780), p. 172.
74. Johnson, 2: 114.
75. Johnson, 2: 74.
76. Johnson, 2: 114.
77. Johnson, 2: 115.
78. Johnson, 2: 115.
79. Johnson, 2: 115.
80. *The Poetical Works of William Wordsworth*, ed. E. de Selincourt and Helen Darbishire. Vol. 2. (Oxford: Clarendon, 1944), p. 430.

3
'This Enormous Contagion of Paper and Print': Making Literary History in the Age of Steam

William R. McKelvy

In the preface to *A New Introduction to Bibliography* (1972), Philip Gaskell would justify the adjective in his title by pointing to his extended discussion of the mechanized modes of textual production that had transformed British print culture in the nineteenth-century. Noting how the previous authority on the topic—McKerrow's *An Introduction to Bibliography for Literary Students* (1927)—had only covered the era of the common hand-press, Gaskell described his work as the attempt 'for the first time to give a general description of the printing practice of the machine-press period.'[1] And yet, despite this theme of novelty, it is striking from today's perspective to witness how Gaskell's *New Introduction* can appear to mark the end of the line for a school of analytical bibliography aiming to produce modern editions that would recapture authorial intentions that had been deformed or obstructed in print shops of the past. Gaskell's work, in other words, does not get a great deal of attention in accounts of the rise of the new book history that is traced to the 1980s. And Gaskell himself conceded that the remarkable learning he displayed might leave literary critics puzzled. Quoting Fredson Bowers, he aligns himself with the view that 'the general scholar' was mostly unable to apply the accumulating knowledge to the business of criticism.[2] No accident, then, that the *Literary Students* courted by McKerrow's earlier work have been excluded from the *New Introduction*'s title-page. We have continued to rely on Gaskell for information about the history of book production, but his work has not done a great deal to shape how book historians have more recently re-approached various cultures of print. This was to be a role reserved for one of Gaskell's students, D. F. McKenzie, the twentieth-century bibliographer who most readily inspired and conspired with the innovative book historians said to have materialized in the 1980s.

I start at this impasse I've associated with Gaskell and his *New Introduction* because I want to make the case that conventional literary history has not yet come to terms in any great detail with the mechanized modes to which Gaskell initially drew attention. When addressing the growth of the nineteenth-century print market, historians of the book in Britain have often been limited to repeating the second of two broad generalizations about Western typography: first, there is the remarkable stability of typographic technologies from the end of the fifteenth century to the first decades of the nineteenth century; and second, there is the fact that this period was followed by an extraordinary expansion of capacities in the 1830s and later to produce print based on the coordinated utilization of mechanized paper production, stereotyping, and steam-powered perfecting machines.[3] Scholars of the seventeenth and eighteenth centuries and the earliest years of the nineteenth century have been given the exciting task of accounting for their own print booms without falling back upon technological determinism.[4] Chroniclers of the nineteenth-century print explosion, by contrast, are often required to engage in an activity rumored to be typical of the Victorians themselves, citing steam-powered statistics that can impress even as they seem to de-humanize complicated social events. Thus we can say, as James Raven has recently done, that while there were 25,000 individual titles published in the years between 1800 and 1835, there were some 64,000 titles published in the considerably shorter period of 1835 to 1865; or that the total volume of publication quadrupled between 1846 and 1916, a period that saw the average price of literature cut in half; or that from 1820 to 1900 paper production, most of it destined for evermore affordable newspapers and other periodicals, would increase 30-fold.[5] And so on. In the end, however, all of this just seems to confirm something sufficiently well-known: that the Victorians were remarkably successful in combining capital, labor, and machinery to make and distribute things faster and cheaper; and thus we arrive at a version of the truth that Gaskell had made so clear in the early seventies, that Western typography has two main periods—the age of the hand-press and the age of the machine press.

Without dispensing with this valid but unwieldy generalization, the following essay attempts a more specific act of historical bibliography by describing the making of two books—Robert Chambers's *History of the English Language and Literature* (1835) and its expanded sequel, the *Cyclopaedia of English Literature* (2 vols, 1842–4)—that were decisively spawned by steam-powered machines.[6] By calling attention to the innovative character of these two works in particular, I aim to demonstrate how the general literary scholar does have good reason to understand the impact of mechanized printing precisely because this new mode of production enabled the first explicit consolidation of our dominant notion of literary history. Chambers's role in popularizing evolutionary theories with his anonymously published *Vestiges of the Natural History of Creation* (1844) has been reconstructed by James Secord; and while Secord and others have recognized how Chambers's slightly earlier *Cyclopaedia* 'was of major importance in defining' a literary canon,[7] this essay adds further reasons to see Chambers as a remarkable pioneer, one whose achievements as a literary historian preceded his covert career as a natural historian.[8]

For as Chambers would have it, his 1835 book was 'the only History of English Literature which has as yet to be given to the world,'[9] a claim that withstands scrutiny mostly thanks to fluctuating definitions of 'literature' and uneasy relations between this privileged field of writing and prose fiction.[10] In Chambers's day, English poetic history (including Shakespeare and other dramatists) had, of course, been well served for some time, but even here there were important limitations. Thomas Warton's *History of English Poetry* (3 vols, 1774–81) did not go beyond the Elizabethan period, while Samuel Johnson's 'Lives' had glaring eccentricities and omissions— no Chaucer or Spenser, for instance. Indeed, the critical and biographical notes that accompanied several post-1774 poetry collections were the closest things to comprehensive English literary histories for the first two decades of the nineteenth century. Inspired and enabled by these, as well as the four large collections of novels published between 1810 and 1833, Chambers was the first single author to compose a narrative literary history that covered both verse and prose fiction during a long period that extended into the nineteenth century.[11]

The rise of the novel—both the increasingly consensual story of its 'origins' in the mid-eighteenth century and the elevation of its status— was an essential trend enabling Chambers's new historiography. But Chambers was not a pioneer historian of the novel per se; and neither the 1835 *History* nor the 1844 *Cyclopaedia* had its origins in an account of the so-called English novel.[12] Rather, these innovative works were more importantly inspired by new kinds of serial publishing enterprises that Chambers would insist represented a key development in literary history on par with the earlier rise of the novel. These projects of serialization were related to older traditions of print production that arose in the eighteenth century.[13] But the serials that inspired Chambers's new sense of literary history were more importantly creatures of the new technologies that defined Gaskell's machine-press period.

As we shall see, Chambers's grasp of the cultural significance of recent events in publishing history made him the innovative literary historian he was to be. His literary histories were products of an intellectual and mechanical network that developed around *Chambers's Edinburgh Journal*, a weekly published for the low price of three halfpence and addressed to a mass audience conceived as being distinct from both radical and affluent middle class audiences.[14] In this setting, the composition of the world's first history of English literature merges with the establishment of a corporate entity—the firm of William & Robert Chambers—dedicated to producing new kinds of reading material for an audience that had been assembled by political and technological innovations. And in this nexus, the poet and novelist Walter Scott, like no other single figure, became an essential model for Chambers as he reconciled the commercial faith, cultural nostalgia, and progressive thinking that enabled him to formulate a new historiography of the literary tradition centered on consumption. Literary history, as we still know it, not only took shape in Thomas Carlyle's 'Age of Machinery.'[15] This new historical form was a product of and commentary on the startling agency of industrialized printing at a time when much print media was still produced with the hand-press, an antiquated technology that experienced its climax and consummation, according to Chambers, in Scott's extraordinary career.

* * *

Chambers's personal acquaintance with Scott went back to February 1822. Scott was then at the height of his prosperity, and the twenty year-old Chambers was a second-hand bookseller. Through the good offices of the publisher Archibald Constable, Chambers had succeeded in gaining an introduction to Scott, who accepted from him the tribute of a manually copied selection of the lyrics in *The Lady of the Lake*.[16] An ecstatic Chambers afterwards described the encounter as 'my own approach to the centre of the Literary System.'[17] Chambers had sought and received Scott's patronage at a propitious moment. In the summer of 1822 George IV made his Royal visit to Edinburgh, and Scott, who had been raised to his baronetcy in 1820, was in a position to get Chambers employed as the calligrapher for a number of honorary addresses presented to the monarch. Through his evolving connections to both Scott and Constable, Chambers also got commissions to contribute volumes to *Constable's Miscellany* (1826–34), what was then an innovative attempt to supply 'respectable' literature at the low rate of 3s per volume.

In the period spanning Chambers's first meeting with Scott and the initial publication of *Chambers's Edinburgh Journal* ten years later, Robert Chambers was a keen observer and self-appointed protégé of Scott. For some time too, he partook of Scott's violent antipathy to the agitations for parliamentary reform. Writing to Scott in March of 1830, for example, Chambers declared,

> The present political excitement ... puts polite literature and all its interests at the wall; and some periodical publications which lately circulated to the amount of 10,000, are now down to a fourth of the amount. This fervor is as fatal to literature as the irruption of the Goths. Nor do I think it near an end: it is rather a beginning. People formerly had a maxim, which history in all its ages showed to be good, that the great object of informed and civilized society was to keep the mob in check; but now the maxim is, that government must reside in the mob.[18]

Less than three years following his linking of mob-rule with declining literary consumption, Chambers would elevate 'the mob' into 'the people' and see in this economically defined body possibilities for new levels of literary circulation in serial forms. The general principles behind *Chambers's Edinburgh Journal*—to supply reading material 'in such a form, and at such a price, as must suit the convenience of *every man in the British dominions*'[19]—were also, to a large extent, the principles that allowed Chambers to produce the first, full-fledged history of English literature. But before doing that, he would give an indication of the new literary history to come in his *Life of Sir Walter Scott*, an astonishingly well-informed biography published on 6 October 1832, ten days after the subject had been buried among the ruins of Dryburgh Abbey, a ceremony Chambers witnessed.

A supplement to the *Journal* priced at three pence, the *Life* is a pivotal work which shows that Chambers had come to understand that the literary historian writing in the shadow of Scott's career was not incidentally but fundamentally an economic historian. Chambers would become a historian of literary genres and forms, but he also saw the necessity of becoming a historian of literary production and consumption. In the broadest sense, Scott was an enabling figure for Chambers because his career embodied the synthesis of poetry and prose fiction that the new English literary histories needed to narrate; and even though Scott himself had never written a comprehensive literary history, he was an active literary historian in ways that would become visibly coherent with the publication of the 'Magnum Opus' edition of his works (88 vols, 1829–36).[20] In a more important and complicated fashion Scott was essential to Chambers's new literary history because his life, as reconstructed in Chambers's biography, was a financial spectacle coordinated with the rise and fall of different literary markets in the context of the social changes ratified by the passage of the Reform Bill in April of 1832. Chambers's version of this spectacle was conventional in its readiness to witness a heroic act in Scott's decision to write himself clear of the debts that he had become responsible for in 1826. But Chambers did more than indulge Scott with the privilege of synthesizing a form of genteel monetary imprudence with a redemptive middle-class recovery through hard work. In Chambers's narrative, Scott's final literary labors are self-defeatingly dedicated to an aristocratic ethos grounded in land-ownership, a desperate dedication to the dream of passing on a title and an estate to a male heir: 'The whole cast of his mind, from the very beginning, was essentially aristocratic; and it is probable that he looked with more reverence upon an old title to a good estate, than upon the most ennobled titlepage in the whole catalogue of contemporary genius.'[21] Scott importantly participates at the end of his life in new modes of publication represented by Constable's Miscellany, Cadell's re-issue of the Waverley novels, Lardner's Cyclopaedia, and Murray's Family Library, but he does so in fealty to his own love of land.

Before detailing the long, drawn-out physical decline, death and funeral of Scott, Chambers implicitly juxtaposed Scott's final adventures in publishing with his more striking inability to adjust to (or even survive) the political changes of the 1830s, changes that turned to a great extent on the claims of new capital against old titles. Chambers described how an enfeebled Scott at an 1831 meeting of the freeholders of Roxburghshire had been hissed by non-voters in attendance, and concluded that 'There can be no doubt that the Jedburgh meeting, and the continued excitement upon the Reform question, did much to sadden the last days of this illustrious man, and perhaps to also accelerate his decline.' Scott 'could not conceal that he believed the Reform Bill ... to be the first step towards the ruin of this mighty empire. In the eyes of the majority of readers, this interpretation of their favorite measure will perhaps be held as indicating great political blindness, or else an interest in the continuance of those abuses which the Reform Bill was designed to abolish.' Identifying his own readership as pro-Reform, Chambers goes on to exculpate Scott's 'political leanings,' describing his conservatism as a matter of 'temperament' rather than an explicit creed born in 'an interest in a bad system, or a deliberate preference of the bad to the good.'[22] Scott joins the ranks of the immortals in the *Life*, but he is also presented as a figure overtaken by a politically reconfigured society, a social body that required new modes of publishing to satisfy new demands for instruction and entertainment.

The defining subject of the *Life of Sir Walter Scott*, in other words, was the print medium itself. And while Scott's personal history would intersect with experimental publishing practices in the late 1820s and early 30s, those enterprises stood out as relatively modest steps in a direction that awaited the bolder calculus of W. & R. Chambers. Here the bottom line was determined by the differences between shillings and pennies. Chambers described the 'Waverley Edition,' for instance, as 'a new cheap uniform series' that was 'adapted to the public convenience.'[23] But at five shillings per volume, it was not a series aimed at those most likely to be reading a three-penny biography in brevier type. This biography thus concludes with a 'Postscript' which links the passing of Scott (and the political and literary systems he represented) to the rise of *Chambers's Edinburgh Journal*. 'The work with which the above narrative is connected,' Chambers explains,

> aims at communicating the largest possible quantity of amusing and instructive reading at the lowest possible charge; each number containing the matter of a small volume at the price of three-halfpence. The Life of Sir Walter Scott, which with a few additions of easy acquirement, would form a half-guinea work, is given in connexion with the Journal ... at a mere trifle, as a still stronger earnest than any hitherto held out, of the desire of the publishers to reduce general literature to the level of the *whole* community.[24]

This goal to supply the whole community with reading material starkly contrasts with Chambers's characterization of Scott's view of 'the people':

> Of the common people, when they came individually before him, it cannot be said that he was a despiser: to them, as to all who came in his way, he was invariably kind and affable. Nevertheless, from the highly aristocratic tone of his mind, he had no affection for the people as a body. He seems never to have conceived of the idea of a manly and independent character in middle or humble life; and in his novels, where an individual of these classes is introduced he is never invested with any virtues, unless obedience, or even servility to superiors, be of the number.[25]

A sincere eulogy for Chambers's central literary hero, the *Life* was nonetheless a valedictory address to the literary and political systems that Scott is made to represent. Released at a time when Chambers was confident of the success of his partnership with his brother, the *Life* reflected a new optimism underwritten by the firm's adoption of a dual stereotyping process that allowed simultaneous publication of their works in both Edinburgh and London. Stereotyping also meant that supplementary works such as the *Life of Sir Walter Scott* could be published according to demand, one that in this case eventually accounted for the sale of 180,000 copies.[26] As Chambers saw increasing evidence of his own agency in the rapidly evolving print market, the dissolution of Scott—both financial and physical—became more than a biographically terminal event; it was to become a literary watershed that Chambers would record and exploit. Invoking the theme of historical supersession central to so much of Scott's work, Chambers the literary historian saw Scott playing a role familiar to readers of the works of 'The Author of Waverley': he was a noble figured destined to yield to a new social accommodation of historical proportions.

Chambers's own biography had put him in a position to identify with Scott—and his literary authority—even as he modeled a professional life in contrast to Scott's. Just as Walter Scott's withered leg and early illnesses were represented as key factors making the writer into a voracious reader, Chambers had early acquired a bookish identity for physical reasons. Born with six digits on each hand and foot, his badly amputated supernumerary toes produced a degree of lameness that made reading his chief childhood occupation.[27] Planning to enter the Church following matriculation at Scott's *alma mater*, Edinburgh University, Chambers had his formal education brought to a sudden end in 1813 when his father, a former manager of hand-loom weavers in Peebles, became financially ruined. The downward spiral of James Chambers had manifold causes and included a problem with drink. Most broadly speaking and in the eyes of the two sons, the father was a victim of his inability to adapt to the transformations being wrought by new modes of mechanization in the textile industries that had been the livelihood of the family. Things were also made worse by the foolhardy extension of credit to a number of foreign officers paroled in Peebles following their capture in the Napoleonic wars. In this final debacle, the father, as Robert Chambers understood it, was gulled by the gentlemanly airs of soldiers who combined 'a proverbial want of principle ... with all their gallantry and enthusiasm.'[28]

Having seen his father overwhelmed by the emergent factory system and a misplaced trust in the honor of an all-male professional class,

Chambers was uniquely poised to appreciate how Scott's financial crisis was linked to his concerns about losing status among his peers by disclosing that he was in effect, not only a knighted writer, but also, through various partnerships, a printer and a bookseller. The combined histories of the two most significant paternal figures in Chambers's life encouraged him to re-conceive his destiny in the thriving republic of letters associated with Edinburgh, a metropolis that despite—and in part because of—its nullity as a political capital was vying to be Britain's cultural capital.[29] Addressing his public from the triumphant setting of '19 Waterloo Place'—home to W. & R. Chambers from 1832–40—he would not fulfill his dreams of authorship in the traditional sense. Instead, he imagined a new kind of literary career that fused author, bookseller, publisher, and printer. Scott remained a model for an Edinburgh-based literary authority that extended its reach to include all of the British dominions. But Scott's life was also a cautionary tale. For while Scott's financial problems were compounded by his secrecy about his involvement in 'the trade,' Chambers would relish the opportunity to advertise his status as a manufacturer of printed matter.

What made all this possible was a new system of textual production described in detail in an article from June 1835, 'The Mechanism of Chambers's Journal.'[30] On a basic level the Chambers Mechanism was a coordinated utilization of mechanized paper production, stereotyping, and steam-powered printing to produce a weekly miscellany. But the details of the Chambers Mechanism began with rudimentary practices such as producing copy on only 'one side of the sheet' so that 'compositors are enabled to cut leaves in pieces, if required, each taking a piece so as to facilitate the work' (6 June 1835: 149). And just as any manuscript copy needed to be divisible, the weekly miscellany itself was composed of many different parts: 'it is of considerable importance for the editor to have a large number of articles in proof, from which he can have a varied selection in making up numbers of his work.' Any given number of the *Journal* was a pragmatically delimited selection from an on-going process of production that normally kept 'as much matter standing in galley proofs as would make at least two numbers' (6 June 1835: 150). This scenario extended to the *Journal*'s description of stereotyping as a method to create 'a fictitious page' that could preserve a particular order of moveable types even while the types themselves were freed up to be re-combined in different sequences to produce new texts (29 Sept. 1832: 278).

The central agent in the Chambers Mechanism, however, was the steam press or printing machine. Under 'the superintendence of a steady person' and 'two boys, one of whom lays on blank sheets, and the other [who] as continuously takes them out,' the printing machine is praised for 'never tiring in its arduous labours and never stopping unless during the night and on Sundays, or when it happens to outstrip the compositors and stereotyper.' Presented as a model employee, the machine is likewise praised for its collegiality and frugality: 'Prodigious as the quantity is of the printing which this excellent machine executes, and great as is its rate of speed, not less astonishing is the smallness of the power employed in keeping it going, and the lightness of the duty of those who attend on its operations.' Describing to readers how eight men used to work two hand presses to produce the journal over a period of six days and nights of continuous work, Chambers depicts a scene of brutality and excess: 'It almost appeared that human nature could not stand up against such violent labor. No amount of wages seemed able to cause the workmen to remain sober. The greater the urgency for the work, and the higher the price paid for its execution, the more extensive were the saturnalia that prevailed' (6 June 1835: 150). With the human employees marring their productive capacities through excessive consumption, the agency of machinery produces a more peaceful—albeit steam-driven—atmosphere that binds proprietors and printing machine in affection. A genuine 'feeling of delight' as the *Journal* put it, 'animated us on first seeing this machine regularly at work'; 'by the quantity and quality of its produce' it afforded 'a joyful prospect of future tranquility': 'Nothing, in our opinion, within the compass of British manufacturing industry, presents so stupendous a spectacle of moral power, working through the means of inert mechanism, as that which is exhibited by the action of the steam-press' (6 June 1835: 151).[31]

Fittingly, W. & R. Chambers would briefly depend on the mechanical networks that were producing Walter Scott's works at the time. As described to its own readers (6 June 1835: 150–51), the *Journal* had suffered its first major crisis in the summer of 1832 when the two hand presses owned by the firm could no longer produce the needed copies of the regular weekly edition. The solution was found in having the printing firm of Ballantyne and Co. take over much of the work, using machines that had first been acquired in April of 1830.[32] A heavy investment had then been made on printing machines based on the presumption that Scott would continue to direct the printing of Cadell's Waverley Edition of Scott's novels to Ballantyne.[33] And thus for a time the same machines used to print the serial re-issue of Scott's novels were also used to print *Chambers's Edinburgh Journal* and its various supplemental works including *The Life of Sir Walter Scott*. This would all change in October of 1833, when W. & R. Chambers acquired their first steam-powered printing machine at a cost of 500 pounds. And that substantial outlay was at least in part made possible by the extensive sale of the three-penny biography of Scott. Thereafter, Chambers would repeatedly use his own products to advertise his status as a proprietor of the world's first industrialized information factory, one that produced a weekly periodical as part of an on-going process of production and reproduction that included other works such as the *History of the English Language and Literature*. The *History* was announced and advertised in *Chambers's Edinburgh Journal* (14 November 1835: 336) where it was also touted as both a free-standing work and as an inaugural installment in yet another serial publication, Chambers's Educational Course.[34] In the week following this initial announcement of the history's publication, the *Journal* also excerpted the first chapter of the *History* as 'Popular Information on Literature: Rise of English Literature' (21 November 1835: 338–9).

Not incidentally, then, Chambers opens his 1835 *History* by portraying it as a response to the contemporary expansion of readers and their options. '[S]uch a work,' as Chambers put it, 'cannot fail to be useful to many besides young persons at school,—to all in short, whose minds have been awakened to a desire of knowledge; guiding them to the stores of English Literature, and distinguishing for them those works which are most worthy of their attention.'[35] Chambers brought this history of purposeful consumption full circle by ending his narrative with 'an account of the cheap and popular system of publication, which has formed so remarkable a feature of the passing age.' Describing the making of a number of serial productions—the Library of Useful Knowledge and the Library of Entertaining Knowledge (both under the auspices of the SDUK), Constable's Miscellany, Murray's Family Library, Lardner's Cabinet Encyclopedia, and the Edinburgh Cabinet Library—Chambers was insisting that the history of English literature had recently been distinguished by the 'production of books, calculated by their price and modes of production for the less affluent and more numerous portion of the community.'[36] Many of these had been mentioned in the earlier biography of Scott, but they now stood out as important signposts in the broader context of national literary history, one that pauses on the threshold of 1832 when 'a step still remained to be taken before full advantage of the cheap mode of publication could be said to have been obtained.'[37] And this event occurs, as recounted in 'the only History of English Literature which has as yet to be given to the world,'[38] with the publication of *Chambers's Edinburgh Journal*, a weekly of 'original and select literature ... in which a quantity of matter equal to that contained in a number of the Library of Useful Knowledge, was offered at a fourth of the price.'[39] Recording the literary significance of W. & R. Chambers in a new kind of book allowed the name of the firm to join a list that included the likes of Chaucer, Spenser, Shakespeare, Milton, and, of course, Scott. Explicitly engaged in retrospective historical pageantry, the *History* also concluded by hailing the arrival of a newly mechanized literary authority that combined author, publisher, and printer and thereby dispensed with what the *Journal* would call 'the old system of publication' (12 Dec. 1833: 296). By ending his *History* with the story of his own *Journal*, Chambers was engaging in self-promotion to be sure. But the claim about the dawn of a new literary age circa 1832 in the wake of Scott's passing, Reform, and the rise of mechanized printing achieved some credibility as it became embodied in a new literary form, one we can now recognize as a type of literary history that discloses its findings in response to inquiries about the production and consumption of reading material. A firsthand witness of the contemporary expansion of steam-powered printing, Chambers was also poised to see the end of Scott's life as materially and symbolically entwined with the passage of the 1832 Reform Bill. Presented with three of the more useful tools for the fashioning of literary periods—the death of a great author, a major political event, and technological innovation—Chambers seized the chance to write and publish a new kind of book in 1835. The rest is literary history–as we know it.

* * *

Conceptually, Chambers's narrative represented a complete departure from the Wartonian model in which historical progress and poetic imagination were discovered to be tragically (one might say romantically) at odds. In the place of this scheme, Chambers's *History* described literary cycles including all kinds of reading matter that operated according to 'a fixed law that an age of vigorous original writing, and an age of imitation and repetition, should regularly follow each other.' At the heart of this view of history was a pattern of consumption that ultimately determined what was original:

> Authors possessed of strong original powers make so great an impression on public taste—their names, their styles, their leading ideas, become so exclusively objects of admiration and esteem, that for some time there is an intolerance of every thing else; new writers find it convenient to compete with the preceding in their own walks,

than to strike out into novel paths; and it is not perhaps, until a considerable change has been wrought upon society, or at least until men begin to tire of a constant reproduction of imagery and the same modes of composition, that a fresh class of inventive minds is allowed to come into operation—who, in their turn, exercise the same control over those who are to succeed them.[40]

This relativistic grasp of a ceaseless parade of changing literary forms and styles would be reiterated in 'Literary Revolutions,' a lead-article in *Chambers's Edinburgh Journal* that first appeared five months before the appearance of the *Cyclopaedia of English Literature*.[41] 'The student of English literary history,' Chambers begins, 'is familiar with the fact, that every successive age has been distinguished by the development of some species of literature distinct in its character from those which delighted the public in the preceding and subsequent ages.' And he goes on to give an account—starting with Scott's popularization of 'the historical novel'—of the rise and fall of a wide range of literary modes and styles (28 May 1842: 145). Assuming that 'the human mind remains fundamentally the same,' Chambers wondered why literary modes were constantly changing rather than moving either toward or away from ideals of perfection. The answer was the fact that once a public's taste had been stimulated by a new style, writers would increasingly seek to satisfy that taste and make it 'the predominanting literary feature of the time—in short, the fashion'—until the 'next great wit carries away the public mind in a new direction' (28 May 1842: 146). Signaling his break with a literary history that pitched rules and correctness against barbarisms and capriciousness, Chambers did not worry over a dilemma between relativistic and universal literary values. He put the relative forward as the universal.[42]

In 'Literary Revolutions' and other essays like it, Chambers was modeling for his readers an ability to combine historical interests with literary veneration even as he was taking an opportunity to fill the pages of the *Journal* by reflecting on his experience as an innovative literary historian. Seven years after it had announced the publication of the *History of the English Language and Literature*, *Chambers's Edinburgh Journal* announced the *History*'s sequel, the forthcoming *Cyclopaedia of English Literature* that would appear in weekly sixteen-page numbers priced at 1 1/2d (22 October 1842: 320). Containing 'the most exquisite productions of English intellect,' the first complete volume was 'a whole English Library fused down into one cheap book' and 'the cheapest volume of its size ever published in Great Britain' (7 October 1843: 304).

Assisted in a great measure by Robert Carruthers, Chambers was not in the traditional sense the author of the *Cyclopaedia* as much as he was its developer and promoter. Illustrated by numerous woodcuts and often culled from prior collectively authored texts, the *Cyclopaedia* was produced by many hands and served many tasks. It was a national history, a biographical dictionary, a copious anthology and a pictorial tour. In its completed form, with its 1476 double-columned pages, it was simultaneously the most comprehensive history of English literature and the most comprehensive English literary anthology (encompassing verse and prose) in existence. An elaboration of the 1835 *History* and incorporating most of that text directly or in some revised form, the *Cyclopaedia* was a major innovation. But its mode of production had been under development since 1832 when Chambers self-consciously began to devise new systems to create printed media.

As often in the functioning of the Chambers Mechanism, the making of the *Cyclopaedia* was enmeshed with the making and remaking of other products. In this particular instance, the pioneering literary history grew out of and departed from another serial of similar scale, a 'New and Improved' version of the *Information for the People* that began to appear in January of 1841. The new *Information* was improved in terms of scope, scale, amount of illustration, price and rapidity of production. The earlier version had been published at a bi-weekly pace in forty-eight eight-page parts costing 1 1/2d; the new version, to be published weekly, would consist of one-hundred sixteen-page parts offered at the same price. It was *Information* supplied at a faster and cheaper rate.[43] 'Complete in two volumes,' as the *Journal* announced, 'it will be A COMPRHENSIVE POOR MAN'S CYCLOPAEDIA, AND PERHAPS THE MOST STRIKING EXAMPLE YET GIVEN OF THE POWERS OF THE PRESS IN DIFFUSING USEFUL KNOWLEDGE' (6 March 1841: 56).

As originally planned, the new *Information for the People* was also to have included among its final installments a number entitled 'English Literature' (6 March 1841: 56), which would have been a re-setting of the 1835 *History*. But rather than reducing that work, it was decided sometime in 1842 to enlarge it on a vast scale and transform it into the *Cyclopaedia of English Literature*, a new serial that would succeed the *Information for the People* in one continuous process. When one project ended 'on Saturday the 3d of December,' the other would commence 'the week following.' And the firm thereby engaged in a form of macro-serialization—producing series of series—where the governing rationale for each serial could productively alternate. The *Cyclopaedia* thus grew out of the idea that a readership having recently been *instructed* was now ready to be *refined*:

> In the *Information for the People*, the Editors aimed at presenting a body of scientific and general knowledge suitable to the wants of the middle and laboring classes. While that work may serve to instruct, there is need for another which may tend to refine. In the Literature addressed at present time to the People, there appears, generally, a lack of something to awaken the higher powers of thought—reflection, imagination, and taste—and to nourish at the same time the finer of the moral feelings. These objects MESSRS CHAMBERS believe will be in some measure accomplished by the work now announced, in which will be concentrated the most exquisite productions of English intellect, from Anglo-Saxon to the present times. (22 October 1842: 320)

Here the production and consumption of the poor man's cyclopedia created the informed man's need for a literary cyclopedia, a need W. & R. Chambers was ready to meet.

Producing the new *Information for the People* and the *Cyclopaedia of English Literature* in tandem also allowed the firm to exploit a flexible concept of serialization in other ways as well. The *Information for the People* was a conventional serial in that each of its parts had an independent structural identity. The *Cyclopaedia of English Literature* by contrast was a virtual serial. Its weekly numbers made no attempt to be integral units; they were numbered gatherings and most often end in mid-paragraph or even mid-sentence. And while the *Journal* had frequently referred to the circulation of individual parts of the *Information for the People*, there was no comparable discussion of the parts of the *Cyclopaedia*. This reflected the fact that it was a serial of a different order, one that had been conceived as a way to produce over the space of some eighty-six weeks the stereotyped plates for a work intended to be consumed in its completed form.

An outstanding exception to this rule came at the strategic moment when Chambers's seventh literary period, 'From 1780 Till the Present Time,' begins. Here was one of the few places that the *Cyclopaedia* participated in a conventional serial gesture that coordinated the conclusion of a part with the design of the whole and created anticipation for a subsequent part. The start of Chambers's present age thus dawns on the last complete page of the fifty-eighth number in two columns of text that give what we would call a summary of the Romantic Age. Concluding with Shelley's paradigmatic empowerment of the imagination—'Poets are the unacknowledged legislators of the world'—the sketch also made a characteristic plea for the potential alliance of inspired minds and useful machinery. 'It has been feared by some,' writes Chambers, 'that the principle of utility, which is recognized as one of the features of the present age, and the progress of mechanical knowledge, would be fatal to the higher efforts of imagination, and diminish the territories of the poet. This seems a groundless fear. It did not damp the ardour of Scott or Byron, and it has not prevented the poetry of Wordsworth from gradually working its way into public favour.'[44] The vignette for the new period was an unmistakable version of Henry Raeburn's 1808 portrait of Walter Scott.[45] Featuring the musing author holding a notebook and pen among ruins in a pastoral setting, the portrait had been commissioned by Archibald Constable—the publisher who had first arranged for Chambers's introduction to Scott—and it captured the poet in the heyday of his initial fame following *The Minstrelsy of the Scottish Border* (1802), *The Lay of the Last Minstrel* (1805) and *Marmion* (1808), books of wide margins and large type that originally sold for prices ranging from 18s to 31s 6d. Transposed to the pages of the *Cyclopaedia*, the portrait was also a visual cue to the fact that the new literary age that began in 1780 was, in Chambers's view, the age of Scott.

In the functioning of the Chambers Mechanism, however, any given text might have a past and a future life in some altered form, and this would be true for imagery as well, as the firm began to produce and collect stereotyped woodcuts for illustrations starting with the first series of the *Information for the People*. In this case, the vignette of Scott would resurface as the initial to the *Select Poetical Pieces of Sir Walter Scott* as it appeared in *Chambers's Miscellany of Useful and Entertaining Tracts* (1845–7), a collection of thirty-two page tracts sold individually (for a halfpenny) and as part of a twenty-volume series. Literally an interchangeable part, the vignette here initiates a different paragraph describing how 'the less opulent classes' could now enjoy 'pieces' of Scott 'principally selected from' *The Lay of the Last Minstrel*, *Marmion* and *The Lady of the Lake*, what then remained Scott's most popular narrative poems.[46] *Chambers's Miscellany* reprinted as well a revised version of the 1832 biography of Scott;[47] and in addition to these portions of Scott's literary legacy, W. & R. Chambers had also issued complete versions of the same narrative poems that had been diced up to make the *Select_Poetical Pieces*: starting with *The Lady of the Lake* in 1838 and followed by *The Lay of the Last Minstrel* and *Marmion* (both 1839), Scott's poems were sold at bargain prices ranging from 6 1/2d to 10 1/2d in yet another series, the People's Editions.[48] As the interest and economic means of a literary consumer grew in the 1840s, we can imagine a reader moving from the lowest priced Scott-related items in *Chambers's Miscellany* to one or more of the complete poems. And in the *Cyclopaedia* this hypothetical reader could admire the author in the larger literary pantheon: 'Assuredly, in our common reverence for a Shakespeare, a Milton, a Scott, we have a social and uniting sentiment, which not only contains in itself part of our happiness as a people, but much that counteracts influences that tend to set us to division.'[49]

This variegated, mutually stimulating form of literary production allowed Chambers to boast in 1846 about being 'at the head of one of the great organizations of industry in this country, whereby more paper is blacked in a week than in many other printing-offices in a twelvemonth.'[50] From October 1833 to the end of 1843 the number of steam-presses powering the Chambers Mechanism had grown to five, and this was then followed by a doubling as profits were re-invested in a substantial expansion of productive capacities (4 January 1845: 1). With its ten printing machines, W. & R. Chambers was not the largest printing office in Britain in 1845. The London firm of Clowes and Company, as Chambers knew, had 19 machines by the early 1840s. But the two firms were fundamentally different. A firm like Clowes was dedicated to printing the works of a constantly shifting supply of authorial agents ranging from individual writers to institutional clients. The machines owned by the Chambers brothers, on the other hand, did nothing but publish the works of W. & R. Chambers. These drew on the authorial labor of many different individuals (with Robert Chambers as the largest single contributor), but the works were part of one enterprise. So while Clowes and Company engaged in industrialized printing on a larger scale, they did so at the employ of various publishers and authorial agents. In the case of W. & R. Chambers, printer and publisher were fused. Earlier innovative publishers such as Archibald Constable, John Murray, and William Blackwood had sought to develop productive relationships between periodicals, series and non-serial publication, but the firm of W. & R. Chambers invented a literary system capable of producing interchangeable texts that could satisfy evolving forms of literary consumption. And any given part of the *Journal* might be excised from its original matrix, united with affiliated parts, and re-issued in another form.

A good deal of the success of W. & R. Chambers was based on a recurrent celebration of Scott's career, one that ironically featured the great author concealing his complicated status as a printer. Having won an introduction to Scott in 1822 after manually copying a selection of lyrics from *The Lady of the Lake*, Chambers by the mid-forties was using the day's most extensive self-contained media factory to retail Scott's life and works on a scale that would have been unimaginable to the best-selling 'Author of Waverley.' Some were not pleased by the spectacle of Scott's works becoming commodified in this way, and Scott's son-in-law and authorized biographer, J. G. Lockhart, sought revenge in the *Quarterly Review* where Chambers was patronizingly described as a 'worthy trafficker' and made an exemplar of a class of self-degraded writers who 'bestowed their ink upon those easier kinds of literature which furnish amusement for the hour, and for which the pay of the hour is sufficiently liberal.'[51] Chambers, though, heard in his machinery a music to which Lockhart was deaf, one that could take its place alongside the recollected songs of tradition being manually inscribed by Scott in Raeburn's portrait. That icon of Scott's role as a medium for reviving the pre-typographical literary culture of bards and minstrels was put into a new historical perspective as Robert Chambers crowned himself Britain's new media mogul. By January of 1845, he would declare that 'there is at this time no literary *system* in the country which approaches ours in magnitude' (4 January 1845: 3): 'We write at present in a huge building of four storeys, flanked by a powerful steam-engine, and with the noise of ten printing machines continually sounding in our ears. ... Upwards of a quarter of a million of printed sheets leave the house each week, being as much as the whole newspaper press of Scotland issued in a month about the year 1833.' As arguably the first historian of English literature (in one sense of the term), Chambers was uniquely qualified to see how such an 'enormous contagion of paper and print' marked 'an entirely new era in literature' (4 January 1845: 1).

Evidence of Chambers's innovative accomplishments can also be gleaned from the reception of François René de Chateaubriand's *Sketches of English Literature* which appeared in July of 1836. British reviews often focused on the inevitable distortions in such a history by a Frenchman.[52] But another significance of the work was perceived from the more distant perspective of the soon to be famous historian William H. Prescott, who noticed the *Sketches* in the *North American Review*. Without mentioning Chambers's work, Prescott unintentionally reaffirmed the Scotsman's claim to priority: 'notwithstanding the interest and importance of literary history,' Prescott wrote, 'it has hitherto received but little attention from English writers. No complete survey of the achievements of our native tongue has been yet produced, or even attempted.'[53] Chateaubriand's work attracted a fair amount of attention in the quarterlies, while those same periodicals had nothing to say about Chambers's earlier work, the *History of the English Language and Literature*. This illustrates how a book's price could determine levels of notice in the periodical press that catered to elite audiences. Chambers's duodecimo work priced at 2s 6d was near the lowest end for the market in newly published books; Chateaubriand's was slightly more than ten times as costly at 24s, a sum that put it close to the expensive three-decker format for fiction. Beyond the economic reach of a sizable reading audience, Chateaubriand's book by the same token fetched a price that made it a fashionable object to discuss. Chambers's *History*, in contrast, fell beneath the notice of 'genteel' readers.

After the publication of Chambers's earliest literary histories there followed a brief period when his pioneering status was acknowledged by the authors of competing texts. In his *Outlines of English Literature* (1849), Thomas Budd Shaw, for instance, noted the 'singular' fact that no comparable work, one 'cheap, compendious, and tolerably readable,' existed in English.' But he also qualified his claim with an acknowledgement that Chambers's works were exceptions with defects that could be quickly summed up: 'Chambers's valuable and complete 'Cyclopaedia of English Literature' is as much too voluminous as his shorter sketch is too dry and list-like.'[54] Priced at 12s, Shaw's volume was about five times more expensive than Chambers's short *History* and roughly the same price as the much larger illustrated *Cyclopaedia* (14s). Shaw's *Outlines* would have been considered 'cheap' by only a small portion of the population. To a status-conscious reader, though, Shaw's book had the added value that it did not come with those helpings of humble pie that accompanied Chambers's works.[55]

In 1853 when the Edinburgh firm of Oliver and Boyd published William Spalding's *History of English Literature* (3s 6d), the author still cited Chambers's *Cyclopaedia of English Literature* as the earliest work 'in which the whole field is minutely surveyed.'[56] Well into the early 1850s books surveying a historically organized literary tradition encompassing verse and prose fiction could still stake some claim to novelty, but this genre rapidly became a staple in the larger print market. It would soon become hard for readers to imagine a time when such books did not exist. Scholars in the twentieth century even began to backdate the genre by referring to Thomas Warton's *History of English Literature*, a pointed distortion of the real title of Warton's book, the *History of English Poetry*.[57] This apocryphal title is something other than a typographical error. It is a professional rumor spawned by a failure to engage closely with a key moment in Britain's era of typography, a moment when an older culture of print initially registered the impact of the printing practices of the machine-press period.

Notes

My thanks to Sondra Cooney for reading a version of this essay and noting several errors that have been corrected.

1. Philip Gaskell, *A New Introduction to Bibliography* (Oxford: Clarendon Press, 1972), Preface, n.p.
2. Gaskell, p. 337.
3. The London *Times* was first printed by steam in 1814, but reliable printing machines for all kinds of work, including book production, were developed in the 1820s and began to account for a substantial amount of the print market only in the 1830s and later. See Gaskell, pp. 251–63. David McKitterick, in *Print, Manuscript, and the Search for Order, 1450–1830* (New York: Cambridge University Press, 2003), also implicitly marks the end of the dominance of the hand press *circa* 1830. See pp. 212–16 for his brief comments on the rise of mechanized printing. James Raven's *The Business of Books: Booksellers and the English Book Trade, 1450–1850* (New Haven: Yale University Press, 2007) commences the period of important technological development in the 1820s while the 1840s mark 'a clearer transition from one age of bookselling to the next' (p. 321).
4. William St. Clair's *The Reading Nation in the Romantic Period* (Cambridge: Cambridge University Press, 2004) stresses the impact of different intellectual property regimes and contends that the subsequent changes in modes of production 'can be regarded as innovations previously prevented or postponed by the industrial structure of the high monopoly period' (p. 114). Raven acknowledges the force of copyright regimes while also stressing non-technical innovations in publishing and bookselling. Commenting on the late eighteenth century's soaring publication rates, he writes 'the most remarkable thing is that all was achieved within the technological constraints of the hand press' (p. 363).
5. For these figures, see Raven, pp. 324–6.
6. In addition to James Secord's *Victorian Sensation: The Extraordinary Publication, Reception, and Secret Authorship of Vestiges of the Natural History of Creation* (Chicago: University of Chicago Press, 2000), my thinking about Chambers is mostly indebted to the work of Sondra Cooney, 'Publishers for the People: W. & R. Chambers: the Early Years, 1832–1850' (Ph.D. diss., Ohio State University, 1970), C. H. Layman, ed. *Man of Letters: the Early Life and Love Letters of Robert Chambers* (Edinburgh: Edinburgh University Press, 1990), and Robert J. Scholnick, "The Fiery Cross of Knowledge': *Chambers's Edinburgh Journal*, 1832–1844,' *Victorian Periodicals Review*, vol. 32, no. 4 (1999), 324–58.
7. Secord, p. 97.
8. For a number of reasons, Chambers's literary innovations have to be understood on economic terms, and this helps to explain why Chambers the literary historian is so rarely welcomed into our standard literary histories. Philip Davis's *The Victorians* (Oxford: Oxford University Press, 2002)

includes astute comments on the *Vestiges* (pp. 63–5, 72, 127), but this literary historian has nothing to say about Chambers's literary histories. For Davis, as for most Victorianists, literary history is something to be practiced not studied. This stands in stark contrast to the habits of scholars of the eighteenth century. For a representative account in which our notion of literary history (as a mode of writing) becomes possible only at the close of the eighteenth century, see Lawrence Lipking's 'Literary Criticism and the Rise of National Literary History,' *The Cambridge History of English Literature, 1660–1780*, ed. John Richetti (Cambridge: Cambridge University Press, 2005), pp. 471–97. For an exception to my generalization about the study of literary history as practiced in the nineteenth century, see Margit Sichert, 'Functionalizing Cultural Memory: Foundational British Literary History and the Construction of National Identity,' *Modern Language Quarterly*, vol. 64, no. 2 (June 2003), 199–217.

9. Robert Chambers, *History of the English Language and Literature* (Edinburgh: W. & R. Chambers, 1835), p. v.

10. Writings on the eighteenth-century 'invention of Literature' are now legion. For a recent account, see Clifford Siskin's 'More is Different: Literary Change in the Mid and Late Eighteenth Century,' *The Cambridge History of English Literature, 1660–1780*, ed. John Richetti (Cambridge: Cambridge University Press, 2005), pp. 795–823. Paul Keen's *The Crisis of Literature in the 1790s* (Cambridge: Cambridge University Press, 1999), esp. pp. 1–22, provides an important discussion of literature's debated status at the turn of the century and after.

11. Mark Phillips, in *Society and Sentiment: Genres of Historical Writing in Britain, 1740–1820* (Princeton: Princeton University Press, 2000), describes the 'perplexing appearance' of the 'history of literary history' during the period: 'On the one hand it is clear that contemporary writers used the term *literary history* without apology or special explanation, an indication that the idea was relatively unproblematic for them. On the other hand, when we look for significant literary histories in this period, we have a good deal of trouble identifying texts that stand, in modern terms at least, as unquestioned representatives of this type of writing' (p. 269). My thanks go to Ina Ferris for pointing me toward this valuable work.

12. The collections of British or English novels—accompanied by critical and biographical material—were: Anna Barbauld's *British Novelists* (50 vols, 1810; reissued in 1820), William Mudford's *British Novelists* (5 vols, 1810–16), Walter Scott's *Ballantyne's Novelist's Library* (10 vols, 1821–4), and Thomas Roscoe's *Novelist's Library* (19 vols, 1831–3). These series have prompted Homer Brown to declare in *Institutions of the English Novel from Defoe to Scott* (Philadelphia: University of Pennsylvania Press, 1997) that 'the eighteenth-century novel was invented at the beginning of the nineteenth century' (p. 183). Speaking of the same collections, Ian Duncan in *Modern Romance and Transformations of the Novel: the Gothic, Scott, Dickens* (Cambridge: Cambridge University Press, 1992) says they mark a time when 'the institutions of national canon-formation began to dignify prose fiction' (p. 4.). Claudia Johnson's "Let Me Make the Novels of a Country': Barbauld's *The British Novelists* (1810/1820),' *Novel*, vol. 34, no. 2 (2001 Spring), 163–79, stresses how that canon was contested.

13. See, for example, R. M. Wiles's *Serial Publication in England before 1750* (Cambridge: Cambridge University Press, 1957), a work brought to my attention by Thomas Keymer.
14. See Jon Klancher, *The Making of English Reading Audiences, 1790–1832* (Madison: University of Wisconsin Press, 1987), p. 44.
15. Thomas Carlyle, 'Signs of the Times' [1829], *Thomas Carlyle: Selected Writings*, ed. Alan Shelston (London: Penguin, 1986), p. 64.
16. The collection, still preserved at Abbotsford, has its title-page reproduced in Layman between pages 88 and 89. It reads: 'TO / SIR WALTER SCOTT, BART. / OF / ABBOTSFORD / THESE SPECIMENS / of / minute / Penmanship / ARE / respectfully presented / BY / AN Admirer OF / HIS / GENIUS.'
17. Quoted in Secord, p. 82.
18. Quoted in Secord, p. 82.
19. *Chambers's Edinburgh Journal* (Feb. 4, 1832), p. 1. Hereafter cited in text by day, month and page.
20. See William B. Todd and Ann Bowden, *Sir Walter Scott: A Bibliographical History, 1796–1832* (New Castle: Oak Knoll Press, 1998), pp. 885–8; and Jane Millgate, *Scott's Last Edition: A Study in Publishing History* (Edinburgh: Edinburgh University Press, 1987), pp. 47–8.
21. Robert Chambers, *Life of Sir Walter Scott* (Edinburgh: W. & R. Chambers, 1832), p. 8.
22. Chambers, *Life of Sir Walter Scott*, p. 10.
23. Chambers, *Life of Sir Walter Scott*, p. 10.
24. Chambers, *Life of Sir Walter Scott*, p. 12.
25. Chambers, *Life of Sir Walter Scott*, p. 12.
26. This extraordinary figure is given in William Chambers's 'Prefatory Note' (n.p.) to the 1871 edition of R. Chambers's biography, the *Life of Sir Walter Scott by Robert Chambers, LL.D. with Abbotsford Notanda by Robert Carruthers, LL.D.*, ed. William Chambers (Edinburgh and London: W. & R. Chambers, 1871). This was yet another republication of the 1832 *Life* that was intended to honor (and profit by) the author's death in the year of the widely celebrated centenary of Scott's birth.
27. See Layman, pp. 55–6.
28. Layman, p. 74.
29. Ian Duncan, *Scott's Shadow: the Novel in Romantic Edinburgh* (Princeton: Princeton University Press, 2007), p. 9.
30. I borrow the term 'system' directly from Chambers. 'Among the labours connected with our business,' as the *Journal* would declare in 1834, 'not the least has been the labour of organising a proper system of printing and publishing. The nature of our publications was, in every respect, so extraordinary, that all old modes of procedure may be described as having fairly broken down under it' (Feb. 1, 1834: 2). Chambers came of age at a time when systems theory was rife. See Clifford Siskin's 'Novels and Systems,' *Novel* vol. 34, no. 2 (2001 Spring), 202–15.
31. For a brief introduction to the wider context for Chambers's intellectual and emotional attachment to machinery, see Herbert Sussman's 'Machine Dreams: The Culture of Technology,' *Victorian Literature and Culture*, vol. 28, no. 1 (2000), 197–204.
32. Millgate, *Scott's Last Edition*, p. 35.

33. This account of Ballantyne's acquirement of printing machines is at odds with Edgar Johnson's unsupported claim, in *Sir Walter Scott: The Great Unknown* (New York: Macmillan, 1970), vol. 2, p. 763, that Scott himself had purchased steam presses during the period (1816–21) when he was sole owner of Ballantyne and Co. This seems unlikely given the fact that an inventory of Ballantyne and Co. at the time of the crash of 1826 includes no printing machines. I am grateful to Jane Millgate for sharing this inventory with me in a personal communication on December 15, 2006.

34. See Cooney, 268ff, for a list of the titles published in the Educational Course between 1835 and 1849.

35. Chambers, *History of the English Language and Literature*, p. v.

36. Chambers, *History*, p. 269. For modern surveys of these series, see Richard Altick, *The English Common Reader: a Social History of the Mass Reading Public, 1800–1900*, 2nd edn (Columbus: Ohio State U P, 1998), pp. 266–77, Millgate, *Scott's Last Edition*, pp. 91–9, and Secord, *Victorian Sensation*, pp. 46–51.

37. Chambers, *History*, p. 271.

38. Chambers, *History*, p. v.

39. Chambers, *History*, p. 271.

40. Chambers, *History*, p. 190.

41. Reprinted in *Select Writings of Robert Chambers* (Edinburgh: W. & R. Chambers, 1847), vol. 3 of 7, pp. 162–8.

42. In this stance, Chambers belongs to a tradition recently described by Christopher Herbert in *Victorian Relativity: Radical Thought and Scientific Discovery* (Chicago: University of Chicago Press, 2001).

43. The new *Information for the People* did not hesitate to put forward the old. These included updated versions of numbers that had appeared in the 1835 collection, but also additional numbers often culled from the *Journal* that had not appeared in the earlier collected form.

44. *Cyclopaedia of English Literature*, 2 vols. (Edinburgh: W. & R. Chambers, 1842–4), vol. 2, p. 256.

45. See www.walterscott.lib.ed.ac.uk/portraits/paintings/raeburn1808.html.

46. 'Select Poetical Pieces of Sir Walter Scott,' in *Chambers's Miscellany of Useful and Entertaining Tracts* vol. 10, no. 95 (Edinburgh: W. & R. Chambers, 1847), p. 1.

47. 'Sir Walter Scott,' in *Chambers's Miscellany of Useful and Entertaining Tracts* vol. 17, no. 144 (Edinburgh: W. & R. Chambers, 1847).

48. These prices are taken from St. Clair, p. 209.

49. Preface, *Cyclopaedia*, vol. 1, n.p.

50. Chambers, *Select Writings*, vol. 1 of 7, p. iii.

51. [John Gibson Lockhart], 'The Copyright Question,' *Quarterly Review* 69 (Oct. 1841), p. 199.

52. See [John Maguire], 'Chateaubriand's *Sketches of English Literature*,' *Dublin Review* 2 (December 1836), 187–98; 'Oliver Yorke at Paris: A Conversation with Chateaubriand on English Literature,' *Fraser's Magazine* (December 1836), 662–80; [E. G. E. Bulwer-Lytton], 'Chateaubriand on the literature of England,' *Edinburgh Review* 64 (January 1837), 506–36; [George Croly], 'Chateaubriand, *On English Literature*,' *Foreign Quarterly Review* 18 (January 1837), 392–418.

53. William H. Prescott,'Chateaubriand's *Sketches of English Literature,'* *North American Review,* vol. 49, no. 105 (Oct. 1839), 318. Remarking on the fact that Johnson's 'biographies were dictated by the choice of the bookseller,' Prescott also said what Thomas F. Bonnell has confirmed in detail in two related studies, 'John Bell's *Poets of Great Britain:* The 'Little Trifling Edition' Revisited,' *Modern Philology,* vol. 85, no. 2 (Nov. 1987), 128–52; and 'Bookselling and Canon-Making: The Trade Rivalry over the English Poets, 1776–1783,' *Studies in Eighteenth-Century Culture* 19 (1989), 53–69.

54. Thomas Budd Shaw, *Outlines of English Literature* (London: J. Murray, 1849), p. iii.

55. The 1835 history was chiefly designed for those seeking 'the rudiments of useful knowledge' (p. v), and the *Cyclopaedia* was addressed to 'the middle and humbler portions of society' (Preface, vol. 1, n.p.).

56. William Spalding, *The History of English Literature* (Edinburgh: Oliver & Boyd, 1853), p. 28.

57. For this error, see the *Oxford Companion to the Romantic Age: British Culture 1776–1832,* ed. Iain McCalman (Oxford: Oxford University Press, 1999), pp. 330, 332, 337, and 747; Marilyn Butler, 'Introduction,' *Northanger Abbey* (London: Penguin, 1995), p. xviii; and Michael Gamer, *Romanticism and the Gothic: Genre, Reception, and Canon Formation* (Cambridge: Cambridge University Press, 2000), p. 49. The latter even has Joseph Ritson compose *Observations on the First Three Volumes of The History of English Literature.* For recent appearances of Warton's non-existent *History* in reputable journals, see James Simpson's review of *The Cambridge History of Medieval English Literature,* ed. David Wallace, *Medium Aevum,* vol. 69, no. 1 (2000), p. 127; and Joseph A. Dane and Svetlana Djananova, 'The Typographical Gothic: A Cautionary Note on the Title Page to Percy's *Reliques of Ancient English Poetry,'* *Eighteenth-Century Life* vol. 29, no. 3 (2005), p. 76.

Part II: Books in the Everyday

4

Canons' Clockwork: Novels for Everyday Use

Deidre Lynch

> I hate to read new books. There are twenty or thirty
> volumes that I have read over and over again, and
> these are the only ones that I have any desire ever to
> read at all.
>
> —William Hazlitt

> [T]he clock, not the steam-engine, is the key machine
> of the modern industrial age.
>
> —Lewis Mumford

More than once in the *Lives of the English Poets* Samuel Johnson depicts the writers whom he is anthologizing as readers. In a manner more rueful than celebratory, Johnson will trace the man's pursuit of poetic fame to the moment when the boy was captivated by illusions: among them, the anthropomorphic illusions that readers cultivate when we construe our encounters with the surfaces of representation as experiences in which we sustain the company of *people*.

This narrative pattern emerges with the first life in the series. Abraham Cowley happens on a copy of the *Faerie Queene* left in the window of his mother's parlour, succumbs to 'the charms of verse' and so becomes, 'as he relates, irrecoverably a poet'. '[I]rrecoverably' is in that passage the loaded term, almost suggesting that Johnson is halfway inclined to narrate Cowley's discovery of his calling as a story of abasement. In fact, Johnson here remembers and bowdlerizes Cowley's own account of how his reading of Spenser 'made [him] a Poet as immediately as a Child is made a Eunuch'. The psychosexual subtext Johnson here opts to bury resurfaces in the oddest of the *Lives'* depictions of the child's sentimental education in book-love, which is found in Johnson's biography of his near contemporary William Shenstone, whose Life was one of the last he wrote. After the young Shenstone learned to read, Johnson recounts, he 'soon received such delight from books that he was always calling for fresh entertainment, and expected that when any of the family went to market a new book should be brought him, which when it came was in fondness carried to bed and laid by him. It is said that when his request had been neglected, his mother wrapped up a piece of wood of the same form, and pacified him for the night'.[1] It is significant, for the purposes of this essay, that this depiction of book-love involves not an abrupt crush – the time-frame of the sudden and irrecoverable that organized Johnson's narration of Cowley's childhood – but instead the time-frame of the routine.

That time-frame becomes key when, seventy years after the *Lives of the Poets*, Johnson's anecdote about Shenstone's bedtime routines gets retold, and Johnson's wary fascination with a compulsive reading that goes beyond the pleasure principle gets sentimentalized and, maybe in a quite precise sense, Romanticized. In 1849 this story of the lessons that a mother administers in the dynamics of desire, loss, and mollifying substitution proves newly useful for an elderly Leigh Hunt – long-lived Romantic poet and erstwhile radical journalist. During the last four decades of his long life, Hunt is at the forefront of the editing, anthologizing, and canonizing enterprises that Samuel Johnson had guided in the previous century. Hunt retells Shenstone's story when he introduces *A Book for a Corner*, a compilation of choice excerpts of eighteenth-century English verse and prose. His motive for that retelling confirms an argument Leah Price has made about how anthologists have tended to downplay, self-effacingly, their own power of selection. Finding it expedient to intimate that 'texts transmit themselves' and themselves select their readers, the anthologist, Price suggests, is more apt to locate difference among Literature's consumers rather than among its producers. And this tendency, she further suggests, indicates how canon-making enterprises are, in the final analysis, not about content but centrally concerned with who reads (or who will be deemed to really read) and how.[2] Hunt's introduction is structured in keeping with this logic: it is less interested in sorting out the kind of poets whose works this *Book for a Corner* collects from those it rejects, than it is in pressing the claims of the kind of readers who are able to appreciate their works. And hence the infant Shenstone's appeal: Shenstone personifies the target audience that Hunt solicits—the special sector of the reading public that is capable of valuing, Hunt explains, 'the placider corners of genius'. Hunt has assembled, in his words, 'passages from such authors as retain, if not the highest, yet the most friendly and as it were domestic hold upon us during life'. And Shenstone, Hunt writes, 'is the sort of child we hope to be a reader of our volume'. Reciprocating that unfailing 'domestic hold' with his own constancy, he is the sort of child able to commit to this lifetime reading plan.[3]

There are two lessons we might extract from these stories of Shenstone's sleeping arrangements. First, the care that Hunt and Johnson take to cast an emphatically oedipal situation as the breeding ground for literacy and literary appreciation might suggest some complexities we have overlooked in our recent efforts to historicize the concepts of literariness, literary heritage, and canonicity that are the groundwork of our discipline. Perhaps that historicizing, which has for the most part involved exposing how instrumental those concepts were for the work of cultural unification and national and imperial consolidation, or for the credentialization that underpinned a new middle-class hegemony, should acknowledge more explicitly the role of the personal attachments that connect readers to the institution of English.[4] Johnson's need to write the story of Shenstone's quirky bedroom rites into the *Lives*, the monumental work that would come to be seen as 'the first history of English letters', indicates that criticism's professionalizing of reading cannot easily be disentangled from the history of the emotions, and of intimacy and private life.[5]

The second lesson we might take away from this bedtime story involves the crucial role it assigns to habit. In Leigh Hunt's hands, Shenstone's bedtime routine does not centre (as it might well have) a fable about the market's power to keep addicted consumers on tenterhooks with its promises of novelty and 'fresh entertainment'. It becomes, instead, a story of a literary attachment that is distinguished by its steadiness, constancy, and capacity to endure even when the thrill is gone. Hunt makes Shenstone a model reader of *A Book for a Corner* by associating him with a mode of literary appreciation we might dub everyday love – an affect that is directed at what is already, unobtrusively and unmomentously, familiar, and an affect that counts as genuine precisely because, unremitting and routine, it does not belong to any one day but has become a quotidian habit.

This essay is about the reciprocal relations between, on the one hand, that ideal of readerly ethics – also, as we will see, an ideal of readerly health – and, on the other hand, the slow emergence in the decades intervening between Johnson's and Hunt's editing projects, of an idea of 'literature' as that which we are always re-reading and never reading for the first time. As far as Hunt is concerned, the crucial point of

Johnson's anecdote about bedtime routines is that the pacification that books proffer the boy never fails. Reassuringly, books are always there for him, even when, markets and mothers failing, they don't show up. And Shenstone in turn reciprocates their steadiness: *he* repeats himself, happily. This, to borrow a pun from the Victorianist Steve Connor, is an account of literature as L-Iterature:[6] Leigh Hunt registers a scheme in which literariness is a quality proper only to those books that both bear *iteration,* retaining their appeal over the long haul, and also mandate it. From the mid-eighteenth century on, the moment when it begins taking on that modern meaning that elevates it above the vast bulk of the market's print products, literature also begins to be reconceptualized as a steadying influence on those who love it.

Though rarely acknowledged explicitly, that steadying has been an important source of the appeal exerted by the idea of a literary canon – a motive for seeking the fellowship available from a restrictive grouping of perennially readable great works. Literature's (L-Iterature's) hour comes back round, again and again, with reassuring regularity. The canon is habit-forming. This is not precisely as he would put it, but there is some resemblance between this proposition and Harold Bloom's recent no-nonsense definition of the canonical text as simply the durable, complex text that demands re-reading (a definition that is supposed to make it seem as if it were simply transient, fly-by-night reading matter that Bloom was denigrating in *The Western Canon,* and not multiculturalism or feminism).[7] To situate the desire to re-read and desire for L-Iterature in history can, however, go a long way toward defamiliarizing Bloom's definition and divesting it of its aura of self-evidence. The promotion of habitual re-reading that this essay seeks to reconstruct helped lay the ground for the disciplinary canon. But I am seeking to recover a neglected aspect of that canonicity, while I try to demonstrate that the act of reading again that Bloom mandates – and which was consistently ennobled in late twentieth-century literary theory – does not have stable meanings over time.[8] Rereading's association with increased edification, with an augmented cognitive mastery, for instance, is neither inevitable nor historically constant. This is worth underlining because, as Michael Warner has recently observed, practitioners of literary studies have a bad track record when it comes to remembering that the 'critical reading' for which they advocate finds its place in the world alongside other, competing ways of processing texts.[9]

Thus the recurrent re-readings that concern me in this essay are not always the homage readers pay to complexity – the term that Harold Bloom uses to make re-readability seem an intrinsic property of select texts rather than the effect of a particular set of socially regulated consumption practices. These recurrent re-readings are often, on the contrary, the homage readers pay to the sensation of comfort, the reassuring feeling that baby Shenstone gets from books' round-the-clock proximity. Conceptualized as virtuous habits, these re-readings are also taken as evidence of readers' regular hours and sober lives, and revered as the means by which a reader might – if only mechanically – bind each day to each in aesthetic piety. Such conceptualizations register how often in the late eighteenth and early nineteenth centuries professional readers' accounts of how other people should read derived from a medico-moral context that valued habit as the guiding mechanism of individual identity and social structure, how often, accordingly, they were intertwined with, for instance, discussions of the benefits of domestic timetables and of regular scheduling in social and mental life, and discussions of the human nervous system's propensity and need for rhythm and repetition.[10] The periodic return engagements with long-loved books that this essay will portray manifest, on occasion, a devotion that is so engaged as to never miss a beat. (One imagines, for instance, that this was the conscientious spirit in which James Boswell undertook the regimen of annual re-readings of *Rassleas* that he enthuses about in the *Life of Samuel Johnson*: a devotee's recreation in a new register of the Christian liturgical year.)[11] But the era between Johnson and Hunt could also, as I have intimated, accord a surprising amount of respect to affections of a more everyday, mundane, and even torpid cast, affections directed at texts so deeply familiar that the emotions that they stir barely register at the level of consciousness.

Talk about art has long gravitated toward a language of eternal verities and situated great books in a numinous territory beyond time. But the institution of literature also depends, again, more mundanely, on alliances that, beginning in the eighteenth century, got forged between literary reception and the temporal order of the everyday and that made eternity a more comfortable and intimate space. The story of canonicity, and in particular, as we will see in the second half of this essay, the story of the novel's belated admission to literary respectability, are tied up with the story of that ordinariness that we measure through a middle-class metric of bedtimes and mealtimes and daily walks. Great books (so classified) are not only socially certified sources of great ideas or artistry. That description doesn't exhaust our transactions with them. The arrangements that canon-makers after Johnson made to cordon off the category of the permanent library from the soon-obsolescent one, and to set apart (in the 1928 words of a Columbia Professor), 'certain books that grow with our maturing experience', from the 'books [that] do not', are also, as we will see, associated with the comforts of the familiar and humdrum.[12] The story of inexhaustibly re-readable Great Books is also that of valetudinarians' health regimens, of the compulsory coupledom of a new marriage culture, of the transformations that reinvented the family and that made a group formerly understood primarily as a unit of economic production into Western culture's primary scene of emotional gratification. This essay seeks to recover some of those less told stories.

Daily textbooks

Appropriately enough, William Shenstone's letters supply the Oxford English Dictionary with its earliest example of a writer who uses the adjective 'everyday' not to designate something that recurs every 24 hours but to identify, instead, those qualities that distinguish normal life, the ordinariness and banality, the repetitive patterns, that become visible over extended time. (The everyday, philosopher Maurice Blanchot wrote in his own definition of that newer usage, is 'what we never see for a first time, but only see again, having always already seen it by an illusion that is, as it happens, constitutive of the everyday'.)[13] Given this role by the OED, Shenstone becomes an even apter mascot for Hunt's purposes. For if the early modern rediscovery of Longinus momentarily made the mind-blowing transports and eruptic moments of upheaval that defined the sublime a useful measure of art's powers, by the nineteenth century accounts of literary value also gestured with increasing frequency toward a notion of the literary object's everydayness – literature's companionability, then, as much as sublimity. Such accounts bypassed the brief encounters of the sublime and gestured towards a structure of feeling that entailed a different, more uniform, and more unruffled experience of time.

Even Wordsworth, whose Romanticism is often construed as consisting in an antipathy toward the emotional torpor induced by the customary and habitual, floats a notion of literature as an occasion for and creator of steadying attachments. Thus the Preface to *Lyrical Ballads*, having identified the 'man of science' as one who seeks 'truth as a remote and unknown benefactor', goes on to demote that man in comparison to the poet, who, by contrast, makes truth present as 'our visible friend and hourly companion'.[14] Wordsworth makes proximity crucial to the personalization that differentiates readers' relation to the poets from their relation to other sorts of benefactors. With that odd adjective 'hourly', he associates poets' beneficence with the regularity and repetitiveness of time's fixed measures.

Identifying Romantic aesthetic theory as the consummation of an earlier discussion of sublime, we have tended to overlook the lessons about the mind's propensity for repetition – and the attendant interest in low-intensity, long-lasting affects like the sensation of comfort – that this theory's architects would have imbibed from their study of their contemporaries' speculations in psycho-physiology: lessons that might underwrite an account of the upkeep of continuity, and the training, not the breaking, of habit as the essence of artistic praxis and that might advance, accordingly, their case for literature's medicinal value.[15] As described by psycho-physiology, the brain was an echo chamber of vibrations and oscillations, whose cerebration consisted largely in a re-activation rivetting habitual associations formed in the past and reassembling patterns already assembled from the happenstance. This account of the mind's operations, combined with beliefs about the evocative power of the word, could underwrite an account of literary experience as the scene in which, in Laurence Sterne's words, the mind has the illusion of reading itself and 'not the book' – that is, as a scene of 'self-reproduction in mirror-circumstances and mirror-texts' (as Jonathan Lamb has put it more recently). (The pleasures of novelty are always being folded back into the pleasures of memory in this aesthetic: the reader's 'own ideas are only call'd forth by what he reads, and the vibrations within ... entirely correspond with those excited', Sterne asserted, striving to explain his belief that the 'true Feeler always brings half the entertainment with him'.)[16]

Something of this portrait of the receptive mind can be glimpsed in Wordsworth's Preface. It informs Wordsworth's portrait of the artist as a creature of healthy habit (endowed 'with such habits of mind ... that, by obeying blindly and mechanically the impulses of those habits, [he] shall describe objects, and utter sentiments' in a way that will of necessity enlighten any audience which is in turn, and reciprocally, 'in a healthful state of association'). It also prompts, as Alan Richardson has noted, the Preface's comments on poetic meter,[17] and, importantly for this essay's purposes, it also motivates Wordsworth as he tests meter's capacity to confer an inexhaustible re-readability on literary representations. Wordsworth insists in the Preface on rhythm's capacity – comprised as it is of 'small, but continual and regular impulses of pleasurable surprise' – to subsume sublimity's intense and incandescent moments into a pattern so that they can no longer ambush us; he also wishes to understand the repetitions of metrical composition as a 'self-regulation

generated by the passionate mind itself'. The Preface accordingly valor-
izes meter as a tonic, one keeping readers, as well as writers, on an even
keel, vibrating steadily.[18] Of course, when, in the Preface, Wordsworth
discusses how the re-readability of Shakespeare's pathetic scenes depends
on a metrical arrangement that tempers over-stimulating excitement as
it introduces 'the co-presence of something regular, something to which
the mind has been accustomed', this praise for the Bard comes precisely
at the expense of the novel. For Wordsworth, Samuel Richardson's *Clarissa*
typifies the distressing writing whose re-perusal health-conscious readers
would avoid. He appeals to 'Reader's own experience of the reluctance
with which he comes to the re-perusal of the distressful parts', whose
Shakespearean counterparts this reader re-imbibes with a contrasting
avidity.[19] Nonetheless, Wordsworth notwithstanding, there are also
signs – ones I will engage shortly – that prose fiction (even Richardson's)
was coming to absorb the remedial functions outlined in the Romantics'
quasi-medical accounts of the virtues of metrical verse.

First, however, let us linger over how the Preface to *Lyrical Ballads*
promotes poetry as an 'hourly companion' and how that phrase almost
makes poetry's high calling depend on its status as an object with
which we may not only spend but also *keep* time. This reference to
around-the-clock reader-friendliness chimes with other formulations
the period coins to valorize literature's soliciting of perdurable attachments. There is, for instance, Coleridge's comment, gesturing toward
the same hydraulic model of poetic action and stress reduction that
we see in Wordsworth's Preface, that a 'genuine admiration of a great
poet' is a 'continuous under-current of feeling … every where present,
but seldom any where a separate excitement'.[20] There is 'the book for a
parlour-window', mentioned by one author after another in the decades
intervening between, at one end, Sterne's *Tristram Shandy* and Johnson's
Life of Cowley (where, as we have seen, the *Faerie Queene* appears in
this guise) and, at the other end, Leigh Hunt's *Book for a Corner*: the
phrase is recurrently recycled as a moniker for a book that itself solicits
perpetual recycling. (Montaigne, with whom the phrase originates, was
vexed that his *Essays* might 'only serve … for a common moveable, a
Book to lie in the Parlour Window', but to be that book that is never
returned to the bookcase but instead left in the open, the book that is
put to everyday use as a source of 'constant recreation', could define
the ambition of Montaigne's eighteenth-century and Romantic-period
successors.)[21] To ponder such coinages alongside the Preface's celebration of the Poet as 'hourly companion' is to acquire some leverage on
an important later-nineteenth-century development in the intersecting

histories of time and of L-Iterature: this is the moment when literary anthologies begin to aspire to the condition of the almanac, aspire, that is, to be the daily remembrancers with which the public will keep time. Victorian titles such as *Birthday echoes from the poets: a selection of choice quotations arranged for every day of the year* commemorate this development, as do the kitschy poem-a-day calendars and literary diaries that may be sitting atop our own desks right now.

The Victorian recipients of such books were promised that they would be able (in the accustomed phrase) 'to go through the year' with the authors, or, more intimately still, with a favourite author (a role assigned by these volumes to, variously, Chaucer, Shakespeare, Milton, Cowper, Burns, Keats, Scott, the Brontës, the Brownings, George Eliot, Dickens, Hardy, Kipling, Longfellow, Whittier, and Brett Harte – not an exhaustive list). These 'remembrancers' and 'birthday books' – whose selections are arranged so as to constitute a 'daily text book', as the subtitle of *The Hemans Birthday Book* explains (*A Selection of beautiful passages from the poems of Felician Hemans, arranged as a daily text book*) – bind the individual's cultivation of her literary sensibility to the practices she uses to mark off the progress of the year, to remember anniversaries, and to keep her appointments. Victorian publishers' recognition that the sensation of dailiness could itself be an object of their marketing earlier conditioned even their handling of the Bible, motivating their mutation of immutable holy writ. The term 'textbook', the OED instructs us, took on a new, specialized meaning circa 1861, as a designation for 'a book containing a selection of Scripture texts, arranged for daily use or easy reference'.

One of the earliest of Leigh Hunt's anthologizing projects, to return for one more moment to the editor of *Book for a Corner*, suggests that one ought to backdate this aspiration to fuse the anthology with the almanac and fuse canonicity with the continuities of daily life. In 1819 that aspiration produced *The Literary Pocket-Book; or Companion for the Lover of Nature and Art*, where Hunt tries out an odd compound of anthology, almanac, commonplace book, London guidebook, and historical primer. To take care of the last of these departments, the Pocket-Book incorporates a 'Chronological list of eminent persons in letters, philosophy, and the arts', which runs from Tristmegistus to Mary Wollstonecraft and Madame de Staël; this account of time as sequence is counterbalanced by a 'Calendar of Nature' (a description of the progress of the seasons and nature's varied appearances through the year) that presents time as cycle. Hunt's Introduction also spells out his hope that, primed by the notations in the Diary section that mark the birthdays of men of 'ORIGINAL genius', the purchaser of *The Literary Pocket-Book* may be tempted after 'he turns, for his ordinary memoranda, to the Diary', 'to make some little homage in the course of the day to the memory of a favourite writer or artist – to drink it after dinner or turn to his life or works'.[22] Almanac and pocket-book makers had by Hunt's day set in place a system of print protocols that might make visible time's uniformity (the empty spaces of identical dimension, one succeeding the other as the almanac's user proceeds methodically through the book). In Hunt's hands, the dailiness of literariness, made to fit this established format, becomes visible too. He has arranged matters so that not only the new poems that he introduces in the volume's section of 'Original Poetry' (by Keats, among others), but also a larger literary tradition, alike end up allied with the steady cyclicity and measured regularity of time. Such a scheme – like another for a *Muses' Almanack* that Thomas Hood floated in 1823[23] – builds bridges between personal experience (the domain of familiar intimacy and everyday routines) and public time, between subjective time and literature's.

Gradually refashioned, along lines like these, as a prop to domestic routine and private intimacies, literature fostered long-term commitments, not mere flings. Where passions were what set the pulses racing in theories of the sublime, now, as befitted a culture increasingly intent on squaring love with marriage, literature occasioned attachment – something more enduring than passion and more healthy than excitement. And if, by the nineteenth century, literature came to be viewed as the one discourse capable, in Ian Duncan's words, of reaching 'across the ... field of public exchange, [of] reaching to and from an inalienable private core of identity',[24] the increasing authority claimed by *novels* in particular within this scheme might be ascribed to the fact that the office Duncan describes may be performed best, not so much when literature annexes life's unrepeatable high points, thrills, and spills, as when it merges, intimately, with life's steady state and the cyclical rhythms of our everyday holding patterns. Novel reading and novel writing are oriented to the long haul. Indeed, one reason to make our histories of reading accountable to the force of habit and the pleasures of banal routine is the better to understand how in the early nineteenth century, the novel form, johnny-come-lately to literariness, could belatedly begin its cultural ascendancy. The fact that novels are long, long enough so that even on its first reading a novel can be something you make a habit of, might have contributed to the form's increasing authority for a culture that wanted its standard texts and favourite authors to be steadying ones.

Voluminous fiction

The discussion of 'Voluminous Authors' that the essayist Mary Russell Mitford includes in her 1851 *Recollections of a Literary Life* thus grants a place of privilege to the novel, as it assesses what Mitford describes as that 'intimate ... familiarity' that a reader develops when living with a book long in itself or when reading through the complete works of a single author. Mitford explains that this familiarity represents the secret of the success, during her lifetime, of a sequence of new series fictions: first, the Waverley Series, and then, in the 1830s, Balzac's Human Comedy, and the novels of James Fenimore Cooper, who (she remarks) 'extended to fifteen volumes the adventures of Leather-Stocking, until every reader offered his hand to greet the honest backwoodsman as if he had been a daily visitor'.[25] Her comment about voluminous fiction's daily calls helps us to think about the historicity of the desires – perhaps we should call them intimacy expectations – at work when we look for a novel that goes on forever, or that we can make go on again and again, that desire that converts some novels from daily visitors into semi-permanent residents on our bedside tables. A significant pre-history informs that particular form of routinized intimacy that is exemplified still by those readers (well known to many of us) who, say, reread every Austen novel every summer vacation or who set aside a Palliser novel for every trans-Atlantic airplane trip. In a century in which the medical profession was promoting habit as a key to health (eating, drinking, sleeping by rule), reading could represent another routine activity that readers would undertake to preserve for themselves a base-line of round-the-clock normality. Mitford's comment about fiction's daily calls thus helps us think about the terms under which novels belatedly obtained medico-moral sanction. Novels last (they go on and on) and maybe that is why they last (are deemed worthy of joining the permanent library).

However over-stimulating or nerve-wracking the consumption of some novels might have been, evidence from the annals of nineteenth-century reading confirms that novelists had been recruited for the regimens and daily rounds that ensured healthy living. The novelist had become an inmate of those households who were lauded for presenting an edifying spectacle of regular hours and uniform habits, who, as historian John Gillis proposes, began, in the nineteenth century, to zealously mark time – conform to daily and weekly schedules for their meals, walks, visits, and devotions, observe anniversaries and birthdays – in ways that were supposed to shield them against time's terrors. Nineteenth-century households were beginning to fashion family time as a time that went, ceremoniously, in circles: thus, in the mid-Victorian period, Gillis writes, 'families began to organize the day into an endless cycle of meals and bedtimes that has changed remarkably little since'.[26] And regularly scheduled appointments with novels provided one metronome the nineteenth century used to adhere to this rhythm method.

It is tempting to imagine that if we could time-travel and take with us an especially sensitive stethoscope, we might as visitors to Britain around the year 1830 actually be able to hear, as if it were a heartbeat, or a kind of bass line, pounding beneath the louder noise of public history, the rhythm that the inhabitants steadily beat out as, turning pages they had turned before, often at the same time of week or year as before, reciting according to schedule the familiar words they had recited before, they conformed to their bookish routines. A kind of low hum might be heard emanating from the nation's domiciles, perhaps soaring into audibility as the several re-reading cycles converge, which they seem to do on winter evenings especially. Hark, our time traveller might say, they are at it again – and not just going through *The Christian Year* with John Keble or using Wordsworth (as John Ruskin attested he did) 'as a daily text-book from youth to age'; but also reading the *Vicar of Wakefield* through every winter (an annual ritual for the poet John Clare, who, he wrote, preferred in his readerly life his old acquaintances and did 'not care to make new ones'); or listening to a Waverley Novel read aloud every Saturday night 'after the candles were snuffed and the fire was stirred' (the custom of the so-called Quaker Poet Bernard Barton, the friend of Charles Lamb, who always on these occasions, his memoirist reported, 'anticipat[ed] with a glance, or an impatient ejaculation of pleasure, the good things he knew were coming – which he liked the better for knowing they were coming').[27] Around 1860 the steady hum gets louder. We have Leslie Stephen making arrangements to secure his household, too, in steady proximity to the Waverley Novels, arrangements commemorated in his daughter's *To the Lighthouse*. And, even more noteworthily, we have the entrance en masse of the Janeites, all those eminent Victorian sages and Oxbridge dons, determined to make Austenian reading inextricable from the resuming, repeating, and remembering of Austenian reading, and programmatically committing themselves to the following schedule: 'all six, every year'. (The phrase is attributed to the philosopher Gilbert Ryle, who is said to have responded with those laconic four words when asked if he ever read novels).[28]

Relevant here is a story that by the early nineteenth century was being shared between the genres of literary biography and medical case history. In the final five years of his life, also the final five years of the eighteenth century, the famous mad poet William Cowper had alternated between walks with his caretakers along the seashore, where, his memoirist reports, his spirit was soothed by 'the monotonous sound of the breakers' and, on days when the weather turned inclement, by a routine deemed equivalent: as others read aloud, he revisited books that he had encountered before, giving preference, we are told, to 'voluminous' fiction, his kinsman John Johnson's term, prefiguring Mitford's, for a category of reading matter constituted first and foremost by Richardson's novels.[29] Richardson in *this* therapeutic regimen (Wordsworth got it wrong), Scott in another: Walter Bagehot said there were no such books as the Waverley Novels 'for the sick-room, or for freshening the painful intervals of a morbid mind'.[30] But Austen's works appear to have been especially likely to focus regularly scheduled ceremonies of readerly fidelity. Or perhaps it would be better to call them readerly doses. The precise way in which the Victorians kept faith with her fiction can sometimes seem less an expression of love than the expression of the solicitude of a valetudinarian scheduling regular appointments with his physician.

D. A. Miller wrote in a 1990 essay of how for many years whenever felled by flu, he needed to 'take to [his] bed', he would take Jane Austen there with him.[31] That confession installed Miller (as, doubtless, he knew) in a pantheon of gentlemen-invalids. For instance, the 'eminent persons' whose opinions of his aunt's novels J. E. Austen-Leigh catalogued in his 1871 *Memoir of Jane Austen* include in their number a certain Lord Holland, who, whenever afflicted by the gout, would also take to bed and have his sister read aloud from 'one of Miss Austen's novels, of which [we are told] [Lord Holland] never wearied'.[32] Meanwhile, at Cambridge, the University Chair of Sanskrit, Edward Byles Cowell, had formed the habit of reading Miss Austen each night 'after his Sanskrit Philology [was] done'; Cowell's former pupil in Persian, the poet Edward Fitzgerald, reported that Cowell found that the novels *composed* him, 'like Gruel'.[33]

Calling to public attention his ordering of the entries in *The Golden Treasury* (1861), pluming himself on the achievement, Francis Turner Palgrave, the Victorian anthologist who followed in Johnson's and Hunt's footsteps, referenced a set of medical truisms about the brain, attention, and time. Strict chronology as a principle of arrangement had its dangers in a book of the *Golden Treasury*'s sort, Palgrave cautioned, because '[t]he English mind has passed through phases of thought and cultivation so various and so opposed during these three centuries of Poetry, that a rapid passage between old and new, like rapid alteration of the eye's focus in looking at the landscape, will always be wearisome and hurtful'.[34] Palgrave's allusion to the perceptual disorders thought to be wrought by railway travel and the attendant experience of speed reminds us that under the aegis of modernity's temporal order it became possible, as usages recorded in the OED also confirm, for people, as well as clocks and machinery, to find themselves 'mistimed'. The adjective designates the digestive disturbances, sleep disorders, and railway brain – the arrhythmic ailments, that is, that were to be counteracted by bedtime routines like the Sanskrit Professor's.[35] A public anxious to forestall modern mistiming could dose itself with its *Golden Treasury*, but novels had also begun to be heralded for their utility as pace-makers. When in 1871 Anne Thackeray Ritchie commends Jane Austen's works, she emphasizes their particular suitability for this office. If, in modern novels, the clocks too frequently run off kilter, Austen's works are different: 'No retrospects, no abrupt flights; as in real life days and events follow one another. Last Tuesday does not suddenly start into existence all out of place; nor does 1790 appear upon the scene when we are well on in '21 ... With Jane Austen days, hours, minutes succeed each other like clockwork'.[36]

What follows if we take seriously the novelist's own seriousness about serving in this office? For a start, that acknowledgement might lead us to rethink the centrality we've granted to *novelty* in our account of the preconditions for the genre's rise. In a recent essay, Franco Moretti has linked the novel's nineteenth-century respectability to a new narrative hierarchy ushered in by Austen and, to a lesser extent, Scott. These two relegate the unheard of and the untoward, earlier fiction's strange, surprising adventures, to the background of the form. At the same time, they relocate to the foreground the more modest events – the walking, talking, eating and shopping, say – that give regularity to existence. In their hands, fillers – materials that are reluctant to narration – triumph over plot, a shift that remakes the novel as, Moretti declares, a 'Weberian form, where time becomes more predictable'.[37] (Moretti might mis-date this remaking. Other evidence suggests that it was in the mid-eighteenth century that the novel began contributing to the labours that would put the spirit of the age on a schedule. 'I must inform you', Lady Bradshaigh, the novelist's biggest fan, wrote to Samuel Richardson in 1749, 'this is another benefit received from your *Clarissa* ... She has also taught me to keep an account of my time'.)[38] Thus for instance

Emma, centred on a set of characters more or less boxed in by their diurnal routines. Over the course of his extended life – extended by his adherence to dietary restrictions, by his horror of late hours and draughts, and by his resolute way of keeping his daughter on a short tether – Mr. Woodhouse, this set's stick-in-the-mud-in-chief, has apparently worked out a full-fledged theory of scheduled sociability, which is out-lined by the narrator in the following passage: 'Mrs. and Miss Bates and Mrs. Godard, three ladies almost always at the service of an invitation from Hartfield, ... were fetched and carried home so often that Mr. Woodhouse thought it no hardship for either James or the horses. *Had it taken place only once a year, it would have been a grievance'.*[39] Emma's stay-at-home dad might suffer from qualms of conscience in contemplating how his arrangements for whiling away his evenings at home unceasingly send his coachman and his horses out of the house. But to appease those qualms he is able, characteristically, to appeal to the alchemy of habit – that queer arithmetic in which augmenting the number of repetitions of an action makes its performance less burdensome.

To what extent did novels cue their readers to their own desire to figure in the homely scenes that they themselves deploy to fill up the space between turning points and to damp down the excitements of plot? Might we connect the form's ascendancy to the public's willing-ness to ratify the proposition that, under ideal conditions, every reading might represent a resumption of an earlier, interrupted reading? This might explain the appeal for Victorians of series like Anthony Trollope's Barsetshire or Palliser Chronicles (whose forte is going over the same ground again), and also, despite the contrast between the sprawl of those Victorian monsters and the chic economy of Austen's novels of everyday life, it might also explain the appeal of Austen, whose works – 'all six, every year' – have often been consumed as if they constituted a series.[40] Leah Price has proposed that novel studies has been disabled by its practitioners' reluctance to remember that novel-reading is as much a matter of impatient skipping and skimming as appreciative lingering.[41] Taking Price's argument in a different direction, one might note that practitioners of novel studies likewise tend to overlook the peculiarities at stake in that mode of appreciative lingering that involves making a habit of a novel. Rereading – and the repetition of rereading – work to release a novel from its internal chronology. This practice guarantees the superannuation of narrative content. It makes the resident more important than the incident. It subordinates closure to continuation. There is more to say about the place within the tradition of the novel of readers' attraction to the genre's sheer protractedness and their strategies for exacerbating it, making a favourite fiction interminable.

Austen critics of the present-day have rarely, however, accounted for the ways in which nineteenth-century people incorporated her works into the periodic practices that, affirming time's underlying homogeneity, made them feel at home in time. Writing on Austen has instead tended to emphasize telos-driven marriage plots.[42] Forgetting about how our own reading practices, semester in, semester out, take us in circles, academic readers represent the experience of an Austen novel as a process in which we ride headlong the forward momentum of a courtship narrative and so hasten together (as *Northanger Abbey* puts it) toward 'perfect felicity'.[43] But within nineteenth-century culture there is a powerful alternative, I've been suggesting, to this normative account of how in *reading* Austen, the reader indulges the fantasy of *being* Elizabeth or *being* Emma and thereby undergoes by surrogate the moral education tracking a heroine for matrimony. Victorian readers, Edith Wharton declared, writing in this instance autobiographically and as a belated member of that group, often forgot the Austen novels' *events*, because they were haunted instead by 'the remembrance of ... [the characters'] little daily round of preoccupations and pleasures'.[44] Confirming Wharton's observation, it appears that in *reading* Austen, many Victorians – or at least the gentlemen-invalids among them – indulge the fantasy of *being* Emma's *father*.

Many Victorians discussed what was paradoxical about the pleasure they took in the tedious prosing of a Mr. Woodhouse, a boring person whom they would shun in real life.[45] As we have seen, however, some of their contemporaries topped this, making their novel-reading a way to replicate and reiterate that old bore's life-long valetudinarian regimen of regular hours, daily constitutionals (all those walks around the Hartfield shrubbery), and, of course, gruel. 'Lord Beaconsfield [Benjamin Disraeli] professed to have read "Pride and Prejudice" 17 times. One wonders no longer that a statesman who was so often in such company should have found himself on the side of the angels'.[46] Their lifetime (re-)reading plans furnished these eminent Victorians – even a prime minister, it would appear – with the pleasures of familiarity, but also, independent of the actual content of the books, with the pleasures that are to be obtained by periodically picking up again where one left off, and of picking up again after one had left off. To be sure, such routines place loveability and take-it-for-grantedness, pleasure and tedium, in a delicate balance. But it is worth noting that one 1824 reviewer, discussing routinization in Scott's Waverley series and the routinization of the

Waverley series, proposed that *the bore* was a 'weighty office ... necessary in every well-regulated novel, as a constitutional check upon the levity of the other characters'.[47]

Fidelity

I want to suggest, by way of conclusion, that acknowledging novels' role in the routines defining this well-regulated, steady state and acknowledging their role in the particular forms of intimacy we associate with everyday life might help us to see something else about the institution we call the canon. This is the programme of moral and psychological assessment – the constellation of diagnostic discourses examining the relationship of feeling to memory, to recollected feeling, and to identity – that this institution came to house. The anthologist Francis Palgrave complains in an 1860 essay for *Macmillan's Magazine* that he lives in an era when 'everything is to be read, and *everything only once*; a book is no more a treasure to be kept ... if deserving that intimacy'. Palgrave decries the contemporary reader – some one unable, Palgrave claims, to 'read even novelties more than once' – as a figure handicapped by (as a modern therapist might put it) his commitment issues. Palgrave's statement suggests the overlap between discussions of the canon and moral and psychological assessments of its readers, as it suggests the supporting role that is played within the institution of literature of those pedagogies that have also put the couple form at the centre of modern erotic life. For that new notion of the canon as a library for all times rests on an account of good readers as those in relationships for the long haul. Thus the peroration with which Palgrave concludes his essay: over and against that reader who reads everything once, he applauds the reader who will read 'mainly the best books, and [who will] begin again when the series is ended'.[48]

'On Readers in 1760 and 1860' reconfirms a premise that Leah Price has made central to the discipline's current discussions of canonicity. As we saw at the outset, when Shenstone's sleeping arrangements gave Leigh Hunt his emblem for the ideal reader of *A Book for a Corner*, discourses on the canon promote not a specific content (a specific book list) but a particular hierarchy of readers and styles of reading. As Palgrave's essay testifies, the idea of literature has been mobilized both as a mechanism for establishing hierarchical differences among readers – for diagnosing some readers' moral failings – *and* as a resource ushering individuals into health-giving unanimity and community. To stop there, however, would be premature, since it's tricky to know how to assess the resemblance that links, on the one hand, Palgrave's praiseworthy public who begin their best books over again to, on the other hand, the book-nerds, slackers, and creatures of habit that, as we have seen, nineteenth-century gentlemen became in their off-hours. That trickiness should interest us: At what point do the commitments demanded by and supporting the idea of a canon become evidence that the reader is in a Woodhouseian rut? How does one distinguish fidelity to 'the best that has been thought and said' from the mental inertia of a creature of habit? (The children of Matthew Arnold – whose definition of culture as 'the best' thinking and saying I have just cited – appear to have been inspired by their father's annual return visits to Austen's fiction when they coined their nickname for him: they called him Mr. Woodhouse.)[49]

To ask these questions is to discern, I suspect, a peculiar overlap between modern canonicity and modern valetudinarianism. Charles Lamb, his contemporary Thomas Noon Talfourd reported, had contrived to miss out altogether on the Waverley Novels, 'preferring to read Fielding and Smollett and Richardson, whose stories were familiar, over and over again, to being worried with the task of threading the maze of fresh adventure'.[50] It is an open question in Talfourd's biography whether Lamb's way with books is being recommended for emulation, or whether this equanimity that takes Lamb beyond the pleasure principle is meant to irk those less fastidious readers who have, after all, managed to break with their routines and read Talfourd.

In the 1821 essay 'On reading old books' that supplied my first epigraph, Lamb's friend William Hazlitt presents himself as the anti-type to female readers who en masse judge of books 'as they do of fashions ... admired only "in their newest gloss"'.[51] As Hazlitt parades his fidelity to the self-same volumes and ability to dispense with new ones, and as he manages thereby to set appreciation and acquisition at odds with each other, he attests to his distinction. The pleasures of the imagination are here wedded to the pleasures of social calculation. Not increasing his literary acquaintance is Hazlitt's way to increase his cultural capital, renegotiate his social position. But attending to the stratagems that advance social mobility will get us only so far in explaining the aspirations to immobility that inform this steady reader's chosen mode of self-fashioning – and that, more generally, inform his contemporaries' ways of incorporating old books into those periodic practices that help people experience time as a steady state.

Hazlitt taps a long history of negative representations of female reading – his contemporaries' innumerable descriptions, in particular, of the novel addict who is always upping her dose. But his disinclination to change his old books for new can, in its turn, look like an addiction to sameness. This is steadiness in a different, less healthful mode. The methodology we bring to the history of reading needs to be supple enough to acknowledge how figures like Hazlitt and Lamb can, observed from one angle, appear paragons of fidelity, but observed from another, appear to be converting a virtuous monogamy into a modern perversion.

Notes

My work on this essay was supported by a fellowship from the John Simon Guggenheim Memorial Foundation. I would also like to thank Tom Keirstead, Laura Mandell, Mary Ann O'Farrell, Adela Pinch, and audiences at the "Bookish Histories" conference, McMaster University, and the University of Madison, Wisconsin for other forms of assistance.

1. 'Life of Cowley', in *Lives of the English Poets*, ed. George Birkbeck Hill (New York: Octagon Books, 1967), vol. 1, p. 2; for the 'Life of Shenstone', Ibid., vol. 3, p. 348. The lines that Johnson recalls in his 'Life of Cowley' are to be found in Cowley's essay 'Of My Self', in *Works of Mr. Abraham Cowley*, eleventh edition (London: J. Tonson, 1710), vol. 2, p. 782.
2. *The Anthology and the Rise of the Novel* (Cambridge: Cambridge University Press, 2000), pp. 71; 70. Also relevant here is Barbara M. Benedict's proposal that the eighteenth-century literary miscellany marks a new acknowledgement of readers as participants in and makers of literary culture, *Making the Modern Reader: Cultural Mediation in Early Modern Literary Anthologies* (Princeton: Princeton University Press, 1996), p. 5.
3. *A Book for a Corner, or Selections in Prose and Verse from Authors The Best Suited to that Mode of Enjoyment* (London: Chapman and Hall, 1849), vol. 1, pp. 8; v; 2.
4. Compare Jonah Siegel's insightful comments on the limitations he finds in much current work on the politics of cultural institutions and the disciplinary effects of disciplines: 'the institutions that contribute to our making are themselves evidently reshaped by needs, confusion, even passions, which have more interesting forms than the ultimately banal ones of coercion, complicity, submission, or resistance. The paradigmatic forms for the relation of self and institution may be best looked for not in the ultimately simple power structures of the prison, but in those suggested by the more complex and inescapable interplay of complicity and resistance that characterizes the self in relation to the family, or by the dark promises and disappointments the family shares with the passions of the erotic life'(*Desire and Excess: The Nineteenth-Century Culture of Art* [Princeton: Princeton University Press, 2000], p. 284 n.1).
5. This characterization of *Lives of the English Poets* is found in Alvin Kernan, *Printing, Technology, Letters, and Samuel Johnson* (Princeton: Princeton University Press, 1979), p. 272.
6. 'Dickens, The Haunting Man (On L-iterature)'. Paper given at the conference *A Man for All Media: The Popularity of Dickens, 1902–2002*, Institute for

English Studies, University of London, 2002, http://www.bbk.ac.uk/english/skc/haunting (accessed 26 December 2006).

7. Bloom, *The Western Canon: The Books and School of the Ages* (New York: Harcourt Brace, 1994), 30; cf. Frank Kermode, 'Institutional Control of Interpretation', *Salmagundi* 43 (1979), 72–86. I receive assistance here from William Paulson, 'The Literary Canon in the Age of Its Technical Obsolescence', in *Reading Matters: Narrative in the New Media Ecology*, ed. Joseph Tabbi and Michael Wutz (Ithaca, NY: Cornell University Press, 1997), pp. 240–1.

8. Re-reading is struggle and suffering in François Roustang's 'On Reading Again', in *The Limits of Theory*, ed. Thomas M. Kavanagh (Stanford: Stanford University Press, 1989), pp. 121–38; see also Matei Calinescu, *Rereading* (New Haven: Yale University Press, 1993); Roland Barthes, *S/Z*, trans. Richard Miller (New York: Farrar, Straus and Giroux, 1974), pp. 15–16.

9. 'Uncritical Reading', in *Polemic: Critical or Uncritical*, ed. Jane Gallop (New York: Routledge, 2004), pp. 13–38.

10. The fact that very few of us can remember a time when we had to *will* our eyes to move across the page, when our reading wasn't something that simply happened was for writers from David Hartley in 1749 (*Observations on Man, His Frame, His Duty, and His Expectations*) to Erasmus Darwin in the mid-1790s (*Zoönomia, or, The Laws of Organic Life* [1794–6]) to George Henry Lewes in 1877 (*The Physical Basis of Mind*) a prime example of the automatic way in which the brain repeats familiar motions, as it shifts from certain physical sensations to the ideas with which those sensations have regularly been associated in the past. For insights into the enduring importance from the mid-eighteenth century until the late nineteenth century of the principles of associationist psychology that David Hume and Hartley set out in the mid-eighteenth century and that continued to govern accounts of cerebration and memory well into the next century, see, *inter alia*, Alan Richardson, *British Romanticism and the Science of the Mind* (Cambridge: Cambridge University Press, 2001); Linda M. Austin, *Nostalgia in Transition, 1780–1917* (Charlottesville: University of Virginia Press, 2007); Nicholas M. Dames, *Amnesiac Selves: Nostalgia, Forgetting, and British Fiction, 1810–1870* (New York: Oxford University Press, 2001), Chapter 3.

11. 'I am not satisfied if a year passes without my having read [*Rasselas*] through; and at every perusal, my admiration of the mind which produced it is so highly raised, that I can scarcely believe that I had the honour of enjoying the intimacy of such a man' (James Boswell, *Life of Johnson*, ed. R. W. Chapman [Oxford: Oxford University Press, 1970], p. 242).

12. The quotation is from John Erskine's 1928 *The Delight of Great Books*, cited in W. B. Carnochan, *The Battleground of the Curriculum: Liberal Education and American Experience* (Stanford: Stanford University Press, 1993), p. 82. A Great Books course entered the Columbia University curriculum in 1920. I quote Erskine as a spokesman for a standard account of the timelessness of classic literature, but his language also evokes particularly aptly the overlooked responses to and exploitations of that category that this essay aims to recover.

13. 'Everyday Speech', trans. Susan Hanson, *Yale French Studies* 73 (1987), 14.

14. Preface to *Lyrical Ballads* (1802) in *The Oxford Authors: William Wordsworth*, ed. Stephen Gill (Oxford: Oxford University Press, 1984), p. 606.

15. John H. Crowley describes the orientation to the comfortable as 'an innovative aspect of Anglo-American culture' in the late eighteenth century, 'one that had to be taught and learned' and identifies an enlightened sub-culture of philosophers who criticized fashionable consumption in the name of comfort in ways that made the public sensible of the discomfort of domestic arrangements – smoky chimneys, for example – it had previously deemed acceptable ('The Sensibility of Comfort', *American Historical Review* 104, 3 [June 1999], pp. 750; 771). In 1794 Mary Wollstonecraft condemns ancien régime France – and establishes France's unreadiness for Revolution – by noting that the French 'have no word in their vocabulary to express *comfort* – that state of existence in which reason renders serene and useful the days, which passion would cheat with flying dreams of happiness'. The French thus, as 'slaves of pleasure or power', are to be 'roused only by lively emotions and extravagant hopes' (*An Historical and Moral View of the Origin and Progress of the French Revolution* [London: J. Johnson, 1794], p. 511).

16. Lamb, *Sterne's Fiction and the Double Principle* (Cambridge: Cambridge University Press, 1989), p. 81; Lamb cites Sterne's letter to Dr. John Eustace on p. 83. In the Romantic period, Francis Jeffrey reprised this account of aesthetic experience while identifying the best kind of poem as opposed to the best kind of reader: this was the kind 'coloured from familiar affections', that 'strike[s] root and germinate[s] in the mind, like the seeds of its native feelings ... propagat[ing] throughout the imagination that long series of delightful movements, which is only excited when the song of the poet is the echo of our familiar feelings' (Rev. of Thomas Campbell's *Gertrude of Wyoming* [1809], rept. in Francis Jeffrey, *Essays on English Poets and Poetry from the Edinburgh Review* [London: Routledge, n. d.], p. 186). Cf. the discussions of Jeffrey in Gordon McKenzie, *Critical Responsiveness: A Study of the Psychological Current in Later Eighteenth-Century Criticism* (Berkeley: University of California Press, 1949), and David Perkins, 'Romantic Reading as Revery', *European Romantic Review* 4 (1994), 183–99.

17. Preface to *Lyrical Ballads*, p. 598; *British Romanticism and the Science of the Mind*, pp. 79–81.

18. Preface to *Lyrical Ballads*, p. 610; Susan J. Wolfson, 'Romanticism and the Measures of Meter', *Eighteenth-Century Life* 16 (1992), 232. As Wolfson puts it, meter, as the 'floating signifier' of the Preface, shuttles back and forth between 'extraordinary and ordinary, ... passion and restraint', but that same shuttling Wolfson highlights as she tracks the shiftiness of the Preface's account of the legitimate language of Poetry also defines the dynamic of mental life as described by the neuro-science of the day. I am also indebted in this section to the discussion of Wordsworth's Preface in Adela Pinch, *Strange Fits of Passion: Epistemologies of Emotion, Hume to Austen* (Stanford: Stanford University Press, 1996), pp. 83–90.

19. Preface to *Lyrical Ballads*, pp. 609; 610.

20. *Biographia Literaria*, ed. James Engell and W. Jackson Bate (Princeton: Princeton University, 1983), vol. 1, p. 23.

21. 'Upon the Verses of Virgil', *Montaigne's Essays*, trans. Charles Cotton, sixth edn (London: Barker, Strahan, Ballard, et al., 1743), vol. 3, p. 71. Compare Sterne in the first volume of *The Life and Opinions of Tristram Shandy, Gentleman*: 'my life and opinions are likely to make some noise in the world,

and, if I conjecture right, will take in all ranks, professions, and denominations of men whatever – be no less read than the *Pilgrim's Progress* itself – and, in the end, prove the very thing which *Montaigne* dreaded his essays should turn out, that is, a book for a parlour-window' (introd. Robert Folkenflik [New York: Modern Library, 2004], p. 4). Cf. William Hone in the Preface to *The Table-Book*, successor to Hone's 1824 *Every-Day Book, or Everlasting Calendar of Popular Amusements, Sports, Pastimes, Ceremonies, Manners, Customs, and Events, Incident to Each of the Three Hundred and Sixty-Five Days:* 'Perhaps, if the good old window-seats had not gone out of fashion, it might be called a parlour-window book – a good name for a volume of agreeable reading selected from the book-case and left lying about, for the constant recreation of the family, and the casual amusement of visitors' ([London: Hunt and Clarke, 1827], n.p.). An 1849 advertisement for Leigh Hunt's essay collection *Men, Women, and Books* cites *The Athenaeum*'s laudatory identification of Hunt as the 'Prince of Parlour-window writers' (back-matter in Charles Hursthouse, *An Account of the Settlement of New Plymouth*, 1849, on the *Early New Zealand Books* website: http://www.enzb.auckland.ac.nz, accessed September 16, 2007).

22. *A Literary Pocket-Book* (London: C. Ollier, 1819), p. 2. This is the first of five volumes: the *Literary Pocket-Book* lasted until 1823. Thanks to Scott Nowka, who helped me navigate the Leigh Hunt Collection at the University of Iowa Rare Books Library. In many respects Hunt's *Pocket-Book* anticipates William Hone's *Every-Day Book*, sharing Hone's ambition (as the latter put it in his Explanatory Address) to provide 'a *Perpetual Guide to the Year* – not to any one year in particular but to every year'. Hunt's Calendar of Nature, for instance, prefigures the 'Floral Directory' that Hone intersperses throughout his annotations of the year's 365 celebrations. Hone's explanation of his reasons for including 'Poetical Elucidations' of this information, and so making the *Every-Day Book*, like the *Literary Pocket-Book*, an anthology of sorts, is suggestive: 'as Cowper says, that, "a volume of verse is a fiddle that sets the universe in motion," it is believed that his remark may be somewhat verified by the pleasant images and kind feelings, with the interspersion of much excellent poetry throughout the work is designed to create in all classes of readers' (n.p.).

23. *The Letters of Thomas Hood*, ed. Peter F. Morgan (Edinburgh: Oliver and Boyd, 1973), p. 686. I owe this reference to Sara Lodge's informative 'Romantic Reliquaries: Memory and Irony in the Literary Annuals', *Romanticism* 10, 1 (2004), 23–40.

24. *Modern Romance and Transformations of the Novel* (Cambridge: Cambridge University Press, 1992), p. 195.

25. *Recollections of a Literary Life, or, Books, Places and People* (1851; rept. New York: Harper and Brothers, 1862), p. 343.

26. 'Making time for family: the invention of family time(s) and the reinvention of family history', *Journal of Family History* 21, 1 (1996), 88.

27. See Kirstie Blair, 'John Keble and the Rhythm of Faith', *Essays in Criticism* 53, 2 (2003), 129–50; Ruskin, 'Fiction, Fair and Foul' (1880), *The Complete Works of John Ruskin*, ed. E. T. Cook and Alexander Wedderburn (London: George Allen and New York: Longmans, Green, and Co., 1902), vol. 34, p. 349; *John Clare by Himself*, ed. Eric Robinson and David Powell

(Ashington, Northumberland and Manchester: Mid Northumberland Arts Group and Carcanet Press, 1996), p. 56; E.F.G. [Edward Fitzgerald], 'Memoir of Bernard Barton', in *The Poems and Letters of Bernard Barton, Edited by his Daughter* (London: Hall, Virtue, and Co., 1849), p. xxxiv. Barton likewise knew by heart 'all of the good things' in Boswell's *Life of Johnson* and would 'sit at table, his snuff-box in his hand, ... repeating some favourite passage, and glancing his fine brown eyes about him as he recited'.

28. I owe this quotation and many insights in this section of this essay to Mary A. Favret's 'Jane Austen at 25', unpublished paper delivered for the 2005 Meeting of the Chicago chapter of the Jane Austen Society of North America. See also Gilbert Ryle, 'Jane Austen and the Moralists', in B. C. Southam, ed., *Critical Essays on Jane Austen* (London: Routledge Kegan Paul, 1968), pp. 106–23.

29. I quote John Johnson's Introduction to Vol. 3 of *The Poems of William Cowper, Containing His Posthumous Poetry, and a Sketch of His Life* (London: T. C. and J. Rivington, 1815), pp. lv and lx, but other biographers – William Hayley in *The Life and Posthumous Writings of William Cowper* (1803) and Robert Southey in *The Life of William Cowper* (1839) – also recount the story of the poet's medicinal use of already-known novels. The American physician Benjamin Rush draws on the example of Cowper in his discussion of the 'hypochondriasis' and of treatments ensuring the 'return of regularity and order in the operations of the mind': *Medical Inquiries and Observations upon The Diseases of the Mind* (1812; rept. New York: Hafner, 1962), p. 210; on Cowper's story see pp. 118; 122.

30. Quoted in Dino Felluga, *The Perversity of Poetry: Romantic Ideology and the Popular Male Poet of Genius* (Albany, NY: SUNY Press, 2005), p. 41.

31. 'The Late Jane Austen', *Raritan* 10 (1990), 55.

32. J. E. Austen-Leigh, *A Memoir of Jane Austen, and Other Family Recollections*, ed. Kathryn Sutherland (Oxford: Oxford University Press, 2002), p. 112.

33. *The Letters of Edward Fitzgerald*, vol. 3 (1867–76), ed. Alfred McKinley Terhune and Annabelle Burdick Terhune (Princeton: Princeton University Press, 1980), p. 240.

34. *The Golden Treasury of the Best Songs and Lyrical Poems in the English Language, Selected and Arranged with Notes by Francis Turner Palgrave*, ed. Christopher Ricks (London: Penguin, 1991), p. 6.

35. The OED's first illustrative quotation is from a publication of 1841, Congregationalist minister Richard W. Hamilton's *Nugae literariae: prose and verse*: 'He has not slept for the last three nights. No wonder he is ill: he is quite mistimed'. The usage is marked as being largely restricted to Scotland and northern England.

36. Anne Thackeray Ritchie, *A Book of Sibyls* (London: Smith, Elder, 1883), p. 201; this reprints a series of *Cornhill Magazine* essays from 1871.

37. Franco Moretti, 'Serious Century', in *The Novel*, vol. 1, ed. Franco Moretti (Princeton: Princeton University Press, 2006), p. 400.

38. Anna Laetitia Barbauld, ed., *The Correspondence of Samuel Richardson* (London: Phillips, 1804), vol. 4, p. 264.

39. *Emma*, ed. James Kinsley (Oxford: Oxford University Press, 1995), p. 17; emphasis added.

40. Laurie Langbauer begins her book on the series in Victorian culture by confessing that she brought her need for a novel that was everlasting even to her reading of Austen: 'Even novels that weren't connected I read as if they were, running straight through Austen's fiction – all just the various adventures possible to one exceptional heroine' (*Novels of Everyday Life: The Series in English Fiction, 1850–1930* [Ithaca, N.Y.: Cornell University Press, 1999], p. 1). For an account of how the Victorians anticipated Langbauer in this understanding of Austen and how Austen's way with time's periodicity influences the chronicling of the everyday that Anthony Trollope and Margaret Oliphant undertake in their Barsetshire and Carlingford Chronicles respectively, see my 'Austen Extended/Austen for Everyday Use', in *Imagining Selves: Essays in Honor of Patrician Meyer Spacks*, ed. Elise Lauterbach and Rivka Swensen (Newark, DE: University of Delaware Press, forthcoming [2009]).

41. *The Anthology and the Rise of the Novel*, 156.

42. Claudia L. Johnson identifies this emphasis on the marriage plot as an artifact of the mid-twentieth-century professionalization of novel studies: 'The Divine Miss Jane: Jane Austen, Janeites, and the Discipline of Novel Studies', rpt. in *Janeites: Austen's Disciples and Devotees*, ed. Deidre Lynch (Princeton: Princeton University Press, 2000), pp. 25–44.

43. Jane Austen, *Northanger Abbey*, ed. John Davie (Oxford: Oxford University Press, 1990), p. 203.

44. Edith Wharton, *The Writing of Fiction* (New York: Scribner, 1925), p. 128.

45. Richard Whately gets this strain of commentary underway in his 1821 *Quarterly Review* essay on Austen, reprinted in B. C. Southam, *Jane Austen: The Critical Heritage*, vol. 1 (London: Routledge Kegan Paul, 1968), pp. 87–105: see p. 98. Compare the poem on Austen's fiction that George Howard, sixth Earl of Carlisle, published in *The Keepsake* of 1835, which includes the line 'Miss Bates, our idol, though the village bore'. The poem is transcribed (and misdated) in J. E. Austen-Leigh's *A Memoir of Jane Austen*, p. 111

46. Adolphus Jack, *Essays on the Novel: As Illustrated by Scott and Miss Austen* (London: Macmillan, 1897), p. 257.

47. Thomas De Quincey, 'Walladmor: Walter Scott's German Novel', in *The Works of Thomas De Quincey*, vol. 4, ed. Frederick Burwick (London: Pickering and Chatto, 2000), p. 236.

48. 'On Readers in 1760 and 1860', *Macmillan's Magazine* 1 (1859–60), 489.

49. B. C. Southam, Introduction, *Jane Austen: The Critical Heritage*, vol. 2 (1870–1940) (London: Routledge Kegan Paul, 1987), p. 13.

50. *Memoirs of Charles Lamb* (1838), ed. Percy Fitzgerald (London: Gibbings and Co., 1894), p. 269.

51. *The Complete Works of William Hazlitt*, ed. P. P. Howe (London: J. M. Dent, 1931), vol. 12, p. 220.

5
Book-Love and the Remaking of Literary Culture in the Romantic Periodical

Ina Ferris

Musing on 'The Book to Come' in a 1997 lecture at the Bibliothèque nationale, Jacques Derrida declared, 'I'm in love with the book, in my own way and forever'. But what is it one loves when in love with 'the book'? Derrida himself (deconstructively enough) does not quite know: 'The word *book* is as difficult to define as the question of the book, at least if the wish is to grant it a sharp specificity, and to cut it out in its irreducibility, at the point where it resists so many neighboring, connected, and even inseparable questions'[1] Such a pure cutting out of the book is of course impossible – Derrida's own subsequent definition of book's essence as 'the idea of *gathering together*' overlays book and archive – but the point is to foreground the displacement whereby 'book' characteristically functions in critical discourse as a sign pointing to contiguous, more conceptual signs such as 'writing', 'print' or 'the work', which then absorb the book. Literary history has long enacted such a conflation, even literary history of a more bookish cast, typically dissolving books into 'literature' on the one hand and into 'reading' on the other (reading itself being understood primarily in terms of imaginative genres). To love books, however, is not necessarily to love either literature or reading, as witness those book-collectors who notoriously never open the books to which they are devoted.[2] But it is always to love *contact* with books, so that in the first instance, we might say, 'the book' names a particular form of material encounter. In the early decades of the nineteenth century, when printed books first achieved an extensive hold in Great Britain, this understanding of the book ramified into the wider culture of literacy in an important way, generating a material imagination of the book whose implications we are only beginning to explore. Imbued with an intense awareness of the presence of books, I want to argue, the period exemplifies a concrete 'book-sense' to be distinguished from the more abstract book-consciousness (a mentality shaped by reading) with which literary studies are more familiar. Articulated in informal bibliophilic writing, which proliferated in these years, and promulgated in the periodical press through the familiar essay, the book-sense of the Romantic period brings into sharp focus the often overlooked spillover effect whereby the moment of the book always exceeds the moment of reading.

Indeed, the book points to a certain fissure in the moment of reading, as made evident in the book-reminiscence beginning to emerge as a standard feature of autobiographical writing at this time. Book memories, as many have noted, often tend to be strangely external, dwelling as much on the physical book and context of reading as on the mental act and products of reading. This is so not just in the case of celebrated bibliomaniacs like Thomas Frognall Dibdin, whose *Reminiscences of a Literary Life* (1836) is one of the earliest examples in English of what Seth Lerer has dubbed 'biblio-autobiography',[3] or in those of professed book-lovers like Leigh Hunt, who rhapsodizes in his autobiography over Cooke's edition of the British poets treasured by him as a school-boy: 'How I loved those little six-penny numbers containing whole poets! I doted on their size; I doted on their type, on their ornaments, on their wrappers containing lists of other poets, and on the engravings from Kirk'.[4] Similar sentiments are echoed by the more scientifically minded Hugh Miller, stone mason turned geologist, who affectionately recalls in his autobiography 'a magnificent old edition of the "Pilgrim's Progress", printed on coarse whity-brown paper, and charged with numerous wood-cuts, each of which occupied an entire page', while a labouring class social reformer like Alexander Somerville fondly recounts his initiation into poetry through a borrowed, well-worn volume of Burns: 'It had been in tatters, and was sewed again together, and I had special charges to take care of it ... and if each leaf had been a bank note, I could not have hugged it in my breast pocket more closely and carefully'.[5]

Repeatedly, early nineteenth-century memoirists and essayists make us privy to the size, look and feel of books they loved (notably in childhood) or to the place of their reading, eliding or subordinating the texts that were being read. So Walter Scott records the 'rapture' with which, as a young boy, he sat in his nightshirt to read some odd volumes of Shakespeare in his mother's dressing-room when he was supposed to be in bed, but he does not tell us what it was of Shakespeare's that he read so rapturously.[6] To some extent such outward turns are a function of the autobiographical genre, motivated by its desire to recapture the world within which a particular consciousness was shaped. But they also point to a peculiar feature of book-memory. William Hazlitt's 'On Reading Old Books' is exemplary, stressing that the simple sight of 'an odd volume' of a familiar author in a book-stall can transport Hazlitt back to the scene of original childhood reading: 'not only are the old ideas of the contents of the work brought back to my mind in all their vividness, but the old associations of the faces and persons of those I then knew, as they were in their life-time – the place where I sat to read the volume, the day when I got it, the feeling of the air, the fields, the sky – return, and all my early impression with them'.[7] What comes back so vividly to adult memory, as Marcel Proust was quick to note, is what at the time of reading often seemed peripheral, external, and may even have been blocked out by the young reader. Proust thus identifies irony as the structure of book memory. 'There are perhaps no days of our childhood we lived so fully as those we believe we left without having lived them', he remarks, observing that reading engraves on memory precisely everything it seemed to be keeping out, so that when we leaf through 'those books of another time', the memories they conjure up of that time are 'so much more precious to our present judgment than what we read then with such love'.[8]

This kind of disjunction between the mental transport triggered by an object in the past and the mental transport it triggers in the present is not unique to books, but it does serve to underscore the way the reading arts intensify a gap between sense data and mental activity. Where arts like music and painting make central to the mental work of imagination the receptivity of the senses (hearing, sight), the language arts typically disjoin the two, defining material response and material vehicle as incidental rather than integral to the experience. They thus produce a heightened split between mind-memory and body-memory with the body inscribing on the brain its own encounter with the book-object at some remove from the inscription made by the mental operation internalizing the text. For this reason, catching sight of an old book generally activates (at least in the first instance) the body's memory-track rather than that of the mind or imagination, dissolving the text into what was marginal to the experiential moment itself. Upon re-encounter, that is, book and words tend to split in a way that pictorial image or musical sound do not. It is true that catching sight of a painting loved long ago, for instance, can equally trigger memories of the context of the initial seeing, but the painting itself anchors the memory and remains firmly within it. This more sharply bifurcated structure of book-memory, however, helps account for how the experience of books fans out in consciousness and culture to achieve a deep purchase on both. When toward the end of his life Hazlitt came to muse, once again, on the working of memory, he lingered on its sense triggers – voices in the street, the sound of crickets, the taste of toast – but most potent of all remained the 'secret and sure charm' of books. Books, he says, are 'the most home-felt, the most heart-felt of our enjoyments'.[9] Moments like this point to the way the Romantic essayists harnessed the surplus power of books to bring them home to a larger public, as well as to make for themselves a personal home in books. Re-inflecting the periodical essay inherited from the eighteenth century on behalf of a broadened notion of literacy, they injected into public discourse a book-sentiment that did not so much privatize what had been public (as we often think) as promote a new public by making a claim on culture based less on the aesthetic pleasures of imagination than on the close, quasi-bodily pleasure of books.

Book discourse

As book historians have demonstrated, for an increasingly broad spectrum of the European population in the early nineteenth century books and reading were quickly becoming incorporated into the architecture and rhythms of quotidian existence. Heather Jackson confirms that by the turn of the century in Great Britain 'reading *does* seem to have become part of the texture of everyday life, seemingly for everyone, as it had not been a generation before', while William St Clair asserts that 'virtually everyone read books, magazines, and newspapers on a regular basis'.[10] If new books were expensive, reprints were readily available; books themselves had become smaller, hence more portable; periodicals in a range of prices and formats flooded the market, appearing at different intervals. This new visibility of printed materials in actual life re-charged the life of books in discourse in a paradoxical way, stripping standard metaphors of the book of their precisely metaphoric value. Thus the venerable trope of books as companions was now understood in a quite literal sense, as when the *Westminster Review* marvelled in 1831 at how the small size of books had in fact rendered them 'perpetual companions': 'if we go abroad they are in the travelling trunk, if we go into the country they are in the carriage pockets, if we are sick they lie by the couch, when we go to bed they are put under the pillow, at breakfast ... they elbow the muffins: in the summer's evening we read them in the garden, in the winter's night by the fire-side'.[11] Underwriting traditional book metaphors was not the material book but the idea of the book with its power to organize what Roger Chartier calls the 'readability' of the physical world: the book of nature, the book of history, and so on.[12] Such metaphors underscore the degree to which the status of the book as a cultural object depended on the detachment of its positive value in culture from its positive existence as an object, and the same holds true when the metaphors travelled the other way, that is, when books were turned into material or social forms (e.g. books as food, books as companions). These kinds of metaphors remained in force in the Romantic period – indeed they are ubiquitous – but the new, intensified sense of the book as a physical object also engendered a peculiar reversal, rendering the book-object rather than the book-idea a source of metaphor or (more strangely) quasi-metaphor. Hazlitt, for example, images the standard notion of a fall-off in literary talent in modern societies in his essay on 'The Periodical Press' by exclaiming, 'If we do not succeed in solid folio, let us excel in light duodecimo'; for his part, Charles Lamb (not entirely whimsically) imagines his friend George Dyer as 'grown almost into a book. He stood as passive as one by the side of the old shelves. I longed to new-coat him in russia, and assign him his place'.[13] As book and body merge, metamorphosing into the figure of the bookman, what obtrudes is not simply the mutual implication of print and persons but the physicality of both reader and book. Such manoeuvres suggest that if the history of reading in the West, as Leah Price has observed, exemplifies 'the progressive disappearance of the reader's body', the bookishness of the early nineteenth century represents something of a swerve, restoring to view the body of the reader through a foregrounding of the body of the book.[14]

Importantly, the book's body is now typically tattered and worn, for Romantic bookishness moves into the foreground the tactile dimension of books: books as objects that have been or are to be handled. It is entirely characteristic that Lamb's 'Detached Thoughts on Books and Reading' registers his delight in the 'sullied leaves and worn out appearances' of circulating library novels and asserts his preference for those editions of Shakespeare 'which have been oftenest tumbled about and handled'.[15] Hunt is equally albeit somewhat more pragmatically attuned to the idea of books-in-use, expressing a wish that his (generally short-lived) periodicals be 'thumbed horribly, and carried about in pockets'.[16] Remarks like this underscore the sociable models of print and books increasingly attracting critical attention, as evidenced by the essays in this section, but they also represent something simpler: an insistence on the experience of literacy as the bringing of printed matter into literal touch with persons. 'I do not care to be anywhere without having a book or books at hand', Hunt sums up in 'My Books'.[17] Underwriting the familiar essay's representation of the culture of literacy is an ethos of close encounter whose rhetorical figure is syllepsis, the master trope of bibliophilia itself. Hunt (whose work as a popularizer of literature remains oddly under-studied[18]) is its most flamboyant practitioner in the period. 'I entrench myself in my books equally against sorrow and the weather', he proclaims in the essay just cited: 'If the wind comes through a passage, I look about to see how I can fence it off by a better disposition of my movables; if a melancholy thought is importunate, I give another glance at my Spenser'.[19] Blocking drafts and blocking melancholy, his books are at once material and mental objects (movables and immutables, so to speak), and his rhetoric bears out Deidre Lynch's argument that the early decades of the nineteenth century witnessed the relocation of library culture to informal private spaces, where it was installed 'within the psychic territory of people's intimate lives'.[20] Thus relocated, however, it not only moved inward but also outward. Hunt's insistence on close bodily contact with books, activating the metonymic logic crucial to his long and tireless campaign to extend the reading public, may represent a shrinking or narrowing of the space of reading in one dimension but it underwrote its expansion in another.

Reduction of distance was the key. As books moved into greater literal proximity, they shed any residual aura. 'Do people nowadays – do even we ourselves – love books as they did in those times?' Hunt asks in 'Bricklayers and an Old Book', and his reply hinges on the new portability that attached persons and books: 'A little book is indeed "a love" (to use a modern phrase)–and fitted to carry about us in our walks and pockets: but then a great book – a folio – was a thing to look up to, ... and therefore it had an aspect more like a religion'.[21] Charles Lamb's campy image of embracing his darling folios ('huge armfuls', as he dryly reports in 'New Year's Eve'[22]) underlines the point of a modern familiarity. Precisely such familiarity prompted the notorious attacks on Hunt and his Cockney circle in the Tory press.[23] The vigorous not to say vicious debate over literature that ensued was in an important way a debate over valorized spacing. Hunt, locating himself squarely within an urban sensibility linked to radical-reformist culture, took a provocative delight in near sight and narrow spaces (spaces where all points are in contact), ostentatiously rejecting open spaces, long views, and sublime landscapes. 'What signifies all this?' he asks of a fine study with views of the sea and mountains. 'I turn my back upon the sea; I shut up even one of the side windows looking upon the mountains, and retain no prospect but that of trees. On the right and left of me are book-shelves; a bookcase is affectionately open in front of me; and thus kindly enclosed with my books and the green leaves, I write'.[24]

As a scene of authorship, 'kindly' enclosure places writers, readers, and books in triangulated intimacy, and Hunt himself is the most consistently personal and informal of periodical practitioners in the first half of the nineteenth century: signing his own name to editorials, adopting a chatty tone, filling his prose with homely details. As Jane Stabler has observed (although she is commenting more specifically on his poetry), Hunt achieved 'an unprecedented level of textual physical intimacy' with his readers.[25] Stabler's suggestive phrasing in 'textual physical intimacy' neatly encapsulates Hunt's desire to infuse print genres with something of the weight and pressure of speaking bodies, a deliberate, provocative vulgarization of the literary word that demys-tifies the category of literature (in both its broad and its more special-ized senses).[26] But while this vulgarization challenged learned and coterie models, it maintained the specificity of literary (that is non-pragmatic) reading in terms of those models. As generally understood, Hunt's aesthetic of intimacy is tied to a model of literature as private shelter, retreat, and comfort, and hence seen as rewriting leisured, gen-try paradigms for the commercial middling classes. His own characteri-zation of his projects amply sustains such a reading. Over and over again, he casts his periodicals as vehicles of relaxation and refuge in an agitating world, while his scenes of reading typically evoke either cosy indoor spaces or home-like outdoor venues such as gardens and parks.[27] At the same time, as Hunt critics have also noted, his insistence on keeping things private ends up scrambling rather than confirming the distinction of public and private. When he began publishing *The Indicator* while continuing to edit *The Examiner* in 1819, for example, he differentiated the two weeklies for his readers in the idiom of public versus private spaces: *The Examiner* is a 'tavern-room', where he holds 'a sort of public meeting with his friends', while *The Indicator* is a 'study', where he holds 'a more retired one' and can himself find a 'retreat from public care and criticism'.[28] But the distinction soon gives way as arti-cles migrate from one to the other under the pressure of deadlines. The crossovers motivated by the demands of a busy journalistic career, how-ever, only underline what had already been apparent in *The Examiner* itself, where literary and political articles were so intermixed despite nominal separation that (to cite Hazlitt's remark in 'The Periodical Press') readers found themselves 'at a loss under what department of the paper to look out for any particular topic'.[29] This does not mean that literary and political folded into one another. On the contrary. The positing of distinct realms was central to Hunt's project as a 'public author': his aesthetic of intimacy seeks not only to render the literary sphere accessible to private persons without a classical education (his targeted periodical audience) but also, more generally, to rewrite the public sphere within which the literary was situated.

'Private publicity'

In an important sense Hunt's authorship is neither public nor private. Rather, understood as a positive intervention in the debate over public culture (rather than its displacement or evasion), it is located on their border. The clearest articulation of his own understanding of his authorship in this way appears in one of his later, less-noticed periodical experiments, the penny halfpenny *London Journal* he launched in April 1834 in an attempt to enter the cheap print market being spectacularly exploited at the time by Chambers's *Edinburgh Journal* and Charles Knight's *Penny Magazine*.[30] Addressing 'enquiring minds' and book lovers all across the nation who had been deprived of educational opportunities, he presents the *London Journal* as a zone of what he calls 'private publicity', wherein (as he explains) he brings into the public realm the conversational discourse of private life in order 'to help break barriers, and hasten utopian time when all will say what they think in public – this has long been the case in political and other public matters – It is desirable that public matters should no longer be supposed exclusively to mean politics, or even parish matters (important as they are). They should comprise knowledge of all sorts, entertainment, the interchange of every kind of advantage'.[31] If the primary point is that 'public matters' should no longer be identified with the official organization of collective life (politics, parishes), Hunt's definitive move is the extension of public discourse in anticipation of a time when 'all will say what they think in public'. Recasting print discourse as familiar, quasi-physical encounter, he strives to bridge the widening public/ private gap in his own time by rewriting the utopian public sphere of the eighteenth century (with its co-implication of public/private) to stretch what counts as legitimate talk in the public forum and by rethinking the relationship of the personal and the 'common'.[32] In keeping with this ambition, Hazlitt and Hunt dropped the editorial masks characteristic of eighteenth-century essayists such as Addison and Steele so as to align their literary activities with the mundane activities they conducted (as Hunt put it) 'in our own proper persons': 'we have avoided the trouble of adding assumed characters to our real ones; and shall talk, just as we think, walk, and take dinner, in our own proper persons'.[33]

Blurring the line between writer and person to place in question the standard valorization of impersonal distance, such familiarity in public also immersed writers and readers in a common temporal flow. Hunt's own rhetoric repeatedly conflates the time of writing and the time of reading, as when he points out in 'Bricklayers and an old Book' (originally published in the *London Journal*) that he is 'at this moment' writing upon the very book he is writing about or when, adding commerce to the mix, he remarks in a number of a later penny daily titled *The Tatler* (1831) that 'the sale is going on while we are writing this paragraph' (or so he hoped).[34] Turning to account the temporality of the commercial periodical, such authorship understands itself as the engendering of a habit over time. 'An author grows upon his readers like a kind of habitual thinking' through periodical publication, Hunt asserts, noting as he does so that '[h]abit does much for intimacies of every sort'.[35] Regular and punctuated, serial publication generates the dispositions that allow for a habitual dwelling within literary culture in a way that book authorship does not. In another of the paradoxes that shape Hunt's career, his promotion of books and bookishness thus depends on a repudiation of the authorship linked to them. The author of books, Hunt observes in an early essay 'On Periodical Essays' in *The Examiner*, comes upon the reader 'at once in all the majesty of a quarto or all the gaiety of a beau duodecimo, smooth and well dressed'. Such authors demand to be preserved in libraries even when they bore you to death, whereas dull periodical authors may be readily eliminated: 'how many pleasant modes are there of getting rid of a periodical essay? It may assist your meditation by lighting your pipe, it may give steadiness to your candle, it may curl the tresses of your daughter or your sister'.[36] If the tone is light, the point is serious: familiar authorship makes its impact in and through time as an intangible relationship rather than as memorable writing; hence its inscriptions are simply disposable marks on paper rather than words to be remembered or reread, abstracted from linear temporal flow.

Immediacy is the mode of such authorship, pleasure its signature. Implicating reading bodies as well as reading minds, literary culture as constructed in the familiar essay is lodged within a spectrum of mundane pleasures, transported ever further into quotidian territory. Hunt's notorious essay 'On Washerwomen', originally published in *The Examiner* and gleefully leaped on by conservative critics when reprinted in *The Round Table* volume, helps to pinpoint this casual genre's critical project.[37] Foregrounding the pleasures that washerwomen carve out for themselves in the intervals of a laborious day (e.g. gossip, a cup of tea), the essay sets out to unsettle 'the fastidious reader, who thinks he has all the taste and enjoyment to himself'.[38] Hunt's 'fastidious reader' recalls and doubles Addison's well-known 'man of polite imagination', a figure predicated on his ability to experience (in Addison's words) 'a great many pleasures that the vulgar are not capable of receiving'.[39] In an important way, the Romantic familiar essay hinges on a rewriting of this statement. On the one hand, it challenges Addison's hierarchy of pleasure by celebrating the vulgar, tactile 'sense of feeling' downgraded by Addison because (unlike the refined sense of sight) it relies on closeness to objects;[40] on the other, it seeks to extend the pleasures of polite imagination to those outside the standard classes of literacy. 'Pleasure is the business of this journal', Hunt announces in the *London Journal*, staking his position on the claim that for those not subject to the strictures of necessity ('if a man is starving, we do not profess to have even the right to be listened to by him'), an expanded consciousness is the desideratum of existence. Pleasure is the trigger of such expansion, with Hunt defining pleasure as a receptivity that 'break[s] open the surfaces of habit and indifference, of objects that are supposed to contain nothing but so much brute matter or common-place utility'.[41] Rehearsing his argument in journal after journal, he risked derision and indeed boredom, but behind Hunt's insistent cheeriness lay a keen sense of the cultural-political stakes of pleasure.

The polemics of pleasure takes its place in the specific period debate over vulgarity recently traced by William Keach, but Hunt's importance lies in his more fundamental assumption that pleasure is a necessary and sufficient principle for inclusion in the culture of literacy.[42] In this assumption he set himself against both political and utilitarian-pragmatic models, which allowed entry primarily under functionalist or disciplinary models of reading. As the nineteenth century wore on, Hunt fought to counter the increasing tendency to restrict the definition of the public sphere to the dissemination of information, the rationale of improvement, and the extension of technical knowledge. From the 'cold' binding of schoolbooks to the drawings of Hogarth (otherwise a much admired artist), he resolutely campaigned against rational-didactic models of cultural dissemination, resistant in particular to instrumental and reductive codings of those outside the literate classes. If he could not quite escape the

ascendancy of utility by the time he founded the *London Journal*, com-
promising enough (at least with its vocabulary) to define the 'gap'
in public reading his journal sought to fill as '*the ornamental part of
utility*', he continued to argue against the restrictive notion of being
posited by utilitarian theory and, importantly, to insist on the extension of pleasure as integral to the 'public intellect': 'as the *Edinburgh
Journal* gives the world the benefit of its knowledge of business, and
the *Penny Magazine* that of its authorities and its pictures, so the
London Journal proposes to furnish ingenuous minds of all classes,
with such helps as it possesses towards a share in the pleasures of taste
and scholarship'.[43]

In an essay on 'The Fate of Pleasure' written some decades ago,
Lionel Trilling turns to the Romantic period as exemplifying an aesthetic of pleasure to set against a modernist aesthetic of unpleasure.
Somewhat unexpectedly, he takes for his theorist of pleasure the austere
William Wordsworth, citing a generally overlooked utterance in the
Preface to the second edition of *Lyrical Ballads* where the poet speaks
of 'the grand elementary principle of pleasure' as constituting the 'the
native and naked dignity of man'.[44] Modern readers, Trilling notes, find
this statement puzzling. We are not used to conjoining pleasure and
dignity; moreover, we are accustomed to identifying the dignity of man
with notions like rights and freedoms. However, as Trilling points out,
'the downward spread of the idea of dignity, until it eventually became
an idea that might be applied to man in general was advanced by the
increasing possibility of possessing the means or signs of pleasure'.[45] It
is no accident that Pierre Bourdieu bases his classic account of social
distinction on the discrimination of pleasures: the vulgar pleasures
of immediacy (instant recognition, sensation, satisfaction) are ranged
against elite pleasures of delay and detour (those that take time).[46]
Enigmatically located at the interface of body and mind, pleasures
generally prove more opaque and intransigent than ideas. It is harder
to understand pleasures not our own than it is thoughts not our own,
for instance, so that in an important way pleasure marks the boundary
of social sympathy.

In fostering pleasure, along with thought, the familiar essay sought
to extend the reach of both literature and sympathy, responding in its
way to what Jon Klancher has termed the 'crisis of sociability' following
the disintegration of the enlightenment model of the republic of letters.[47] By exploiting the periodical's fragmented and miscellaneous
form, the Romantic essayists sought to generate precisely affiliations
and associations but on the basis of a more capacious model of culture.

Aligning literary pleasures with a range of mundane activities without denying its canonical pleasures, they adumbrate an understanding of culture as a set of everyday practices, customs and rituals possessing meaning but refusing systematic readability. As they celebrate activities such as card-playing, eating, walking, attending a boxing match or muse on the habit of shaking hands, the size of modern hats, the custom of grace before meals, the essays constitute a type of proto-cultural criticism that answers to the heightened visibility of quotidian practices in the early nineteenth-century intellectual field (and anticipates in many ways the cultural turn of our own day). If such interests had always characterized the miscellaneous essay, the practice of miscellaneous and informal representation was newly charged in the Romantic period by pressure from two related directions: first, a vigorous debate over what made for public culture in an intensely self-reflexive periodical sphere obsessed with questions of dissemination (should one have public lectures on poetry? what was the point of publishing antiquarian anthologies? what were periodicals themselves doing these days?); second, a more particular debate over taste in which politeness found itself under increasing siege from what Denise Gigante has called the 'gustatory trope', which gave prominence to the bodily appetites and pleasures of the senses ruled out in polite taste.[48] The Regency period in particular, as Gigante shows, saw the emergence of subcultures devoted to what went on bodies or into them (e.g. the dandy, the gourmand). Like the bibliomaniac (who flourished at the same time), however, such figures embraced and refined specialist pleasures; hence they represent that expansion of pleasure in one dimension which makes for coterie culture. By contrast, the bookishness of the familiar essayists promoted the material-mental pleasures of print as accessible general pleasures, part of a valorized expansion of the spectrum of pleasure in the familiar periodical. In so enlarging the range of experiences that entered into public discourse to form what Hunt called 'the public intellect', their bookishness opened out a notion of literary culture that was not at the same time a cult of literature.

Notes

Research for this essay was undertaken with the help of a grant from the Social Sciences and Humanities Research Council of Canada. My thanks to the Council for its support.

1. *Paper Machine*, trans. Rachel Bowlby (Stanford: Stanford University Press, 2005), pp. 16, 4.

2. Bibliophiles themselves have been more alert to the distinction. Thus Andrew Lang emphasizes that the love of books 'for their own sake' (i.e. as physical and psychological objects) is 'distinct from the love of literature', *Books and Bookmen* (New York: George J. Coombs, 1886), p. 71.

3. Seth Lerer, 'Epilogue: Falling Asleep Over the History of the Book', *PMLA* 121 (Jan 2006) 230.

4. *The Autobiography of Leigh Hunt. A New Edition, Revised by the Author; With Further Revision, and an Introduction by his Eldest Son* (London: Smith, Elder, 1860), p. 69.

5. My Schools and Schoolmasters; or, the Story of My Education (Edinburgh, 1854), p. 28; The Autobiography of a Working Man (London, 1848), p. 87.

6. *Scott on Himself: A Selection of the Autobiographical Writings of Sir Walter Scott*, ed. David Hewitt (Edinburgh: Scottish Academic Press, 1981), p. 26.

7. *The Complete Works of William Hazlitt*, ed. P. P. Howe, vol. 12 (London: Dent, 1933), p. 222.

8. *On Reading Ruskin*, trans. and ed. Jean Autret, William Burford, and Phillip J. Wolfe (New Haven and London: Yale University Press, 1987), pp. 99, 100.

9. *Complete Works*, vol. 17, p. 376.

10. H. J. Jackson, *Romantic Readers: The Evidence of Marginalia* (New Haven and London: Yale University Press, 2005), p. 52; William St Clair, *The Reading Nation in the Romantic Period* (Cambridge: Cambridge University Press, 2004), p. 13. Also see Kathryn Sutherland, '"Events ... Have Made us a World of Readers": Reader Relations 1780–1830', *The Romantic Period*, ed. David B. Pirie (London: Penguin, 1994), pp. 1–48.

11. Rev. of *Mothers and Daughters*, *Westminster Review* 14 (Apr. 1831) 420.

12. *The Order of Books: Readers, Authors, and Libraries in Europe between the Fourteenth and Eighteenth Century*, trans. Lydia G. Cochrane (Stanford: Stanford University Press), p. 90.

13. Hazlitt, *Complete Works*, vol. 16, p. 219; Charles Lamb, *The Complete Works and Letters of Charles Lamb* (New York: Modern Library, 1935), p. 11.

14. 'Reading: The State of the Discipline', *Book History* 7 (2004) 303–20.

15. *Complete Works and Letters*, pp. 147, 148. Henry Crabb Robinson commented that Lamb himself had 'the finest collection of shabby books I ever saw', *Diary Reminiscences and Correspondence*, ed. Thomas Sadler (London, 1869), 2: 265.

16. *London Journal*, No. 61 (27 May 1835), p. 161

17. *Essays (Selected) by Leigh Hunt* (London: Dent, 1929), p. 347.

18. The recent upsurge of interest in Hunt, while widely assuming his role as a popularizer of literature, has devoted surprisingly little critical attention to this facet of his career. Nicholas Roe, for example, does not include popularization in the list of Hunt's influence in his introduction to the important collection *Leigh Hunt: Life, poetics, politics* (London and New York: Routledge, 2003) nor is this side of Hunt much represented in the new multi-volume edition of his writings, *The Selected Writings of Leigh Hunt*, ed. Greg Kucich and Jeffrey N. Cox, 6 vols (London: Pickering and Chatto, 2003).

19. *Essays*, pp. 339–40.

20. Deidre Lynch, '"Wedded to Books": Bibliomania and the Romantic Essayists', *Romantic Circles-Praxis Series* (Feb 2004), http://www.rc.umd.edu/praxis/libraries/lynch/lynch.html.

21. *Essays*, p. 226.
22. *Complete Works and Letters*, p. 28.
23. See Kim Wheatley's detailed account, 'The *Blackwood's* Attacks on Leigh Hunt', *Nineteenth-Century Literature* 47 (Jun 1992) 1–32.
24. *Essays*, p. 340.
25. Jane Stabler, '"Leigh Hunt's Aesthetics of Intimacy' in Roe, p. 97.
26. On legitimation of 'the vulgar' by second-generation Romanticism see, in particular, Gregory Dart, 'Romantic Cockneyism: Hazlitt and the Periodical Press', *Romanticism* 6/2 (2000): 143–62 and Ayumi Mizukoshi, *Keats, Hunt and the Aesthetics of Pleasure* (Basingstoke: Palgrave Macmillan, 2001).
27. See Elizabeth Jones 's reading of Hunt in relation to the suburban aesthetic of 'the gardenesque' developed by John Claudius Loudon, 'Suburban Sinners: Sex and Disease in the Cockney School' in Roe, pp. 78–94.
28. *The Indicator*, 20 Oct 1819, p. 10. Jeffrey N. Cox cites this passage as exemplary of Hunt's sense of his periodicals as 'social and interactive texts', *Poetry and Politics in the Cockney School: Keats, Shelley, Hunt and Their Circle* (Cambridge: Cambridge University Press, 1998), p. 73).
29. *Complete Works*, 16: 229.
30. Hunt had made a foray into cheap print years earlier when he published the penny *Tatler* in 1808, but it was even more short-lived than most of his ventures.
31. *London Journal*, 16 April 1834, p. 17.
32. The debate over public writing initiated by the Romantic essayists continued to be redrawn and replayed throughout the century, notably in the controversy over journalistic anonymity in the 1880s; see Richard Salmon, '"A Simulacrum of Power": Intimacy and Abstraction in the Rhetoric of the New Journalism', *Nineteenth-Century Media and the Construction of Identities*, ed. Laurel Brake, Bill Bell, and David Finklestein (Basingstoke: Palgrave Macmillan, 2000), pp. 27–39.
33. *The Round Table* (Edinburgh, 1817), 1: 3.
34. *Essays*, p. 265; *Prefaces by Leigh Hunt, Mainly to His Periodicals*, ed. R. Brimley Johnson (Port Washington, NY: Kennikat Press, 1967), p. 81.
35. *Prefaces by Leigh Hunt*, p. 23.
36. *The Examiner*, 10 Jan. 1808, p. 26.
37. See, for example, the review of *The Round Table* in the *Quarterly Review* 17 (Apr. 1817) 154–9.
38. *Essays*, p. 53.
39. *The Spectator*, no. 411, *The Papers of Joseph Addison, Esq.* (Edinburgh, 1790), 3: 244.
40. Denise Gigante helpfully sums up the way in which Romantic revisions of taste deposed sight from its 'lofty eminence' in eighteenth-century taste theory in her introduction to *Romantic Gastronomies, Romantic Circles Praxis Series* (Apr. 2007), http://www.rc.umd.edu/praxis/gastronomy/gigante/gigante_essay.html.
41. *London Journal*, 2 April 1834, p. 1.
42. See his chapter on 'Vulgar Idioms' in *Arbitrary Power: Romanticism, Language, Politics* (Princeton: Princeton University Press, 2004).
43. *London Journal*, 2 April 1834, p. 1.

44. Wordsworth, *Poetical Works*, rev. ed. Ernest de Selincourt (London and Oxford: Oxford University Press, 1969), p. 735.
45. *Beyond Culture* (New York: Viking, 1965), p. 63. In a related point, Elizabeth Jones notes, in her discussion of *Blackwood's* attack on Hunt, that 'to have abundance and leisure without birthright' was in fact to pose the profoundest threat to the constitution of society defended by Tories like Lockhart, 'Suburban Sinner', p. 91.
46. Pierre Bourdieu, *Distinction: A Social Critique of the Judgement of Taste*, trans. Richard Nice (Cambridge, MA: Harvard University Press, 1984).
47. 'Discriminations, or Romantic cosmopolitanisms in London', *Romantic Metropolis: The Urban Scene of British Culture, 1780–1840*, ed. James Chandler and Kevin Gilmartin (Cambridge: Cambridge University Press, 2005), pp. 64–82.
48. See her book on *Taste: A Literary History* (New Haven and London: Yale University Press, 2005), as well as the issue on *Romantic Gastronomies* in *Romantic Circles Praxis* cited above.

6
The Art of Sharing: Reading in the Romantic Miscellany

Andrew Piper

Assorted books

'Sharing is more difficult than you think.'[1] This was the advice offered to the Major by his friend in Goethe's novella, 'The Man of Fifty', and it concerned the difficulties of transmitting the *Verjüngungskunst*, the art of rejuvenation, that the Major required in order to remain vital and youthful for his niece who, in a typical Goethean fantasy, had fallen in love with him. 'The Man of Fifty' had initially appeared in part in 1817 in Cotta's *Ladies' Pocket-Book*, and it was a story that was in fact largely concerned with the problem of the part – with the parting, imparting, and parting with things. It would later be included in Goethe's last novel, *Wilhelm Meister's Travels* (1821/29), where it would achieve its fame as one of his most important prose works, and yet its initial placement within Cotta's miscellany disclosed an important fact about the culture of nineteenth-century miscellanies in which it first appeared: that the question of the part, imparting and parting with – in a word, *sharing* – was integral to the miscellanies' success as a literary format in the nineteenth century.

In the first half of the nineteenth century whether in France, England, the German states, or the United States, a vast amount of writing was circulated through eclectic collections of poetry, short fiction, essays, and anecdotes. These were enormously influential books during the romantic period, books that have until recently largely been left unexplored by literary historians, much like the book itself. Recent work by Barbara Benedict, Leah Price, Ina Ferris, Kathryn Ledbetter, Seth Lerer, and Meredith McGill in English, York-Gotthart Mix, Hans-Jürgen Lüsebrinck, and Siegfried Wenzel in German, Armando Petrucci in Italian, and Ségolène Le Men in French have put the miscellany back onto the literary historical map.[2] The theory of reading 'the whole book', put forth by the medievalists Stephen Nichols and Siegfried Wenzel, has drawn our attention to the way texts can interact with one another in the physical space of the codex, opening up new spaces of readerly activity.[3] Unlike another essential romantic bibliographic format, the collected edition, the miscellany was not organized around the unifying figure of the author, but instead, as Barbara Benedict has suggested in her study on the early modern miscellany, around the figure of the reader.[4] Where the collected edition aimed to canonize its author and in the process create a literary canon, the miscellany was far more a document of the impulse to undo such rules, standards, or means. With the absence of any obvious organizing principle and with the simultaneous presence of high, low and outright weird texts, the romantic miscellany authorized the reader to create the linkages between such cultural strata. Like the stitching that bound together the loose leaves of the book, it was the reader who provided the intellectual threads that connected the book's diverse parts. As Leah Price has suggested, anthologies and miscellanies 'determine not simply who gets published or what gets read but who reads, and how'.[5] In their capacity to slice, select, condense, combine, and reproduce, miscellanies' prominence during the romantic period reflected, as Ina Ferris has shown in the case of Isaac D'Israeli's *Curiosities of Literature*, the rising importance of the elsewhere and the afterward, transmission and excision, to romantic literary culture.[6]

The miscellany was of course not a new bibliographic format to the romantic period. It had played an important role both as a printed book since the early modern period and as a manuscript book since the Middle Ages. But the romantic period did give birth to a particular type of miscellany, one that has traditionally been classified according to different names depending on which language one is working in. We speak of *almanacs* in French, *Taschenbücher* in German, and *gift-books* or *literary annuals* in English, a fact of nomenclature that I suspect has had much to do with why the study of these books has been so nationally focused. While there were of course important differences between these regional articulations of the miscellany, I want to suggest that there was a fundamental continuity in the cultural work that such books performed during the romantic period.

In drawing upon the much older book format of the 'almanac' or 'calendar' that appeared in yearly instalments, nineteenth-century miscellanies were drawing upon one of the oldest available bibliographic genres and thus engaging in that familiar romantic quest for origins.

As Leigh Hunt said in his introduction to the English miscellany, *The Keepsake* (1828), 'The history of Pocket-books and their forerunners, Almanacks, Calendars, Ephemerides, &c. is ancient beyond all precedent: even the Welshman's genealogy, the middle of which contained the creation of the world, is nothing to it'.[7] But in mapping such serially appearing collections onto the seasonal rhythms of nature – most visible in the calendrical tables that often appeared in these books' front matter – the romantic miscellany also played an important role in marking the transition from the cyclicality to the seriality of cultural production that would become a hallmark of both nineteenth-century literature and twentieth-century mass media more generally.[8] At the same time, in the small size captured in the notion of the *Taschenbuch* – the book that could fit in one's pocket – the miscellanies articulated the increasing reproducibility and affordability of printed books that brought with it a growing sense of losing control that surrounded the book's accessibility. The appellation of 'gift book', on the other hand, captured the way these books were increasingly being explicitly produced as gifts in both their content and design.[9] While books had always functioned as gift objects, the miscellaneous 'gift book' was emerging at precisely the moment when books were overwhelmingly being defined by their status as commodities. In replacing a system of anonymous circulation with a more intimate system of exchange between friends and family, the gift book was a means of compensating for, but also propelling, the new commercial proliferation of books. Finally, what all of these books had in common was the *mixed* nature of writing that appeared within them. They reflected, and indeed celebrated, the growing heterogeneity of writing within the larger literary market. As the editors argued in the miscellany, *Curiositäten-Almanach* of 1825, which was dedicated to 'friends of encyclopedic entertainments', such collections were expressly for people who read 'fragmentarisch'. The miscellanies thus represented a powerful challenge to assumptions about the book's capacity to promote sequential reading habits.

It is precisely the mixedness at the core of writing in the miscellanies that I want to explore in this essay, a mixedness understood not just as the diversity of form, but the diversity of ownership, too. By returning to the bibliographic scene of Goethe's reflections on sharing – by reading the linguistic and material codes of this particular genre of books – I want to suggest that the book format of the romantic miscellany functioned as a particularly acute space in which the mutual relationship of sharing and owning – a common right and copyright to writing – could be rehearsed during the first half of the nineteenth century. How *was* one to know how to share something with someone else, to have it in common without losing it completely? With so much material moving about with ever greater ease, how was one to reliably negotiate the complex contours between the mine, the yours, and the ours? Sharing was integral to writing's diffusion in the nineteenth century, making it increasingly available at the same time that writing's availability made sharing that much easier. But the more writing was shared and shareable, the more difficult it became to claim something as one's own. The more one shared, the less one paradoxically had to give away. As Goethe suggested, sharing *was* more difficult than one might have thought.

Following on the work of Martha Woodmansee, there have been numerous excellent studies in the course of the last two decades on the origins and evolution of the notion of copyright, the long and contentious process of establishing the conditions for the proprietary ownership of ideas that emerged out of the eighteenth and early nineteenth centuries.[10] What we know less about, are the numerous ways that this period emphasized the sharing, and not the owning, of information. As Natalie Zemon Davis argued in an essay that remains a key contribution to the history of intellectual property, 'We have concentrated on the book as a commodity rather than on the book as a bearer of benefits and duties, on copyright rather than common right'.[11] In our emphasis on the proprietary, we have overlooked how sharing has served as a crucial site for literary or intellectual innovation both during and after the romantic period. At the same time, we have overlooked just how complicated and contentious such a practice was and continues to be, the complexity of trying to work out the principles of parting, imparting, and parting with something.

By turning to the history of a *common* right and not a copyright to writing, then, we can begin to see how our current predicament over file sharing, for example – where writing, in the form of computer code, is now the basis of all of the arts – is not something distinctly new, but reflects a persistent problem that has always surrounded writing as an allographic art, that is, as an art form that can be reproduced without degrading or changing its value.[12] With each new innovation in writing technology, with each new contribution towards the *reproducibility* of writing, the question of sharing only seems to emerge with renewed force. Rather than offering another trenchant critique of the current institutional exuberance for stricter and stricter mechanisms of copyright,[13] I want to identify the richness of a literary and intellectual tradition of sharing and sharedness, so that we can begin to understand contemporary digital practices not as essentially aberrant, but as standing in a long and legitimate history. We can begin to see how sharing and owning should not be seen as agons, as mutually exclusive of one another – as they are increasingly understood today – but as standing in a necessary, mutual, and always tangled formation with one another.

As I will try to show, it is precisely when we take into consideration the romantic miscellany as a material object, when we attend to the range of paratextual elements such as bindings, front matter, and dedicatory leaves, that we can observe the intricate ways that miscellanies dramatized questions of sharing and the sharedness of writing during this crucial moment of media change. At the same time, I am interested in illustrating how text and book worked in concert with one another to incubate such a culture of sharing. By focusing on one work in particular, Washington Irving's, 'An Unwritten Drama of Lord Byron', which appeared in the miscellany *The Gift* (1836), we can see how literature, too, functioned as a key space for readers to think about and adapt to the changing nature of their own bibliocosmos. As in Goethe's 'The Man of Fifty', Irving's work offers an emblematic instance of a piece of writing that elaborately turns around questions of sharedness and ownness, the complicated bipolar project of imparting something and owning it at the same time at the core of the romantic miscellany. It is only when we combine these two very different spaces of analysis that we can see the full extent of the *Kulturtechnik*, or cultural engineering, employed through the medium of the romantic miscellany to facilitate nineteenth-century readers' adaptation to their increasingly bookish world.

Book-keeping

In the introduction to the first issue of the English miscellany, *The Keepsake* (1828), Leigh Hunt writes:

> What renders a book more valuable as a keepsake than almost any other, is, that, like a friend, it can talk with and entertain us. And here we have one thing to recommend, which to all those who prize the spirit of books and or regard it above the letter, can give to a favourite volume a charm inexpressible. It is this: that where such an affectionate liberty can be taken either in right of playing the teacher, or because the giver of the book is sure of a sympathy in point of taste with the person receiving it, the said giver should mark his or her favourite passages throughout (as delicately as

need be), and so present, as it were, the author's and the giver's minds at once.

(16)

Hunt's alignment here of the categories of the book and friendship was a familiar strategy that dated back at least to Erasmus's choice to frame the commercial printed text as common property, beginning with the choice of 'Friends hold all things in common' for the opening adage of his adage collection. Equating the book with a friend was not simply a way of enlivening the dead letter on the page as Hunt suggested. It was also a way of replacing the anonymous distribution of mass-produced objects with a model of intimate circulation of personalized copies among friends, however paradoxical such a notion of the 'personalized copy' might have been. The discourse of friendship and the practice of gift-giving under which miscellanies were produced and circulated were intended to counteract precisely the anonymity of mass circulation that the format itself was engendering during the romantic period.

Perhaps no other practice facilitated this mode of intimate exchange more than the act of *inscription*, the placement of the giver's handwriting alongside, or in front of, the printed text. As Hunt intoned, 'One precious name, or little inscription at the beginning of the volume ... is worth all the binding in St. James's' (17). Numerous miscellanies, including *The Keepsake* for which Hunt was writing, contained a printed space that was designed to allow givers to dedicate these books to their recipients. Whether it was ornamental presentation leaves or dedicatory poems that included a blank space to write in the dedicatee's name, miscellanies consistently used white space to encourage their users to write within them. Unlike the white space that would emerge in another key romantic bibliographical format, the critical edition, which functioned as a kind of immaculate border insulating the author's work from the work of the editor, white (or blank) space in the miscellanies was an invitation to co-ownership, to cross the boundaries between reader and reader and reader and author to produce the presence of multiple hands on the page.

If we look at individual copies of nineteenth-century miscellanies – and here I will be drawing on examples from the holdings of the American Antiquarian Society – we find numerous instances of inscriptions, a practice that was of course not limited to the miscellanies, but was nonetheless uniquely solicited within them. On December 25, 1849, for example, Mary Hinsdale received a copy of *The Garland* from her 'Uncle Beardsley', and in a copy of *Hyacinth* from 1849, we find the note, 'Christmas present for Sarah J. Lord, North Berwick; from her bro. Charles', written to his sister when she was ten years old. Miscellanies were not only given by men to women – as in a copy of *The Token* of 1830 where we find the inscription, 'Mrs. Julia A. Jackson from her husband' – but also functioned as a means of establishing a matrilineal network of reading. Sarah M. Park of Groton, Massachusetts, received a copy of *Robert Merry's Annual for All Seasons* in 1840 from Mrs. Eliza Green when she was seven, and in *The Gift for All Seasons* (1844) we find the note, 'Abby M. Gourgas from her afftn. Aunt Anne. Jan 1, 1843', given to Abby when she was six. At the age of ten she would also receive a copy of Longfellow's *Evangeline* (fifth edition) from 'Mrs. Tyler'. In an interesting case in a copy of *The Literary Souvenir* of 1838, we find *two* dedications, 'Mary F. Quincy from Mr. J. M. Newhall' (when Mary was nineteen) and 'Lizzie Quincy from sister Mary' (when Lizzy was sixteen), suggesting how it was probably not uncommon that such gifts were regifted in an ongoing extension of the network of readers. Finally, there were also examples of these books being given to men from women, as in a copy of *The Rose of Sharon* from 1852 in which Miss Achsa Hayford of Abington, Mass., dedicated the book to Daniel Temple Noyes on November 25.

What such examples illustrate is that at the historical juncture when we witness the gradual disappearance of the vertical dedication of author to patron in books (as Balzac dramatically said: 'Madame, the time of dedications is past'[14]), we find the growing profusion of horizontal dedications between *readers* in books specifically designed to foster such exchanges. When we look at the various ages of the recipients of such gifted books, we see how the miscellany was most often transferred at moments marking crucial biological thresholds, either when one was beginning to read or becoming a young adult, husband, or wife. The horizontal exchange was simultaneously reverticalized, only now in the opposite direction. Where the book was formerly 'given' upwards to an aristocratic patron through the book's dedication as a sign of the recipient's power, the inscription and the book it gave away downwards now marked the power of the giver. Instead of an acknowledgment of debt, the romantic inscription transferred debt from one reader to another.

On one level, then, the inscription was part of a larger cultural matrix in which the acquisition and deployment of handwriting played a pivotal role in the socialization of nineteenth-century readers and writers.[15] As we know from nineteenth-century handwriting handbooks, the production of manuscript involved an extraordinary investment of one's entire body to the execution of this technology.[16] If handwriting manuals served as treatises on the incorporation of writing – of bringing the letter into the body – miscellanies and their inscriptions served as sites for the opposite process of bringing the body into the book and, by association, the world of books. Unlike printed dedications of authors to patrons, which inscribed the private into an otherwise public mode of address, the handwritten dedication – writing in a book – endowed this seemingly private mode of address with a certain publicness. But the important message that it communicated, beyond any well-wishing included in the often prescribed dedicatory lyrics, was that the printed writing in the book was something that was fundamentally shareable between readers. The inscription conveyed the ease with which printed objects could be transferred from one reader to another, shared in the sense of held in common.

Hunt's introduction went one step further to motivate another kind of writing in books and thus another mode of shareability: that between *author and reader*. When Hunt instructed owners of the book to further 'mark' the text beyond the inscription ('the said giver should mark his or her favourite passages throughout (as delicately as need be)'), this act of handwriting was not understood as an act of giving away, but conversely, as one of taking. Instead of authorizing the shareability of books, such marking with the hand authorized the shareability of ideas within them. It instructed readers on how to make the ideas in the book their own property, just as their 'property' was importantly being framed as a selection of someone else's ideas.

The inscription thus functioned as a starting point – a portal – to initiate more writing in books. But where the handwritten inscription emphasized the importance, and the singularity, of the material object of the book (this copy is special because it bears my personal handwriting), Hunt's invocation for readers and givers to move beyond the signature and to mark-up the text was not a way of prizing the book as an object, but as a bearer of ideas ('to all those who prize the spirit of books and or regard it above the letter'). The individual book was transformed in Hunt's injunction into a space of literary work. When Hunt concluded this invitation to write in miscellanies with the words, 'and so present, as it were, *the author's and the giver's minds at once'*, he was granting to handwriting an extraordinary power, suggesting that the reason to write in books was to endow writing in books with authorial status. By marking the book with one's hand, the giver – or more generally the reader – was in some sense making the ideas *her own*.

Her markings would create a new work within the material space of the book; she would occupy, as Hunt suggested, the same space and thus the same status as an author.

According to the textual economy of the miscellanies, then, writing was not only a product of more writing, it was even more significantly founded on the critical act of selection, not origination. Following Hunt's directions, when the giver shared a selection of readings (a miscellany) gleaned from a particular selection of texts (another miscellany), she was modelling an activity for the receiver to create her own miscellany within the miscellany. She was illustrating for her how to participate in this system of marking one's debts and forwarding one's credits. Whether handwritten or print, writing in the miscellanies was conceived as miscellaneous, as a practice of (medial and transactional) mixing. It was always framed as a share and thus shareable.

Hunt's instructions to mark-up these books was not only a rhetorical extension of the typographical invitations of the miscellanies' dedicatory leaves. It was also an extension of a more general visual logic in the miscellanies' front matter that encouraged readers to mark their books. There was an intimate connection between the cosmos of book formats that all fell under the heading of the romantic 'miscellany' and typographical invitations to get readers to write in books. Such note-taking was mobilized by designs such as financial ledgers, for example in *The American Ladies' Calendar* (1818) or the German *Taschenbuch der Liebe und Freundschaft gewidmet* (1805–7); diary spaces found in books like *Le Souvenir* (1826) or a later issue of *Taschenbuch der Liebe und Freundschaft gewidmet* (1808); or, finally, wallet bindings that were common to such miscellanies and into whose pockets readers could place their own writing. Goethe had done this for example in his many shipments of his writings to his English translator, Thomas Carlyle, where he would place his own poems in the pockets of the books' bindings (one of which was called *Ein Gleichniß*, or *A Likeness*, and was an exquisite comparison of the practice of translation to a vase of cut flowers).[17] In all of these cases of writing in books, readers' writing was importantly being framed as a part – a share – of a larger universe of writing. Typographical spaces like the accounting tables or the diary sheets encouraged readers to learn to narrate their own lives – to *re*count and thus *a*ccount for their actions – but these autobiographical spaces were of course not taking place in blank books, but books with other writing in them. There was a transactional logic to such writing that was also encoded in the 'in' and the 'out' of those accounting tables. In framing the reader's writing according to the logic of book*keeping*, such writing was framed not as an act of keeping books, of possession, but as a way of mapping lines of exchange.[18]

Yet unlike the popular early-modern book format comprised of the collection of textual parts, the commonplace book, the miscellany did not take excerpts of what was 'out there' and inscribe them 'in here' in one's own personal book, but rather inscribed the individual into a book *already composed* of textual parts. As in Lucy Walsh's copy of *The American Ladies Pocket Book* (1818) or Edward King's copy of *The Gentleman's Annual Pocket Remembrancer* (1816), which bear their readers' annotations, the act of writing no longer took place on the blank page of the commonplace book, but on the printed page of the miscellany. Indeed, in Prudence Carter's copy of *Le Souvenir* (1826), we can see how her own annotations mingle with those of another, a certain William A. Howard of Charlestown, who has written some occasional poems on the theme of friendship on the tissue paper that covers the book's images. When the Major in Goethe's 'The Man of Fifty' looks over his commonplace books in order to select a citation to adorn his poem that was to be sent in a kind of pocket-book (a *Brieftasche*) that has been woven by the beautiful widow, we can see how Goethe's novella was staging precisely this bibliographic transition from the handwritten collection of one's own writing to the 'woven' collection of the writing of others.

In drawing attention to these manuscriptural spaces within printed books, my aim is to expand the study of romantic book culture to include observations of the *simultaneity* of various writing technologies within what we have traditionally called 'print culture'. As Margaret Ezell has illustrated in her study of late-seventeenth- and early-eighteenth-century manuscript literature, handwriting continued to have an important role to play in literary communities even with the ascent of print in the eighteenth century.[19] In Ezell's words, 'public' did not always mean 'publication'.[20] And as Meredith McGill, Pat Crain, and Bernhard Siegert have shown, handwriting continued to play an important role in literary culture well after Ezell's timeframe into the nineteenth century.[21] As Wilhelm wrote to Nathalie in Goethe's *Travels*, 'One has no idea how much people write today. I'm not even talking about what is printed, although that is still plenty. One can only imagine what is circulated in silence through letters and essays about the news, letters, stories, anecdotes and descriptions of individual lives'.[22] If Wilhelm's observation was true and manuscript production far exceeded print production at the turn of the nineteenth century, can we still reliably speak of a 'print culture'?

Rather than simply move from one category to the other, rather than conceive such manuscriptural work as an *alternative* writerly space to print (which has achieved the status of a scholarly commonplace these days),[23] I'm interested in exploring the ways that handwriting and printed writing were brought into contact with one another, the way these two very different technologies could literally overlap in the space of a single book. It is precisely the book as an object of inquiry that allows us to see how such different writing technologies intersected with and depended upon one another. Unlike Laurence Sterne's use of handwriting in the printed book, for example, who signed copies of the first edition of *Tristram Shandy* to keep it from being pirated,[24] the miscellanies did not use such invitations to write with one's hand to *authorize* the printed book, but instead to frame the book as a *shared* space, either between one reader and another or between readers and authors. An inscription was crucially *not* a signature. The singular identity of the hand in Sterne's sHANDy starkly contrasted with the commonality of hands framed by the miscellany's typographical layout and that was captured in the familiar miscellany title, 'by *several* hands'. The invitation to handwriting in the miscellanies thus did not serve a compensatory function – an articulation of an alternative, human space in a world of mechanized, mass-reproduced objects – but served instead as a kind of initiation into a way of thinking about writing more generally within the printed public sphere as a space of commonality. Reformulating writing as a share was not a means of capturing some larger sense of modern fragmentation, but was the precondition, indeed the foundation, upon which a culture of intellectual ownership was being built in the romantic period and that found one of its most successful articulations through the bibliographic genre of the romantic miscellany.

Textual hollows

> The reading world has, I apprehend, by this time become possessed of nearly every scrap of poetry and romance ever written by Lord Byron. It may be pleased, however, to know something of a dramatic poem which he did not write, but which he projected – and this is the story: – [25]

This was the opening of Washington Irving's 'An Unwritten Drama of Lord Byron', which appeared in the miscellany *The Gift*, for the year 1836. The contribution was based on information that Irving had recorded in his journal in 1825 under the heading, 'Unpublished note by Capt. Medwin'.[26] The note that Irving received and then transcribed in his journal was itself based on Medwin's conversations with Byron in Italy about a play that Byron intended to write that was in turn based, so Irving tells us, on a play by Calderon entitled, *Embozado de Cordova*. No such play existed, but Calderon's *El Purgatorio de San Patricio*, which was based on a long tradition of reusing the St. Patrick myth (perhaps most notably by Marie de France), was translated by Shelley and read by Byron, who eventually incorporated elements of it into his *unfinished* drama, *The Deformed Transformed*.[27] To begin to recover the story of 'An Unwritten Drama' is not only a means of reconstructing a literary history in miniature, a chronicle of the borrowing, sharing, misreading, transcribing, and transforming of ideas and motifs that make up the field of literature. It is also a means to understand the medium of the book in which this contribution appeared. As we will see, Irving's short piece is a telling lens to understand the culture of sharing that was being promoted by the bibliographic format of the romantic miscellany.

Irving and the American literary culture to which he did (and did not) belong are of particular interest here because both his fame and subsequent marginalization within the European and American romantic canons has rested on the overt miscellaneity that surrounded his writing (and by extension 'American' writing before the American Renaissance). Few writers were more associated with the miscellany and the genre of the 'short story' that emerged out of this format than Washington Irving.[28] Indeed, he would one day become a miscellany himself: *The Irving Gift* of 1853. At the same time, few writers have seemed both so central and yet so marginal to literary history, much like the genre of the miscellany itself.[29] Irving is at once the father of the short story and the American Renaissance as well as a deeply derivative writer whose work was far surpassed by his followers, a patriarch, like Rip van Winkle, always out of sync with his place and time. In trying to address the diminution of Irving within American literary history, Paul Giles has suggested that it is largely a function of nationalist critical perspectives. 'Irving is perhaps the best example', writes Giles, 'of an American author whose stature is diminished by a forced affiliation with agendas of literary nationalism, but whose subtleties can be appreciated more readily once he is situated within a transnational context'.[30] Michael Warner, on the other hand, has suggested that Irving's troubled reception is a function of Irving's own 'rhetoric of anachronism' and the problematic relationship to futurity staged in his own writing.[31]

What I want to suggest, by contrast, is that Irving's sinking fortunes have a bookish rationale, that the decline in his reputation has been closely related to the decline of a bibliographic format with very distinct gender associations and with which his writing was most intimately associated. The ambiguity of his patriarchy, in other words, was tied to both the femininity and the secondarity of this bibliographic genre that had little in common with the later critical biases of the profession. In resurrecting Irving around the genre of the 'short story' and not the miscellany, we overlook in the process the diversity and the very real derivative quality that surrounded his writing. The derivative that promoted the practice of derivation – as though such derivation was one's own – was precisely the complex point of Irving's literary programme, one that could be seen in crystallized form in 'An Unwritten Drama'.

What does it mean to write about something that has *not* been written? There is something wonderfully strange about the title of this work. In its emphasis on the *unwritten* and not the *unfinished*, Irving's piece posed an initial problem of genre, a problem whose availability was a function of the format of the miscellanies themselves with their constant jostling of genres. Was a work about something unwritten a work of fiction, an act of imagination, or was it philology, an act of textual criticism? In invoking the 'scraps of poetry' of Byron's writing, he aligns his work with the tireless energies of nineteenth-century manuscript-hunting editors and philologists. And yet at the same, when he writes, 'and this is its story', he assumes a narrator's stance, transforming his contribution back from philology to fiction. Irving's opening mirrored the fictional editors of so much romantic fiction, thus capitalizing on the referential ambiguity at the heart of romantic writing. And yet instead of a twice-told tale, a retelling of what has already been recorded, what we are about to hear is something that has *not* been written. At first glance it looks like the exact inverse of Borges' *Pierre Menard* whose title character's crowning authorial project was to write *Don Quixote* word for word *again*. Instead of writing the same work, Irving writes a work that does not exist. But it is still said to belong to another author, as it hovers between the generic spaces of imaginative writing (fiction) and commentary (criticism) that were both so prevalent in the miscellanies.

The opening to this work is as remarkable as its title, and its function seems to be precisely to make an opening. Beginning with the words, 'The reading world', as a replacement of, 'Dear reader', marks that all-important romantic shift from a familiar, coterie audience to a scene of mass communication, from a closed to an open system. The first main verb in the sentence, 'become possessed', performs a clever parody of the ideals of completion and proprietariness – the possibilities of closure and enclosure – that suffused projects of nineteenth-century bibliomania. To want 'every scrap of poetry and romance ever written' was indeed to 'become possessed'. *Possession* embodied the bibliographic obsessions of the nineteenth century at the same time that it illustrated the impossibility of such projects in a world of overproliferation. To offer an *unwritten* drama was thus both to feed this possession of possessiveness as well as to confound it: how could you possess that which had not been written? To whom did the *unwritten* drama belong? It was to call the whole project of possession – the genitive case in the title ('*of* Lord Byron') – into question.

Thus we are offered something that is both there and not there at once, Byron's, but also Irving's, a poem 'which he did not write, but which he projected'. It is 'an unwritten drama *of* Lord Byron', at the same time that another 'I' emerges merely five words into the story, set-off in its own privileged grammatical universe through the use of commas ('The reading world has, I apprehend'). The key word that Irving uses to negotiate this predicament of possession – the very predicament that makes Irving's authorial project possible – is that verb 'project'. The author is no longer equated with a *creator* in Irving's piece, but with a *projector* in a double sense: as someone who projects so that others will write (here represented by the proper name Byron) and as someone who projects – who throws forth (*projectere*), but also imagines – what others have *partially* written (here represented by the proper name Irving). Writing is established as a shared practice (collaborative *and* partial, transactional *and* creative), but also as a crucially intermedial one as well. Writing is reformulated as a kind of adaptation, as the *un*written drama is written, the *un*published note is published. The author – or each author – is only one component in this larger technological undertaking. In equating writing with projecting, the opening establishes, in numerous ways, an opening for more writing.

The story that Irving goes on to tell is about a Spanish nobleman, Alfonso, whose passions have become 'ungovernable' and who is soon plagued by a mysterious figure who remains 'masked and muffled up' and follows Alfonso 'at every turn' ('like the demon in Faust, he intrudes in his solitude'). The pursuer destroys Alfonso's 'zest' ('the sweetest cup of pleasure becomes poison to him') and soon Alfonso suspects that he is seducing Alfonso's lover. A duel ensues and Alfonso kills the pursuer only to learn that he is himself: 'The mask and the mantle of the unknown drop off, and Alfonso discovers his own image – the spectre of himself – he dies with horror!' (89).

Byron's/Irving's tale belonged, of course, to the rapidly expanding corpus of works about the *Doppelgänger* in the first half of the nineteenth century. The *Doppelgänger* has most often been thought of in psychologized terms, as a sign, in Christoph Forderer's words in a recent monograph on the topic, of the 'diffusion of identity [Identitätsdiffusion]' or the 'dedifferentiation of the I-Pronoun [Entgrenzung des Ich-Pronomens]'.[32] The proliferation of literary doubles was supposed to be the most emphatic sign of the growing psychologization of literature in the nineteenth century, the orientation of the literary as an exploration of an interiority that was undergoing both a remarkable expansion as well as internal division. The double was, according to Friedrich Kittler, where we learned to read properly, to see ourselves in our books and thus forget our books. 'The printed word was skipped and the book forgotten', writes Kittler, 'until somewhere between the lines a hallucination appeared – the pure signified of the printed sign. In other words, Doubles in the era of classical Romanticism originated in the classroom where we learn to read correctly'.[33]

I want to pause for a moment and ask whether this rather common reading of the proliferation of the romantic double is not in need of some revision. If the encounter with the double in romantic fiction was most often a threatening one, why would such an agonistic figure function as a mechanism of *identification* between reader and medium? Why would the traumatic experience of one's double lead a reader to see *through* the medium of the book? Why is the double a figure of the double self, in other words, and not just a figure of doubleness more generally? Instead of a figure of narcissistic personification or psychological division, perhaps the story of the double – the story about the proliferation of sameness – offered an extremely attractive plot to address a mediaspace defined by increasingly reproducible cultural objects. In capturing the crisis that surrounded the singular and the unique, the story of the double did not so much articulate some new psychological reality or a larger programme of psychologization at all, but represented with striking precision the material reality of a new communications environment. It represented the sheer discomfort of inhabiting a world constituted by so much of the same thing, or put differently, of a world of so little originality. The duel with the double was not so much an invitation to identify with the characters in books as it was a means of contending with the discomforts of so much sameness.

If the double captured a more general concern with reproducibility and sameness that inhered in the emerging nineteenth-century mediascape, the crisis of singularity at its heart also disclosed, on a more specific level, something essential about Irving's project of 'projection' and the culture of sharing surrounding the romantic miscellany. 'Diffusion of identity' and the 'dedifferentiation of the I' were as much at the heart of those spaces of bibliographic inscription in the miscellanies as in Irving's project of writing the 'unwritten'. Irving's story of the double – of the reproducibility but also shareability of writing – was at the same time also a story about the 'ungovernable', about the difficulties of order and classification that the growing shareability of writing produces. That is why the crowd plays such a crucial role here ('he follows him in the crowded street, or the brilliant saloon; thwarting his schemes, and marring all his intrigues of love or ambition'), a connection that would be elaborated in later stories of the double such as Poe's 'The Man of the Crowd' or Grillparzer's 'Der arme Spielmann'. That is why the concluding event that leads to the hero's downfall is the disruption of the dance: 'In the giddy mazes of the dance, in which Alfonso is addressing his fair partner with the honeyed words of seduction, he sees the stranger pass like a shadow before him; a voice, like the voice of his own soul, whispers in his ear; the words of seduction die from his lips; *he no longer hears the music of the dance*' (89; emphasis added). The order of the dance ('the giddy mazes') gives way to the disorder of the crowd, the hero's form-giving powers of orchestrating intrigues disappears ('marring all his intrigues'), along with the orchestrating power of the music *that he can no longer hear*. The harmony of the dance is replaced by the disharmony of the whisper, the key mode of communication from E.T.A. Hoffmann's tour de force narrative of an emerging culture of the copy, 'The Uncanny Guest'. Following this whisper, 'the words of seduction die from his lips', as we no longer know the content of speech. Speech is crucially hollowed-out here as closed forms like the 'intrigue', 'scheme', or 'dance' are replaced by forms without form that challenge the notions of governance and singularity that were essential to social and narrative order. A story that opens with an opening about openings is no less itself about openings.

Irving's story (if we can call it that) ends (if we can say that) also in proto-Borgesian fashion (idem):

How far the plan he had in view agreed with the Spanish original, I have not been able to ascertain. The latter was said to be by Calderon; but it is not to be found in any edition of his works that

I have seen. My curiosity being awakened on the subject, I made diligent inquiry while in Spain, for the play in question, but it was not to be met with in any of the public libraries, or private collections; nor could the book-sellers give me any information about it. Some of the most learned and indefatigable collectors of Spanish literature informed me that a play of the kind, called the Embozado of Cordova, was somewhere in existence, but they had never seen it. The foregoing sketch of the plot may hereafter suggest a rich theme to a poet or dramatist of the Byron school. (90)

We are offered a textual universe that consists of a chain of writers (Irving, Byron, Calderon) at the same time that the status of each preceding node in the network is called into question. The drama that Byron did not write, which Irving is merely summarizing and thus not 'writing' (in the sense of creating), is based on a drama that Calderon himself might not have written. Like Byron's unwritten drama, Calderon's drama is said to exist, but has never been seen. Irving consults all of the relevant nodes of the print economy (the library, the book-seller, the collector), but the textual gap continues to exist. The conclusion of the story creates yet another opening. The incapacity of Calderon's work to be possessed seems to be the very condition upon which its continued circulation depends, much like Irving's own project that is intended to motivate the possibility of future writing ('The foregoing sketch of the plot may hereafter suggest a rich theme to a poet or dramatist of the Byron school'). The bibliographic economy is conceptualized, like the crowd in the story, as necessarily incomplete, unwhole, and open.

To summarize Irving's story, and to interpret it, is thus to perform an amazing feat of repetition: like Susan Sontag's 'Description (of a Description)', we are summarizing a summary (articulated most forcefully in the wonderfully vague temporal markers that populate Irving's story, such as 'at first', 'by degrees', 'at length', 'soon after', 'at every turn'). But Irving's summary is not intended as a *summa*, a totality, but instead as a *projection*, as something to produce more writing. In her essay on nineteenth-century miscellanies, Laura Mandell has argued that miscellany contributions very often dramatized what she calls an act of 'productive consumption', where 'the poems, stories, and pictures in literary annuals are often about viewing, listening to, and reading works of art',[34] and on one level, we could say Irving offers an exemplary instance of this. But it is precisely the element of sharedness, which suffused these books and their contents, that problematizes the dualism of Mandell's terms of producing and consuming. Sharing stood outside of the binary logic of both production and consumption, challenging such market rationale from within. In calling his story 'An Unwritten Drama *of* Lord Byron', Irving was emphasizing the ambiguity surrounding the ownership of literary property, challenging the possibilities and even the legitimacy of possession that demarcated the twin, autonomous spaces of production and consumption. At the same time, in calling his story 'An *Unwritten* Drama of Lord Byron', he was also demarcating a space for future writers to call their own. Just as the origin of Byron's work (Calderon) could not be recovered, the origin for Irving and future writers was not there either. Writing what was *unwritten* was a way of simultaneously affirming and effacing the work's own origins, its indebtedness and sharedness to another writer. Like the complicated semiotics of the inscription, Irving was both inviting the practice of textual sharing at the same time that he was producing boundaries to facilitate the paradoxical sense of originality, of a space of one's own, within this shared space.

To conclude, then, however small or partial this particular miscellany entry of Irving's might have been – indeed precisely because of its summary and partiality – I want to suggest that it can serve as an excellent entry-point for understanding the larger questions of sharing and owning that surrounded romantic miscellanies more generally. Unlike Irving's more famous 'tales', pieces like 'An Unwritten Drama' have not been anthologized with any regularity (if at all) and have most often been treated as textual anomalies in the critical literature. As the editors of Irving's critical edition write, 'No information is available as to the impetus which led Irving during the summer of 1835 to prepare his sketch for publication in an elegant gift-book ... Since he was extremely busy – revising and proofreading the second and third volumes of The Crayon Miscellany, purchasing and renovating a home, and overseeing the researches of his nephew Pierre for Astoria – it seems unlikely he would have written the work at this time unless solicited to do so'.[35] At work on more important miscellanies of his own, we have little idea why he would contribute a ten-year-old journal entry to another miscellany. Like the blank spaces that populated the miscellanies, Irving's contribution to *The Gift* is read as a kind of unmotivated blank space within Irving's own corpus of miscellaneous writing, itself a persistent blank space in the narrative of American literary history.

And yet 'An Unwritten Drama' has much to tell us about the bibliographic importance of Irving's writing that has been more properly classified as 'tales', whether it was the doubling of 'Rip van Winkle', the borrowings of 'The Art of Book-Making', the incompletions found in 'The Student of Salamanca', or the literal hollows of 'A Legend of

Sleepy Hollow'. In each case it was the figure of the hollow or the hollow text that served as a crucial figure for thinking about a poetics of the derivative. 'An Unwritten Drama' was thus no random contribution to randomly organized books – miscellaneity *in extremis* – but rather a very considered piece of writing that engaged with the principles of writing encoded in these increasingly prominent media objects. In exploring a notion of writing as projection – and all of the related, technologized ideas of amplification, division, processing, calculation and computation that accompanied it – Irving's work was engaging with the sharedness of writing that the miscellanies themselves were in the process of promoting, but of course also trying to control. Like the miscellanies, Irving's work made sharing a central principle in the creative process, but like the miscellanies, it also attempted to negotiate textual openings as well, to carve out writing spaces of one's own. As a part itself, it attempted both to impart and part with writing. Like the hero of Goethe's novella, 'The Man of Fifty', who eventually lost his front tooth and thereby quite literally fell to pieces, such romantic texts were compelling explorations of what happened when the body of writing fell to pieces too. 'An Unwritten Drama' suggests that sharing was not only more difficult but also far more important to the romantic *bibliocosmos* than we have traditionally thought.

Notes

A note on illustrations: all images related to this article can be found at my website: http://piperlab.mcgill.ca.

1. Johann Wolfgang von Goethe, *The Man of Fifty*, trans. Andrew Piper (London: Hesperus Press, 2004) 12.
2. Kathryn Ledbetter, *A Woman's Book: The Keepsake Literary Annual*, Diss. University of South Carolina (1995); Barbara Benedict, *Making the Modern Reader: Cultural Mediation in Early Modern Literary Anthologies* (Princeton: Princeton UP, 1996); Leah Price, *The Anthology and the Rise of the Novel: From Richardson to George Eliot* (Cambridge: Cambridge UP, 2000); Seth Lerer, 'Medieval English Literature and the Idea of the Anthology', *PMLA* 118.5 (2003): 1251–62; Ina Ferris, 'Antiquarian Authorship: D'Israeli's Miscellany of Literary Curiosity and the Question of Secondary Genres', *Studies in Romanticism* 45.4 (Winter 2006): 523–42; Meredith McGill, 'Common Places: Poetry, Illocality, and Temporal Dislocation in Thoreau's "A Week on the Concord and Merrimack Rivers"', *American Literary History* 19.2 (Summer 2007): 357–74; Stephen G. Nichols and Siegfried Wenzel, eds., *The Whole Book: Cultural Perspectives on the Medieval Miscellany* (Ann Arbor: Michigan UP, 1996); Paul Gerhard Klussmann and York-Gotthart Mix, eds., *Literarische Leitmedien: Almanach und Taschenbuch in kulturwissenschaftlichen Kontext* (Wiesbaden: Harrassowitz, 1998); Hans-Jürgen Lüsebrink, 'La littérature des almanachs: réflexions sur l'anthropologie du fait littéraire', *Études françaises*

36.3 (2000): 47–63; Armando Petrucci, 'From the Unitary Book to Miscellany', *Writers and Readers in Medieval Italy: Studies in the History of Written Culture* (New Haven: Yale UP, 1995): 1–18; and Ségolène Le Men, 'Quelques définitions romantiques de l'album', *Art et métieres du livre* (Jan. 1987): 40–7.

3. Stephen G. Nichols and Siegfried Wenzel, eds, *The Whole Book.*
4. Barbara Benedict, *Making the Modern Reader* 40.
5. Leah Price, *The Anthology and the Rise of the Novel* 3.
6. Ina Ferris, 'Antiquarian Authorship'.
7. Leigh Hunt, 'Pocket-Books and Keepsakes', *The Keepsake* (London: Hurst, Chance & Co., 1828) 4–5.
8. On the importance of the series for mass media environments, see Umberto Eco, 'Serialität im Universum der Kunst und Massenmedien', *Streit der Interpretationen* (Konstanz: Universitäts-Verlag, 1987) 49–65.
9. Writing of the emergence of the modern, commercial function of the Christmas holiday, Nissenbaum writes, 'Books were on the cutting edge of a commercial Christmas, making up more than half of the earliest items advertised as Christmas gifts'. Stephen Nissenbaum, *The Battle for Christmas* (New York: Vintage, 1997) 140–55; 140.
10. Martha Woodmansee, 'The Genius and the Copyright: Economic and Legal Conditions of the Emergence of the "Author"' *Eighteenth-Century Studies* 17.4 (1984) 425–48 and *The Author, Art, and the Market: Rereading the History of Aesthetics* (New York: Columbia UP, 1994). See also Mark Rose, *Authors and Owners: The Invention of Copyright* (Cambridge: Harvard UP, 1993) and Heinrich Bosse, *Autorschaft ist Werkherrschaft. Über die Entstehung des Urheberrechts aus dem Geist der Goethezeit* (München: Schöningh, 1981). For a discussion of contemporary issues in copyright, see Peter Jaszi, 'Toward a Theory of Copyright: The Metamorphoses of "Authorship"', *Duke Law Journal* (1991): 455–500. For a discussion on the common rights of copyright, see Trevor Ross, 'Copyright and the Invention of Tradition', *Eighteenth-Century Studies* 26.1 (1992): 1–28.
11. Natalie Zemon Davis, 'Beyond the Market: Books as Gifts in Sixteenth-Century France', *Transactions of the Royal Historical Society* 5.33 (1983): 69.
12. 'Let us speak of a work of art as *autographic* if and only if the distinction between original and forgery of it is significant; or better, if and only if even the most exact duplication of it does not thereby count as genuine ... Thus painting is autographic, music non-autographic, or *allographic*'. Nelson Goodman, *Languages of Art: An Approach to a Theory of Symbols* (Indianapolis: Hackett, 1976) 113.
13. Two of the most powerful recent critiques are Siva Vaidhyanathan, *Copyrights and Copywrongs: The Rise of Intellectual Property and How It Threatens Creativity* (New York: New York UP, 2003) and Lawrence Lessig, *Free Culture: How Big Media Uses Technology and the Law to Lock Down Culture and Control Creativity* (New York: Penguin Press, 2004).
14. Cited in Gerard Genette, *Paratexts: Thresholds of Interpretation*, trans. Jane Lewin (Cambridge: Cambridge UP, 1997) 123. Genette writes, 'Tending to disappear at the beginning of the nineteenth century, therefore, are two features, obviously connected: the most direct (economic) social function of the dedication, and its expanded form of the laudatory epistle'.
15. For an excellent discussion of the socialization into writing in the eighteenth and nineteenth centuries that does not however touch on the role of the

miscellanies, see Patricia Crain, *The Story of A: The Alphabetization of America from The New England Primer to The Scarlet Letter* (Stanford: Stanford UP, 2000).

16. For example, see *Dean's Universal Penman* (1808), where he advises, 'Sit at a convenient distance, avoid leaning hard on the pen, and incline the left side of the body toward the desk, without leaning upon, or even touching it ... The forefinger should lie on the top of the pen, and be just as low as the top of the nail of the second finger ... Lay the third or ring finger, over the little finger inward, and when writing, rest lightly on the end of the little finger' (unpaginated). It was also not uncommon for manuals to call for a system of tying-up pupils' limbs. See Ray Nash, *American Penmanship 1800–1850* (Worcester: American Antiquarian Society, 1969) 33.

17. Carlyle writes to his mother in 1827: 'News came directly after breakfast that the packet from Goethe had arrived in Leith! ... In the box containing the necklace [for Mrs. Carlyle], and in each pocket of the pocket-book were cards, each with a verse of poetry on it in the old master's own hand'. Charles Eliot Norton, ed., *Correspondence between Goethe and Carlyle* (London: Macmillan, 1887) 28.

18. For an excellent recent material example of this intersection of accounting and fiction, see Borges' manuscript for the *Library of Babel* – a story that is overwhelmingly concerned with the infinite interchangeability of writing – that was written on ledger paper. On the relationship of bookkeeping to modernist fiction, see Stanley Corngold, 'Bookkeeping in the Modernist Novel', *Approaching Modernism*, eds Astradur Eysteinsson and Vivian Liska (Amsterdam: Benjamins, 2007) 367–81.

19. Margaret J.M. Ezell, *Social Authorship and the Advent of Print* (Baltimore: Johns Hopkins, 1999). She writes, 'In contrast to existing interpretations of the heroic, democratizing impact of print technology in the seventeenth century, I explore the cultural world of the script author and the 'hidden' female participation in it as author and as reader ... We still need histories of authors and readers – often women – who resided away from the centers of publishing and technology of 'modern' authors. In short, we still need studies that are not focused on the 'advanced' or modern concept of authorship during this period of transition but instead on all the varied aspects of the material culture of literature' (11–12).

20. Margaret J.M. Ezell, *Social Authorship* 25.

21. Tamara Plakins Thornton, *Handwriting in America* (New Haven: Yale UP, 1996); Meredith McGill, 'The Duplicity of the Pen', *Language Machines: Technologies of Literary and Cultural Production*, ed. Jeffrey Masten, Peter Stallybrass, Nancy Vickers (New York: Routledge, 1997) 39–71; and Bernhard Siegert, *Relays: Literature as an Epoch of the Postal System*, trans. Kevin Repp (Stanford: Stanford UP, 1999).

22. J.W. Goethe, *Wilhelm Meisters Wanderjahre. Sämtliche Werke*, vol. 10, ed. Gerhard Neumann (Frankfurt/Main: Deutscher Klassiker Verlag, 1989) 339.

23. For an explicit and exemplary argument of the differentiation of script and print in their evolution, see Thornton, who writes that Americans around the turn of the nineteenth century 'came to understand handwriting in contradistinction to print and to make handwriting function in contradistinction to the press, as the medium of the self'. Tamara Thornton, *Handwriting in America* 30. See also Michael Warner, *The Letters*

of the Republic: Publication and the Public Sphere in Eighteenth-Century America (Cambridge: Harvard UP, 1990) 7–9.

24. Kenneth Monkman, 'The Bibliography of the Early Editions of *Tristram Shandy*', *Library: A Quarterly Journal of Bibliography* 25 (1970): 11–39.

25. Washington Irving, 'An Unwritten Drama of Lord Byron', *The Gift* (Philadelphia: Carey & Hart, 1836) 166–171. Reprinted in Washington Irving, 'An Unwritten Drama of Lord Byron', *Miscellaneous Writings 1803–1859*, vol. 2, ed. Wayne R. Kime (Boston: Twayne, 1981) 88–90.

26. 'Textual Commentary', *Miscellaneous Writings 1803–1859* 2: 394.

27. For a discussion of the sources of both Byron's and Irving's work, see Charles E. Robinson, 'The Devil as Doppelgänger in the *Deformed Transformed*: The Sources and Meanings of Byron's Unfinished Drama', *The Plays of Lord Byron: Critical Essays*, ed. Robert Gleckner (Liverpool: Liverpool UP, 1997) 321–46. Robinson's move from calling it an 'unwritten' drama to an 'unfinished' one in his scholarly essay indicates the way these different terms underwrote different genres and also shows the generic ambiguity that the term 'unwritten' could provoke and that necessitated its replacement.

28. On Irving as father of the American short story, see Eugene Current-Garcia, 'Soundings and Alarums: The Beginning of the Short Story in America', *Midwest Quarterly* 17 (1976): 311–28.

29. On Irving as ambiguous patriarch, see Edward Wagenknecht for a summary of this position: 'Irving's position in American literature is a rather odd one. So far as his name goes, he is still one of the most famous American authors. There is also a conventional honor paid to him as the Father of American Literature. Yet the living body of his work is small, and in the critical estimate generally placed upon his effort as a whole, he now ranks below any of the others who enjoy a comparable fame'. Edward Wagenknecht, *Washington Irving: Moderation Displayed* (Oxford: Oxford UP, 1962) ix.

30. Paul Giles, 'Burlesques of Civility: Washington Irving', *Transatlantic Insurrections: British Culture and the Formation of American Literature 1730–1860* (Philadelphia: Pennsylvania UP, 2001) 142–63; 143. For a discussion of Irving in a similar vein through a reading of his biographies of English writers, see James Chandler, *England in 1819: The Politics of Literary Culture and the Case of Romantic Historicism* (Chicago: Chicago UP, 1998).

31. Michael Warner, 'Irving's Posterity', *ELH* 67.3 (2000): 773–99.

32. Christof Forderer, *Ich-Eklipsen. Doppelgänger in der Literatur seit 1800* (Stuttgart: Metzler, 1999) 25.

33. Friedrich Kittler, 'Romanticism – Psychoanalysis – Film: A History of the Double', *Literature, Media, Information Systems*, ed. John Johnston (Amsterdam: G&B Arts, 1997) 90.

34. Laura Mandell, 'Hemans and the Gift-Book Aesthetic', *Cardiff Corvey* 6 (2001): unpaginated.

35. 'Textual Commentary', *Miscellaneous Writings 1803–1859* 2: 394.

7
Getting the Reading Out of It: Paper Recycling in Mayhew's London

Leah Price

Until not much more than a century ago, most reading matter was made from old rags, and much of it went on to be recycled in turn. Newspapers were handed down a chain of households as their contents staled: letters were torn to light a pipe, broadsheets pieced out dress patterns or lined pie-plates or wiped shit. In their passage from hand to hand and use to use, loose sheets corroborate Natalie Davis's description of the book as 'not merely a source for ideas ... but a carrier of relationships.'[1]

Or a carrier of food: as late as 1911, the *Encyclopedia Britannica* continued to define paper as 'the substance commonly used for writing upon, or for wrapping things in.' If pages can make readers forget hunger, as in so many accounts of prison reading, paper serves as a reminder of the need to ingest and excrete. At least, they *did* serve as such a reminder, because this chapter will suggest that two phenomena that usually get explained in terms of the rise of electronic media in the late twentieth century—the dematerialization of the text and the disembodiment of the reader—in fact have more to do with the rise of woodpulp paper in the late nineteenth century, and also, in the twentieth, of plastics.

In an age of taxed paper, reading constituted only one point in a cycle: beginning its life as rags no longer worth wearing, the page dwindled back into paper once its content was no longer worth reading. Once, common readers—as well as literary critics—noticed the prehistory and afterlife of legible objects. In the wood-pulp era, only bibliographers continued to. But even bibliographers need limits. Can the study of printed books stop short of forestry and the second-hand clothing market? Does the interpretation of graffiti require expertise in brickmaking? In the opposite direction, how far downstream should reception theorists venture: to the archive, the depository, the dumpster?

To think about the preservation of paper is to think about the contingent, the unmentionable, and the mundane. Much of the vernacular Chinese fiction now extant has reached our hands by accident, unearthed from tombs or stumbled across in the backing material for other books.[2] In Europe, the same 'secondary causes' that destroy books have preserved pages. Some of those unintended consequences are bibliographic (binder's waste), others more vulgarly domestic (trunk linings).[3]

Nothing more embarrassing than a book past its read-by date. What's no longer worth reading, however, still needs to be handled, if only to get it out of the way. And at the opposite level of abstraction, what's no longer fit to read may remain good to think with. Such thinking, I want to suggest, stands at the heart of Henry Mayhew's *London Labour and the London Poor*, the loose, baggy ethnography of the urban underclass that swelled out of a messy series of media: eighty-two articles serialized in the *Morning Chronicle* (October 1849–50) provided the raw material for freestanding weekly numbers published between December 1850 and February 1852, which in turn were expanded, revised and collected in volume form in 1861–2.

My question is why Mayhew's 'cyclopaedia of the industry, the want, and the vice of the great Metropolis' so encyclopedically catalogs the uses to which used paper can be turned. In the city that *London Labour* describes, books and newspapers never stand still: they're sold to fishmongers, to middlemen who distribute them to fishmongers, to a fly-paper manufacturer, and even to a member of what the narrator terms the 'sham indecent trade,' whose sealed packets, advertised as 'not [to] be admitted into families,' turn out to be stuffed with 'a lot of missionary tracts and old newspapers that [the vendor] got dirt cheap at a 'waste shop.'[4] Wrapping, wadding, padding, lining: why so much attention to paper, so little to the page?

The answer that you might expect is that Mayhew's informants aren't literate. That explanation seems to me neither accurate nor relevant—and not just because he does represent them reading (including previous installments of *London Labour* itself). More specifically, Mayhew takes pains to attribute the reading of texts and the recycling of papers to the same agents.[5] As a result, those actions are distinguished not by who performs them (gentlemen read, street urchins recycle) or even by which genres or media invite them (bibles are for rereading, newspapers for wrapping), but rather by successive moments in the life-cycle of the *same* piece of printed matter. And even that minimal distinction gets broken down, I'll argue, as Mayhew replaces the conventional timeline in which wrapping follows reading by a counternarrative in which food packaging gets resurrected as legible text.

What, then, if we were to replace 'illiteracy' with a more positive term? 'Orality' would be one obvious candidate, given how central speech is not just to the informal economy described in *London Labour*, but to its own formal structure. Books signify bankruptcy, if only because the waste paper described is as likely to consist of financial and legal manuscripts as of printed books. One waste-seller offers Mayhew 'railway prospectuses, with plans to some of them, nice engravings; and the same with other joint-stock companies. ... Old account-books of every kind. A good many years ago, I had some that must have belonged to a West End perfumer, there was such French items for Lady This, or the Honorable Captain that' (2.114).

Contrast that memento mori with the busy street vendor who tells Mayhew that 'it's all headwork with us' (2.24)—by which he means that he operates, as they say, 'off the books.' The more lifeless the papers that Mayhew describes, the more vivid the voices that he quotes: padded packets provide a foil to street cries, waste paper to oral interviews. In this analysis, the illusion of immediacy that *London Labour* so uncannily creates would be thrown into relief against the backdrop of dead media.

Another possible explanation is more reductive: you could say that paper gets resold in Mayhew's London simply because everything does. Readers today—at least in the West—will be even more struck than middle-class Victorians were by the ubiquity of reuse in *London Labour*. Unable to afford either to buy new things or to discard old ones, his informants lack the luxury of ignoring the past and future of their possessions. When we're told of one man that 'his dress could not so well be called mean as hard worn, with the unmistakable look of much of the attire of his class, that it was not made for the wearer' (2.65), the narrator's self-correction encapsulates a characteristic stutter step. Mayhew begins by gesturing toward the possibility of pricing an object on the basis of the amount of labor or quality of materials that went into its original manufacture; but he goes on to upstage that logic by a competing explanation that bases price on the position that the object occupies in a chain of successive owners and uses. The literary genre that he's drawing on here is the object narrative: the story narrated by a banknote, or a pocket-watch, or a coin as it circulates among a series of owners. In borrowing from that eighteenth-century genre, Mayhew is invoking a providential model of the market in which, far from exhausting or depreciating objects, circulation animates and invests them with fresh value.

In this analysis, 'after-uses' would provide Mayhew with a lever to topple books from their taxonomic pedestal—to simultaneously defamiliarize and deflate printed matter by lumping it among a long list of humbler commodities that lose value as they pass from hand to hand. (Such a list would encompass every consumer good that turns up in the pages of *London Labour*, with the possible exception of women's stays (2.29): in Mayhew, no such thing as what Igor Kopytoff calls 'terminal commodities,' those which make only one journey from production to consumption.[6]) The question of whether bookstands outside the market become a test case of whether anything at all stands outside the market. Anything, or even anyone: the value of used paper provides a measure for the value of the human beings who sell it: 'one dealer in 'waste' (paper) … had been brought up as a compositor, but late hours and glaring gas-lights in the printing-office affected his eyes, he told me; and … a half-blind compositor was about of as little value, he thought, as a 'horse with a wooden leg'' (1.289). From waste-paper to blind person to lame horse: as so often in Mayhew, what sounds like a hyperbolic analogy will turn out in retrospect to have been a perfectly serious cross-reference, because the price of the goods and services derived from horse carcasses will form the subject of a tabular breakdown in the next volume (2.9). Books, persons, and horses are all expected to form privileged categories, exempt from base uses. (Or at least, this is the case in England; the French, Mayhew reminds us, are less sentimental about their horses.) Yet each exemption dwindles with age: what can't be eaten turns out to be not horses, but young horses; what can't be pulped turns out to be new books, not books in general.

If books begin their life as an exception, they end up exemplifying the rule. Mayhew's uncertainty about whether to place books in parallel with, or contradistinction to, other kinds of objects prefigure the tension between internalist accounts of book history and those that draw on non-bibliographical analogies, situating debates about copyright in the context of pharmaceutical patents or reducing the history of authorship to a subset of the history of branding. Structurally, that tension between exceptionality and typicality can be measured by the placement of paper within *London Labour*. The volume devoted to the resale trade opens—before moving briskly along to second-hand backgammon boards and used mattress-ticking—with a set-piece describing 'a body of men in London who occupy themselves entirely in collecting waste paper.'

> It is no matter what kind; a small prayer-book, a once perfumed and welcome love-note, lawyers' or tailors' bills, acts of Parliament, and double sheets of the Times, form portions of the waste dealers'

stock. ... [M]odern poems or pamphlets and old romances (perfect or imperfect), Shakespeare, Molière, Bibles, music, histories, stories, magazines, tracts to convert the heathen or to prove how easily and how immensely our national and individual wealth might be enhanced, the prospectuses of a thousand companies, each certain to prove a mine of wealth, schemes to pay off the national debt, or recommendations to wipe it off [a bad pun?], auctioneers' catalogues and long-kept letters, children's copybooks and last-century ledgers, printed effusions which have progressed no further than the unfolded sheets, uncut works and books mouldy with age—all these things are found in the insatiate bag of the waste collector.

(2.9)

The breathlessness of Mayhew's syntax levels generic 'kinds' into undifferentiated 'matter.' But the reduction of absorbing reading to absorbent paper doesn't necessarily imply a social fall, because Mayhew repeatedly attributes wrapping and reading to a single agent. 'Some of the costermongers who were able to read,' the narrator tells us, 'or loved to listen to reading[,] purchased their literature in a very commercial spirit, frequently buying the periodical which is the largest in size, because when they've 'got the reading out of it,' as they say, 'it's worth a halfpenny for the barrow' (Mayhew and Neuburg 27).

What might it mean to 'get the reading out of' a newspaper? Before woodpulp, esparto grass, and other raw materials began to replace rags in the decades following the publication of *London Labour*, the obvious answer would have been that paper outlasts its contents: the read-by date rarely coincides with the sell-by limit.[7] That quality isn't unique to paper, of course. Mayhew notes elsewhere that brass doorplates fetch a fraction of their original value when they fall into the hands of scrap metal dealers after their owners' death: there, too, the value of the material medium paradoxically hastens the erasure of the text (2.10). But there's something especially poignant about measuring the ephemerality of the message against the adaptability of the medium, because that contrast inverts the traditional hope that words will survive the surfaces on which they're inscribed—whether brass, stone, or marble and gilded monuments, much less paper. Within that tradition, pages transcend the temporal limits that paper embodies. If texts (in the sense of verbal structures) broker a transhistorical meeting of minds, books (in the sense of material objects) can never break free of a particular location in space and time. Mayhew turns that contrast on its head, pitting the durability of paper against the disposability of words.[8]

In pairing the afterlife of paper with the death of text, Mayhew inverted a paradox most succinctly stated by Drummond of Hawthornden in 1711, the year when paper taxes began the climb that would end the year before the volume publication of *London Labour*. 'Books have that strange Quality,' he observed, 'that being of the frailest and tenderest of Matter, they out-last Brass, Iron and Marble.'[9] Stone is immortal, paper ephemeral. Or is it? On the one hand, the high resale value of stone makes it likelier to be erased;[10] on the other, ephemerality makes paper cheap, and cheapness allows each text to be produced in multiple copies that will go on to be stored in multiple locations and transmitted through multiple channels—channels that include the pastry-cook as often as the librarian. Redundancy thus forms at once an effect of, and a counterweight to, the fragility of paper. Texts survive in proportion as books decay. Bibliographers all know that preservation varies inversely with use: not only do small books circulate most widely and reach libraries most rarely, but the genres that get the most handling (such as almanacs) are the hardest for modern scholars to lay their hands on.[11] As Thomas Adams and Nicolas Barker note, 'popularity tends to operate positively on the text and negatively on the book' (Adams and Barker 33): the more readings a work undergoes, the more reprintings are likely to be produced, but the less likely any given copy is to survive.

In Mayhew's own time, the battle lines were clearly drawn between those who saw circulation as life-giving and life-shortening—or, more specifically, who credited or blamed the library either with putting books into circulation, or withdrawing them from use. Because bibliographic debates draw on the language of saving and exchange, it comes as no surprise that economists were among the most prominent participants in early debates about free library funding: Jevons, for example, acknowledged that free-library books wore out faster than those in private collections, but insisted 'how infinitely better it is that they should perish in the full accomplishment of their mission, instead of falling a prey to the butter-man, the waste-dealer, the entomological book-worm, or the other enemies of books which Mr. Blades has so well described and anathematized.'[12] The image of books as heroes 'perishing in the full accomplishment of their mission' makes a valiant attempt to translate the life-cycle of books into a martial language. But its mock-heroics can do little to counter the less high-flown imagery of a 1871 article on circulating libraries which observes that if unpopular books have a short life-span (because no one reprints them), popular books die for the opposite reason: too 'torn, dirtied, and read-to-death' to serve even as food wrapping, 'they will not carry butter; nor will they 'to the trunk-makers.' Their purpose is—for manure!'[13]

In one direction or the other, both models overlay the relation of text to book onto a timeline. But the more obvious axis onto which those terms get plotted is social. If waste paper looms large in the slums that Mayhew describes, the simplest explanation is that the Victorians associated mental operations (such as reading) with the upper classes, manual gestures (such as wrapping) with the lower. This contrast reflects not simply the price of paper itself, but also the lack of materials manufactured specifically for packaging. Today, books themselves are one of the few commodities that, even in the developed world, continue to be packaged in used paper rather than new plastic: what reader of this page has not unwrapped a secondhand book from the outdated local newspaper of an online bookseller in some never-visited small town? For us, however, wastepaper wrapping is the exception; for the Victorians, it remained the rule. And if we use it to wrap other texts, they associated it with decidedly non-textual contents. Before the invention of the paper bag—first produced for sale in the same decade as *London Labour*—and the even more spectacular rise of plastics, old paper was inextricably linked to food: to the kitchen and the privy, to the market and the body.[14]

The context in which Mayhew's contemporaries would have expected to come upon such references to grocery packaging was neither ethnographic (as in his costermongers) nor economic (as in Jevons's 'butterman'). On the contrary, food wrapping had by the nineteenth century come to occupy a central role in esthetics, because a long satirical tradition ensured that the easiest way to insult a work of literature was to mention it in the same breath with groceries.

A few examples out of many: The *Monthly Review*'s 1792 attack on Charles Harrington's *The Republican Refuted* concludes with two lines: 'Here, boy! throw this to the great heap that lies there, in the corner, for the cheesemonger: it may be of some use to him, though we can make nothing of it in *our way*.'[15] By 1830, Macaulay could demolish Montgomery's *Satan: A Poem* in the pages of the *Edinburgh* by remarking, a propos of nothing in particular, that 'the fashionable novels of eighteen hundred and twenty-nine hold the pastry of eighteen hundred and thirty.'[16] Sometimes ethnic slurs could reinforce class hierarchies: thus, a review of 'Railway Literature' in the *Dublin University Magazine*:

> There is upon record a story of the late Mr. Daniel O'Connell, which is not inapplicable to our subject. Meeting one day an author newly-fledged, and greatly elated by the hit of his literary first-born, he shook him heartily by the hand.

'Well, my dear fellow, I congratulate you sincerely on the success of your book; I have seen something extremely good in it.'

'What was it—eh?' said the delighted author, rubbing his hands and blushing.

'A mutton pie, my dear fellow,' replied the Liberator, chuckling slyly.[17]

But authors, too, could smear their own writings by association with household uses, as in *Biographia Literaria*:

Of the unsaleable nature of my writings I had an amusing memento one morning from our own servant girl. For happening to rise at an earlier hour than usual, I observed her putting an extravagant quantity of paper into the grate in order to light the fire, and mildly checked her for her wastefulness; la, Sir! (replied poor Nanny) why, it is only 'WATCHMEN.'[18]

The value of the paper proves the worthlessness of the page.

In the hands of a hostile reviewer, books dramatize the mortality that they're expected to counterbalance. And outside of the pages of book reviews, waste paper prompts authors to confess their own mortality. On January 4, 1821, Byron's diary records

I was out of spirits—read the papers—thought what fame was, on reading, in a case of murder, that 'Mr. Wych, grocer, at Tunbridge, sold some bacon, flour, cheese, and, it is believed, some plums, to some gipsy woman accused. He had on his counter (I quote faithfully) a book, the Life of Pamela, which he was tearing for waste paper, etc. etc. In the cheese was found, etc., and a leaf of Pamela wrapt round the bacon.' What would Richardson, the vainest and luckiest of living authors (i.e. while alive)—what would he have said could he have traced his pages from their place on the French prince's toilets (see Boswell's Johnson) to the grocer's counter and the gipsy-murderess's bacon!!!

What would he have said? what can any body say, save what Solomon said long before us? After all, it is but passing from one counter to another, from the bookseller's to the other tradesman's—grocer or pastry-cook. For my part, I have met with most poetry upon trunks; so that I am apt to consider the trunk-maker as the sexton of authorship.[19]

The 'leaf of Pamela wrapt round the bacon' prefigures our own metaphor which describes worthless information by analogy with spam.

In fact, Byron's elegiac tone has more in common with twenty-first-century information overload than it does with the rags-to-pages triumphalism elaborated a century earlier by one of the periodicals most frequently named in Mayhew's inventories of waste-dealers' stock (e.g., 1.293). The *Spectator* for May 1, 1712, begins by observing that 'When I trace in my Mind a bundle of Rags to a Quire of *Spectators*, I find so many Hands employ'd in every Step they take thro' their whole Progress, that while I am writing a *Spectator*, I fancy my self providing Bread for a Multitude'; but he goes on to confess that

> I have lighted my Pipe with my own Works for this Twelve-month past; my Landlady often sends up her little Daughter to desire some of my old *Spectators*, and has told me, more than once, the paper they are printed on is the best in the World to wrap Spice in. They likewise make a good Foundation for a Mutton pye.

The shift from metaphorical food ('I fancy myself providing bread') to its literal counterpart ('they make a good Foundation for a Mutton pye') echoes the demotion of 'paper' from a count noun (a 'Spectator paper') to a mass noun ('the paper they are printed on').

The essay counterbalances that fall, however, by a celebration of the benefits that papermaking diffuses among classes and even nations. 'It is pleasant enough,' Addison adds (the word here connotes pleasure as well as the older sense of 'comic')

> to consider the Changes that a Linnen-fragment undergoes, by passing through the several Hands above-mentioned. The finest pieces of Holland, when worn to tatters, assume a new Whiteness more beautiful than their first, and often return in the shape of Letters to their Native Country. A Lady's Shift may be metamorphosed into Billet-doux, and come into her Possession a second time. A beau may peruse his Cravat after it is worn out, with greater Pleasure and Advantage than he ever did in a Glass. In a word, a piece of Cloath, after having officiated for some Years as a Towel or a Napkin, may by this means be raised from a Dung-hill; and become the most valuable piece of Furniture in a Prince's Cabinet.[20]

Where Mr Spectator's writing descended from study to kitchen, here cloth rises from the hands of a servant ('a Towel or a Napkin') to a prince's study.

If Byron invokes the obituary, Addison channels the it-narrative. Tracing the book's origins exalts; predicting the book's fate degrades: a similar symmetry links *Sartor Resartus*'s reflection on the mortality of books—'is it not beautiful to see five million quintals of Rags picked annually from the Laystall; and annually, after being macerated, hot-pressed, printed on, and sold,—returned thither; filling so many hungry mouths by the way?'—with Carlyle's boast that a letter from John Sterling attacking *Sartor Resartus* would be 'made into matches.'[21] (The material quoted within the novel itself is presented as having reached the narrator's hands via wrappings: 'Round one of those Book-packages, which the *Stillschweigen'sche Buchhandlung* is in the habit of importing from England, come, as is usual, various waste printed-sheets . . . by way of interior wrappage; into these the Clothes-philosopher, with a certain Mohammedan reverence even for waste paper, where curious knowledge will sometimes hover, disdains not to cast his eye' [Carlyle 211].)

None of these jokes gets much of a laugh today. But the idea of paper falling into the hands of a servant—or tradesman, or Irishman, or woman—led a long and happy life in the most recyclable of genres, the anecdote (Donaldson 4). Between 1791 and 1823, Isaac D'Israeli's six-volume *Curiosities of Literature* catalogued a mind-numbingly comprehensive series of variations on this theme. One antiquarian 'left [old manuscripts] carelessly in a corner, and during his absence his cook used them for culinary purposes';[22] another 'one day at his tailor's discovered that the man was holding in his hand, ready to cut up for measures—an original Magna Charta' (D'Israeli 22). If servants recycle what masters once read, women discard what men create. In a third anecdote retailed by D'Israeli, a scholar's 'niggardly niece, although repeatedly entreated to permit them to be published, preferred to use [his] learned epistles occasionally to light her fires!' (D'Israeli 54)[23] When Harriet Taylor's maid kindled a fire with the first draft of Carlyle's *French Revolution*, she walked straight into a literary convention.

In the era of wood-pulp and Tupperware, with fireplaces and servants both on the wane, the trope should have died. Instead, it adapted, by substituting a figurative for a literal maidservant, and a preserver for a destroyer. As early as 1881, Andrew Lang declared that 'the book-collector may regard his taste as a kind of handmaid of critical science';[24] and as late as 1939, the *Cambridge History of English Literature* pronounced that 'bibliography ... is only the handmaid of literature [and] ... it is only because of their loyal services to letters that [bibliographers] can claim a place in these pages.'[25] The maid subsides into metaphor: a figure for those scholars, such as bibliographers, whose relation to the text has never made the leap into New Critical idealism and abstraction.

The fall from gentlemen's minds to servants' bodies pivots on a linguistic shift, from the figurative to the literal. Thus, the O'Connell anecdote hinges on competing senses of the preposition 'in': does 'I've seen something good in your book' refer to the content of the text or to the contents of the object? When the playwright in *La Bohème* sacrifices his manuscript to heat an icy garret, he describes its contents in a series of equally broad doubles-entendres, as 'scintillating' and 'ardent.'[26] The ambiguous class position of the bohemian is announced, in this opening scene, by the fact that we watch him burning papers before he is ever shown marking them. We know that we stand outside of the class system, in Murger's imagined Latin Quarter, when we see a single person combining composition (the mental labor of a gentleman) with destruction (the proper work of a maid).

Mayhew places such puns in the mouth not of his narrator, but of informants themselves. The narrator's indifference to literary genres ('it is no matter what kind') finds its foil in a fly-paper manufacturer's comically elaborate taxonomy of newspapers:

> I use the very best 'Times' paper for my 'catch-em-alives.' I gets them kept for me at stationers' shops and liberaries, and such-like. I pays threepence a-pound, or twenty-eight shillings the hundred weight. That's a long price, but you must have good paper if you want to make a good article. I could get paper at twopence-a-pound, but then it's only the cheap Sunday papers, and they're too slight.
>
> (3.32)

An 'article,' of course, usually refers to a news item, just as a 'paper' designates a periodical. By the same token, 'cheap' and 'slight' figure prominently among the insults dear to Victorian literary critics. By stripping each term of its metaphoric or metonymic charge, Mayhew shifts our attention from texts to objects. Not for nothing does his informant call the paste that gums the paper a 'composition.'[27]

'Composition' in the usual sense remains absent from Mayhew's pages. Where Addison starts from a legible object and goes on to trace its afterlife, Mayhew's descriptions of the resale trade open *in medias res*: third- or fourth-hand paper forms their starting-point, not their punch-line. By exploring from the inside the uses to which the formerly legible can be put, Mayhew forbids his readers to dismiss recycling as a disraelian 'curiosity,' much less an addisonian joke or a carlylean disaster.

By extension, Mayhew refuses to align the life-cycle of paper with the social class of its users. The anecdotes that I quoted a moment ago delegated to servants the dirty work of noticing paper's material attributes: its impermeability, its inflammability, its absorbency. Here, in contrast, the middle-class implied reader (or should that be implied handler?) is never allowed to forget his or her own body. *London Labour* constantly reminds us that we're wearing out its pages, if only because the weekly numbers published in 1851–2 were protected by wrappers printed with letters from readers and answers from Mayhew. At the level of the text, the wrappers incorporated readers' writing; at the level of the object, though, they kept dirty hands at a distance. In the long run, they've proven the most disposable, missing from most library copies today because they were tossed aside when the consecutively numbered pamphlets were bound into volumes. Mayhew himself termed the wrappers 'waste'—as if pamphlets could be packaged like pies—and his publisher announced that 'the outer pages of this periodical will, in future, be used as a wrapper, intended to be cut off in binding.'[28] In anticipating its own disposal, *London Labour* drags its readers down to the level of grocers. Where most Victorian social reformers leveled up—asking middle-class readers to endow working-class characters with an interiority that mirrored their own—Mayhew levels down, reducing the page in front of us to tomorrow's fish and chip paper.[29] The handling of paper replaces the reading of text as the activity that unites different social classes.

We can see now that the costermonger who chooses the largest newspaper, in anticipation of the moment when he will have 'got the reading out of it,' collapses into a single person the functions traditionally parceled out between gentleman-scholar and female servant. But Mayhew undermines temporal priority as strenuously as social precedence: that is, he doesn't simply reveal handlers of food as readers of books, but also scrambles the order in which one follows the other. One 'fancy-cabinet-maker,' now unemployed thanks to the underselling of slop-masters,

> enjoyed no reading, when I saw him last autumn, beyond the book-leaves in which he received his quarter of cheese, his small piece of bacon or fresh meat, or his saveloys; and his wife schemed to go the shops who 'wrapped their things from books,' in order that he might have something to read after his day's work.
>
> (2.114)

Where D'Israeli represents women confusing texts with pie-plates, here it's the wife's job to spot literary value in cheese packaging.

Mayhew himself seems to endorse that literary value—in contrast, for example, to a contemporaneous review which insults a novel by imagining it falling into the hands of a female Irish street-vendor: "Hawkstone'—if it has not gone to the butter-shop, and enlightened Irish barrow-women before that time—'Hawkstone,' if surviving, will teach [the reader] how important it was once thought to furnish a model-prot-estant hero with a rosary.'[30] It's not entirely clear where to situate the irony in 'enlighten': whether the reviewer is implying that book will go from cradle to grave, from press to barrow, without ever finding a reader, if only because the hypothetical barrow-women aren't literate; or whether, on the contrary, the point is that to read a page of *Hawkstone*—even for a barrow-woman—would be the reverse of 'enlightening.'

Butter in the review of *Hawkstone*, sandwiches in the *Dublin University Magazine*: traditionally, to couple books with food is to strip them of their textual value. In the resolutely materialist landscape of *London Labour*, however, the specificity of 'bacon or fresh meat, or saveloys' comes across as poignant, not comic. Another vendor complains that 'we should both be tired' if he were to inquire too closely into the con-tents of his waste papers, but adds: 'Very many were religious, more's the pity. I've heard of a page round a quarter of cheese, though, touch-ing a man's heart' (2.114). Think back to the *Monthly Review* article that ends by ordering an imaginary servant to throw the book to the cheese-monger. Nothing lower than cheese: even butter would be less smelly. For Mayhew, in contrast, wrapping doesn't preclude reading: the paper may touch the cheese, but the page still touches the heart.

In Mayhew's miraculous logic (and this is what makes his pages touch the heart of any literary critic) entropy can always be reversed.[31] A miracle, or an accident—if only in the typographical sense of the word. Blackstone's *Commentaries* famously claimed that 'the identity of a lit-erary composition consists entirely in the *sentiment* and the *language*,' while 'the paper and print are merely accidents' by which 'that com-position [is 'conveyed'] to the ear or eye of another.' Mayhew's readers don't just have ears or eyes; he also endows them with hands and noses. Although the mentions of 'once perfumed love-note' reminds us that papers lose some of their sensory attributes as they age, the persist-ence of excremental humor points in the opposite direction, toward a materiality that intensifies over time. The items listed in a West-End Perfumer's account-books may have lost their fragrance, but books themselves accrue smells over the course of their life-cycle.

In fact, in twentieth-century book history, smell has often figured as a synecdoche for the inadvertent traces of earlier readers' bodies: if the researcher's sight allows him to spot intentional actions (a fingernail mark, the trace of a pen), the smell of food that lingers on old pages points to less conscious, more embodied acts. Paul Duguid, for example, explains the importance of non-verbal information through an anecdote about his own experience working in an archive where (as an asthmatic) he reads while holding his nose; in the next seat, however, he notices another researcher passing letter after letter under his nose without even glancing at the contents. The researcher turns out to be sniffing for vinegar, in order to tell whether the port from which the letter was sent was under quarantine at the moment corresponding to the date on the letter; the lesson that Duguid learns is that digitizing a paper document can cause relevant information to be lost or changed. The shock value of his anecdote comes as his own persona shifts from brainy researcher to embodied asthmatic; he chokes, quite literally, on the realization that the nose can convey more information than the eye.[32] A similar mind-body contrast structures another early-twenty-first-century argument against digitization, Sean Latham's and Robert Scholes's 'The Rise of Periodical Studies,' which faults an editor for failing to reproduce the advertisements from a 1711 *Spectator*. The example given is an advertisement for a 'Tincture to restore the Sense of Smelling, tho' lost for many Years. A few Drops of which, being snuff'd up the Nose, infallibly cures those who have lost their Smell, let it proceed from what Cause soever.'[33] For them as for Duguid, to think of the book as something more than words is to recover a long-lost body.

'The paper and print are merely accidents': in Mayhew's world, texts reach readers not via the mind but via the body, thanks not to intentions but to accidents, errors, contingencies, and side-effects. In making a virtue of those necessities, his informants silently draw on what any Victorian reader would have recognized as the parable of the sower—the master trope of contemporary religious tracts, eventually to be secularized in the metaphor of 'broadcasting' (Matthew 13).[34] Leslie Howsam has described one missionary, shipwrecked in 1814 off the African coast, consoling himself for the natives' seizure of his goods by reflecting that 'my having been cast away, may perhaps be the saving of many of those into whose hands these Bibles have fallen, or shall fall in the future.'[35] Dispersal didn't need to mean disposal: in some cases, it could become the most effective means for the providential spread of the Word.

Mayhew shifts the trope of broadcasting from a religious to an economic register. But the two frameworks are not, of course, mutually exclusive. On the contrary, as Howsam has shown, the relation of textual gifts to bibliographic commodities found its most sophisticated analysts in the British and Foreign Bible Society, which devoted considerable ingenuity to wresting Bibles out of older free distribution networks and into market mechanisms, however heavily subsidized. Mayhew, more profanely, lumps tracts together with every other form of free—and therefore worthless—print: thus, 'sham indecent' packets are described as being stuffed with 'a religious tract, or a slop-tailor's puff' (1.241). And the pious remark that 'Mr. Mayhew is ... afraid that the distribution of [religious] tracts among the profligate is a pure waste of good wholesome paper and print' is later undercut by the speculation that 'could the well-intentioned distributors of such things ... see what is done with the papers they leave, they would begin to perceive, perhaps, that the enormous sum of money thus expended ... might be more profitably applied.'[36] It's only because used paper is always good for a scatological laugh that Mayhew can leave 'what is done' with tracts to the imagination. Again, when he cites a pickpocket as authority for the report that tracts are good to light pipes with, he borrows the strategy that we've seen already in book reviews, where a social inferior can be made to dispose of competing publications.[37] But political tracts prove just as hard to get rid of: 'the anti-Corn-Law League paper, called the *Bread Basket*, could only be got off by being done up in a sealed packet, and sold by patterers as a pretended improper work' (241). Free tracts, junk mail, bill-sticking: Mayhew testifies to a moment when the auditory overload of early modern cities was giving way to the curse of cheap paper.

Let me wrap up (if you'll forgive the pun) on a more personal note. I began thinking about the relation of reading to handling when I was working on the reception history of eighteenth- and nineteenth-century novels. Part of what maddened me, and has frustrated so many other scholars, was how few traces of use were verbal. For every pencil mark in the margin, ten traces of wax or smoke; for every ink stain, ten food spills. Such traces bring us back to the accidental; but the absence of intention doesn't need to imply an absence of meaning. The dog's-eared page, the uncut page, the faded page, even the page that smells of cheese—each of these can tell us something about the thoughts and feelings of a reader, and not simply in the case of a cookbook.

Every scholar knows how hard it is to untangle transmission from destruction. This is true for material objects (think of printer's waste), but also for verbal texts (think of the relations between editing and expurgation). The literary trope has women destroying what men compose, but in practice, we owe the survival of many manuscripts to the efforts of wives and daughters—not to mention stenographers, typists, and other female professionals.[38] To compare the bibliographer to a 'handmaid,' in this context, is not simply to reduce bibliography to a service industry; it's also to remember how close the archive lies to the pantry, the oven, and the toilet.

The anatomy of non-textual uses of paper that Mayhew elaborates looks backward, as we've seen, to a literary tradition that's also a literary-critical tradition. But it also looks forward to the question that faces historians of the book: how to disentangle reading from handling. *London Labour* forbids us to parse that difference as hierarchy: to position the text as prior to the book (the book as a residue left over once the text has been used up), or as superior to the book (the book as the province first of illiterate grocers, then of theoretically-illiterate bibliographers), or the text as purer than the book (the book as manual, the text as digital; the book as the dusty residue clogging up our libraries, the text as abstract thought streaming into an ethereal future). Mayhew reminds us that books are objects—but ones 'out of which,' in the costermonger's words, one can never finally 'get the reading.'

Notes

For helpful suggestions on this essay, thanks to Natalka Freeland, Catherine Gallagher, Celeste Langan, Deborah Nord, John Plotz, and Susan Wolfson; for research help, thanks to Maia McAleavey and Sol Kim-Bentley.

1. Natalie Davis, *Society and Culture in Early Modern France* (Stanford: Stanford University Press, 1975), 192.
2. Judith Zeitlin, 'Xiaoshuo,' in *The Novel, 2001–2003, vol. 1*, ed. Franco Moretti Princeton: (Princeton University Press, 2006), 254. Polastron observes that books buried in tombs are at least protected from wear and tear: 'it is certainly possible to view as a fairly honest conservation system this egotistical practice that wipes them from the face of the earth' (Lucien X. Polastron, *Books on Fire: The Destruction of Libraries Throughout History*, 1st U.S. edition [Rochester, VT: Inner Traditions, 2007], 10).
3. Thomas R Adams and Nicolas Barker, 'A New Model for the Study of the Book' in *A Potencie of Life: Books in Society*, ed. Nicolas Barker (London: British Library, 1993), 31.
4. Henry Mayhew, London *Labour and the London Poor; Cyclopaedia of the Condition and Earnings of Those That Will Work, Those That Cannot Work, and Those That Will Not Work* (London: Griffin Bohn, 1861) 1.289–90, 3.33, 1.40; subsequent references will appear in the text.
5. For informants reading earlier installments of *London Labour*, see, e.g., 3.214. For a subtle analysis of Mayhew's characterization of his informants' literacy, see Patrick Brantlinger, *The Reading Lesson: The Threat of Mass Literacy in Nineteenth-Century Britain* (Bloomington: University of Indiana Press, 1998), 85. On the other hand, one waste-paper dealer who declares that 'the people as sells 'waste' to me is not such as can read' adds that 'I don't understand

much about books'; the point is proven a moment later when he describes a customer asking 'Have you any black lead?,' by which Mayhew's readers can only understand 'black letter' (2.110). On Victorian attitudes toward waste, see Natalka Freeland, *Trashing the Novel: Ephemeral Reading and Disposable Culture* (unpublished ms.), to which my argument is indebted; on waste paper more specifically, Talia Schaffer, 'Craft, Authorial Anxiety, and 'the Cranford Papers,'' *Victorian Periodicals Review* 38.2 (2005), which takes middle-class women's domestic paper handicrafts to exemplify the 'material evolution, as it were, when rubbish could be reshaped into treasure, or inexpensive common things made to bear uncanny resemblances to precious materials'—the middle-class domestic equivalent of the working-class trades described by Mayhew (223). On paper more generally, see Kevin McLaughlin, *Paperwork: Fiction and Mass Mediacy in the Paper Age* (Philadelphia: University of Pennsylvania Press, 2005), which focuses more on nineteenth-century representations of paper than representations on paper; Lee Erikson, *The Economy of Literary Form* (Baltimore: Johns Hopkins University Press, 1996), whose analysis of the relation of paper to nineteenth-century literature is weakened by its emphasis on technology at the expense of changing taxation regimes; and, out of period but still suggestive, Andrea Pellegram, 'The Message in Paper,' *Material Cultures: Why Some Things Matter*, ed. Daniel Miller (Chicago: University of Chicago Press, 1998) xi, 243, an ethnography of paper use in present-day London.

6. Igor Kopytoff, 'The Cultural Biography of Things' in *The Social Life of Things: Commodities in Cultural Perspective*, ed. Arjun Appadurai (Cambridge: Cambridge University Press, 1986), 75.

7. Dard Hunter, *Papermaking: The History and Technique of an Ancient Craft*, 2nd edition (New York: A.A. Knopf, 1947), 555.

8. Compare Thomas Adams and Nicolas Barker's argument that 'popularity tends to operate positively on the text and negatively on the book' (Thomas R. Adams and Nicolas Barker, 'A New Model for the Study of the Book,' *A Potencie of Life: Books in Society*, ed. Nicolas Barker (London: British Library, 1993), 33).

9. William Drummond et al., 'Bibliotheca Edinburgena Lectori,' in *The Works of William Drummond, of Hawthornden: Consisting of Those Which Were Formerly Printed, and Those Which Were Design'd for the Press: Now Published from the Author's Original Copies* (Edinburgh: Printed by James Watson in Craig's-Close, 1711), 222.

10. James N. Green and Peter Stallybrass, *Benjamin Franklin: Writer and Printer* (New Castle, DE; London: Oak Knoll Press; British Library, 2006), 21.

11. As Jane Kamensky points out to me, this paradox resembles that governing the survival of clothing: ceremonial articles and those made for infants are preserved in disproportionate numbers.

12. William Stanley Jevons, 'The Rationale of Free Public Libraries,' in *Methods of Social Reform: And Other Papers* (London: Macmillan, 1882), 30.

13. Hain Friswell, 'Circulating Libraries,' *London Society* 20 (1871): 522. Compare another discussion of Mudie's: 'There is, however, such a thing as a charnel-house in this establishment, where literature is, as it were, reduced to its old bones. Thousands of volumes thus read to death are pitched together in one place. But would they not do for the butterman?

was our natural query. Too dirty for that. Not for old trunks? Much too greasy for that. What were they good for, then? For manure! Thus, when worn out as food for the mind, they are put to the service of producing food for our bodies!' Andrew Wynter, 'Mudie's Circulating Library,' *Victorian Print Media: A Reader*, eds John Plunkett and Andrew King (Oxford: Oxford University Press, 2005), 278.

14. On the paper bag, see Henry Petroski, *Small Things Considered: Why There Is No Perfect Design* (New York: Alfred A. Knopf Distributed by Random House, 2003), 99.
15. 'The Republican Refuted; in a Series of Biographical, Critical, and Political Strictures on Thomas Paine's Rights of Man,' *The Monthly Review* 7 (1792): 84; thanks to Paul Keen for suggesting this example to me.
16. Thomas Babington Macaulay, 'Mr. Robert Montgomery,' *Critical and Historical Essays, Contributed to the Edinburgh Review*, vol. 1 (London: Longman, Brown, Green, and Longmans, 1843) 279.
17. 'Railway Literature,' *Dublin University Magazine* 34 (1849): 280.
18. Samuel Taylor Coleridge, *Biographia Literaria*, eds James Engell and W. Jackson Bate (Princeton: Princeton University Press, 1983), 187.
19. George Gordon Byron Byron and Leslie Alexis Marchand, *Byron's Letters and Journals: The Complete and Unexpurgated Text of All the Letters Available in Manuscript and the Full Printed Version of All Others*, vol. 8 (Cambridge, MA: Belknap Press of Harvard University Press, 1973) 11–12; thanks to Susan Wolfson and Betty Schellenburg for this reference.
20. Joseph Addison. *Spectator* 367 (1 May 1712), in 'The Spectator,' ed. Donald Frederic Bond (Oxford: Clarendon Press, 1965), 380–1.
21. Thomas Carlyle, *Sartor Resartus*, eds Kerry McSweeney and Peter Sabor (Oxford UP, 1987), 35, 233.
22. Isaac D'Israeli, *Curiosities of Literature* (London: Frederick Warne, 1881), 54.
23. On bibliophilic misogyny, see Willa Silverman, 'The Enemies of Books? Women and the Male Bibliophilic Imagination in *Fin-De-Siècle* France' (unpublished paper), and Holbrook Jackson, ed., *The Anatomy of Bibliomania* (Chicago: University of Illinois Press, 2001).
24. Andrew Lang, *The Library* (London: Macmillan & Co., 1881), 23.
25. A. R. Waller and Adolphus William Ward, *The Cambridge History of English Literature* (Cambridge [Eng.]: The University Press, 1932), 12.362; see also W.W. Greg's description of bibliography as 'the handmaid of literature': W. W. Greg, 'What Is Bibliography,' *Transactions of the Bibliographical Society* 12 (1914): 47. On the bibliographer as service worker, see Jon Klancher, 'Bibliographia Literaria: Thomas Dibdin and the Origins of Book History in Britain, 1800–1825' (unpublished paper), and, on the feminization of the literal Margaret Homans, *Bearing the Word: Language and Female Experience in Nineteenth-Century Women's Writing* (Chicago: University of Chicago Press, 1986).
26. The libretto copies this scene roughly from chapter 9 of Henri Murger's eponymous novel: there, the 'dénouement ne fit que flamber et s'éteindre' Giacomo Puccini and Henri Murger, *La Bohème* ([Paris]: Calmann-Lévy: Erato, 1988), 293.
27. The term puns on writing, but also on printing: the 'secret composition' that makes the flypaper sticky bears some resemblance to the mixture of

glue and treacle used to ink the device known as a 'composition roller.' See Carey, n.d. #3858@105.

28. Henry Mayhew and Bertrand Taithe, *The Essential Mayhew: Representing and Communicating the Poor* (London: Rivers Oram Press, 1996), 87.

29. Listeners of Elvis Costello will recognize this formulation as borrowed from his 1981 song 'Fish 'N' Chip Paper.'

30. 'The Progress of Fiction as an Art,' *Westminster Review* 1853: 361.

31. See Christopher Herbert's analysis of 'semiological entropy, in which cultural artifacts lose their power to represent social values' (218)—a process counterpointed by Mayhew's understanding of street life as a 'striving to invent cultural value out of almost nothing' Christopher Herbert, *Culture and Anomie* (Chicago: University of Chicago Press, 1991), 221. For a related argument about the relation of waste to raw material in Dickens, see Michal Peled Ginsburg, 'The Case against Plot in *Bleak House* and *Our Mutual Friend*,' *ELH* 59.1 (1992): 179.

32. John Seely Brown and Paul Duguid, *The Social Life of Information* (Boston: Harvard Business School, 2002), 173.

33. Sean Latham and Robert Scholes, 'The Rise of Periodical Studies,' *PMLA* 121 (2006): 526.

34. On the history of the metaphor, see James Hamilton, 'Unearthing Broadcasting in the Anglophone World,' in *Residual Media*, ed. Charles R. Acland (Minneapolis: University of Minnesota Press, 2007), 283–300, and John Durham Peters, *Speaking into the Air: A History of the Idea of Communication* (Chicago: University of Chicago Press, 1999), 52.

35. Leslie Howsam, *Cheap Bibles: Nineteenth-Century Publishing and the British and Foreign Bible Society*, Cambridge Studies in Publishing and Printing History (Cambridge [England]; New York: Cambridge University Press, 1991), 150.

36. 'Answers to Correspondents,' 47.5 (1 November 1851), reprinted in Henry Mayhew and Bertrand Taithe, *The Essential Mayhew: Representing and Communicating the Poor* (London: Rivers Oram Press, 1996), 212.

37. Richard Altick, *The English Common Reader: A Social History of the Mass Reading Public, 1800–1900* (Chicago: University of Chicago Press, 1998), 108.

38. As Hannah Sullivan has pointed out, Eliot himself discarded drafts of *The Waste Land* later saved and edited by his wife: here it's the man who dismisses the paper as waste, the woman who invests it with value (PhD diss., Harvard University 2008).

Part III: Remapping the Literary Field

8
Reading Collections: The Literary Discourse of Eighteenth-Century Libraries

Barbara M. Benedict

This essay explores the confluence of two, great eighteenth-century passions: collecting and books. Both are phenomena that embody the political and cultural strains of the period because both challenge contemporary concepts of learning and ownership. The two are intimately connected: indeed, although the term 'museum' is currently identified with national collections of objects, historically it denoted 'a place for learned occupations,' and was traditionally understood primarily as a library, and only secondarily as a repository of objects.[1] In the eighteenth century, collectors of books often also collected objects, and vice versa, since books and collections were similarly conceived as vessels of knowledge. Both collectors and intensive readers were engaged in the enterprise of learning—or, at least, of displaying knowledge, which is not quite the same thing.

Both were also undergoing a shift in cultural status. The rhetoric and cultural concerns surrounding collections transfer to libraries, indeed book collections in general, and forefront key issues in the period. Although collections of natural and artful objects had drawn satire since the seventeenth century, in the eighteenth they were becoming the center of British culture. In 1753, in fact, collecting was established as national practice when Sir Hans Sloane's curiosity collections, along with his library, were institutionalized as the British Museum; and by the end of the century, the tradition of the Grand Tour, with its concomitant loot-gathering, the spread of antiquarianism, and the discoveries at Herculaneum made collecting seem a way to understand history and to master the world's cultures. As new social ranks—people from the middling classes and even workers—began accumulating things, the question of the purpose, meaning, and value of collections and objects became a cultural preoccupation. The concurrent explosion of printed culture in the period also became a widespread topic of debate, since more books might, or might not, indicate a more learned society, depending on the value—material or intellectual—of the books. Thus, while collecting things and books was becoming a sign of the laudable British empirical thrust to learn and conquer, it was simultaneously represented as decadence, greed, and deviance. This struggle plays out the great shift throughout the century as changes in production, consumption, and social relations transformed the relationship of individuals to culture, and in particular made aristocrats and gentry—those who in the early century ruled cultural production—instead subject to it. These strains pulling at the practice of collecting inflect the rising cultural institution of the library.

Libraries represented a national ideal and a personal statement of identity. Like collecting objects, collecting, and in theory reading, books signified the ambition to improve the self through knowledge.[2] This ambition, along with its signature of collected objects and books, indicated the great social sea-change of the eighteenth century whereby individual enterprise could remake a person's social class. Whereas book collections had traditionally symbolized an elite culture, they were becoming a luxury that was possible for members of a wealthier and more leisured middle class, especially since the invention of the printing press and changes in copyright laws had made books inexpensive and prolific.[3] This transformation of a tradition of rarified learning into an increasingly popular practice prompted several key concerns for eighteenth-century collectors and writers. For collectors, the primary question was what to collect—in terms of category, quality, and quantity. This, however, entailed other questions that especially occupied observers and commentators: who collected books and things, and especially why they did so. The doubts implied by these concerns center on the social function of collecting and reading. *Is* there one? asked moralists, or are hoarding books and objects, like reading novels privately, acts of antisocial, even masturbatory, obsession? Correlative with the dubious social aspects of the practice of collecting was the value of it, as writers attacked and defended the kind of knowledge collecting and bibliomania involved. Does merely owning something, looking at it cursorily or reading it through rapidly, constitute understanding it?

These issues galvanize the discourse that surrounds the library in eighteenth-century literature. A library, by the definition in the *OED*, is 'A place set apart to contain books for reading, study, or reference,' and can encompass a building, a set of rooms, a single room, or even a bookcase. In the ancient world, libraries symbolized cultural control: indeed, the Alexandrian library stood as the center of civilization, and its fate epitomized the barbarism of the unlearned mob throughout the eighteenth century.[4] While lending books had been an early monastical practice, the term 'library' comes into use in the Medieval period, when lending libraries were already well established, and was historically associated with religious and antiquarian study. Indeed, since collections of books had an ancient lineage, unlike collections of objects of natural philosophy like rock or human fragments, they not only connoted piety, but carried the patina of historical legitimacy. However, once individuals possessed and used collections of books for secular and personal purposes, the library became an ambiguous symbol of social change. Libraries brought to the fore the spectacle of a consumer culture spiraling into opulence and out of social control. Collections of books thus represented the threat and liberation of unmonitored private knowledge.

Collecting and the presentation of accumulation

Conventions dictating the practices of what to collect and how to display it existed before the eighteenth century, and resulted from the history of collecting and collections. The most common, public pre-eighteenth-century collections in Britain lay in churches. These small repositories typically contained religious relics, sacred ritual items, valuable books, and a scattering of oddly-formed natural and artful items, probably acquired and exhibited in order to stimulate awe at God's mysterious ways.[5] Books, and learned reading, thus traditionally sat alongside revered objects. However, royalty and high gentry also possessed collections that, albeit technically private, were usually open to display by visitors with the correct, elite credentials. In the Renaissance, such collections typically boasted a single, exquisite example of a class of item: a coca-de-mer from the Indian Ocean, a finely-tooled clock, a Roman coin, a Chinese porcelain vase. Before the late-seventeenth-century fad for scientific exactitude, elite collectors did not attempt to adhere to the scientific principles set out by Aristotle that sketched the way to find meaning in observed, natural phenomena. Since these collectors intended primarily to elicit respect by displaying their wealth, plenty, and power to find rarities, rather than to present an argument about nature, they concentrated on accumulating spectacular, rather than informative, things.[6] Nonetheless, by the later sixteenth and early seventeenth centuries, elite status was becoming identified with cutting-edge information. Accordingly, collections became increasingly scientistic in orientation, designed to exhibit the owner's modern knowledge of discoveries overseas as well as his wealth and taste.

The twin principles of acquisition and categorization often clash in collections. Since collecting originated long before John Locke's empirical epistemology had become fashionable, collections in churches and curiosity repositories typically displayed their loot in a fashion that loosely melded Catholic reverence for sacred relics, the showman's wish to elicit wonder, and sheer pride of accumulation. Most private collections similarly present cultural phenomena as examples of man's ingenuity at the command of the powerful collector/owner, while natural phenomena are typically crowded together in odd juxtapositions, and thus hover between being presented as examples of the divine power to overturn nature's rules at will, and as evidence for a rough conception of nature's classifications. Collections thus supported both a superstitious and a learned approach to nature and culture: they encourage an unlearned indulgence in wonder, a reverent admiration at the collector's power to possess the world in miniature, and a speculative exploration of the riches of the earth, all at the same time. No matter who the collector-church, state, dignitary, natural philosopher, or traveler-quantity, quality, and fashionableness were the key principles, and so they remained for collections of books.

The organization of collections remained a problematic issue throughout the seventeenth and early eighteenth centuries. The practice of juxtaposing objects to increase the effect of incongruity, and thus stimulate deeper wonder, was transferred from grand collections to personal curiosity cabinets, which redirected the elicited, spectatorial wonder from God to the collector. Sir Richard Steele mocks this in his treatment of Leonora's 'Ladies Library,' in which, as we shall see below, such luxurious items of fashionable consumption nestle beside learned books. However, by the later seventeenth century, the empirical principles of the Royal Society generally served to organize important collections. These principles ostensibly followed a Lockean system of comprehension: objects were placed in an order that reflected the collector's close observation of their physical characteristics, and his consequent determination of their relationship to one another, logically reasoned from his observations. Natural philosophers thus attempted to position their collections according to evolving definitions of classes or categories of creatures and materials, thus making the collection an exhibition of genealogy or natural history.

This procedure also turned collections into an enactment of the educational processes of observation and reflection. By minute and value-free description, it prompted visitors, and indeed any readers of the catalog, to employ their own empirical prowess and make an order from what they saw. This is exemplified in the catalog of the Royal Society's collection. Its author, Nehemjah Grew, a passionate advocate and member of the Royal Society and the College of Physicians, explicates the new scientific ideal in his preface to *Musaeum Regalis Societaties, Or, a Catalogue & Description of the Natural and Artificial Rarities Belonging to the Royal Society* (1681). His method, he explains, is to describe the contents of the museum so minutely that observers can draw conclusions, even make discoveries, from reading them. He thus provides a verbal representation of the seen object, making reading *about* the thing as important, perhaps more important, than actually observing it:

> In the Descriptions given, I have observed, with the Figures of Things, also their Colours; so far as I could, unless I had view'd them Living, and Fresh. And have added their just Measures. Much neglected by Writers of Natural History. If any object against their length: perhaps they have not so well considered the necessity hereof, for the cleer [*sic*] and evident distinction of the several Kinds and Species, in so great a Variety of Things known in the World. And wherein also regard is to be had, to all that after Ages may discover, or have occasion to enquire after. ... It were certainly a Thing both in it self Desirable, and of much Consequence; To have such an Inventory of Nature, wherein, as on the one hand, nothing should be Wanting; so nothing Repeated or Confounded, on the other. For which, there is no way without a cleer and full Description of Things. Besides, that in such Descriptions, many Particulars relating to the Nature and Use of Things, will occur to the Authors mind, which otherwise he would never have thought of. And may give occasion to his Readers, for the consideration of many more.[7]

For Grew, seeing a phenomenon is the primary avenue to knowing it, yet this seeing must itself be informed by a learned way of looking that can be reproduced in a language that notes every detail but refuses to accept unthinkingly prior authorities, the language that Thomas Sprat celebrated as that of empiricism itself.[8]

Like all Royal Society scientists, Grew rejects received history and Aristotelian dicta in favour of each observer's independent, empirical discovery; this method, he avers, will make all of nature 'cleer.' Grew also employs an exhaustive descriptive mode that multiplies categories and names, finding individuation in place of broad classes, and places natural phenomena in a hierarchy with man at the top. He explains that he rejects 'the reason which *Aldovandrus* gives for his beginning with the History of *Quadrupeds* with the Horse: *Quod praecipuam nobis utilitatem praebet*. Being better placed according to the degrees of their Approximation, to Humane Shape, and one to another: and so other Things, according to their Nature. Much less should I choose, with *Gesner*, to do by the Alphabet. ... As to the Names, where they were wanting, (which in our own Language were many) I have taken leave to give them' (preface). This organization becomes characteristic of most catalogs of natural collections: Ralph Thoresby employs it, as too does Sir Hans Sloane.[9] Grew thus sets out five vital principles for organizing collections: a plenitude of categories in order to represent each phenomenon properly; a refusal to employ moral language; a rejection of authority; a reliance on fresh observation; and a tolerance, indeed hospitality, for the acquisition of any thing, even bits of thing or being, like human skin and animal feet. No longer the Renaissance representative cabinet, the natural history collection dramatized the contemporary desire, the privilege of wealthy men and state institutions, to accumulate and map *everything*.

Throughout the long eighteenth century, these principles were widely ridiculed. In the seventeenth century, satirists including Samuel Butler, Aphra Behn, and Thomas Shadwell characterize the Royal Society's idealistic quest to name the physical world as a distortion of social values, and the hazardous replacement of humanistic meanings with an anti-human mechanization of nature.[10] By the early eighteenth century, Jonathan Swift, Alexander Pope, John Gay, John Arbuthnot, and, later, Henry Fielding transfer Grew's procedure from the natural to the literary world, depicting it as a Scriblerian mania for detail, profusion and originality over economy, efficiency, beauty and meaning. Perhaps most vehemently, all these satirists represent the idealistic determination to 'inventory' the entire natural world as a gross ambition, as much misguided and hopeless as presumptuous. This ambition is incarnated by the collection itself. In this satirical discourse, the collection perfectly embodies the chaotic greed of a culture addicted to accumulation over selection. Moreover, as the collection blurs distinctions between natural and cultural phenomena, it represents the individual's desire to exert mastery not merely over the physical world, but over society itself. Collecting thus appears as the visible sign of aristocratic arrogance—whether exercised by aristocrats themselves, or, even worse, by those mimicking them.

Eighteenth-century book collections

Books, as physical items and vessels of impalpable ideas, are both like and unlike other objects, yet libraries attract cultural commentary similar to that of other objects. Eighteenth-century libraries themselves were seen as paradoxically both public and private places. In his 1755–6 *Dictionary*, Samuel Johnson defines the library as 'a large collection of books, publick or private,' and even earlier, libraries had gained their association as being primarily public institutions.[11] Under Queen Anne in 1708 the term designates 'a public institution ... charged with the care of a collection of books, and the duty of rendering the books accessible to those who require them.'[12] Eighteenth-century libraries come essentially in three forms, differentiated by their principles of acquisition, procedures of consumption, and consumers: private, subscription, and circulating. Before the eighteenth century, 'private' libraries, which had existed in Europe for centuries, had been the prerogative of royalty, nobility, clergy, and high gentry. Requiring space to house, wealth to acquire, and leisure to consume, these libraries denoted their owners' social status, as well as their intellectual and political prominence. When rulers owned these collections, they served as symbolic public possessions, demonstrations of the wealth of the entire culture. Indeed, national and urban libraries had formed one of the traditional tourist stops for European travelers since the Renaissance. Like palaces, castles, and repositories, they were seen to embody the historical significance and political clout of a culture. Such libraries, often lodged in churches, sometimes contained remarkable art works or exotic artefacts. The library thus carried powerful connotations as a place of spiritual contemplation, and a space for displaying a nation's cultural identity.[13]

Similarly, private libraries, which became endemic in the landed classes in the eighteenth century, were often patriarchal strongholds, testaments of a noble lineage of acquisition and intellectual prominence. They were thus, paradoxically, public places albeit used privately, and therefore a pressure-point in what Habermas has termed the structural transformation of the public sphere.[14] Typically, eighteenth-century private libraries contained both classical works renowned by history and recent ones, critically applauded: owners had to maintain the tradition of judicious but generous cultural selection. When in Jane Austen's *Pride and Prejudice* the sycophantic Caroline Bingley compliments Mr. Darcy on 'add[ing]' to his impressive ancestral library at Pemberley – 'the work of many generations' – by 'always buying books,' he replies, 'I cannot comprehend the neglect of a family library in such days as these.'[15] Austen shows that libraries thus embodied the literary learning of the ruling class, the accumulation of power and knowledge over history.

As Darcy's comment reveals, books' *physical* status complicates their cultural identity. The principles of book acquisition and the organization of book collections, both physical libraries and catalogs of book collections, do shadow those of natural collections. Like physical phenomena, books come in different sizes, or formats, and book collectors perforce organize books accordingly, beginning with the generously-presented folios and proceeding downward to the miniature duodecimos. Book catalogs from libraries and auctions invariably list their volumes in this fashion. John Binns' 1789 *A Catalogue of Books, containing Several Valuable Libraries*, for example, itself an accumulation of book accumulations, provides an initial Index that categorizes the goods for sale by topic, but organizes the catalog by format.[16] However, the size of the book (unlike that of the animal) itself reflects a prior choice by the bookseller: folios were expensive to produce and, since they took up space, to display, so they were reserved for literary works deemed worthy of a long shelf-life, or, as Binns' Index shows, works with expensive illustrations. On the other hand, the duodecimo, small enough to carry in pocket or reticule, was usually expected to be worn to shreds. Thus, book collections mirror the Grew's hierarchy that opens with creatures closest to mankind by placing the important texts foremost, and the least significant last, bringing up the rear. Furthermore, the more elaborately and expensively packaged a book, the more status and wealth it manifests.

Nonetheless, several factors complicate this organization of book-by-appearance. Whereas Grew suggests that looking *at* objects can enable spectators to forge knowledge, merely looking at a book indicates a different kind of forgery. In *Characters*, Samuel Butler identifies the deluded Virtuoso – an antiquarian addicted to collecting coins and books – with the jackets of his library: 'He is like his Books, that contain much Knowledge, but know nothing themselves.'[17] The invention of the identity of the bibliomaniac reflects this common charge of preferring '*looking*' at books to 'actually reading them.'[18] Moreover, as wealth spread to the trading classes and lesser gentry, writers often satirized private libraries as examples of consumerist self-display. This itself was a cliche: as early as 1622, Henry Peacham in *The Compleat Gentleman*, advised, 'Affect not as some do that bookish ambition to be stored with books and have well-furnished libraries, yet keep their heads empty of knowledge; to desire to have many books, and never to use them, is like a child that will have a candle burning by him all the while he is sleeping.' In the eighteenth century, however, this reproof gains force as books appeared in elegant editions, pleasing to the eye but untouched by the mind.[19] Mr. Town in George Colman and Bonnell Thornton's mid-century periodical *The Connoisseur* attacks thoughtless consumption with the image of 'the beau blockhead,' who never removes a book because his library, 'though it contains many books finely bound and gilt, is designed merely for shew, and it would spoil the backs or rumple the leaves to look into the contents of them.'[20] Henry Mackienzie's periodical persona, the Lounger, notes that one host whom he visits exhibits 'an unwillingness ... to let me take down any of the books, which were so elegantly bound and gilt, and ranged in such beautiful order, that is seemed contrary to the etiquette of the house to remove any of them from the shelves.'[21] The accumulation and expensive packaging turns the book collection into a boastful display of the owner, rather than a source of information for owner and visitor alike.

The eye-catching beauty of books ranged in order and so positioned as not to be read is only one aspect of the way book collections can transform books into objects, and pervert them from their cultural meaning. Another is their sheer quantity. Oliver Goldsmith fictionalizes this dilemma in his idealized Chinese traveler, whose study of Confucius and knowledge of 'the characters of fourteen thousand words,' enables him to 'read a great part of every book that came his way.'[22] In Austen's Regency novel *Northanger Abbey* (1818), the self-important General Tilney grandly exhibits his library to advertise his class to Catherine Morland, whom he intends his son to wed:

> [T]hey proceeded into the library, an apartment, in its way, of equal magnificence, exhibiting a collection of books, on which an humble man might have looked with pride—Catherine heard, admired, and wondered with more genuine feeling than before—gathered all she could from this storehouse of knowledge, by running over the titles of half a shelf, and was ready to proceed.[23]

This library functions not only as a 'storehouse of knowledge,' but as a 'magnificent' hoard of culture reserved for privileged use. Significantly, Catherine, herself a mis-reader of life and fiction, only gleans superficial knowledge of this collection by scanning the titles; probably most of them concern politics or history, rather than the fiction to which she is addicted. Such libraries as the General's both proclaim his public identity and hold too much to know intimately. As Catherine instinctively recognizes, the General wants *too much*: too much money, property, status, and power. His library dramatizes this greed.

Both the Lounger's protest and Catherine's cursory glance reveal another complication in the acquisition, display, and cultural significance of book collections: categorization. As generic categories for literature multiplied throughout the century, thanks to the ingenuity of hungry booksellers and competing writers, the ideal of collecting every important book that has been the principle of patriarchal collections became increasingly difficult. However, the fluidity of genre that marked the period made it equally difficult to choose which books, or what kind of books, to collect.[24] Book auction and library catalogs particularly from the final third of the century demonstrate this multiplicity by a roster of mini-classes of literature. William Cater's 1780 *Catalogue of several valuable libraries and collections of books*, for example, characteristically lists books by format, but within each category appear further classes of literature that are themselves – like 'Miscellanies' – often little libraries.[25] In his circulating library catalog, the prominent bookseller John Bell, who himself popularized mini-libraries, and issued *The Poets of Great Britain complete from Chaucer to Churchill* from 1777–87, attempts further classification to ensure that his readers can locate precisely what they wish. Yet even he resorts to categories like 'Romances, Novels, and other Books of Entertainment,' along with the ubiquitous 'Miscellanies.'[26]

Moreover, certain classes of books become associated with certain kinds of collections. Novels, for example, quickly adopt the form of the three-volume octavo, yet their cultural status remained low for most of the period. Furthermore, the addiction to novelty inflected the expected reception of a book, particularly as books multiplied. Fresh works outranked old ones, while some works had become virtually canonical: in 1716, the important bookseller Jacob Tonson issued the six volumes of John Dryden's valuable and culturally celebrated *Miscellany Poems*, for example, in tiny duodecimo to garner a fresh audience when Dryden's reputation seemed to be fading. Just as certain items in curiosity cabinets dramatize faddishness, like the fabled unicorn's (narwhale's) horn, and Egyptian crocodile, so the newest poem by Pope or satire published by Edmund Curll simultaneously represented the slavish adherence to fashion and glamorous cosmopolitanism. Especially as books proliferate, the questions of fashionableness, use (is the book ever really read?), and reception (how does the book affect the reader?) become central to the question of whether, what, and how to collect books.

Despite the existence of subscription libraries, book clubs, and patri-archal collections, it was circulating libraries, first established in 1740, that came to embody the book collection in public consciousness. These libraries shifted the onus of accumulation from the individual to the merchant. Usually costing a guinea for the entrance fee and a guinea annually for membership, these libraries, like all lending libraries, struc-tured literary consumption by rules regulating waiting lists, late returns, acquisitions, and so on. Such regulations suggest that the patrons shared reading tastes and purposes to a large degree. Although circulating librar-ies notoriously provided romantic fiction supposedly aimed at young women, in fact the shared tastes of the audience, which comprised men as well as women, encompassed a great variety of books, according to contemporary classification. In his 1778 catalog for his enlarged circu-lating library, holding 50,000 volumes, John Bell advertises: 'History, Antiquities, Voyages, Travels, Lives, Memoirs, Philosophy, Geography, Novels, Divinity, Physic, Surgery, Anatomy, Arts, Sciences, Plays, Poetry, Husbandry, Trade, Commerce, Gardening, Coins, Minerals' (title page). Albeit self-serving, Bell's classificatory fragmentation reflects a common trend, one that appears in all auction, bookselling, and library catalogs. In mirroring the mushrooming categories in catalogs of natural history collections like that of Sir Hans Sloane or Ralph Thoresby, such catalogs represent literature as highly differentiated, and the library as an all-encompassing collection: the world in books. The library is the model of culture organized into a reference-room.

However, as accumulation became the task of book-purveyors like Bell, the value of this madly productive book trade came under scrutiny. This itself was a traditional discourse. Even the ancients had grumbled against a ballooning production of literature that made it impossible to read everything.[27] In Britain in the long eighteenth century, however, similar complaints shaped the task of choosing what to read into a dec-laration of identity. As many critics have noted, this ideal of conscious readerly choice entailed a backlash against libraries as providing new spaces for reading, both physical and imaginative, and as licensing new ways to read. Whereas in the early century public reading spaces like coffeehouses, many of which carried newspapers or even small book collections, presented reading as a social prompt to conversation and consumption, lending libraries facilitated private reading at home.[28] This certainly could be social: in Jane Austen's *Northanger Abbey*, Isabella Thorpe and Catherine Morland 'shut themselves up to read novels together,' and William Gilray depicts a small group of rotund, female readers gasping over a similar horror tale in his famous caricature.[29]

However, most conservative critics considered private reading of publicly lent books self-indulgent, a perversion of the habit of pious literary contemplation into a practice of self-stoking passion—particularly, of course, because readers borrowed books too ephemeral to buy. Small libraries, indeed, merely lent books out, and although large circulating libraries furnished reading rooms, they were provided mostly with periodicals and newspapers for clients; in such resorts as Bath, books were read at home while libraries served as community centers, offering cards, games, and even dancing 'after the blinds had been drawn to cover the bookshelves.'[30] Although certainly social venues, most libraries nonetheless limited kinds of reading: while reading books—especially since users had no access to the open shelves and had to order their choices by catalog number—remained largely private, the selection of books to read was highly public. In Lackington's library in Finsbury Square, for example, clerks retrieved, indeed recommended, books for customers in the vast, panopticon-like warehouse.[31] Libraries hence functioned as liminal spaces between a public and private identity. Even the private patriarchal library retains this quality. Although designed as the patron's refuge from the social melee, it was also used to entertain guests or as the place to issue orders to servants. The domestic library or private closet in the middle-class home similarly represented a very public kind of privacy. It encouraged women and middle-class men to enjoy solitary reading, yet also symbolized to others their refinement. If, as many critics suggest, the novel facilitates the new practice of solitary reading, the library serves as the place where this private practice is formally recognized as a part of identity.

Clearly, both membership in circulating libraries and acquisitions rose dramatically in the final years of the eighteenth century and into the Regency. The Bristol library increased its membership by a third between 1782 and 1798, but its titles increased five times to 4987. Kaufman documents that, in its first ten years from 1773 to 1784, the Bristol library saw 13,497 withdrawals of 900 titles, demonstrating the importance of sharing texts. The catalog for *The Ayr-Shire Circulating Library for Gentlemen and Ladies* (1760), for example, characteristically consists 'of Books Ancient and Modern, Instructive and Entertaining,' and in its preface, the proprietor James Meuros boasts of the variety of his wares, which span the usual travels, moral works, fiction, geography, divinity, philosophy and so on, down to 'Small Chapmen history books.' Meuros remarks that 'even works of pure imagination, and fictitious lives and memoirs ... serve to unbend the mind after vigorous application to business.' He adds that 'there are many persons in every county, whose taste and inclination for reading greatly exceeds their ability to gratify their taste, by purchasing the numerous productions they would choose to read.'

These public libraries became the imaginative center of shared literary experience in the eighteenth century. They manifest the transformation of eighteenth-century literary culture from one segregated into what might be called practical texts—sermons, histories, and manuals—read by professionals, and imaginative ones, poetry, prose fiction, travels, and history, read by gentry.[32] Characteristically, they present *all* texts as equally available to all readers, and even while all sorts of specialty libraries persisted—institutional, educational, corporate, ecclesiastical, and so on—these public libraries were broadly dedicated in significant measure to literary entertainment.[33] Significantly, their origin lay partly in the book clubs, organized by a band of neighborly enthusiasts, which had probably existed since the seventeenth century. By 1821 Paul Kaufman estimates there were some 500 book clubs, serving at least 15,000 readers. These organizations differ from libraries in their practice of regular, usually monthly, meetings and their dedication to convivial-ity, often of a liquid variety.[34] They are, however, significant in the tra-dition they establish of a coterie-consumption of literature. Reporting on an early account of the forerunner of the London Library, Kaufman observes that 'the books—which were rarely bought by farmers or even gentlemen—became family friends and exerted a strong molding influence on individual and social character'; moreover, as bookseller complaints register, 'each loan served a number of readers.'[35] Collected books thus represented a social bond, a commodity for consumption, and a personal acquisition.

These contrasting ideas of the library as a door either to self-improvement or to self-indulgence intensify by the late eighteenth century. Sentimental novelists frequently use the private library to denote their heroes' superior intellectual and spiritual refinement. In *The Mysteries of Udolpho* (1794), for example, the family of the heroine Emily St. Aubert possesses a library so large that it 'occupied the west side of the chateau and was enriched by a collection of the best books in the ancient and modern languages.' This library symbolizes the ideal of paternal wisdom so strongly that his open book there 'appeared [to Emily] sacred and invaluable.'[36] Radcliffe ties Emily's sensitivity and virtue directly to her book-heavy education. Austen, however, play-fully mocks this cliché by depicting Caroline Bingley, who exhibits tinsel accomplishments rather than true taste, attempting to flatter Mr. Darcy in *Pride and Prejudice* by declaring, 'I declare after all there is no enjoyment like reading! How much sooner one tires of anything than of a book! When I have a house of my own, I shall be miserable if I have not an excellent library' shortly before yawning and throwing her book aside.[37]

The ideal library

As these literary references demonstrate, book collections become a central motif through which writers and booksellers expressed their critique or their concept of contemporary values. Starting early in the eighteenth century when books were growing relatively affordable, unconventional readers—middle-class and professional people, and especially women—were also represented as beginning to collect books. Writers portray these private libraries as spaces in which idiosyncratic tastes might meet public literary fashion, a process of individual self-fashioning depicted as either admirable or absurd—depending both on its size and its contents. Whereas most eighteenth-century novelists employ the term rarely, and only to satirize bad reading, it appears quite frequently and more ambiguously in periodical literature stretching from Joseph Addison and Richard Steele's *The Spectator* (1711, 1712–13) to Henry Mackenzie's *The Lounger* (1785–7). As they record the transition from the library as an idea to the library as a commodity, these periodicals depict the struggle between accumulation and selection as cultural value.

As libraries sprouted all over Britain, the library gained increasing valence as a concept. Eighteenth-century booksellers frequently used the title 'library' to designate the completeness and variety of their contents. Especially after the Becket v. Donaldson trial and 1774 copyright decision, booksellers such as John Bell produced uniformly-packaged series of plays, poems, and novels as 'libraries,' and moral compendia like *The Young Lady's Pocket Library, or Parental Monitor* (1790), which contained several texts. The titular claim of 'library' served to advertise the consistency and multitude of the contents: it informs readers both that they need no *other* text since all the pertinent information is contained in this one, and that this book contains more than one opinion or source—a sign of the new value for multiplicity over consistency.[38] Typically, like library catalogs, the contents are digested under narrative heads such as 'Knowledge of the World,' and/ or numbered. Such an organizational system encourages readers to compartmentalize experience and to use the book as a reference. Although these libraries ostensibly offer a variety of opinions on a topic, they usually present multiple examples of the same point of view. The 'library' has become a hybrid mini-genre.

The idea of the library as a personal arena for self-fashioning also stimulated the literary conceit of the imaginary library. This was an ideal place of tasteful, personal cultural selection that offered a rational blend of entertainment and instruction, consumption and reflection: both a physical location and an intellectual concept. At the same time, it served as a symbol of the consumerist misuse of culture for appearances' sake. This construct served as a figurative link between the unmonitored and proliferating literary market and the ideal of disciplined education. The most famous imaginary library was doubtless Sir Richard Steele's 'Ladies Library,' advertised in *The Spectator* no. 37 for Thursday 12 April 1711. In this issue, Mr. Spectator, snared by a 'Curiosity' to see a *'Lady's Library,'* examines Leonora's closet, noting 'a great many of her Books, which were ranged together in a very beautiful Order.' The detailed description includes an account of the items interspersed with the books: 'great Jars of *China*,' 'a Pile of smaller Vessels, which rose in a delightful Pyramid,' and 'Tea-Dishes of all Shapes, Colours and Sizes' separate formats, and,

> That Part of the Library which was design'd for the Reception of Plays and Pamphlets, and other loose Papers, was enclosed in a kind of Square, consisting of one of the prettiest Grotesque Works that ever I saw, and made up of Scaramouches, Lions, Monkies, Mandarines, Trees, Shells, and a thousand other odd Figures in *China* Ware. In the midst of the Room was a little Japan Table, with a Quire of gilt Paper upon it, and on the Paper a Silver Snuff-box made in the shape of a little Book. I found there were several other Counterfeit Books upon the upper Shelves, which were carved in Wood … I was wonderfully pleased with such a mixt kind of Furniture, as seemed very suitable both to the Lady and the Scholar, and did not know at first whether I should fancy my self in a Grotto, or in a Library.[39]

Clearly Steele intends to poke fun at this fashionable treatment of literature, which categorizes books by size, and places them in counterpoint with other elite consumer items. Like the porcelain and the toy books, they appear empty vessels, cherished for their exterior beauty and faddish appeal. At the same time, however, the personalness, or personality, of the library is both gendered and individuated.[40] It consists of a privately-designed space for a variety of intellectual pleasures and humors: aesthetic, moral, practical, gastronomic, political.

Nonetheless, Mr. Spectator obviously ridicules the way books had become objects of display or fetish, rather than vessels of information. He remarks of the Lady's Library, for example, that, 'I found there were some few which the Lady had bought for her own use, but that most of them had been got together, either because she had heard them praised, or because she had seen the Authors of them.'[41] None of these reasons suffices. Collecting a book as a souvenir or relic of the Author whom Leonora has seen smacks of superstition or sexual fixation; at the very best, it suggests the book serves as a prompt to allow her to show off to the visitors. In *The Bee*, Oliver Goldsmith similarly indicts books whose appeal lay in the eye, and 'the vulgar [who] buy every book rather from the excellence of the sculptor [whose engravings adorn it] then the writer.'[42] Display, certainly, is the purpose of collecting books Leonora has 'heard praised,' while even the Lady's 'use' indicates reading as self-advancement or self-pleasuring. In an issue of *The Connoisseur* in 1754 that derides virtuosi for theft, Mr. Town speaker complains that, 'If the libraries and cabinets of the curious were, like the peacock in the fable, to be stripped of their borrowed ornaments, we should in many see nothing but bare shelves and empty drawers.'[43] In targeting virtuosi for stealing single volumes to spoil and thus reduce the value of a set, for purloining rare editions, and for counterfeiting coins, Mr. Town articulates the distrust of those who collect books and things for self-pleasuring. In implicit contrast to this cynical or solipsistic use of books lies Mr. Spectator's ideal: collecting books that one has chosen for oneself and for one's own moral improvement or sophisticated pleasure, to be read and re-read.

Although Steele smiles at her consumerist approach to literature, Leonora's collection demonstrates the new value for *selecting* books to form a collection. Works of literature, classical and modern, shoulder natural philosophy, morality, grammar, novels, a courtesy manual, politics, history, and prayer (as well as Steele's own *Christian Hero*), all linked by the owner's *personal* connection to the content. Importantly, the library is not extensive but selective: it holds a few, sometimes only one, representative text from each category of literature, including Dryden's *Virgil*, a spelling book, a dictionary, Newton's *Works*, Locke's *Essay on Human Understanding*, and political, practical, moral, and religious works. Moreover, the Spectator's correspondents who advise him on a ladies' library demand the inclusion of their favorite texts, each catering to a particular humor: plays for entertainment, devout readings for improvement, conduct works for practical advice. Steele himself indulged one of these correspondents when publishing the anthology of pious conduct advice as his own *Ladies Library* in 1714. Leonora, however, prefers the idea of a library as a representative collection, neither exhaustive nor thematic, but rather choice.

Leonora's personal and feminized space corresponds to the ideal owner's mind. Recounting that the Lady of the library, widowed after an unhappy marriage, 'has turn'd all the Passions of her Sex into a Love of Books and Retirement,' the Spectator muses,

> how much more Valuable does she appear than those of her Sex, who employ themselves in Diversions that are less Reasonable, tho' more in Fashion? What Improvements would a Woman have made, who is so susceptible of Impressions from what she reads, had she been guided to such Books as have a tendency to enlighten the Understanding and rectifie the Passions, as well as to those which are of little more use than to divert the Imagination.[44]

Albeit a blatant lure to draw readers, real and invented to discuss gender and polite literature, this observation also sketches the dream that libraries promoted: the ideal of furnishing the mind with a plenitude of sources and resources that would shape character and provide principles for action in the future.[45] This conservative recipe for literary culture persisted. Mr. Town echoes it in *The Connoisseur* no. 24 (Thursday 11 July, 1754), and 60 years later, Mackenzie's *Lounger* also describes a lady who has 'her own library for Sabbath or rainy days ... ranged in a little book-press in the parlour.' Like Steele's Lady's Library, this also contains representative texts, and even fewer: religious works, *The Spectator* and *The Guardian*, poetry, including the omnipresent Dryden, history, a heraldic reference text, and cookery.[46]

All these kinds of libraries embody choice, but a highly socialized choice as Johnson's quotations in the *Dictionary* illustrate: 'Make choice of all my library, / And so beguile thy sorrow' from Spencer, and from Dryden, 'I have given you the library of a painter, and a catalog of such books as he ought to read.' The choice of texts thus may demonstrate the reader's private desire or taste, but within a socialized realm, as the Spencerian quotation suggests, or his/her desire to possess fashionable, public knowledge. In their Dedication of *The Spectator* to Charles Lord Halifax, the authors express the hope that 'this Book may be placed in the Library of so good a Judge of which is Valuable, in that Library where the Choice is such, that it will not be a Disparagement to be the Meanest Author in it.'[47] As a model of the objectified mind, Lord Halifax's library becomes the space the writer seeks to inhabit, the bridge between private and public identity. Thus, as a concept, like the literary anthology, itself the library's miniaturized mirror, the library reconciles the contradictory principles of inclusion and exclusion, both in texts and in readers.

Libraries not only garnered criticism as collections dramatizing proliferation and decadence, but also contradictorily as cathedrals to the value of the book over other things. Much of this reflects traditional ambivalence about books themselves, but it gains force from the familiar attacks on accumulation as cultural practice that segregates things from use. As an ideal way to understand culture and the self, the secular library challenged not only religious authority, but practical politics. In eighteenth-century literature, the rivalry between learning from worldly experience as opposed to learning from books and schooling forms a common, sometimes comic discourse. 'The study of man is abundantly more necessary than the study of books,' asserts La Rouchefoucault.[48] Characters who model life on literature, familiar in satire since Cervantes' *Don Quixote*, took on new life when books burgeoned. Novels, of course, were seen especially to target novel-reading women by flattering them into a mad, rebellious self-love, like Charlotte Lennox's Arabella in *The Female Quixote* (1752), or Jane Austen's Catherine Morland in *Northanger Abbey* (1818). This charge gained force, however, because of the sheer number of novels. Indeed, it was as much their number as their nature that shook contemporary critics: there were a lot, they were all the same, and they were all bad.[49] These charges colour contemporary discourse about the private, usually female, library. In the Marquis's 'large and well furnished' library, for example, there were 'unfortunately for [Arabella] ... a great Store of Romances, and, what was still more unfortunate, not in the original *French*, but very bad translations.' When she attempts to indoctrinate her lover Glanville to her way of thinking by requiring him to read her books, she believes that she is selecting only a few:

> Arabella, having ordered one of her Women to bring *Cleopatra, Cassandra, Clelia*, and the Grand Cyprus from her Library, *Glanville* no sooner saw the Girl return, sinking under the Weight of those voluminous Romances, but he began to tremble at the Apprehension of his Cousin laying her Commands upon him to read them ... [which] appeared to him an *Herculean* Labour. ... *Glanville* sat rapt in Admiration at the Sight of so many huge Foilio's written, as he conceived, upon the most trifling Subjects. ... I have chosen out these few, said *Arabella* (not observing his Consternation) from a great many others, which compose the most valuable Part of my Library.[50]

The library thus embodied the fallacy that more is better—either in quality or quantity.

Libraries also seemed to some to offer a false notion of education: that choosing more of the same was, in fact, selectivity in action. Not only did they hold bad books—morally and aesthetically—but they held irrelevant ones. In the famous number in *The Mirror* to which Mrs. Morland refers when scolding Catherine for her discontent at domestic work, Mackenzie indicts over-refined women whose reading incapacitates them for the honest labor their social status requires. In it, a spoiled young lady recounts that, 'When I came to the country I proposed to pass great part of my time in my favourite amusement of reading' but quickly discovered that her farmer-father's library only contains five books: the Bible, *Dickson's Agriculture*, a 'treatise on *Farriery*,' a book of *'Domestic Medicine*,' and *'the Compleat House-wife*.'[51] Mackenzie here seems to condemn an opulent literary culture, yet it is the very culture to which his own periodical belongs.

In fact, this ambivalence colors virtually all literary attacks on literature as illusion. Chesterfield explains the relationship between books and experience as a process of application and heightened perception: 'The knowledge of the world is only to be acquired in the world, and not in a closet. Books, alone will never teach it you; but they will suggest many things to your observation which might otherwise escape you; and you own observations upon mankind, when compared, with those you will find in books will help you to fix the true point.'[52] Indeed, although novelistic rhetoric appears to endorse direct experience over book-learning, this rhetoric is continually undermined by the fact that it is pointed at readers who learn *not* to value reading as experience by, in fact, reading. In Henry Fielding's *Joseph Andrews* (1742), for example, Parson Adams exemplifies the naivete of the book-learned idealist who repeatedly suffers trickery and contempt from his wordly-wise acquaintances. On the other hand, of course, Fielding intends *his* reader to value Adams' perspective, indeed to learn it from his very novel. Austen similarly plays on reading as knowledge in *Northanger Abbey*. Whereas General Tilney's books are intended to represent him, has he read them? Certainly, he has not learned to read such men as John Thorpe. Catherine Morland's Gothic reading at least informs her of the possibility of deception, ignorant as she is of how to apply the knowledge. Austen's *own* reader, however, learns the fallacy of misreading both books and people precisely by reading about it. In Richard Brinsley Sheridan's *The Rivals* (1793), it is the antiquated marplot Sir Anthony Absolute who intones, 'a circulating library in a town is, as an ever-green tree, of diabolical knowledge!'[53] The very prevalence in imaginative literature of these warnings against imaginative literature underscores the contemporary assumption that, because there are so many books, readers will take literature with a grain of salt.

This ambivalence about the plenitude of books, and the double role of the library as a private and also a public space produced corresponding ambivalence about the library. On the one hand, the library embodied the classical ideal of retirement from the vanities of politics and society, a refuge and retreat. On the other hand, this ideal itself validated a social withdrawal that came to seem antagonistic to human nature and the moral obligations of society. In *The Lounger*, Hortensius laments the 'inactive uselessness' that eats away his spirit when, disgusted at the 'world,' he escapes to the country, and purchases 'a considerable library of books' in order to experience 'an elysium of enjoyment, a life of philosophic ease and happiness.' Instead of delighting in 'the renewal of the studies of my early days' and the conviction that 'my taste was every day improving,' he feels 'a craving void in my heart,' and warns his audience that 'Men were born to live in society; and from society only can happiness be derived.'[54] Samuel Johnson declares in *The Rambler* that, 'No place affords a more striking conviction of the vanity of human hopes, than a publick library; for who can see the wall crouded in every side by mighty volumes, the works of laborious meditation, and accurate enquiry, now scarcely known but by the catalog, and preserved only to encrease the pomp of learning, without considering how many hours have been wasted in vain endeavours.'[55] Libraries dramatize the inadequacy of writing, learning, culture itself; their very plenitude diminishes the importance of what they contain.

As antiquarianism rose and public libraries multiplied in the mid-century, libraries also came to embody national cultural wealth. They offered the promise of completeness. The British Museum library was seen to parallel its natural history holdings, and embody British literary learning. This became a matter of national pride: Tobias Smollett's fussy Matthew Bramble complains to Dr. Lewis that, 'It would be a great improvement, with respect to the [British Museum's] library, if the deficiencies were made up, by purchasing all books of character that are not already in the collection.'[56] Johnson laments the loss of the Alexandrian library for draining the modern world of vast stores of knowledge in history, law, philosophy, politics, and literature, and promoting scholarly confusion: had it 'been spared, how much might we have known of which we are now doomed to be ignorant; how many laborious enquiries and dark conjectures, how many collations of broken hints and mutilated passages might have been spared.'[57]

At the same time, libraries stifle novelty. They are both a treasure-house and a tomb. Mr. Town complains that 'It hath been generally imagined, that learning is only to be acquired in the closet, and by turning over a great number of pages; for which reason men have been assiduous to heap together a parcel of dusty volumes ... as if knowledge was shut up in a library, and chained to the shelves together with the folios.'[58] Johnson himself notes that the burning of the Alexandrian library permits new writers to flourish, and himself as Idler to write 'a disquisition on the loss.'[59] Similarly, he salutes libraries as places of cultural preservation and guarantors of authenticity, regretting that 'The original Copy of *Burnet*'s History, tho' promised to some public Library, has never been given; who then can prove the fidelity of the publication.' He even includes a footnote suggesting that 'It would be proper to reposite, in some publick Place, the manuscript of *Clarendon*, which has not escaped all suspicion of unfaithful publication.'[60] Yet he derogates a scholar because 'after many years past in Biography, [he] left his manuscripts to be buried in a library because that was imperfect which could never be perfected.'[61] While libraries preserved and authenticated culture, they also froze it: removed from the current of conversation and thought, books in libraries moldered.

By the end of the century, however, literary discourse, a professional book trade, and a tradition of literary consumption had largely reconciled these opposing notions. Book collections were shown to be a *means* of socializing. This appears in a genre dedicated to bridging the gap between reading and the world: urban guidebooks. An early nineteenth-century fad, these books characteristically advertise the city as the avenue to the world, and themselves as the map visitors—or even native urbanites—require. *The Picture of London, for 1802*, for example, bears the subtitle 'being a Correct Guide to All the Curiosities, Amusements, Exhibitions, Public Establishments, and remarkable Objects, in and near London.'[62] Significantly, this guidebook dwells on the role of reading in acquiring urban sophistication, and the role of publishing as a sign of British progress. The author Sarratt advertises London as the center of publishing, noting that about 800 new books and pamphlets are regularly published there annually, amounting in value to about 240*l* for one copy of each work. He claims that the gross annual returns approach half a million pounds, and that the book trades provide employment to nearly 2000 persons. Moreover, the guidebook includes an 11-page list of London's circulating libraries, including foreign, professional, and specialist bookshops, and the three private libraries most important for their 'magnitude and value.'[63] The author assumes that his readers will

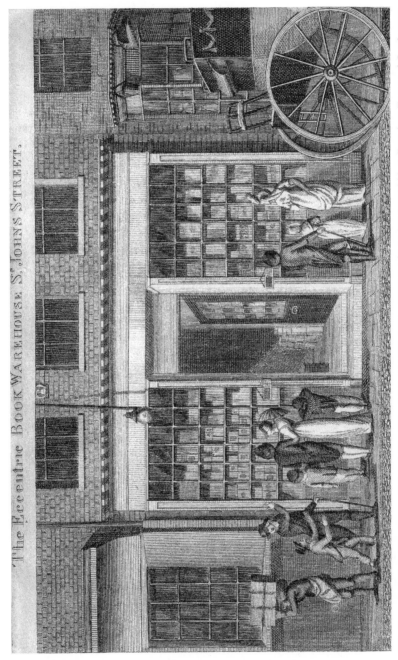

The Ececentric Books Warehouse, St. John's Street from H.J. Sarrett, A New Picture of London For 1803–4 (London: Tegg and Castleman, 1804). This engraved frontispiece depicts the plenty and the oddities of urban literary culture to awe-struck spectators.

wish to read other works, and informs them that, 'By applying to the Librarians or to the Committee, any genteel person may obtain permission to attend the reading-room at stated times; by which he will have an opportunity of perusing some very valuable publications, and making extracts which are equally interesting and improving.'[64]

Bookshops, as well as libraries, have a key role as an urban luxury because they provide not merely topical or fashionable reading, but *lots* of it: a wide choice. Furthermore, books in their multitude offer experience equivalent to touring, history, and spectacle. Tegg and Castleman's *New Picture of London For 1803–4*, for example, includes as its subtitle: 'A Guide through this Immense Metropolis ... containing Comprehensive Descriptions of the *Publick Edifaces, Collections of Curiosities*, and Places of Entertainment; interspersed with Diverting, Authentick, and VALUABLE ANECDOTES, many of which are historical, and record events which have happened several hundred years ago.'[65] The frontispiece, however, ignores the Tower of London, St. Paul's, or any of the conventional London sights for 'The Eccentric Book Warehouse, St. John's Street,' showing figures outside the windows staring at books **(Plate 1)**. This plate illustrates the consumer attitude toward literature and identifies it with travel, urban luxury, and social experience.

Conclusion

Book collections, from the literary conceit to the public library, prompt debate on topics vital to British culture in the long eighteenth century. While other collections of things—museums, repositories, both religious and secular, and curiosity cabinets—present the issues that faced book collectors when books became the new thing to accumulate, books had a particular status as revered cultural and national art, in part because they were simultaneously unique and replicable. Fine books had always formed part of a nobleman's cultural hoard, yet by the later eighteenth century, books were produced in increasing numbers and copies. The library thus encapsulates the struggle between modern commercialism and traditional values. Both collectors' own practices and satire on these underscore the debate between quantity and accumulation, and quality or selection, and this becomes a central motif in the discourse surrounding collections of books. Moreover, the debates about principles of organization, categorization, and learning that surround the establishment of the early museum carry over to discussions about books and book collections. Libraries are part of the great eighteenth-century enterprise to accumulate and collect, and like advertisements, catalogs, dictionaries, encyclopedias, magazines, miscellanies, anthologies, guidebooks, and bookshops, they dramatize verbal and informational opulence, authority and yet also unreliability. By the century's end, there were so many books that only public libraries would serve readers. This process intensified the tensions between the ideal library as complete, like the lost library of Alexandria, and the ideal of the library as select. Eighteenth-century libraries are bastions of public culture, with an historical resonance of privilege and spiritual superiority; they are also private spaces for individual pleasure and self-improvement. They embody the usurpation of privilege by commercialism and also a reverential, quasi-religious regard for the text. They are public places for self-display and sociability, monuments to national history yet prisons of dead culture. As places that preserve, entomb, liberate and confine, where knowledge is chained to the shelves and also fetched by clerks, the library is the eighteenth-century arena in which a new notion of cultural consumption as the paradox of individual choice in a public theater is realized.

Notes

1. Michael Hunter, *Science and the Shape of Orthodoxy: Studies of Intellectual Change in Late Seventeenth-Century Britain* (Woodbridge, Suffolk: Boydell Press, 1995), p. 148, citing Charlton T. Lewis and Charles Short, *A Latin Dictionary* (Oxford: Clarendon Press, 1975).
2. See John Brewer, *The Pleasures of the Imagination: English Culture in the Eighteenth Century* (London: HarperCollins, 1997).
3. John Feather, *A History of British Publishing* (London: Routledge, 1998), pp. 84–105, passim.
4. James Raven, *Lost Libraries* (Cambridge University Press, 2007).
5. Susan M. Pearce, *Museums, Objects, and Collections: A Cultural Study* (Leicester and London: Leicester University Press, 1992), p. 92, passim.
6. See Lorraine Daston and Katharine Park, *Wonders and the Order of Nature* (New York: Zone Books, 1998).
7. Nehemjah Grew, *Musaeum Regalis Societatis, or, a Catalogue & Description of the Natural and Artificial Rarities Belonging to the Royal Society. And preserved at Gresham Colledge [sic]. Made by Nehemjah Grew M.D. Fellow of the Royal Society and of the Colledge of Physitians. Whereunto is Subjoyned the Comparative Anatomy of Stomachs and Guts. By the same Author.* London: by W. Rawlins, for the Author, 1681.
8. See Thomas Sprat, *The History of the Royal Society of London, For the Improving of Natural Knowledge* (London: J. Martyn, 1667).
9. See *Museum Thoresbyanum. A Catalogue of the genuine and valuable* COLLECTION Of that well known Antiquarian the late Ralph Thoresby, Gent. *F.R.S.* [1725]; also M. Day, 'Humana: Anatomical, Pathological and Curious Human Specimens in Sloane's Museum', in *Sir Hans Sloane: Collector, Scientist, Antiquary, Founding Father of the British Museum*, ed. Arthur MacGregor (For the Trustees of the British Museum: British Museum Press in association with Alistair McAlpine, 1994): 67–9.

10. John Sitter, *Arguments of Augustan Wit* (Cambridge: Cambridge University Press, 1991), p. 124; Brean S. Hammond, 'Scriblerian Self-Fashioning', *YES* 18 (1988): 118.

11. Samuel Johnson, *A Dictionary of the English Language* (London: W. Strahan, 1755–6).

12. Paul Kaufman, *Reading Vogues at English Cathedral Libraries of the Eighteenth Century* (Rept. from the *Bulletin of the New York Public Library*, Dec. 1963: Jan., Feb., March 1964; vols. 67, 68; nos. 1–3), p. 653; 1708 Anne Act 7, c. 14, p. 1.

13. John Ray, *Travels through the Low-countries, Germany, Italy and France, with Curious Observations* (London: J. Walthoe, et al., 1738), vol. 1, pp. 32, 72, 84, 208–9, 293, 329; vol. 2, pp. 453–4.

14. These conflicting ideas appear in Shakespeare's *The Tempest*, when the magician Prospero loses his Dukedom because of his obsession with books: 'My dukedom was library enough', he declares, admitting that 'Knowing that I loved my books, he furnished me/From my own library with volumes that/I prize above my dukedom' (I, ii, 109; I, ii, 166–8). See Jurgen Habermas, *The Structural Transformation of the Public Sphere: An Inquiry into the Category of Bourgeois Society*, trans. Thomas Berger, with ... Frederick Lawrence (Cambridge, MA: MIT Press, 1989).

15. Jane Austen, *Pride and Prejudice*, ed. R. W. Chapman (Oxford University Press, 1987), v.1, ch. 8, p. 38. The arriviste Mr. Bingley presses 'all that his library afford[s]' on Elizabeth Bennet, in a well-intended but over-eager attempt to amuse her, another example of the attempt to imitate the well-born Darcy (p. 37).

16. John Binns, Bookseller, Stationer, Print-Seller, and Music-Seller, *A Catalogue of Books, containing Several Valuable Libraries, lately purchased ... to be Sold ... October, 1789* (Leeds: John Binns, 1789).

17. Samuel Butler, *Characters*, ed. Charles W. Daves (Cleveland and London: The Press of Case Western Reserve University, 1970), p. 124.

18. Philip Connell, 'Bibliomania: Book Collecting, Cultural Politics, and the Rise of Literary Heritage', *Representations* 71 (Summer, 2000): 27.

19. Richard B. Sher, *The Enlightenment and the Book* (Chicago: The University of Chicago Press, 2006).

20. [George Colman and Bonnell Thornton], *The Connoisseur. By Mr. Town and Censor-general* (London: R. Baldwin, 1755–56), vol. 2, no. 103 (Thursday 15 January 15 1756), p. 624.

21. Henry Mackenzie, *The Lounger*, (vol. 3, no. 89, Saturday 14 October, 1786: p. 193).

22. Oliver Goldsmith, *The Bee* (J. Wilkie, 1759), 'On the Instability of Wordly Grandeur', p. 187.

23. Jane Austen, *Northanger Abbey*, ed. Barbara M. Benedict and Deidre LeFaye (Cambridge: Cambridge University Press, 2006), vol. 2, ch. 8, p. 188.

24. J. Paul Hunter, *Before Novels: The Cultural Contexts of Eighteenth-Century English Fiction* (New York: W.W. Norton, 1990), esp. ch 5.

25. William Cater, *A Catalogue of Several Valuiable Libraries and Collections of Books ... to Be Sold ... on Monday, May 1, 1780* (London: William Cater, 1780).

26. John Bell, *A New Catalogue of Nell's Circulating Library, Consisting of above Fifty Thousand Volumes ...* (London: John Bell, 1778).

27. Elizabeth L. Eisenstein, *The Printing Revolution in Early Modern Europe*, 2nd edn (Cambridge: Cambridge University Press, 2005), p. 343; see also Ann Blair, 'Reading strategies for coping with information overload c. 1550–1700', *Journal of the History of Ideas* 64 (Jan. 2003): 11–28.

28. Paul Kaufman, 'Coffee Houses as Reading Centers', *Libraries and Their Users: Collected Papers in Library History* (London: Library Association, 1969), pp. 115–18.

29. Jane Austen, *Northanger Abbey*, vol. 1, ch. 5, p. 30.

30. Charlotte Stewart-Murphy, *A History of British Circulating Libraries: The Book Labels and Ephemera of the Papantonio Collection* (Newtown, PA: Bird and Bull Press, 1992), p. 27.

31. Barbara M. Benedict, 'Jane Austen and the Culture of Circulating Libraries: The Construction of Female Literacy' in *Revising Women: Eighteenth-Century Women's Fiction and Social Engagement*, ed. Paul R. Backscheider (Baltimore and London: Johns Hopkins University Press, 2000), p. 159, passim.

32. Stewart-Murphy, *History*, pp. 33–4; 49.

33. *The Ayr-Shire Circulating Library for Gentlemen and Ladies ...* By James Meuros (Kilmarmock, 1760.), p. viii.

34. Kaufman, 'The Community Library: A Chapter in English Social History', in *Libraries and Their Users*, pp. 188–9; also 'English Book Clubs', pp. 48, 61.

35. Kaufman, *Libraries*, p. 38; Stewart-Murphy, *History*, p. 30.

36. Ann Radcliffe, *The Mysteries of Udolpho*, 4 vols (London: G. G. and J. Robinson, 1794), vol. 1, ch. 1, p. 6; vol. 1, ch. 13, p. 354.

37. Jane Austen, *Pride and Prejudice*, v.1, ch. 11, p. 55.

38. This contains in addition to the titular text the Marchioness de Lambert's *Advice of a Mother to her Daughter* (c. 1695, first published in English in 1727); John Gregory's *A Father's Legacy to his Daughters* (1774); and John Moore's *Fables for the Female Sex* (1744). See too the popular *The Gentleman's Library; Being a Compendium of the Duties of Life in Youth and Manhood* (Edinburgh: Williamd and Joseph Deas, 1808) containing Chesterfield's *Advice to His Son*, and *Observations on Men and Manners*, along with the *Polite Philosopher* and La Rochefoucault's *Maxims*, with passages from the works of Hugh Blair and James Fordyce.

39. Joseph Addison and Sir Richard Steele, *The Spectator*, vol. 1, 3rd edn (London, 1714), no. 37, Thursday 2 April 1711, pp. 138–9.

40. Mr. Spectator notes in another issue, on the surprising discovery of literary works in scraps of waste paper, that his own 'Library' contains, 'upon the Shelf of Folios, two long band-boxes standing upright among my Books ... both of them lined with deep Erudition and abstruse Literature. I might likewise mention a Paper Kite, from which I have received great Improvement; and a Hat-Case, which I would not exchange for all the *Beavers* in Great Britain' (No. 85, vol. 2, p. 16).

41. *Spectator*, 1: 154.

42. Goldsmith, *The Bee*, p. 59.

43. *The Connoisseur* vol. 1, no. 18 (30 May 1754), p. 105.

44. *Spectator*, pp. 140–1.

45. See, for example, No. 79 for Thursday 31 May, containing a reader's reply urging religious texts (pp. 305–9), or no. 92 for Friday 15 June (vol. 2, 1713, pp. 41–4).

46. Henry Mackenzie, *The Lounger*, no. 87 (Saturday 30 September, 1786): vol. 3, pp. 174–5.

47. Joseph Addison and Sir Richard Steele, *The Spectator*, 2nd edn (London: for S. Buckely; and J. Tonson, 1713), Dedication.

48. Duke de la Rochefoucault, *Maxims, and Moral Reflections* (Edinburgh: William and Joseph Deas, 1808), p. 32, no. 261.

49. Raven, *Judging New Wealth*, p. 9.

50. Charlotte Lennox, *The Female Quixote; or, the Adventures of Arabella*, vol. 1 (London, 1752), bk. 1, ch. 1, pp. 3-4; ch. 12, p. 70.

51. Henry Mackenzie, *The Mirror*, vol. 2 (Edinburgh: W. Creech; London: W. Strahan and T. Cadell, 1981), no. 51, Tuesday 20 July 1779, p. 136.

52. Chesterfield, pp. 52–3.

53. Richard Brinsley Sheridan, *The Rivals* (Dublin: Messrs. C. Brown, et al., 1793), I, ii, 27.

54. Henry Mackenzie, *The Lounger*, no. 9 Saturday 2 April, 1785 (Dublin: for Messrs. Colles, Burnet, et al., 1787), vol. 1, pp. 77–80.

55. Samuel Johnson, *The Rambler*, vol. 4 (London: for J. Payne and J. Bouquet, 1752), no. 106, Saturday 23 March 1751: p. 47.

56. Tobias George Smollett, *The Expedition of Humphy Clinker*, vol. 1 (London: W. Johnston, and B. Collins in Salisbury, 1779), 147.

57. Johnson, *The Idler*, 1: 74.

58. *Connoisseur*, vol. 2, no. 86 (Thursday 18 September 1755), p. 517.

59. Johnson, *Idler*, 1: 77.

60. Johnson, *Idler*, 1: 71.

61. Johnson, *Idler*, 1: 73.

62. *The Picture of London, for 1802, The Picture of London, for 1802*; being a Correct Guide to All the Curiosities, Amusements, Exhibitions, Public Establishments, and remarkable Objects, in and near London; with a collection of appropriate tables. By Lewis and Co (London, 1802), p. 4.

63. *Picture of London*, p. 240. In particular, the author cites five French and three German booksellers, and dealers in valuable and second-hand books (16 of them), medical booksellers (2) and Juvenile Libraries (Harris's on the corner of St. Paul's churchyard, and Tabart's No. 157 New Bond st.), and Law booksellers (3). The author also advocates a subscription library: 'It is a disgrace to the metropolis, that it contains no Public Subscription Library, on a liberal and extensive plan, similar to those which exist at Liverpool, Bristol, Burmingham, and other places. Those paltry establishments which now assume the name of Public Libraries, as far as respects the practical and effectual purposes of literary accommodation, are wretchedly contemptible, and unworthy even of the small degree of patronage which they meet with. A public library in the metropolis ought to fill the Pantheon in Oxford-street, or the Lyceum in the Strand, be provided with duplicate and triplicate copies of new books, with journals, foreign and domestic, and be conducted on the broadest and most liberal principles' (p. 240).

64. 'A new reading-room has been erected for that purpose. Any person who wishes to see the British Museum has only to leave his name and address with the porter; a day will be appointed on which he is to call and get a printed ticket free of any expense. Except Saturdays and Sundays the Museum is open every day of the week' (Sarratt, p. 179).

65. H. J. Sarrett, *A New Picture of London For 1803–4* (London: Tegg and Castleman, 1804).

9
Imagining Hegel: Bookish Forms and the Romantic Synopticon

Michael Macovski

I

Post-Enlightenment scholarship is marked by a range of textual responses to the burgeoning of the archive. Keepsakes, annuals, miscellanies, compendiums, anthologies, treasuries, souvenirs, almanacs, catalogs, and other examples of what we might term 'mediated forms' continue to challenge theorists—including those seeking to define the rationale behind compilations that often strike us as at best randomly organized.

Perhaps in response to this diversity of forms, the Organization of Knowledge has become a key field within the area of Book History. And at least part of this recent emphasis is a direct outgrowth of insightful scholarship on the eighteenth- and nineteenth-century history of the encyclopedia. Such scholarship includes not only the pioneering work of Robert Darnton in this field, but also a host of scholars including Ernst Behler, David S. Ferris, and Richard Yeo.[1] In this paper, I begin with this history of the era's encyclopedias, because it represents the best and most far-reaching approach to characterizing the epistemic trajectory and organization of the archive during the era. That is, if we would begin to explain the explosion of knowledge, information, and literature during this period—especially as they are reflected in the collective forms I have noted—we would do well to consider the theories that have tracked the organization, categorization, and classification of knowledge, both during and after Diderot's famous project.[2]

My contention is that the most influential and pervasive systems for organizing knowledge during the Enlightenment derive not so much from such celebrated works as Diderot and d'Alembert's *Encyclopedie*, or from the early Scottish *Encyclopedia Britannica*—as they do from Hegel's encyclopedism, as expressed in his 1817 Introduction to his tripartite *Encyclopedia*.[3]

Hegel's theory of the encyclopedia stems from German Idealism; it envisions a compilation in which individual subjects are presented not in isolation but as part of a totalizing, connected sweep of knowledge. This fundamental connectedness of knowledge—in which discrete disciplines cohere within a single circle—looks to a synthesis of thought. The key term is systematicity. Whereas purely alphabetic modes of organization concentrate on ready retrieval, more systematic structures tend to bring out the interdisciplinary web that links ostensibly isolated fields.

For Hegel, moreover, this vision of a holistic, encyclopedic knowledge emerges from his view of an all-embracing philosophy. In this context, philosophy itself is encyclopedic. As he writes, 'Philosophy is the encyclopedia of the philosophical sciences, ... and it is a philosophical encyclopedia insofar as the differentiation and the connection of its parts are presented according to the necessity of the concept.' It is this unifying 'connection of its parts' that defines Hegel's synthesized organization of encyclopedic knowledge—what he terms a 'circle of totality,' a 'circle of circles.' He writes, 'Since philosophy is rational knowledge throughout, each of its parts is a philosophical whole, a circle of totality containing itself within itself. ... The whole presents itself then as a circle of circles in which each circle is a necessary moment, so that the system of its characteristic elements constitutes the whole idea, which also appears in each individual part.'[4]

In this sense, disciplines that appear discrete unto themselves can be linked—both historically and synchronically—to 'one and the same whole.' In Hegel's terms, the 'principle of true philosophy contains all particular principles in itself. Philosophy demonstrates this both in itself and in its history: on the one hand, the philosophies that appear different in history are only one philosophy at different stages of development; and on the other hand, the particular principles that underlie particular systems are only branches of one and the same whole.'[5] This 'philosophical whole' of interconnected, disciplinary 'circles' comes to illustrate, again, Hegel's recurrent reference to 'system.' 'Philosophizing without a system can not be scientific,' he suggests. 'Moreover, if it expresses for itself primarily a subjective perspective its contents are contingent. For the contents are only justified as a moment of the whole, and outside of the whole rest on ungrounded presuppositions or have only subjective certainty.'[6] Only this noncontingent, post-subjective vision can effect Hegel's encyclopedic 'totality' of knowledge: 'Philosophy is also essentially encyclopedic, since the true can only exist as totality, and only through the differentiation and determination of its differences can it be the necessity of totality and the freedom of the whole. It is, therefore, necessarily systematic.'[7] Hegel concludes this discussion by distinguishing his vision of a philosophical encyclopedia from other approaches to this field: 'The philosophical encyclopedia can be distinguished from other, ordinary encyclopedias,' he suggests, 'by the fact that the ordinary one is an assemblage of sciences, taken up in a contingent and empirical manner, and it sometimes includes topics that merely bear the names of sciences but are otherwise only collections of bits of information.'[8]

Hegel's philosophy of the encyclopedia tends to permeate many approaches to the organization of knowledge during the Romantic era. Coleridge, for instance, briefly considers editing an encyclopedia, to be called the *Encyclopedia Metropolitana*. Similar to Hegel, he envisions a totalizing system whose 'integral parts or members ... are interdependent and reducible to one and the same law.'[9]

I would suggest, moreover, that Hegel's encyclopedist theories also have profound implications for other collective forms of the eighteenth and nineteenth centuries—including several of those mediated genres listed above. Of course, the differences between encyclopedia forms and these other collective genres are considerable. Yet it is also vital to recognize that both textual categories are essentially *aggregations*—compiled collections that must necessarily and recurrently address the issue of how disciplinary knowledge is to be organized.[10] I would argue, in fact, that we can reconsider several of these collective genres in terms of the Hegelian theory of the interconnectedness of knowledge—the totalizing sweep of synthesized thought. That is, we can illuminate the organizational rationale behind forms like the keepsake, the annual, and the souvenir if we reconceive them as part of what I term the synoptic vision of Romantic epistemology. As we shall see, this synoptic vision stands in direct contrast to the more particularistic, divided, and partitioned view of organized knowledge that is occasionally invoked during the era. I will suggest, moreover, that while the foregoing *contrast* between interconnected, synoptic, or universalist perspectives and more divided or particularistic organization often applies, they at times overlap—and for this reason must be further elaborated and refined in order to account for the remarkable diversity of collective genres that come to define the era.

II

As the foregoing discussion of encyclopedias suggests, then, the era under discussion promulgates several concepts of organized knowledge that extend across disciplinary—and generic—boundaries. As I have noted, one of my intentions in this paper is to reveal just how the era envisions the evolving archive. Put another way, we are examining just how the period comes to '*see*' the world. Hence, to illuminate these distinctive forms of seeing—what is in effect the period's epistemic *perspective*—I will also be turning to a field that, to my knowledge, has never been applied to either the history of the book or the organization of knowledge—namely, optics. For both the eighteenth and nineteenth centuries witness the discovery and development of several optical devices that directly capture and represent the kind of broad epistemological view that we are discussing. We will accordingly be looking beyond Foucault's (often metaphorical) notion of panoptical power and restraint, in order to ascertain how the *actual* instruments of the era come to refract its vision of knowledge.

III

We can further refine the divergent purposes—as well as the individual categories or classifications—of these mediated forms when we look analytically at some particular examples.[11] In fact, the very self-presentation of these volumes—as defined by their title pages, prefaces, frontispieces, list of plates, tables of contents, and other prefatory (or ancillary) material—serves as compelling evidence of how each editor envisions the epistemic organization and classification of a particular volume. Consider, for example, the following title-page text:

The Bibliographical and Retrospective Miscellany, Containing Notices of, and Extracts from, Rare, Curious, and Useful Books, in all Languages; Original Matter Illustrative of the History and Antiques of Great Britain and Ireland; Abstracts from Valuable Manuscripts; Unpublished Autograph Letters of Eminent Characters; and Notices of Book Sales. By Rev. Edward Richard Poole. London: Printed for John Wilson, 19, Great May's Buildings, St. Martin's Lane. 1830.

Here, we see a compilation intended to serve as an ongoing, continually 'Useful' storehouse of knowledge. Its editor clearly envisions it as a synthesized compilation, a pointedly *representative* set of 'Extracts.' In this particular example, moreover, the editor sees this totalizing sweep of knowledge as quintessentially historical and nationalistic, containing 'Manuscripts' (and other documents) from his country's history—each of which is specifically selected to be 'Illustrative of the History and Antiques of Great Britain and Ireland.' In this sense, the volume stands as a kind of encyclopedic compendium of the country's literary and documentary history—its specifically 'Bibliographical' heritage. Although this heritage is necessarily limited by British perspectives, it nevertheless constitutes this editor's requirements for synoptic knowledge. What is more, the 'Rare, Curious, and Useful Books' he mines are emphatically 'in all Languages.' The intention, then, remains clear: such a comprehensive vision must underlie any 'Illustrative' organization of knowledge.

The impetus for this pointedly 'Bibliographical' compilation becomes even clearer in the 'Introduction' to this volume. There, the editor Poole makes it clear that he intends his *Bibliographical and Retrospective Miscellany* both to represent and 'preserve' the textual heritage of his nation—what he terms the 'countless literary and pictorial collections, that had remained for centuries undisturbed in public institutions, or the repositories of private individuals.'[12] Accordingly, it is this synthetic sweep of textual knowledge that he seeks to excerpt in his miscellany. Although most of these 'collections' have been lost, Poole can still provide an indication of their national value and breadth to the 'major portion of the community.' Yet to reach this majority, the bibliographical form and price of his volume is particularly vital. Unlike those who can afford Dibdin's celebrated, encyclopedic lists of bibliographic heritage, the readers of Poole's *Bibliographical and Retrospective Miscellany* will be spared the 'expence' that 'acts as a prohibition to the acquiring of' such national knowledge. Hence the form of the necessarily adumbrated and excerpted *Miscellany*.

For Poole, then—and other 'lovers of English literature'—this bibliographical selection represents a holistic, national 'repository.'[13] What is more, collecting such a heritage is especially urgent since it has come under siege: although 'Great Britain has enriched herself, as regards such objects of *virtu*, since the year 1814,' the 'numerous dispersions of important libraries' have effectively ceded such studies to European rivals—and 'left us far behind them in the prolific field of Bibliographical research.'[14] In order to 'redeem the credit of our nation,' then, these 'literary and pictorial collections'—and the aggregate of synthesized knowledge they represent—must be perpetuated. Much as Hegel's compendium of encyclopedic knowledge abjures what he calls 'mere assemblages of information,' so too do many nineteenth-century miscellanies seek, in the words of this 'Introduction,' to go beyond a 'mere enumeration of the various editions of rare works, their dates, &c.' Instead, they invoke a grand design of interconnected knowledge: the overarching 'plan upon which this work is to be pursued.'[15] Only this systematized 'plan'—this Hegelian synthesis of encyclopedic thought—can represent the national body of organized knowledge.

IV

This desire for an interconnected, synthesized body of knowledge finds its most explicit optical correlative in the another collection, *The Telescope*—a volume that embraces 'a TELESCOPIAN utilitarianism' in order to effect the goal 'looking forward and looking far.' The title page reads:

> *The Telescope. A Miscellany of Literature, Science and Religion*. Edited by the Rev. Thomas Smith, Missionary of the General Assembly of the Church of Scotland. Vol. I. September 1840 to April 1841. Calcutta: Printed by W. Rushton and Co., Ballantyne Press, and Published by G.C. Hay.

Here, the titular instrument emblematizes the synoptic, panoramic perspectives of expansive knowledge that we have been discussing. In fact, for this editor, such a telescopic approach signifies not only a broad, distanced perspective but also one that is less pragmatically utilitarian than its Benthamite contemporaries would have it. Indeed, the editor excoriates those who criticize the 'man of literature ... as a very idler.' In the 'Introductory Statement, By the Editor,' Thomas Smith characterizes his journal's broad, interdisciplinary organization of knowledge—or, in this case, its compendium of 'literature'—as part of the 'national honor' and the 'national wealth.' Much as the foregoing editor (of the *Bibliographical Miscellany*) exhorts 'lovers of English litera-ture' to regard their dispersed collections as a national, bibliographic 'repository,' so too this editor praises the 'man of literature' for elevat-ing what he calls the 'national character.' And for him, the English language is the 'depository of the richest stores of literature.'[16] Yet it is also crucial to recognize that, within *The Telescope*, the 'national wealth' inheres in 'all knowledge'—that is, in the panoramic compilation of all 'literature, science, and religion.' Only such a panorama can embody the 'enlarged ideas' requisite 'to raise up a community.'[17] For this editor, 'all knowledge, be it of what kind it may, is capable of being turned by its possessor to good account.' Since a man is 'responsible for the use he makes of all the knowledge communicated to him,' he can—and must—acquire as much and as diverse an amount as possible. Indeed, earlier in his introduction, the editor stresses that the express purpose of the volume is to begin 'diffusing the greatest possible amount of knowledge.'[18] As a result, he goes on to conclude, 'We therefore set out with this as our starting declaration, that no department of human knowledge is to be considered as foreign to our province; and how vast, how immeasurable a field does the declaration spread out before us!'[19]

No matter 'how vast, how immeasurable a field' the miscellany must cover, its editor will contrive to represent every 'department of human knowledge.' As he says, the coverage of this synthesized totality, this 'immeasurable field,' is his grand 'design.'[20]

Again, moreover, we should bear in mind that—for this editor, at least—what enables the preservation and diffusion of the 'greatest possible amount of knowledge' is the English language itself. He writes, 'For this end we hold it to be a high privilege to find in this country, from which sound knowledge had well high fled, so large a band of those who understand a language the best fitted of all for communicating all sound knowledge—a language which is the depository of the richest stores of literature—a language rendered capable by a long course of improvement of expressing all the ideas that have yet entered into the mind of civilized man.'[21] In this sense, only the historical depth of the English language—the *lingua franca* of epistemological diffusion—can 'express all the ideas that have yet entered into the mind of civilised man.' It accordingly becomes the 'depository' of 'all sound knowledge.'

Finally, in enumerating the panoramic 'division of all knowledge'—as contained in the 'full compass of [his] design'—this editor turns to the same field that guides Hegel's encyclopedic organization of knowledge: namely, Philosophy. He writes:

> Lord Bacon, the father of modern philosophy, makes a three-fold division of all knowledge, into history, poetry and philosophy, corresponding to the three principal faculties of the human mind— memory, imagination and reasoning. ... All these branches of knowledge we deem within our province; and not these alone, but also their various combinations and mutual dependencies. The history of poetry and philosophy, the poetry of history and philosophy, the philosophy of history and of poetry, will be among the most interesting of the topics that will claim our attention. All these are real and distinct branches of knowledge, each claiming a distinct and serious attention.[22]

Although Bacon's 'branches' or 'divisions of knowledge' turn out to be more pragmatic and disparate than those within Hegel's vision, both philosophers stress these discrete fields' 'mutual dependencies.' For this editor, all such fields fall within his synthesized 'totality': 'All these branches of knowledge we deem within our province.' He will accordingly seek to establish epistemological 'modes' of gathering and organizing this breadth of knowledge—systems capable of 'handling so vast and various a compass of subjects.'[23] What is more, in facing this daunting task, his 'Introductory Statement' offers the following analogy: 'Because no instrument has yet been invented by which we can satisfy all our curiosity regarding the various heavenly bodies, shall we, therefore, for ever shut our eyes, and refuse to look upon these heavenly bodies at all?'[24] Here again, the most telling analog of Hegelian comprehensiveness—the 'circle of circles'—is optical. Although even his titular telescope will prove inadequate, it still represents the kind of distanced, all-encompassing perspective that the era seeks to capture.[25]

V

In terms of etymological history, Hegel's sense of an all-embracing 'circle of learning' emerges most tellingly in the early eighteenth century, when the abbreviated rubric 'Cyclopaedia' comes to connote not only the full cycle of knowledge but also the material volume that contains it. The title page of the following compendium, for instance, reads as follows:

The Cabinet Cyclopedia. Conducted by the Rev. Dionysius Lardner, LL. D, F.R.S. L & E. M.R.I.A. F.R.A.S. F.L.S. F.Z.S. Hon. F.C.P.S. & c. &c. Assisted by Eminent Literary and Scientific Men. History. *The Chronology of History*. By Sir Harris Nicolas, K.C.M.G. London: Printed for Longman, Rees, Orme, Brown, Green, & Longman, Paternoster-Row; and John Taylor, Upper Gower Street. 1833.

Following the title page, the editor announces the particular subject category of this Cyclopedia—namely, 'History.' This page reads, 'The Chronology of History, Containing Tables, Calculations & Statements, Indispensable for ascertaining the dates of Historical Events, and of Public and Private Documents, from the Earliest periods to the present time.'

Of course, like many of our exemplary volumes, the purposes of such a compilation differ from those of other genres and types. (Indeed, each of these volumes diverges from the others; they serve discrete purposes, distinctive constituencies—in disparate formats.) Yet it is vital to ascertain that—in the words of the volume's 'Preface'—this 'Cyclopedia' seeks to establish, here again, a 'system.' Much as Hegel stresses a 'systematic' organization of knowledge, this compendium puts forth an expansive 'system for computing time' and historical evolution. In this sense, the generic boundaries between the divergent compendia we are discussing are inherently fluid. And it is precisely because these collective genres overlap that we can directly compare their organizational systems—and again draw some conclusions about the organization of knowledge during the era.

This edition of the *Cabinet Cyclopedia* itself includes a series of brief entries on historical 'Eras and Epochs,' followed by several chapters listing various chronological methods for correlating diverse calendrical systems and dating historical events. It is also worth noting that, here again, its systematic organization diverges from the kind of alphabetically-organized 'cyclopedias' developed in France and Scotland. Still, the proto-Hegelian 'system' of this 'Cyclopedia' is again clear. In this case, however, such a system is inherently causal and historiographic: it envisions history as a 'long chain of events,' linked by 'cause' and 'effect.' As the editor writes:

> Every event in history arose from, and depended in a great degree upon, some preceding circumstance, and became in its turn the parent of other events of greater or less moment; hence, however trifling either of them may be in itself, or, if viewed without relation to other circumstances, however immaterial, the precise time of its occurrence, there are few which, as tributary streams to the great current of human affairs, had not some influence on the political state of the nation in which they took place, and not unfrequently also on those of neighboring countries.[26]

Here, history is by definition interconnected and systematic. 'Every event' both 'arose from' and 'depended upon' others; every event had at least 'some influence' on others. As such, each event constitutes a 'tributary stream' that links up to the 'great current of human affairs.'

It is this great, systematized 'current,' then, that organizes the editor's historical volume into what our previous examples have termed a master 'plan' or 'design.' In this case, moreover, its logic inheres in a Humean linkage between cause and effect—a desire to 'trace transactions to their causes, and, when these are known, to discover their general consequences.'[27]

We should recognize, too, that this editor's other motivations for his compendium also parallel the aims of our foregoing examples. He believes, for instance, that the 'archives of a country should be carefully preserved.' At the same time, he further suggests that England is losing ground to French systems of historical archiving and chronology.[28] Finally, it is this panoramic system or perspective, which—here again—is best characterized in optical terms: 'Chronology and Geography have been justly called the 'eyes of History,'" writes the editor, 'without the lights of which all is chaos and uncertainty.'[29]

VI

This impulse toward the synoptic emerges still more dramatically in the following title-page text: *The Souvenir Keepsake, with Fine Engravings*. London: Reynolds & Son, and all booksellers. In the Preface to this volume, the 'compiler' opines that he is 'fully convinced that those who read it in the same spirit in which it was selected, will be made wiser, than by wading through volumes of other works. It is hardly necessary to descant on the great advantage of having comprised in so small a book, extracts from the writings of some of the wisest and greatest men the world has produced.'[30] Here, the preface clearly stresses the representative, even synoptic vision of the compiler's 'selection' or 'compilation.' His 'small volume' stands as a distillation, obviating the need for 'wading through volumes of other works.' Though we may question his criteria, his carefully chosen 'extracts' are specifically intended to *represent* the best (and thus presumably the most expansive) body of knowledge available—from what he terms the 'writings of some of the wisest and greatest men the world has produced.'

At the same time, not only historical collections but literary compendiums as well claim to have achieved this same representative, synoptic status. The editor William Kennedy, for instance, in his preface to *The Continental Annual*, insists that the 'taste' the collection seeks to address 'will endure as long as man retains the faculty of imagination.' Assured of this generalized, universalist endurance, then, he goes on to express confidence in his 'selection' 'from the varied walks of literature.'[31]

VII

Much as the foregoing volume, *The Telescope*, presents itself as a 'Miscellany of Literature, Science and Religion', so too do the many biblical collections of the era claim to embody this sense of a unified collection—this totalizing synthesis. Consider, for instance, the following title-page text:

The Youth's Biblical Cabinet. No. I. New Series. Leicester: Printed and Published by T. Cook, 26, Granby-street, (to whom all communications must be addressed.) London: Simpkin & Marshall, Houlston & Stoneman, and W. Brittain; and sold by all Booksellers. Price Twopence.

Here, the reference to a biblical 'Cabinet' carries heightened significance. To begin with, we know that the pre-codex bible was essentially a collection of scrolls, stored in a literal cabinet or cupboard.[32] In this sense, the compendium's use of the title 'Cabinet'—to indicate a compilation of biblical commentary and paraphrase—may in fact recall the bible's early bibliographic status as an *actual collection* of fragmentary (and often unauthorized) pieces. At the same time, moreover, envisioning any bible as itself a kind of special collection—or 'selection,' to use a term common during the eighteenth century—may also suggest that all bibles are actually selections or 'extracts' from God's Word, which is available in its entirety only in heaven. This implication is, in fact, embodied in the following title-page text:

> *A Golden Treasury for the Children of God, Whose Treasure is in Heaven; Consisting of Select Texts of the Bible, with Practical Observations in Prose and Verse, for every Day in the Year.* Written by C.H. v. Bogatzky. With a Preface of the Author, on the Right Use of this Book. And now for its great Usefulness translated from the 19th Edition of the German. London: Printed for A. Linde, in Catherine-Street in the Strand. 1754.

In this volume, then, the 'Select Texts of the Bible' emerge as synecdochic. That is, this 'Golden Treasury' or collection of texts is actually presented as a 'Selection' of another, transcendent treasury—the 'Treasure in Heaven.' As such, it is intended for those 'Whose Treasure is in Heaven.' Only this godlike, nonmaterial 'Treasury' can represent the kind of totalized, all-embracing knowledge we have discussed.

VIII

As we have also suggested, when the foregoing editors seek to emblematize their systematic, panoramic compendiums of knowledge—what might be called their broad-brush perspectives—they often turn to one governing metonym: namely, the optical conceit. Such a trope is not extraordinary, however, when we consider that this same era witnesses the rapid development of some of the most influential optical devices in the history of perspective. As Timothy Brownlow has noted, the Romantic 'way of seeing was made possible by the increasing fascination with the mechanics of vision during the eighteenth century. The development of optical instruments is an intriguing foretaste of the camera, and ultimately the cinema. By 1800 there was a profusion of such instruments, including the magic lantern, the Claude glass, the *camera obscura*, the *camera lucida* and a whole family of panoramas, dioramas and other offspring.'[33] Brownlow's list of optical machines—to which we might add the stereoscope as well—indicates that such devices serve many functions in the development of image culture during the late eighteenth century. From our perspective, however, what distinguishes these various devices is their ability to encapsulate an entire scene—to capture it in its entirety.[34] It is not surprising, then, that the miscellanies, keepsakes, encyclopedias and other mediated forms we have been discussing repeatedly invoke such optical emblems of panoramic perspective. These devices come to suggest the period's recurrent interest in not only a totalized perspective but also a *literally* synoptic vision of the organization of knowledge.

IX

On several levels, then, the widely-used optical devices of the eighteenth century also emblematize the broad, panoramic perspective that characterizes the era's all-embracing view of knowledge. This synoptic perspective accordingly parallels the organizational model suggested by Hegel, with its emphasis on a broad, interconnected sweep of knowledge. Both approaches thus shed light on the foregoing compendiums and their totalizing collections of diverse concepts. For many editors of these volumes, the goal is to schematize a recognizable corpus of knowledge—one that pointedly *represents* the total knowledge necessary for the targeted reader. That is, each volume purports to synopsize—or, in Hegel's terms, to systematize—a synthesized view of the 'writings of … the wisest and greatest men the world has produced.' In this context, each volume is inherently synecdochic.

By specifically representing such a totality—by providing a 'selection' or indicative set of 'abstracts'—these popular compendiums thus stand as a permanent record of what many editors see as universally requisite knowledge. Such permanent records of knowledge are intended to become, quite literally, keepsakes—in that they concretize idealized knowledge for years to come, for 'posterity.' Indeed, many editions are also termed 'Forget-Me-Nots'—mnemonic compilations that encapsulate, in one synchronic moment, a spectrum of necessary insight. In this sense, they are literally 'souvenirs'—mechanisms of memory.

Yet in establishing an organization of knowledge, this synthesized, totalizing schema is also inherently paradoxical. While appellations such as 'Keepsake' and 'Forget-Me-Not' suggest a *permanent* record of knowledge, the full titles of many of these compendiums also imply a more *transient* perspective—one that is quite literally 'Annual' or 'Historical.' Such rubrics thus seem to imply a *temporary* gathering of knowledge, provided for a given year. Consider, for instance, the following representative titles: *The New Year's Gift, for MDCCCXXXIV*; *Peter Parley's Annual: A Christmas or New; Year's Present for Young People; The Religious Keepsake; for Holiday Presents; The Continental Annual, and Romantic Cabinet, for 1832; The Historical Souvenir, and Literary Cabinet; Retrospective Miscellany;* and the *Retrospective Review.* Of course, some of these volumes are specifically designated as giftbooks or presents for a given year. In other cases, the assumption behind 'Annuals' may also be that one must collect them, year by year, in order to sustain, reinstate, or refresh one's permanent record of requisite concepts. In either case, though, such designations appear to suggest an organization of knowledge that is not only synoptic and synchronic—but one that can operate historically as well. Such an organization would thus include both 'local knowledge,' in Geertz's sense, and totalized knowledge as well. Indeed, the very titles of these volumes capture this epistemic duality: as we have begun to suggest, they are both 'Annuals' *and* 'Keepsakes'; occasional (that is, periodical) *and* historical (that is, 'Retrospective'); youth-oriented advice *and* lifelong guides. They are also both transient catalog *and* permanent collections. In fact, the recurrent use of the title 'Cabinet' clearly implies a kind of material permanence—a perdurable, lasting fixity—that seeks to moor knowledge, to serve as a bulwark against the fluid, mutable, and erratic evolution of the overall print archive. Like the actual antiquarian cabinets of the period, these textualized 'Cabinets' position themselves as stable, enduring records—secure against the river of information that yearly washes over the era's readers. And that the same volume would present itself as *both* such a 'Cabinet' and an 'Annual' may actually reflect what I would call the epistemic tension or paradox of the era—the sense that the print archive is simultaneously necessary for the educated reader's overall knowledge and also ultimately inassimilable.

We can conclude, then, that the foregoing genre of collective volumes may also indicate a concept of knowledge that tends at times toward the *segmented, sequential, and divided*—that is, an organization of knowledge that is not *always* and completely totalizing. Such a revision serves not to negate our previous discussion of synoptic thought, but rather to suggest that such a synthesis is often balanced by a countervailing force—one that reveals the epistemological dichotomy of the era's print culture. In this context, we are now expanding on the Hegelian concept of totalized, universalist knowledge—adding another model that is, here again, more inherently partitioned, segmented, divided, even fragmented—yet still sequential.

We may also need to build on the Hegelian model in another way as well. For if Hegel's concept of encyclopedic Idealism encompasses a single, synchronic record of synthesized knowledge, the foregoing list of titles also suggests a model that is more chronological and, in a word, *narrative*. We can say, in fact, that many collective volumes of the era seek to add a *diachronic* perspective to their synoptic—and synchronic—organization. Within this schema, a given editor may attempt to represent the temporal progression of 'annual' knowledge—a kind of yearly epistemology—with ongoing, narrative '*re*-collections.' Consider, for instance, the words of William Kennedy, editor of *The Continental Annual, and Romantic Cabinet, for 1832*, who informs his readers that 'we purpose rambling from year to year, hoping to lead the adventurous reader' on the 'fairy track of Romance.' In thus progressing 'year to year' (as the title 'Annual' implies), Kennedy affirms the chronological, narrativized desire of his collection. And much as Kennedy's volume postulates a progressive 'track' for his readers, the editor of *The Historical Souvenir, and Literary Cabinet* seeks to lead 'youth' along the diachronic 'road of happiness'—and thus 'correct the heart' over time.

X

Here again, such diachronic paths and publications suggest an attempt to capture, at least momentarily, the evolution of chronological knowledge. It is as if one could contain a progression of narrative years—or moments—within a single volume. Indeed, it is almost as if one could contain narrative time—which is exactly what, in another context, the era is attempting to do.

I am referring here to the revolutionary development of the pocket-watch during this same era—the device that does, in one sense at least, capture narrative time. As Stuart Sherman has noted, the pocketwatch emerges during this period as portable, self-contained, and indicative of a paradigm shift in the way that narrative time is encapsulated. It is important to note that the eighteenth century's signal development of the sprung mechanism, as used in the steel-spring pocketwatch, represents a quantum leap within watchmaking history—and essentially introduces the accurate pocket-watch to the Early Modern era. Within the context of the present discussion, moreover, we must also recognize that the eighteenth-century pocketwatch serves as a historical emblem of incorporated, contained, narrative duration within the ongoing organization of knowledge.

Hence, by alluding to the diachronic dimension of their epistemological schemas, the foregoing volumes suggest that the era's organization of knowledge contains a paradox: readers must 'keep up' with the chronological expansion of the print archive while at the same time maintaining or 'keeping' access to the timeless cabinets of the historical record.

Notes

1. See Ernst Behler, 'Language, hermeneutics, and encyclopaedistics,' *German Romantic Literary Theory* (Cambridge: Cambridge University Press, 1993), pp. 260–98; David S. Ferris, 'The Question of a Science: Encyclopedistic Romanticism,' *The Wordsworth Circle* 35.1 (2004): pp. 2–6; and Richard Yeo, *Encyclopaedic Visions: Scientific Dictionaries and Enlightenment Culture* (Cambridge: Cambridge University Press, 2000), p. 277.
2. See Robert Darnton, *The Business of the Enlightenment: A Publishing History of the Encyclopedie, 1775–1800* (Cambridge, MA: Harvard University Press, 1979).
3. G. W. G. Hegel, *Encyclopaedia of the Philosophical Sciences in Outline*, trans. Stephen A. Taubeneck, *Encyclopedia of the Philosophical Sciences in Outline and Critical Writings*, ed. Ernst Behler (New York: Continuum, 1990), pp. 45–263.
4. *Encyclopaedia*, p. 51.
5. *Encyclopaedia*, p. 52.
6. *Encyclopaedia*, pp. 51–2.
7. *Encyclopaedia*, p. 151. See also Clifford Siskin, *The Work of Writing: Literature and Social Change in Britain, 1700–1830* (Baltimore and London: The Johns Hopkins University Press, 1998), 29–102. Siskin, too, discusses the field of Philosophy as what he calls the 'happy center' of diverse specialization—though he is not concerned with Hegel's perspective on this center nor with the textual forms behind this 'unified diversity' (such as encyclopedias, miscellanies, almanacs, annuals, keepsakes). Instead, he focuses on questions of disciplinarity and professionalism—including how these ideas are influenced by schools, gender, nationalism, and the comparison between British education and the 'Scottish philosophical mix.' As part of his argument, he also considers a move from Philosophy to broadly canonized writing or capital-L 'Literature'—as well as a potential move from a centering Philosophy to 'subject-specific' specialization. My own argument is that the era's emphasis on a synoptic, centering Philosophy not only persists and evolves throughout the era but also has crucial implications for textual history, eighteenth-century historiography, Humean causality, narrative temporality, and the textual history of collective forms (keepsakes, encyclopedias, and so on).
8. *Encyclopaedia*, p. 53. The best discussion of Hegel's Encyclopedism is Tilottama Rajan's 'The Encyclopedia and the University of Theory: Idealism and the

Organization of Knowledge,' *Textual Practice* 21.2 (2007): 335–58. (See esp. pp. 337–41.) See also the historical summaries in Behler; Pierre Bourdieu and Loic J. D. Wacquant, *An Invitation to Reflexive Sociology* (Chicago: University of Chicago Press, 1992), pp. 97–101; Ferris; Michel Foucault, *The Order of Things: An Archaeology of the Human Sciences* (New York: Vintage, 1973), pp. 312–18; Philippe Lacoue-Labathe and Jean-Luc Nancy, *The Literary Absolute: The Theory of Literature in German Romanticism*, trans. Philip Barnard and Cheryl Lester (Albany: State University of New York Press, 1988), pp. 39–40, 122–3; Friedrich Schlegel, 'Introduction to the Transcendental Philosophy,' in *Theory as Practice: A Critical Anthology of Early German Romantic Writings*, ed. Jochen Schulte-Sasse et al. (Minneapolis: University of Minnesota Press, 1997), p. 255; Gianni Vattimo,*The Transparent Society*, trans. David Webb (Baltimore: Johns Hopkins University Press, 1992), p. 1; and Yeo.

9. Qtd. in Rajan, p. 339.

10. As we shall see, much as the eighteenth and nineteenth centuries become the era of collecting various ephemera, so do they become the era of collecting—and organizing (or classifying)—knowledge. This association is just one of the connections between the textual collection and actual, physical collections of objects.

11. For excellent background summaries of the history of the *Keepsake*, see Paula Feldman and Frederic Mansel Reynolds, *The Keepsake for 1829* (Peterborough, Ont.: Broadview Press, 2006); Laila Ferreira, 'Selling Romanticism: Wordsworth and Public Discourse in the Literary Marketplace' (Unpublished Paper, 2007); Terence Allan Hoagwood and Kathryn Ledbetter, *Colour'd Shadows: Contexts in Publishing, Printing, and Reading Nineteenth-Century British Women Writers* (New York and Basingstoke, England: Palgrave Macmillan, 2005); Peter J. Manning, 'Wordsworth in the Keepsake 1829,' in *Literature in the Marketplace*, ed. John O. Jordan and Robert L. Patten (Cambridge, Eng.: Cambridge UP, 1995), pp. 44–73; and Charlotte Sussman, 'Stories for the Keepsake,' in *The Cambridge Companion to Mary Shelley*, ed. Esther Schor (Cambridge, Eng.: Cambridge UP, 2003), pp. 163–79.

12. *Bibliographical and Retrospective Miscellany*, p. i.

13. *Bibliographical and Retrospective Miscellany*, pp. i–ii.

14. *Bibliographical and Retrospective Miscellany*, pp. i, ii.

15. *Bibliographical and Retrospective Miscellany*, p. iii.

16. *The Telescope*, pp. 1, 2.

17. *The Telescope*, p. 2.

18. *The Telescope*, p. 2.

19. *The Telescope*, p. 3.

20. *The Telescope*, p. 3.

21. *The Telescope*, pp. 2–3.

22. *The Telescope*, p. 1.

23. *The Telescope*, p. 1.

24. *The Telescope*, p. 3.

25. The panoramic intentions of *The Telescope* are also evident when the editor suggests that the 'truth' of a 'Miscellany' depends specifically upon 'Extracts'—that is, careful selections which enable a work to claim a quintessentially *representative* status.

26. *Cabinet Cyclopedia*, p. v.

27. *Cabinet Cyclopedia*, p. v; see also p. vi.
28. *Cabinet Cyclopedia*, p. vii.
29. *Cabinet Cyclopedia*, p. vi.
30. *The Souvenir Keepsake*, 'Preface' unnumbered, single page.
31. *The Continental Annual*, p. v; see also p. vi. Similarly, the 'Advertisement' to *The Religious Keepsake; for Holiday Presents* takes pains to point out that, after a series of editions, it has garnered the 'universal approbation of its readers.'
32. For useful discussions of the Bible as a collection, see Stephen Prickett's introduction to *The Holy Bible*, ed. Robert Carroll and Stephen Prickett (Oxford: Oxford University Press, 1997); and also Anthony Harding, *Coleridge and the Inspired Word* (McGill, Canada: McGill-Queen's University Press, 2003).
33. Timothy Brownlow, *John Clare and Picturesque Landscape* (Oxford: Clarendon Press, 1983), p. 11.
34. See Jonathan Crary, *Techniques of the Observer : On Vision and Modernity in the Nineteenth Century* (Cambridge, MA: MIT Press, 1990), Chapters 2, 3. Perhaps the most telling example of this desire for optical synthesis—throughout the eighteenth- and nineteenth centuries—is the pervasiveness of the *camera obscura*. As Jonathan Crary has demonstrated, this device operates as an epistemological model throughout the era. Prior to the turn of the century, for instance, the camera obscura stood 'as model, in both rationalist and empiricist thought, of how observation leads to truthful inferences about the world' (Crary 32). For Crary, moreover, this synthetic truth—this synoptic vision—inheres in the individual. We might say, in fact, that the single individual's vision becomes a model for the all-encompassing perspective that we have been discussing. By the early 1800s, however, such a vision begins to fragment: although it still centers on the individual, Crary notes that he or she now must now be 'made compatible with new arrangements of power: the body as worker, student, soldier, consumer, patient, criminal.' (Crary 147). Similarly, by the 1840s, we witness the 'division and fragmentation of the physical subject into increasingly specific organic and mechanical systems.' (Crary 81). Nevertheless, although the concept of a singular truth begins to break down during this later period, the idea that that this fragmented vision might still be seen and encompassed by a single observer (or individual) appears to persist throughout the period. See *Techniques of the Observer*, pp. 32, 147, 81. For another useful discussion of this optical concept, see Gary Shapiro, *Archaeologies of Vision: Foucault and Nietzsche on Seeing and Saying* (Chicago and London: The University of Chicago Press, 2003).

10

'The Society of Agreeable and Worthy Companions': Bookishness and Manuscript Culture after 1750

Betty A. Schellenberg

There may be something a little perverse about contributing to a volume on the bookishness of the eighteenth and nineteenth centuries a reflection on the persistence of manuscript culture in the second half of the eighteenth century. Yet as I have reflected for the past several years on a number of matters seemingly unrelated to one another – the miscellaneous nature of the novelist Samuel Richardson's later correspondence, the origins of innovative book projects such as Robert Dodsley's *Collection of Poems by Several Hands*, the emergence of a discourse of Lake District tourism in London-based print, and the roles of intellectual women in determining the reception of other women's publications – I have found myself encountering questions which are slowly cohering into one more fundamental inquiry. The chameleon-like shifts in roles played by Richardson in his letters depending on his correspondent; the inaccuracy of the labels of 'editor' and 'publisher' for William Shenstone's and Robert Dodsley's contributions to latter's poetic miscellany volumes IV to VI; the presentation of the eighth edition of Daniel Defoe's *A Tour thro' the Whole Island of Great Britain* (1778) as 'modern' because of the contributions of leisured gentlemen; and the power of the socially inflected, unpublished assessments of a handful of Bluestockings to control the reputations of women writers respected by their fellow professionals and well received by reviewers and the reading public – all these phenomena have led me to try to pry my way into a black box that is the manuscript culture of 1750 to 1780.

While it is commonly asserted that by the eighteenth century England was in the latter stages of a definitive transition from orality and manuscript to print as the medium dominating not only communicative practice, but also the individual subject's imagining of her- or himself as a participant in culture, I am not the first to note that manuscript production and circulation persisted in its own right in this period, and not merely as a preliminary step towards print publication.[1] However, even where this has been acknowledged in passing, the tendency has been to treat such practices as anachronistic, aberrant, or at best, isolated.[2] While not denying the shift in balance from scribal to print publication which prompts such characterizations, my concern is to imagine the workings of a scribal culture whose continuities extend not only into the past, but across the eighteenth-century present in a still-intact, though increasingly finespun, web. To what extent might the norms of manuscript circulation continue to hold sway over its adherents and also over the wider reading public, whether in precedence to those of the print medium, or in competition with them, or in some sort of hybrid structure? And how might our own scholarly landscape be altered if we developed a habit of seeing, say, those awkward print fictions of reading a written dialogue aloud in a novel, or of claiming to have received a treatise in a letter from a gentleman, not as symptoms of crude technique or a naive obsession with truthfulness, but rather as the invocation of contemporary and authoritative modes of exchange?[3]

In this approach I am indebted to the important arguments of Harold Love, Margaret Ezell, and Donald Reiman, who, although they have not noted a significant scribal culture operating beyond 1750, have established some ground rules for talking about the persistence of such a culture well into the 'age of print'. Love, for example, has argued for a definition of publication that is not attached to a particular medium, but rather attends to the movement from the private realm of what he calls 'creativity' to the public realm of consumption, marked by the moment 'at which the initiating agent (who will not necessarily be the author or even acting with the approval of the author) knowingly relinquishes control over the future social use of that text', thereby creating a potential availability which may or may not be realized.[4] In addition, these writers have noted that scribal circulation tends to occur within spaces that blur rigid public-private distinctions – communities whose boundaries are defined by social groupings such as kinship, common beliefs or interests, shared membership in institutions such as the church or the military, or geographical proximity[5] – hence the terminology of 'social authorship', 'reserved publication', or 'confidential publication'.[6] Ezell has opened up intriguing possibilities by providing case studies in which manuscript and print cultures 'existed simultaneously (and ... competitively and companionably)'.[7] And Love and Ezell, again, have identified certain characteristic qualities of scribal culture and publication – such as a deep-rooted habit of transcription, a relative informality and frankness of style, a 'delight in mixture', and a relative unconcern to distinguish between individual authors contributing to a collection or to attribute works accurately[8] – to which we might add, a persistent association with a social elite, which I will argue constituted the greatest factor in the continuing influence of coterie publication.[9] Finally, Reiman has offered the important insight that the meaning of this manuscript production cannot be assumed to be static, that in fact the manuscript's cultural place was adapting along with the shifting functions of print. In this essay I will briefly review three sites of ongoing coterie practice from the perspective of their intersections with commercial print production – the Shenstone network of manuscript circulation, the development of Lake District tour writing, and the discussion of coterie writing that followed upon the *Donaldson vs. Becket* judgement in 1774 – in order to sketch out characteristics of a manuscript culture specific to the 1750s to 1770s. I will pay particular attention to how this culture was represented by, and in turn shaped the presentation of, printed books, suggesting that late eighteenth-century 'bookishness' was at least in part an effect of the persistent influence of social authorship.

The Dodsley-Shenstone circle

Michael Suarez has described the final three volumes of the bookseller Robert Dodsley's popular anthology *A Collection of Poems by Several Hands*, which appeared in a total of six volumes between 1748 and 1758, as largely consisting of 'poems scavenged by Dodsley's gentleman editors', emphasizing in particular 'the strong presence of [William] Shenstone's friends and neighbours' in the latter three volumes, published in 1755 (Volume 4) and 1758 (Volumes 5 and 6).[10] Another twentieth-century commentator has designated Shenstone as 'virtually [the] editor' of these volumes, based on his role in supplying and commenting on about one-fifth of the poetry comprising the final two volumes.[11] A careful examination of Shenstone's correspondence with Dodsley and others, however, suggests that it might be more illuminating, rather than assuming a print-publishing model, as these terms do, to consider the extent to which Shenstone's – and perhaps more surprisingly, Dodsley's – working schema for literary production and circulation in this case was that of coterie publication.

Shenstone, a sedentary country gentleman residing on the small estate of Leasowes from 1744 to his death in 1763, polishing poetry and perfecting the garden design of his *ferme ornée*, was in the first instance much more contact and conduit than editor. He was an ideal supplier of poems because of his established practice of manuscript exchange with overlapping circles defined by his student days at Oxford and his geographical location in the Birmingham area.[12] Thus Dodsley gained through his friendship with Shenstone access to materials which were actively circulating, but had not yet appeared in the medium of print.[13] These materials came to Dodsley with the hallmarks of coterie practice – transcribed by Shenstone, often revised by him and others, and unidentified by individual author.[14] Rather than carry out a wholesale production process with these materials for the new medium, Dodsley treated them as already published – in other words, as coterie publications, a fact that is initially evidenced by the title's invocation of the gathering together of poems in their physical state, the manuscripts produced by various hands. Thus he focused on the tasks of collecting and ordering, apparently not finding any need to identify authors, obtain their permission to print, or send them proofs for correction (increasingly the practice for single-author publications).[15] Significantly, only a minority of the authors seem to have objected, and their objections were mildly surprising to him. Dodsley's replies to such complaints may seem ambiguous, even cagey: in some cases, he responds that he supposed Shenstone had obtained permission to submit the work; in others, he regrets that the poems are now in proof, and so it is too late to withdraw them. But together they suggest the notions that the poems had already been published in the act of relinquishing control of the manuscripts to a coterie circle, that coterie circulation was a process of collaborative correction and perfecting, and therefore that the texts he saw were, rather than unpolished originals, already at the copytext stage.[16] This assumption was based on some experience, since he often received letters from members of the Shenstone circle mentioning pieces that were being passed in all directions for mutual entertainment and improvement. He seems also to have believed that his membership in this coterie network (he sent his own work to Shenstone, Richard Graves, and others in the group for their comments, as they did to him) entitled him to further circulate the work – this time in print.[17]

If such groups were a profitable source of material pre-edited and polished for the press, the notion that the bookseller was an unscrupulous thief of manuscript materials appears not to have arisen. The distinctly commercial realm of print is recognized in this correspondence, but primarily in the sense of shared concerns – about obtaining enough poetry to fill a volume, publishing it before the London season ended, wanting to sell one edition before a new one was announced – or of recognizing

Dodsley's expertise in knowing how to bring material before the public effectively, in judging what would sell. What did the authors who appeared in the *Collection of Poems by Several Hands* gain that they saw as a fair exchange for any profit accruing to the bookseller from their work? Although many of the poems in these three volumes were published anonymously, their authors seem to have viewed their inclusion as an act of friendly homage, facilitating the circulation of their work in 'the world' and preserving their reputations for posterity.[18] Suarez observes insightfully that the *Collection of Poems* was not intended to represent a select compendium of the best poetry of the time. Unlike the anthologies produced by John Bell and others in the latter decades of the century, this was a 'distinctive, even exclusive' gathering; '[Dodsley] was marketing poems by his coterie of authors and by the friends of his close associates for a particular readership'.[19] In short, for the coterie, printing was an extension of their publishing practices, to similar ends. This colonization of print is also demonstrated in the triangular working relations of Dodsley, Shenstone, and the innovative type-designer John Baskerville, to whose specialized press in Birmingham, near Leasowes, both Dodsley and Shenstone turned (or, in Shenstone's case, endlessly *intended* to turn) for small editions of works destined for delimited audiences.[20] Shenstone's phrasing to Richard Jago regarding a possible printing of the manuscript miscellany he was compiling and revising in the last years of his life nicely illustrates this extension of the localized scribal community: 'Be not apprehensive: there shall nothing appear in print of your composition any more, without your explicit consent – And yet I have thoughts of amusing myself with the publication of a small Miscellany from neighbour Baskerville's press, if I can save myself harmless as to expense – I purpose it no larger than a "Landsdown's", a "Philips's" or a "Pomfret's Poems"'.[21]

Love suggests that one reason for the decline of scribal publication was the decline of the political or religious need to maintain separate ideological communities among the governing classes.[22] As Shenstone's placement of himself in a tradition defined by Lansdowne, Philips, and Pomfret reveals, however, the eighteenth-century country gentleman, if politically marginalized, retained his desire to be recognized as a leader in cultivated taste.[23] Shenstone in particular built for himself a reputation as aesthetic arbiter in poetry and gardening through his participation in two forms of circulation – of manuscripts and of travellers between landscape gardening projects. Of course the two activities were culturally related, associated with a freedom of physical movement which allowed one to form and maintain select connections, which in turn came with leisure and independent means; a notable thread in the Dodsley and Shenstone correspondences refers to written descriptions of gardens visited or built by their gentleman correspondents.[24] I suggest that it is because of this association that, even in this age of efficient postal service, manuscript circulation in Shenstone's circles remained tied to the physical circulation of visitors through Leasowes – Dodsley in fact travelled there regularly in the summers of the latter, prosperous years of his life, at once to work with its proprietor on each other's manuscripts in progress, and to admire and consult over the ongoing landscaping work, while Shenstone was extremely reluctant, despite Dodsley's persistent pleading, to simply *mail* his work to the bookseller. This stance of reluctance, preserving a sense of difficult and limited access, of viewing as a hardwon privilege, maintaining the link also between the text and its physical source in the author, seems to have been a part of Shenstone's persona as leader in taste, which was in fact heightened by its contrast to the technologies of convenience advancing around him. Deliberately working in allegedly 'anachronistic' or 'devalued' media, Shenstone established his contemporary reputation as 'a forerunner of a later generation' (in the 1933 phrase of Marjorie Williams) through his aesthetic of rural simplicity, his interest in the Gothic and in antique ballads (extensive correspondence shows that he served as a trusted advisor to the younger Thomas Percy in the *Reliques of Ancient Poetry* project), and his cultivation of the picturesque.[25]

But this reputation, based on the social cachet of activities such as gardening and coterie exchange, was secured for literary history by the appearance of his work in print, particularly in Dodsley's *Collection of Poems*, reissued repeatedly, and in the same publisher's posthumous edition of his friend's works.[26] As Barbara Benedict has noted, from the perspective of the readers of such print publications, 'literary collections ... exhibit a clique yet aim at a general audience. ... Collections paradoxically popularize the exclusivity of public printed culture'.[27] From the perspective of the clique, however, with the exhibition of the exclusive textual origin, one which remains sealed off to the reader, who only gains access to its products, the desired end has arguably been achieved. Love has suggested that Walter Benjamin's notion of the aura of the work of art prior to the age of mechanical reproduction can be applied to manuscript publication's authority in the age of print. This 'aura' in a reductive commercialized sense is certainly exploited by printers of travel accounts, and demystified by commercial authors attacking coterie circles, as discussed below; Shenstone's approach to his writing and gardening activities might thus be seen as a continuation of aesthetic practice that takes on an aura of authenticity in inverse proportion to the increasing dominance of urban print culture.[28]

Manuscript circulation and the gentleman traveller

The link I have just suggested between circulating bodies and manuscript culture offers insight into another of the major sites of manuscript circulation in the latter half of the eighteenth century: writing about domestic travels. If one constructs the tradition of domestic tourism as it is articulated in late eighteenth-century prefaces to printed accounts of such tours, one easily establishes a list of the influential writers – John Brown, Thomas Gray, Arthur Young, and Thomas Pennant are named repeatedly. Further investigation, however, takes some revealing turns. First, many of these publications either established their reputations through manuscript circulation before appearing in print, or presented themselves as based on such activity. I will give three brief examples. Brown's *Description of the Lake at Keswick (and the adjacent country) in Cumberland. Communicated in a letter to a friend*, originally written in about 1753 to his friend and mentor George, Lord Lyttleton, circulated for years in manuscript before coming into print posthumously, first its prose portion in 1767, and finally in 1776 its poetic component, in a collection of odes by Richard Cumberland, who introduces the poem as taken from a manuscript he has been 'favoured with'. As a result of this scribal publication, Brown was known by 1755 within the Lyttleton circle as 'the Columbus of Keswick', apparently influential in fuelling interest in travel to the Lakes long *before* his letter appeared in print.[29]

A second case is that of Gray's *Catalogue of the Antiquities, Houses, Parks, Plantations, Scenes, and Situations in England and Wales, Arranged According to the Alphabetical Order of the Several Counties. ...* Even as this text moves into print, it sheds its scribal features only gradually. William Mason first privately printed the catalogue in 1773, two years after his friend Gray's death, referring to the author in the 'Advertisement' only as 'a person of too much eminence to be mentioned on so slight an occasion'. A mere one hundred copies were printed, and these were interleaved with blank pages so that 'those, *to whom they shall be presented, may at their leisure* make such short remarks as their *own personal knowledge* of the several counties enables them to do; and in these *to add or expunge* what they may think proper'. Mason as anonymous editor situates this printed work even more explicitly in a culture of controlled circulation when he explains that 'as many of [the Cataloguer's] friends had *transcribed* it in his life-time, and many more have *requested copies* since his decease, it was thought best to print it in this pocket form; not only for their present gratification, but as the most likely means of *rendering this little work complete*, and of fitting it hereafter for the eye of the public'.[30] By contrast, when the *Catalogue* finally makes its fully public debut under the imprint of a London bookseller in 1787, it is attributed directly in its title, *A Supplement to the Tour through Great-Britain, containing a Catalogue of the Antiquities, ...*, to *'the Late Mr. Gray, Author of the Elegy written in a Country Church-Yard, etc.'*. The former coterie of the cataloguer and his collaboratively engaged friends has been refashioned as an authoritative author reaching out to a large, undifferentiated audience ('the World') imbued with a passion for domestic tourism, yet ignorant and submissive: its 'Publisher' notes in the 'Advertisement' that 'What Mr. Gray thought important enough to engage his attention, those for whose use it is intended will not receive with neglect. Scenes, Situations, Seats, and Antiquities, selected as worthy of notice by the elegant Author of the Church-Yard Elegy, will be visited with a degree of respect unfelt before. To his taste no person will venture to dissent, and to his judgement few but will readily subscribe'.[31]

Thirdly, Thomas Pennant, an Oxford-educated estate-owner and member of the Royal Society with connections throughout Britain and Europe, published in 1771 an account of a Northern tour that was constructed partly upon the responses of 'the Gentlemen and Clergy of *North-Britain*' to questionnaires circulated in advance of his travels. In a 1774 expanded edition Pennant celebrates 'the liberal spirit of communication among the Gentlemen of the Northern parts of this Kingdom', which has enabled him to produce this edition 'freed from some errors that must unavoidably attend the performance of a rapid traveller, notwithstanding all his wishes to be accurate', while in a 1774 account of a tour which included the Lakes, he notes the contribution to knowledge of, and 'all the comforts that arise from the society of', his 'agreeable and worthy companions', the two clergyman-friends who accompanied him.[32] Pennant first publishes each book locally in Chester, and dedicates his work initially to his neighbour and patron in Flintshire and later to Sir Joseph Banks, as one of those 'generous volunteers of rank and fortune, who distinguishing themselves by the contempt of riches, ease, and luxury', travel for the sake of furthering knowledge.[33] With these strategies Pennant imports into his commercially successful publications the flavour of the gentleman scholar, member of a coterie of amateur specialists whose private correspondence and travels are being offered to a wider public in pursuit of a general increase of knowledge.

In each of these cases of travel writing, print at first appears parasitic on manuscript form, bringing the aesthetic and learned authority of coterie writing into play as a marketing device. Yet the metaphor of parasitism implies a gradual weakening of the host, whereas in this instance, the practice simultaneously reinforces the identification of good taste with manuscript production and its restricted modes of circulation. This paradoxical valorization of the manuscript mode is arguably the most historically persistent feature of the manuscript-print contact zone, and in the short term might even have led to a strengthening of certain elements of manuscript culture in the third quarter of the eighteenth century; again, such publications 'exhibit a clique'. Thus for travel writing, just as in the case of poetry, the purported observations of a gentleman conveyed to a bookseller seem almost obligatory as the origin or basis of authority of a printed work, and even as the sign of modernity. And so the final eighteenth-century edition of Defoe's *Tour thro' the Whole Island of Great Britain*, appearing in 1778, trumpets that modernity at every turn, from the streamlined typeface with reduced use of capitals and italics to the repetition of 'modern' or 'modernized' four times in the four-page preface to describe the text, the maps, and, of course, the 'modern geographical state of *Great Britain*' itself; yet it begins by anchoring its authority in 'the informations of gentlemen resident on, or in the neighbourhood of, the spots they have described', adding this resource to the accounts of 'travellers of independent fortunes' and to the 'assistance' of 'many of the first literary characters of the age, at the two universities, and in most capital towns'.[34]

If there is parasitism here, it may in fact be on the part of that supposedly weakened host, the circulating manuscript. For just as scribal publications were being credited with creating a tradition of Lake tour writing, the role of the print medium in creating the new taste for domestic travel was simultaneously being elided. Defoe's *Tour*, after all, first appeared in print in 1724–6 without the claimed assistance of gentleman-correspondents or even of a named and celebrated author; these features were added to the *Tour*'s paratexts in the 1742 and 1769 editions, respectively. Similarly, the role played by commercial print authors such as Thomas Amory, in his 1755–6 *Life of John Buncle, esq.*, in popularizing domestic tourism, and particularly tourism to the north-western counties, was lost to literary history. Amory's fiction alternates between accounts of utopian idylls established by beautiful, intelligent, Unitarian women, and appreciative, aestheticized descriptions of the narrator's travels in a wild, virtually unpopulated and uncharted Westmoreland which he describes as 'the most romantic and the most beautiful solitude in the world' (2.267). These descriptions were influential enough that a 1770 reviewer of Arthur Young's agricultural tour to the North, quoting at great length Young's description of a 'sublime' mountain scene, suddenly concludes, 'All this is very fine, but the painting is certainly too much in the style of John Buncle'.[35] Yet apart from Anna Letitia Barbauld's passing comment that Amory's book, which 'was much read, possibly contributed to spread that taste for lake and mountain scenery which has since been so prevalent' and the recent suggestion that Amory's style may have influenced Wordsworth's *Excursion*,[36] neither eighteenth-century nor much more recent accounts of the tradition of Lakes travel acknowledge this role. Was Amory's rarefied, romanticized style by some roundabout sequence of associations absorbed into manuscript travel writing, only to re-emerge as part of the aura of that writing itself, in the constructed 'tradition' of picturesque and sublime descriptions of the Lakes?[37]

Coterie culture under fire

A series of late 1770s attacks on manuscript exchange as a social phenomenon suggests that at least some print authors felt threatened by its continued cultural power.[38] Often these attacks reflect coterie publication's one-time role as a form of opposition discourse by associating it with the circulation of scandal manuscripts.[39] In Frances Brooke's 1777 novel *The Excursion*, for example, the representative target is a female writer of scandal, Lady Blast, but the critique is not a specifically gendered one – rather, the narrative portrays the power wielded by *'a certain set'* of wealthy, urbanized aristocrats, through the promiscuous circulation and publication in scandal magazines of authorless manuscript narratives, to destroy the social reputations of unsuspecting individuals. The narrator seeks to persuade the consumers of print to boycott such publications: 'It is in your power alone to restrain the growing evil, to turn the envenomed dart from the worthy breast. Cease to read, and the evil dies of itself: cease to purchase, and the venal calumniator will drop his useless pen'. The very urgency of the address, however, serves to affirm the extent to which the press has allowed itself to depend on such copy and readers have become addicted to the voyeuristic thrill of glimpsing manuscript material supposedly meant for restricted circulation.[40] A similar representation is that of the scandal club created by Richard Sheridan in his 1778 comedy *The School for Scandal*, whose 'circulate[d] ... Report[s]', especially when they reach the published papers, are the boasted cause of multiple broken matches, disinherited sons, 'forced Elopements', 'close confinements', 'separate maintenances', and divorces. Within the confines of the play, the club is ultimately exposed and rendered impotent, but the persistent power of scandal writing is affirmed by a framing prologue that mocks the 'Young Bard' who 'think[s] that He/Can Stop *the full Spring-tide* of Calumny'.[41]

As I have already noted, some critics have seen these satiric attacks as aimed at an easy target, as a sign of the anachronistic status of the coterie, but I would suggest that in their focus on a form of publication, they rather demonstrate that commercial authors could feel their own status or success challenged by the productions of such circles. My final example is located where such concern might be acutely felt: that of a woman writer in the literary profession. It has been noted that in the late seventeenth and early eighteenth centuries women might choose scribal publication of their work as a means of reinforcing or even enhancing their social and literary status, and of establishing a position of strength from which to approach print.[42] With the emergence of Bluestocking women as cultural leaders in the 1750s, the patronage power of such coteries, rather than declining, arguably became stronger than ever before, as demonstrated by the extensive support this group marshalled through letter-writing and word-of-mouth for subscription publications by Sarah Fielding, James Woodhouse, Ann Yearsley, and others. In the case of Hannah More, whose first play circulated extensively in manuscript for ten years and became her entrée into London society before it finally appeared in print in 1773, acceptance into this coterie launched her into the position of fame and influence she sought. But coming to the attention of this group could also have negative consequences. As I have argued in more detail elsewhere, the fact that novelist, translator, and critic Charlotte Lennox displeased the Bluestockings Catherine Talbot and Elizabeth Carter with the poem 'The Art of Coquetry', published at the start of her career, seems to have been detrimental in the long term to her earning ability and her reputation, despite the active support of Samuel Johnson, Andrew Millar, and Samuel Richardson, the positive response of reviewers, and her considerable print success. Thus Frances Burney, entering into Bluestocking circles in the late 1770s, discovered that, although Lennox had written novels which Burney judged to be 'far the best of any *Living* Author', 'her *Books* are generally approved, [but] Nobody likes *her*'.[43]

This context provides a suggestive backdrop to Burney's very critical treatment of a coterie literary circle in her play *The Witlings*, written and then suppressed in 1779. In *The Witlings*, a coterie circle called the 'Esprit Club', whose leader in several respects resembles the Bluestocking leader

Elizabeth Montagu, is less a source of scandal writing than a group with pretensions to literary production and to leadership in critical taste. The Club is portrayed as a ridiculous vestige, playing coy games of scribal circulation – 'if you'll promise not to take a Copy, I think I'll venture to trust you with the manuscript – but you must be sure not to shew it a single Soul' – but in fact lost in a wilderness of print, struggling to maintain some semblance of originality and authority in a cultural field dominated by the poetic reputations of Pope, Swift, and Gay. Thus the amateur poet Dabler, informed that his wish for a short memory has already been expressed somewhere, 'either in Pope or Swift', laments: 'I've just finished an Epigram on that very Subject! I protest I shall grow more and more sick of Books every Day, for I can never look into any, but I'm sure of popping upon something of my own'.[44] This unthreatening characterization of the coterie is belied, however, not only by the severity of the satire, but also by Burney's acquiescence in her advisors' decision that the play ought to be suppressed. By contrast, when Burney needed to maximize her profits from the sale of her 1796 novel *Camilla*, she turned to her Bluestocking contacts to keep books of subscription receipts for her, resulting in the largest English novel subscription to that date.[45] The Brooke, Sheridan, Lennox, and Burney examples together suggest that even seasoned and well-known print authors felt the need to remain alert to, and if possible, contain and harness, the cultural power of a group that circulated its views through oral and manuscript means, and through these means also held a certain sway over the printing press and the reading consumer.

Yet these prickly representations of scribal practices coincide precisely, not only with the 1778 *Tour thro' the Whole Island of Great Britain* in its association of gentlemen's travel manuscripts with modernity, but also with the appearance of the first volumes of John Bell's *Poets of Great Britain* and the rival *Works of the English Poets* for which Johnson wrote his biographical and critical prefaces, events Ezell describes as definitively establishing 'all the mechanisms for the presentation of bulk literature to a consuming public', and thereby firmly placing literature into the category of commercial commodity to be purchased and consumed rather than, as in the social authorship model, created and sustained.[46] Such highly commercialized publications promise, as both Barbara Benedict and Leah Price have noted, writing that has been authorized by the best judges, offering entertainment and utility, and thereby participation in national literary culture, to a broadly inclusive audience.[47] And in 1780, the poet John Duncombe appealed in *The Gentleman's Magazine* to James Dodsley to improve his brother's

Collection of Poems by providing the names of the many unnamed authors, while another contributor, 'J. W'., proposed the revision of the collection to gather up the 'Many pieces, not inferior in poetical merit, [which] are handed about in manuscript at both our universities, and in other parts of the kingdom', in order to 'be rescued from their present obscurity'.[48] Although 'J. W'. allows that individual printed pieces might be suffering a similar fate, this conjunction of events suggests to me that with the late 1770s, the desire of middle-class consumers for access to literary culture was shifting the balance from the manuscript, with its intimacy, flexibility, and social embeddedness, to the book, with its ability to preserve, order, and transmit across social and geographic boundaries.

Thus the next chapter in the history of manuscript-print relations, the 'intense bookishness' of the late eighteenth and early nineteenth centuries to which this volume's editors refer, would reflect a growing confidence in print, specifically in the book, as the cultural archive, as well as the increasing organization of literature around 'celebrated', and ultimately canonized, authors. As my case studies have suggested, this development was furthered, rather than hindered, by the dissemination of the values of coterie culture through their representation in print. Ironically, in this new dynamic, the manuscripts and mere autographs of these select authors took on symbolic and commercial value through their source in the originating author, their 'aura' heightened even as their functionality in a system of social authorship was reduced.[49] It might also be hypothesized that the early collaborative writing practices of the Romantic author Samuel Coleridge were self-conscious efforts to reconstitute the sort of coterie context for poetic creation that was now most often experienced at one remove, through the printed book.[50] For as my argument has sought to demonstrate, the ongoing vitality of manuscript culture in the third quarter of the eighteenth century at once nurtured, and was sustained by, a book trade that in the process learned to market the insider access, approved taste, and elegance-by-association signified by scribal publication.

Notes

I wish to thank Victoria Burke, Heather Ladd, Michelle Levy, the participants in the Bookish History conference, the editors of this volume, and the Palgrave readers for their helpful suggestions in my development of this argument.

1. Donald H. Reiman devotes an entire study to what he designates as 'modern manuscripts' – those originating in the period of print dominance, between the beginning of printing in the late fifteenth century and the shift to

electronic modes of text transmission in about 1975 (*The Study of Modern Manuscripts: Public, Confidential, and Private* [Baltimore: Johns Hopkins UP, 1993]). In *Social Authorship and the Advent of Print* (Baltimore: Johns Hopkins UP, 1999), Margaret J. M. Ezell argues that 'the older notion of the text as a dynamic and collaborative process coexisted [with a proprietary view of authorship based in print technology] well into the mid-eighteenth century' (p. 141); for Ezell, 'By denying the significance of script authorship, manuscript circles, and social texts, we have in the name of democracy [associated with print] apparently disenfranchised the participation of the majority of the literate population of the period' (p. 102). In her view, the definitive shift to print did not occur until the emergence of the marketed literary series (eg. Bell's *British Poets*, 1777–89, and the London-based *The English Poets* with Johnson's prefaces, 1779–81) in the late 1770s. However, she does not discuss any cases of social authorship beyond the 1730s. See also George L. Justice and Nathan Tinker's edited collection *Women's Writing and the Circulation of Ideas* (Cambridge: Cambridge UP, 2002), particularly the essays by Leigh A. Eicke on Jane Barker, Kathryn R. King on Elizabeth Rowe, Isobel Grundy on Lady Mary Wortley Montagu, and George Justice on Frances Burney, which collectively imply a case for some sort of ongoing scribal practices in the eighteenth century. In more general terms, Nicholas Barker has argued that manuscript culture itself did not exist until it became an alternative to participation in print exchange during the sixteenth century; it then took shape as 'a new kind of communication, linking writers with readers through a system of diffusion, that all its participants cultivated to serve complex and sometimes conflicting ends' (Nicholas Barker, 'In Praise of Manuscripts', in *Form and Meaning in the History of the Book: Selected Essays* (London: British Library, 2003), p. 27).

2. Justice, for example, in his discussion of the suppression of Frances Burney's *The Witlings*, applies the term 'anachronistic' to the coterie culture Burney is satirizing, though it is not entirely clear whether for him that culture is *indeed* so, or whether Burney is attempting to make it *appear* a thing of the past ('Suppression and Censorship in Late Manuscript Culture: Frances Burney's Unperformed *The Witlings*', in Justice and Tinker, eds, pp. 201–22); see my discussion of *The Witlings* below. Harold Love sees manuscript circulation as increasingly devalued from the reign of George I onward, and as 'aberrant' from at least 1800, because of an increasing association of print publication with a required standard of quality; 'What was kept in manuscript was increasingly what lacked the quality required for print publication' (*Scribal Publication in Seventeenth-Century England* [Oxford: Clarendon, 1993], p. 288).

3. Two quick examples might be the juxtaposition of a reading of Home's printed play *Douglas* with the manuscript letters of Sidney Bidulph to her friend Cecilia, as the narrative frame of Frances Sheridan's novel *The Memoirs of Miss Sidney Bidulph* (1761) and Edmund Burke's representation of his *Reflections on the Revolution in France* in the form of *A Letter Intended to Have Been Sent to a Gentleman in Paris* (1789). In Burney's 1778 *Evelina*, on the other hand, the public discovery of manuscript verses praising the heroine above all the women at Bristol brings nothing but embarrassment and misunderstanding. The verses are purportedly written by the heroine's

mysterious, romantic, but unstable acquaintance McCartney. This portrayal is congruent with Burney's consistently and assertively negative stance toward manuscript culture, discussed below.

4. Love, p. 36–9.
5. Love, p. 83.
6. These terms are used by Ezell (*Social Authorship*), Love (in Chapter 7 only), and Reiman, respectively.
7. Ezell, *Social Authorship*, p. 16. Ezell's most developed example is that of Alexander Pope. See also King's study of Rowe's publishing practices throughout her writing career, concluding with the extremely successful print publication in 1728 of *Friendship in Death*, which 'shows Mrs. Rowe, in the last decade of her life, seeking to re-enter the marketplace of print from within the protected precincts of the feminine manuscript networks she had cultivated since the 1690s' ('Elizabeth Singer Rowe's Tactical Use of Print and Manuscript', in Justice and Tinker, eds, p. 169).
8. Love, pp.199–200; 189; 282; Ezell, 'Posthumous Publication', p. 130.
9. This observation is central to my argument, despite Ezell's objection that it is dismissive to view 'non-commercial texts as "aristocratic", "amateur", and "vulnerable"' (*Social Authorship*, p. 17).
10. Michael F. Suarez, SJ, 'Trafficking in the Muse: Dodsley's *Collection of Poems* and the Question of Canon', in *Tradition in Transition: Women Writers, Marginal Texts and the Eighteenth-Century Canon*, ed. Alvaro Ribiero, SJ, and James G. Basker (Oxford: Clarendon, 1996), pp. 297–313.
11. Ian A. Gordon, *Shenstone's Miscellany 1759–1763* (Oxford: Clarendon, 1952), p. xii; Suarez comments on this over-estimation in the Introduction to his 1997 facsimile edition of the *Collection of Poems by Several Hands* (London: Routledge/Thoemmes, 1997), pp. 33–4.
12. Principal members of these circles were Richard Jago, Richard Graves, Anthony Whistler, Lady Luxborough, William Somervile, George Lyttleton, John Scott Hylton, John Pixell, a Miss White (later Pixell's wife), and later in life, Robert Dodsley, Joseph Spence, and Thomas Percy.
13. Suarez has, by contrast, emphasized the poems in these three volumes which were reprinted from Dodsley's then-defunct periodicals *The Museum, Philomel*, and the *Public Register* ('Trafficking', p. 307).
14. See James E. Tierney, ed., *The Correspondence of Robert Dodsley 1733–1764* (Cambridge: Cambridge UP, 1988), pp. 115–16 n3.
15. See, for example, *Correspondence*, pp. 171–2. In a related case, Dodsley is able to supply only nine of 15 names when Shenstone asks to know the authors of a number of poems in the *Collection's* fourth volume (*Correspondence*, pp. 198–9).
16. Richard Jago writes, 'I am sensible, Sir, how advantageous Mr. Shenstone's Recommendation is, and that it is no inconsiderable Compliment to be admitted to a Place in a Collection under so judicious a Compiler: At the same Time Sir, You must permit me to claim such an Interest in my own, as to give my Consent both to the Dress, and the Manner of its Insertion,' to which Dodsley replies that he thought Jago had been informed of the submissions, which have already been printed off (*Correspondence* pp. 298, 301–2). Richard Graves, by contrast, writes with gratitude of Shenstone 'endeavouring to rescue more of my Rhymes from utter Oblivion', worries

about exposing himself to the public, then decides he is 'safe in the Hands of a Person of your Judgment & Character', but asks 'to know, in one Line, what particular Piece or Pieces of mine, you have honour'd wth yr approbation' (*Correspondence*, p. 336).

17. See *Correspondence*, pp.230, 233, 265f, 274 for references to the circulation of Dodsley's tragedy *Cleone* and his poem *Melpomene*.

18. Ezell has argued that posthumous publications tended to claim that the author's friends would recognize the printed text's fidelity to the manuscript and the author, thereby suggesting that such publications were viewed as extensions of manuscript culture, rather than repudiations of it ('The Posthumous Publication of Women's Manuscripts and the History of Authorship', in Justice and Tinker, eds, pp. 128–9). This view matches that of John Pixell, one of Shenstone's coterie connections, about the posthumous Shenstone edition published by Dodsley; he writes, 'You have certainly done your utmost to hand [the Writings of Mr Shenstone] down to Posterity in the most elegant manner, which must be esteem'd as the highest Instance of your friendly Zeal for his Fame & Reputation' (*Correspondence*, p. 487).

19. Suarez, 'Trafficking', p. 312. In an illuminating study of the eighteenth-century literary collection, Barbara Benedict has elected to treat the anthology and the miscellany as one form, arguing that distinctions between the former's focus on previously published material 'selected for consistency and quality' and the latter's compilation of new and more heterogeneous material were at the time not only blurred, but insignificant from the perspective of the reader who turned to these for '"dip, sip, and skip"' reading ('The Paradox of the Anthology: Collecting and *Différence* in Eighteenth-Century Britain', *New Literary History*, 34 [2003], 231–56). From the perspective of production rather than reception, however, the miscellany's association with a more informal gathering of scattered materials is a genealogically important one, linking it to a culture of scribal circulation.

20. Graves's response to Shenstone's thoughts of having Baskerville print a volume of his own elegies articulates a more print-culture-oriented view: 'I told him It would give him the Air of a *local* Author – & that for my part, I should not have so high an opinion of any Production, that did not make its first appearance in the Metropolis – And I believe there are many people that have the same prejudice – It puts one in mind of one Doughty's *country* Sermon – preach'd in a *country* Church – & published at ye request of a *Country* Congregation' (*Correspondence*, p.408). Baskerville himself made the occasional foray into scribal publication; John Hylton writes to Dodsley of 'a very sensible and smart Letter in vindication of himself', in response to a local aspersion of his character, 'which is shown about privately' (*Correspondence*, p. 261).

21. Marjorie Williams, ed. *The Letters of William Shenstone* (Oxford: Blackwell, 1939), p. 503. The sensitive Jago had earlier protested Shenstone's submission of his poems to Dodsley without permission, as discussed above. It is noteworthy that of the poets Shenstone names here, at least Landsdowne was known principally as a coterie poet. For a fuller discussion of Shenstone's careful production of this manuscript, see Gordon's introduction to his edition of the miscellany.

22. Love, pp. 288–93.

23. It might in fact be possible to draw a line of authorial descent from elite coterie circles including writers such as Anne Finch, Elizabeth Rowe, and Lady Hertford, through Lady Luxborough and George Lyttleton, to Shenstone. Relevant here is J.G.A. Pocock's account of a shift in the defining components of a gentleman's identity from property, leisure, and public engagement to commerce, leisure, and cultivation ('The Mobility of Property and the Rise of Eighteenth-Century Sociology', in *Virtue, Commerce, and History: Essays on Political Thought and History, Chiefly in the Eighteenth Century* [Cambridge: Cambridge UP, 1985], pp. 103–23).

24. See, for example, *Correspondence* 424–6 regarding Joseph Spence's description of Persfield after a visit there.

25. Williams, *William Shenstone and His Friends* (London: The English Association, 1933), p. 9 (although critics now might question the progressivist bias of Williams' assessment of Shenstone as 'far ahead of the Augustans' in his criticism); Gordon, pp. xi–xii, xvii–xviii.

26. I am not suggesting that Shenstone proceeded along a developmental trajectory from manuscript to print: in fact, as I have already indicated, while communicating with Dodsley late in his life about publishing his elegies, he was simultaneously preparing a manuscript miscellany by multiple authors, of which Dodsley appears not to have been aware, and which posthumously became part of Percy's library. Ian A. Gordon's account, in his 1952 edition of the miscellany, of its compilation, composition, and reception by Percy illustrates the typical scribal-culture features of the project.

27. Benedict, 'The Paradox', p. 234.

28. Walter Benjamin, 'The Work of Art in the Age of Mechanical Reproduction', *Illuminations*, ed. Hannah Arendt and trans. Harry Zohn (NY: Harcourt Brace and World, 1968), pp. 217–50.

29. Many critical accounts of the growth in popularity of the Lakes tour refer to the posthumous publication in 1767 of the prose portion of this letter as the point of departure; see, for example, Esther Moir, *The Discovery of Britain: The English Tourists, 1540–1840* (London: Routledge and Kegan Paul, 1964), p. 139. For evidence of the manuscript influence of the letter, see Donald D. Eddy, 'John Brown: 'The Columbus of Keswick', *Modern Philology* 73.4, Part 2: A Supplement to Honor Arthur Friedman (1976): S74–S84.

30. Thomas Gray, *A catalogue of the antiquities, houses, parks, plantations, scenes, and situations in England and Wales, arranged according to the alphabetical order of the several counties* (London, 1773), pp. iii–v, emphases mine.

31. Thomas Gray, *A supplement to the tour through Great-Britain, containing a catalogue of the antiquities, houses, parks, plantations, ... by the late Mr. Gray, ... To which are now added, by another hand, several additions* (London, 1787), pp. iv–v. Even here, the text retains an aura of secrecy regarding 'another Hand' which, we are told, has made 'Several Additions' (the hand is thought to have been that of Horace Walpole); blank spaces again are provided, at the end of the volume, 'to enable every Traveller or Reader to make his own Remarks or Corrections' (title page).

32. Thomas Pennant, *A tour in Scotland. MDCCLXIX* (Chester, 1771), 287; *The additions to the quarto edition of the Tour in Scotland, MDCCLXIX. And the new appendix. Reprinted for the accomodation of the purchasers of the first and second editions* (London, 1774), p. iii; *A tour in Scotland, and voyage to the Hebrides; MDCCLXXII* (Chester, 1774), iii.

33. Pennant, *A Tour in Scotland; and Voyage to the Hebrides; MDCCLXXII*, p. ii.
34. Daniel Defoe, *A Tour thro' the Whole Island of Great Britain*, 8th edn (London: Strahan et al., 1778), vol. 1, n.p.
35. *The Monthly Review* 42 (April 1770), 263.
36. Anna Letitia Barbauld, Introduction to *The British Novelists*; James Mulvihill, 'Amory's *John Buncle* and Wordsworth's *Excursion*', *Notes and Queries*, 235 (1990), 25–6.
37. Ironically, the 'sequel' to *John Buncle*, the anonymous 1776 *John Buncle, Junior, Gentleman*, displays an insistently print-media consciousness, devoting its first 80 pages to lengthy discussions between the narrator and a bookseller about title pages, editions, and dedications. It is as though, with the increased tensions surrounding the manuscript-print interface that I discuss in the next section, this spurious continuation jettisons the coterie trappings of the rural idyll and enthusiastic tour in favour of a firm alignment with print technology, retaining nothing but the claim to having been produced by a gentleman.
38. An even earlier satiric treatment occurs in Oliver Goldsmith's 1766 *Vicar of Wakefield*, where two ladies of the town, posing as aristocrats, discuss privately circulated verses as well as contributions to the *Lady's Magazine*. In this case, however, the prostitutes are mimicking aristocratic refinement, and the butt of the satire would seem to be the Primrose family's inability to distinguish false gentility from true.
39. George Justice, in his discussion of Burney's *The Witlings*, observes this association of later eighteenth-century coterie writing with scandal (pp. 217–20), extrapolating from Love's emphasis on scribal publication as the vehicle of lampoons and oppositional writing (Love, pp. 209–10, 279–81).
40. Frances Brooke, *The Excursion*, ed. Paula R. Backscheider and Hope D. Cotton (Lexington, KY: Univ. Press of Kentucky, 1997), pp. 19–20; 118. Brooke's novel concludes, not with the heroine's successful London production of her tragedy, but with a return to a select country coterie that will mount productions of her manuscript tragedies for its own pleasure. It would seem that, as a peripheral member of Shenstone's social network, Brooke was prepared to endorse his social mode of authorship as a way out of the danger that arises when a limited coterie readership is replaced by an uninformed, yet debased urban audience. However, the focus of her commentary at this point is not print publication, but the despotic theatrical government of David Garrick.
41. Richard Brinsley Sheridan, *The School for Scandal* in Vol. 1 of *The Dramatic Works of Richard Brinsley Sheridan*, 2 vols, ed. Cecil Price (Oxford: Clarendon, 1973), pp. 359; 356; emphasis in original.
42. See King's analysis of Rowe's career, cited above.
43. Betty A. Schellenberg, *The Professionalization of Women Writers in Eighteenth-Century Britain* (Cambridge: Cambridge UP, 2005), pp. 166–70; 173–4; Frances Burney, *The Early Journals and Letters of Frances Burney, Vol. III: The Streatham Years, Part I (1778–1779)*, ed. Lars E. Troide and Stewart J. Cooke (Montreal and Kingston: McGill-Queens University Press, 1994), pp. 105–6 (emphasis in original).
44. Frances Burney, *The Witlings* in Vol. 1 of *The Complete Plays of Frances Burney*, 2 vols, ed. Peter Sabor, contributing editor Geoffrey M. Sill (Montreal and Kingston: McGill-Queen's UP, 1995), Act 2, ll. 323–5; 187; 190–3.

45. Peter Sabor, Introduction to *The Subscription List to Frances Burney's 'Camilla'* (Montreal: Burney Centre and Burney Society, 2003), pp. 12–13.
46. Ezell, *Social Authorship*, p. 131.
47. Barbara M. Benedict, *Making the Modern Reader: Cultural Mediation in Early Modern Anthologies* (Princeton: Princeton UP, 1996), and Leah Price, *The Anthology and the Rise of the Novel: From Richardson to George Eliot* (Cambridge: Cambridge UP, 2000), especially chapter 2, 'Cultures of the Commonplace'.
48. Quoted by Suarez in his Introduction to the *Collection of Poems*, pp. 74–5.
49. Reiman lists the growing interest in authorial autographs and manuscripts, as well as the nostalgia for ancient manuscripts, as characteristic of the meaning of manuscripts in the Romantic era (pp. 24–6).
50. For a discussion of Coleridge's early idealization of collaborative authorship set within an intimate social context see Michelle Levy's 'Coleridge, Manuscript Culture, and the Family Romance', in *Family Authorship and Romantic Print Culture* (Basingstoke: Palgrave Macmillan, 2008), pp. 45–69.

11
The Practice and Poetics of Curlism: Print, Obscenity, and the *Merryland* Pamphlets in the Career of Edmund Curll

Thomas Keymer

Samuel Johnson was not thinking of scandalous usages like 'Curlism' when he lamented that, even as his great dictionary of 1755 was being printed, 'some words are budding, and some falling away'.[1] Yet this eloquent eighteenth-century term (with 'Curlicism', the jeeringly ornamented version favoured by Daniel Defoe) is a good enough instance of the mutability he regretted. A malicious coinage that was recognized by everyone in the Grubstreet milieu of Johnson's early career, 'Curlism' was now already fading from the language, even though its inspiring figure, the flamboyant bookseller-publisher Edmund Curll, had been dead for less than a decade. The word could still be used without explanation a generation later ('I know the art of Curlism, pretty well', writes Thomas Chatterton in 1770[2]), and the phenomenon flourished for longer still, albeit without the gleeful panache of its first and greatest exponent. But one looks up 'Curlism' in vain in Johnson's or any other dictionary of the period,[3] and later lexicographers ignored the term. Even the inhibition-free *OED Online*, which cites Curll himself just twice (as the earliest source for two entirely characteristic locutions, 'onanism' and 'onanist'), yields no results. 'Bowdlerism' survives from the lexicon of pre-Victorian publishing to denote prudish expurgation; Curlism, which typically involved the opposite, does not.

Yet Curll was an unforgettable man, and one whose brazen professional practices epitomized, for Pope, Swift, and lesser critics of commercial modernity in the eighteenth century, everything that was morally deplorable and culturally corrosive in the thriving book trade of the day. It was this Scriblerian view that prevailed after Curll's death, and for the next two centuries literary scholars and book historians were more or less content to settle for the terse recommendation of his first obituarist. 'Yesterday died ... Mr. Edmund Curl, Bookseller, in Rose-Street,

Covent-Garden', reported the *General Evening Post*: 'His Character may be found in Pope's and Swift's Works'.[4] This willingness to let Curll's posthumous reputation be defined by his fiercest adversaries does no real injustice in human terms, not only because Curll was quite as cynical, shameless, and exploitative as Pope alleges, but also because his characteristic response to defamation was not denial; instead he embraced it as a compliment, to be regretted only if it understated his impudence or guile. In this context, the goal of the present chapter is not rehabilitation, though I also argue that, especially as Curll's career went on, the practices and postures to which his enemies objected became a matter of self-conscious performance – even, as Chatterton's wording implies, a calculated form of art. In everything from his sly and fantastic title pages to his unabashed defiance in the pillory, Curll's presence in the public arena was an act of self-fashioning no less ingenious than Pope's or Sterne's, and it demands a certain appreciation. 'Curlism' was above all an art of effrontery, and to retrieve its defining routines is to find in Curll a fitting adversary for the impressive list of authors who lined up to attack him: not only Pope, his fellow Scriblerians, and their allies at the *Grub-street Journal*, but also other prominent figures such as Defoe and (more genially) Fielding. By focusing on key instances of Curll's publishing activities, and on contemporary representations of and objections to these activities, I hope to restore 'Curlism' to view as a distinctive and scandalous set of book-trade practices at the time, and as a category worth reviving as a tool for measuring the norms and limits of eighteenth-century print culture, particularly with reference to the questions about commercial ethics, literary property, and obscene publication that Curll's career conspicuously raises.

By his own (of course unreliable) account, Curll was born in the west country in 1683, and in an early publication he implicitly claimed kinship with Bishop Walter Curll of Winchester, a distinguished cleric who had been ejected for his royalist allegiance in the 1640s.[5] The truth may have been more prosaic, but like much else Curll's personal background remains obscure, and the main source for his early life is a malevolent biography of 1745 that details various Shandean misadventures, including a botched circumcision, and offers copious back-handed praise of a proleptic kind. 'He shew'd an early Inclination to Letters, and Plagiarism', alleges 'J. H.', the otherwise unidentified supporter of Pope who penned this attack: 'But his early Love of Bawdry, &c. was what was even more remarkable'.[6]

Curll entered the London book trade at an opportune moment, a few years after the system of precensorship that had unevenly regulated the seventeenth-century press at last collapsed in 1695, and a decade or so before the first effective copyright statute was passed in 1710. He never became a member of the Worshipful Company of Stationers, a body of ongoing prestige but declining authority that had lost its ability to exert monopoly power. Nor was he ever a member of any of the congers, more or less stable consortia of leading bookseller-publishers who would pool resources in major ventures: so called, a contemporary alleged, 'because as a large conger eel is said to devour the small fry, so this united body overpowers young and single traders'.[7] Sometimes the younger traders would bite back, and Curll's special genius was to operate as predator and parasite at once, always for his own ends, though often also in short-term tactical partnerships and alliances that spread the cost of new projects while also, where necessary (as it often was), disguising or deflecting attention from his own role. By 1706 he was operating as an independent bookseller, and several of his early successes involved piracy of previously printed material, unauthorized publication of stolen manuscripts, and false attribution of unrelated material to marketable names – though sometimes the authors and booksellers concerned (leading figures like Matthew Prior and his bookseller Jacob Tonson) could take advantage of Curll's depredations as pretexts for decently bringing out new authorized editions.[8] This kind of manoeuvre was used most elaborately by Pope, decades later, to elicit from Curll a pretext to publish an official version of his own correspondence,[9] and it illustrates an enduring pattern of uneasy symbiosis or hidden reciprocity between Curll and more respectable branches of the trade. In this context we should check whatever temptation we might feel to polarize book-trade identities into simple, opposing categories of legitimate or illegitimate, high or low, or to construct narratives of absolute or constant enmity between Curll and those who reviled him. Across the span of his career as a whole, there can be few leading book-trade professionals in London who did not at one time or another, in some way or another, collaborate knowingly with Curll, and his close association with ambiguous, undiscriminating figures such as James Roberts, four times Master of the Stationers' Company but also a regular and willing front for dubious Curll publications, meant that even fewer could operate at more than one degree of separation from him.

As Curll's business position strengthened during the reign of Queen Anne, his early reliance on partnerships diminished, but he had collaborated with at least forty other members of the trade by 1714, and it is from this point that the distinctive lineaments of 'Curlism' become most visible. Paul Baines and Pat Rogers track the minutiae of his career in their superb recent biography, cutting their way with expert vigilance through the maze of obscure, misleading, and often downright fraudulent imprints that have hitherto shrouded their subject. They promise a follow-up volume in due course, 'a full analytic bibliography of more than 1,000 books associated with Curll'.[10] In this ambition lies Curll's apotheosis, yet also in a sense his defeat, for a full bibliography will at once reveal his true importance in publishing history while also overcoming his lifelong project of subterfuge and mystification. It is also an ambition that needs guarded expression, for mere 'association' may still be the only link that can safely be drawn between Curll and much of his output.

Curlism displayed

So what was Curlism, exactly? The simple answer is anything emanating from, associated with, or even just faintly reminiscent of the publishing output and business ethics of a figure whose reputation for sharp and shameless practice has never been eclipsed. For a better answer, the character of Bookweight in Fielding's comedy *The Author's Farce* (1730) is a good place to start, and Bookweight's hack-filled establishment in the play was widely recognized at the time (though Thomas Lockwood adds caveats to the identification) as a satire on Curll's notorious 'Literatory', a sweatshop for the mass production of worthless textual commodities.[11] Here ignorant scribblers and penniless dunces translate Virgil out of prior translations, thrash tedious verses out of dictionaries of rhyme, and manufacture or prolong pointless controversies simply to sell more print. Fielding resumed his mockery in the *Champion* a decade later, accumulating over time a comic anatomy of Curlism and its distinctive gestures and ruses: the bogus attributions, the fictitious title pages, the plagiarisms and thefts, the comprehensive suspension of all integrity, sincerity, and taste. But Fielding also betrays a hint of relish for the shameless brio of Curll's operations, including his goading of the Pope circle by publishing spurious sequels with titles like *One Thousand Seven Hundred Thirty Nine* and numerous works by a writer with the suspicious name of 'Joseph Gay'. Also noted by Fielding is Curll's instant but poisonous responsiveness to any opportunity: 'Several Mushroom, or rather Toadstool Performances have sprouted up ... in the Nursery of one Mr. *Kurl* a Gardener'.[12]

Somewhat oddly, amidst all this, Fielding ignores the relentless and increasingly imaginative obscenity that had been at the core of Curll's output since such prurient early publications as *The Case of Sodomy,* in the *Tryal of Mervin Lord Audley, Earl of Castlehaven* and *The Case of John Atherton, Bishop of Waterford in Ireland; Who Was Convicted of the Sin of Uncleanness with a Cow, and Other Creatures* (both 1710).[13] Later publications linger on a more exotic range of proclivities, and as time went on there were few niches in the market for pornography to which Curll failed to cater, from plain vanilla (*The Pleasures of Coition*, 1721) to religiously inflected lesbianism (*Venus in the Cloister; or, The Nun in Her Smock*, 1724) and early modern S&M (*A Treatise of the Use of Flogging in Venereal Affairs*, 1718).[14] Crucially, Fielding also passes by the transparent, or at least diaphanous, pose of righteous indignation that Curll typically used to veil, while also somehow spicing further, his most lubricious publications. He certainly noticed the technique, however, and beyond Curll's own output there are few better examples of Curlism in the period than Fielding's own catchpenny pamphlet of 1746, *The Female Husband*, which documents and condemns, in salacious detail, a true-life case of lesbian imposture and bigamy. Covertly published (but eventually acknowledged) by Andrew Millar, 'the Maecenas of the age', this pamphlet also demonstrates the permeation of Curlism into the publishing mainstream.[15]

It was *Onanism Display'd* (1718), an insalubrious pamphlet that seven years later Curll claimed to have sold '*with universal Approbation, thro' nine Editions of* 2000 *each*',[16] that lured Defoe into a torrent of outright denunciation and unguarded free publicity in the pages of *Mist's Weekly Journal*. In the midst of it, he coined a promotional label that Curll then coolly embraced in his published response, *Curlicism Display'd* (1718). Writing with unusual loss of control (Defoe scholars have suspected collusion with Curll, though Baines and Rogers offer convincing evidence of real and enduring hostility), Defoe rails against the 'verbal Lewdness' and '*printed Bestiality*' of the modern press, and lays responsibility at the door of a vividly described individual:

> From him the Crime takes the just Denomination of *Curlicism*: The Fellow is a contemptible Wretch a thousand Ways: he is odious in his Person, scandalous in His Fame, he is mark'd by Nature, for he has a bawdy Countenance, and a debauch'd Mein, his Tongue is an Echo of all the beastly Language his Shop is fill'd with, and Filthiness drivels in the very Tone of his Voice.[17]

Defoe misses nothing here except the squint that notoriously afflicted Curll, and marked, for other critics, the slyness and mobility of a publishing operation that glanced in all directions at once, but never met or returned an honest gaze. For one minor antagonist, Curll 'would look *nine Ways at once* ... and tell you as many L – – s into the Bargain'; another noted his recklessness in the face of danger, who 'looking nine Ways couldst not spy | What might be seen with half an Eye'.[18]

Other writers had personal reasons for joining the attack on Curll and Curlism, above all Pope, whose decades-long feud with Curll did more than anything to fix the latter's image for posterity, and Pope's fellow Scriblerians Swift and Arbuthnot, whose response to another trademark Curll genre, the instant posthumous biography, was to proclaim the publisher 'one of the new terrors of Death'.[19] For Pope and his allies at the *Grub-street Journal*, Curlism meant not only smut but also towering hypocrisy, as manifest in ruses such as the use of affected denunciation to promote and renew an existing illicit success. By 1727, another satirist could write that 'every Body is now acquainted with *Curlism*, or the Tricks which Booksellers put upon the World, in order to raise their Market',[20] and over the next few years these tricks were scathingly anatomized in the *Grub-street Journal*, beginning with a letter to the journal in which 'Kirleus' claims (with little exaggeration of Curll's authentic voice) that 'the mystery of bookselling has been carried to a greater height by me, than by any, either of my Predecessors or Contemporaries'. All his devices and activities – the fake imprints, the bogus attributions, the cheap piracies – have worked 'to the great advancement of learning and knowledge', Kirleus claims, and his selfless efforts have always been for the same of 'extending the liberty of the press, the source of all our other liberties'. Later issues of the *Grub-street Journal* resume this attack, playing especially on the term 'Literatory' (a name Curll coined for the ambitious new premises he opened in 1729) to represent his establishment as a production line of sweated hack labour. In one paper, 'your Literatory is a lively representation in miniature, of three famous Hospitals, St. Bartholomew's, Bridewell, and Bedlam'. Elsewhere, an engraving represents Curll as a grotesquely squinting devil who prints off casuistry and pornography ('Cases of Impotency', 'Cases of Conscience') with no discrimination of value. The accompanying text describes 'a particular bookseller, stripped of all his false ornaments of puffs, advertisements, and title pages ... putting up his own and other peoples copies, books, some of pious devotions, others of lewd diversion, in his literatory' (**Plate 1**).[21]

All these insinuations, like those of Fielding, take their cue from *The Dunciad*. But Pope handled Curll with a malicious creative surplus that was all his own, and the locus classicus of anti-Curll lampooning is certainly the richly annotated footrace in Book II of *The Dunciad Variorum*,

Curl's 'Literatory' as seen in the _Grub-street Journal_ 147 (26 October 1732). Courtesy, The Lilly Library, Indiana University, Bloomington, Indiana.

where Curll slithers on the residue of his mistress's chamber-pot with results that recall (beyond the mock-heroic echo of Ajax) how Curll's forays into the gutter had returned to haunt him: 'Obscene with filth the Miscreant lies bewray'd, | Fal'n in the plash his wickedness had lay'd'.[22] Here and elsewhere, Pope's satire insistently associates 'Curl's chaste press' – the irony suggests not only obscene output but also promiscuous origins and prostituted standards – with bodily effluvia and excreta, and he famously enacted the allegation by slipping Curll an emetic in a tavern and then detailing the prank in a gloating pamphlet. With his characteristic ability to bounce back unabashed from punishment and humiliation, Curll later described the episode himself in *The Curliad* (1729), a virtuoso display of literary chutzpah written in counter-attack against *The Dunciad Variorum*; better still, in 1735 he provocatively renamed his establishment 'Pope's Head', with shop-sign effigy to match, so retaliating against the emetic and later attacks with a symbolic decapitation.[23]

But Curll was far too mercurial a figure, and far too clever an entrepreneur, to confine himself to a single market. Many of his publications escape the stereotype promoted by Pope and his allies, and not only because an output of such prodigious extent could hardly fail to include the occasional respectable item. He was a genuinely enthusiastic antiquarian who helped research some of the studies he published (his robust notes survive from a tour of Oxfordshire churches, where he met 'Mr. Tuder of Checkendon, Rich Large, Lame, Lecherous and Impertinent'), and he was handsomely credited by John Nichols in the nineteenth century 'for his Industry in preserving our National Remains'.[24] Although he was often guilty of political posturing – a characteristic nicely caught in the *Grub-street Journal* passage about literary piracy as English liberty – there was also something of substance in the anti-ministerial attitudes he struck. He could worry as much about his efforts to revive the poetry and political prose of Andrew Marvell as about his latest exercise in scandal, and it may well be that his promotion of Marvell's republicanism was among the activities that landed him in trouble in the mid 1720s. In his Preface to *The Case of Seduction: Being, An Account of the Late Proceedings ... against the Reverend Abbée, Claudius Nicholas des Rues, for Committing Rapes upon 133 Virgins* (1725), he voices anxiety 'lest this FACTUM for Abbée *des Rues*, and the Revival of MARVELL's *Works*, should *heap more Coals of Fire upon my Head*', and then adds defiantly that 'as to the Principles of MARVELL I will avow them *while I have any Being*'.[25] A characteristic red herring, perhaps, but also a reminder, just as Walpole was strengthening his hold on power, that

Curll did more than anyone before Thomas Hollis in the 1760s to keep alive Marvell's posthumous reputation as a writer of oppositional prose, and incidentally as a poet.

Curll's intertwining of seduction and sedition as transgressive threads of his output was a feature targeted and exploited by the authorities, and his belated prosecution for publishing pornographic titles including *Venus in the Cloister* was largely a proxy, as Baines and Rogers authoritatively show, for his publication of politically embarrassing memoirs by John Crawford, alias Ker, a double agent between Walpole's ministry and the Jacobite court. Here Baines and Rogers reassert and clarify a longstanding assumption recently challenged by Alexander Pettit, who argues that in the eyes of the prosecuting authorities Ker's *Memoirs* were 'an additional irritant, nothing more', and that *Venus in the Cloister* cried out for punishment because its erotic content 'neutralizes masculine power while positing lesbianism as unbound by rigid models of power', so transgressing conventions and limits that made other pornography tolerable.[26] This ingenious reading of the offending text notwithstanding, the comprehensive account that Baines and Rogers provide of the legal harassment suffered by Curll between 1725 and 1728, in which proceedings for obscene and seditious libel became mutually entangled, leaves no doubt that the decisive interest at work in Curll's prosecution was that of the ministry in particular, not patriarchy in general. Indeed, Curll's typically outrageous defence of *Venus in the Cloister* as a salutary work of anti-Catholic satire even seems to have won a degree of acceptance, and one of the judges involved recorded his opinion that, far from being suppressed, the work ought 'rather to be published on Purpose to expose the *Romish* Priests, the Father Confessors, and Popish Religion'.[27] As it turned out, the severest part of Curll's eventual sentence related to the Ker offence, and this included an hour in the public pillory which he then brilliantly stage-managed as a piece of oppositional street theatre, posing now as a Tory: 'for being an artful, cunning (though wicked) fellow he had contrived to have printed papers dispersed all about Charing-Cross, telling the people, he stood there for vindicating the memory of queen Anne: which had such an effect on the mob, that it would have been dangerous to have spoken against him: and when he was taken down out of the pillory, the mob carried him off, as it were in triumph, to a neighbouring tavern'.[28] Perhaps Curll's triumphant showmanship at this point owed something to his antagonist Defoe, who had famously pulled off a similar trick when punished for his *Shortest Way with the Dissenters* a quarter of a century beforehand; both were later satirically accused of having lost their ears.[29]

Rogering in Merryland

Similar stunts and subterfuges mark the remainder of Curll's career, albeit less theatrically played out. With his ruses, feints, and elaborate false trails, indeed, he retained the ability to hoodwink readers even from beyond the grave. As the work of Baines and Rogers incidentally shows, his fake imprints and bogus title pages remain a force for havoc in scholarly bibliographies and library catalogues to the present day, and he even scores a posthumous victory or two over their own expert and determined efforts to set the record straight.

Curll's culminating succès de scandale was *A New Description of Merryland* (1740), the first in a quickfire series of ribald, innuendo-laden publications about the lush topography of a fantasy island, all playing relentlessly on a sexual sense of 'merry' that was standard early modern slang. Here was yet another of Curll's obscene publications, flogging a single schoolboy joke to death, yet also winning an avid furtive readership and a reputation for daring wit. As a superficially hostile commentary called *Merryland Display'd* alleged a year later, the whole enterprise had begun when one of Curll's hack authors, working his way through an otherwise unimpeachable geography textbook by Patrick Gordon, chanced on an inadvertent double entendre in Gordon's survey of the Netherlands: 'viz. *"the Country lying very low, it's Soil is naturally very wet and fenny"*. Ha! said he, the same may be said of a **** as well as of *Holland*; this Whim having once entered his Noddle, he resolved to pursue the Hint, and try how far he could run the Parallel'.[30]

What lends credibility to this snide account of the origins of *Merryland* in a smutty private joke is that its author and the author he derides were one and the same person. This flexible hack was the otherwise untraceable Thomas Stretzer or Stretser, whose name survives on manuscript receipts acknowledging that Curll had given him 'full Satisfaction for the sole right and title to the copy' of both *Merryland* and *Merryland Display'd*.[31] The extent of this full satisfaction is not specified, but no doubt it was Curll, not Stretzer, who made the real money from this venture. ('Missing from the annals', as Baines and Rogers laconically note in another context, 'is any record of a writer who got rich through his labours for Curll'.[32]) Inescapably, he was up to his well-tried tricks again, probably commissioning, and certainly publishing, not only the original pamphlet but also a strident attack on it, penned by the same hand. Indeed, pronounced similarities between *Merryland Display'd* and Curll's much earlier *Curlicism Display'd* suggest that he was guiding the direction of Stretzer's bogus attack with some closeness. Here was

Curlism at work in its most efficient and impudent mode, maximizing the payoff from a limited resource and fanning the lucrative flames of scandal under cover of an effort to douse them.

In the opening pamphlet alone, Stretzer was able to run his parallel for more than seventy pages of puerile though occasionally amusing sexual innuendo. Presented as a tittering burlesque of voyage narrative, his description lingers on the hidden contours of an eroticized female bodyscape, a mysterious world of opulent labial inlets and luxuriant vaginal creeks, and as such it combines the appeal of pornography and satire. Whatever the accidental inspiration, indeed, Stretzer's text also belongs to a subgenre that was firmly established by the time he wrote, and its obscenity flows from the same parodic impulse that marks Scriblerian and other send-ups of scientific discourse in the period, albeit with clumsier execution. Two prior works of drolling erotica in a similar vein, though with botanical as opposed to geographical referents, are also routinely attributed to Stretzer, and the locus classicus of the subgenre is a Restoration fantasy entitled *Erotopolis: The Present State of Bettyland* (1684), an exuberantly obscene misapplication of the directions issued by the Royal Society to scientific voyage-writers.[33] *Merryland* clearly outsold all these, prompting not only Curll's sequels and associated reprints but also a rash of overnight imitations by other publishers.[34]

Aside from all the spin-offs generated by *Merryland*, of course, we have only Curll's word for it that this teasing exercise in veiled obscenity was successful enough to reach the ten editions he claimed to have published within two years. Not all of these supposed editions survive, and it was one of his favourite techniques to freshen up yellowing old remainders with new title pages. But Stretzer's pamphlet unquestionably made a splash, and Baines and Rogers's narrative of the whole murky episode, already a standard point of reference in the burgeoning scholarship on early pornography and its suppression, leaves the whole affair much clearer than before.[35]

That said, there remain some strange loose ends in the account they give. Although they eventually reject the attribution, Baines and Rogers give close discussion to a preface in which Stretzer claims to have inherited the text of *Merryland* in manuscript from a recently deceased Irishman named 'ROGER PHEUQUEWELL', and their analysis ends in the guarded conclusion that here 'Pheuquewell emerges more as a representative type than as the portrait of a real individual'.[36] So he does – but representative of what? As Stretzer helpfully adds in the genealogy he supplies of this putative author, the Pheuquewell family are 'remarkable for their being Red-Headed ... and of *long standing* in that Country',[37] and it is hard not to suspect the presence here of what linguisticians call a coincidental homophone. Readers familiar with the tradition behind *Merryland* would no doubt have recognized Roger Pheuquewell's kinship with 'the learned *Leonhard Fucksius*', an obsessive botanist in an earlier pamphlet possibly written by Stretzer,[38] and to make things still clearer Curll even seems to have had his printer use a damaged 'E' in some editions, so that the surname look more like 'PHFUQUEWELL'. As for 'Roger', this was soon to become the trademark verb of Boswell's London journal. See, for example, Boswell's famous vow of abstinence after falling under the moral influence of Johnson in 1763: 'Swear to have no more rogering before you leave England except Mrs. —— in chambers'.[39]

The blatancy of these double entendres notwithstanding, the ghost of Roger Pheuquewell, like other Curll inventions, continues to pheuque up the bibliographical record. He even invades the online Eighteenth-Century Short Title Catalogue as the alter ego or pseudonym of Stretzer himself, who is listed as 'Stretzer, Thomas, d. 1738', presumably by confusion with the fictional Pheuquewell's vital dates. For 1738 is the year in which, as Stretzer tenderly reports, Pheuquewell at last dies from exhaustion brought on by his addiction to rogering in Merryland, where he has been 'almost continually going and coming, and spent so much'.[40] Stretzer himself was alive and well more than three years later, writing the sequel to his bestselling work, and still signing on to the payroll at Curll's literary.

Perhaps, in the penultimate chapter of their groundbreaking and normally very vigilant study, Baines and Rogers have at last tired of detecting Curll in all his wiles, stunts, and decoys. But in handling the *Merryland* pamphlets they seem unduly trusting about questions of publication as well as authorship. *A New Description of Merryland* begins by announcing the first edition as a Bath publication, 'printed for W. Jones, and sold by W. Lobb there, and by the booksellers of London and Westminster'. Other early editions name Jones and/or Lobb alongside the strategically unspecified London retailers, and there was also a piracy under the fictitious (and in context somewhat predictable) imprint of 'J. Wagstaff'. Only from the 'fifth' edition onwards does Curll display his name on the title page, still maintaining the fiction that his publication emanates from Bath, and presenting himself as junior partner in the enterprise to the leading bookseller James Leake, a man whose prestigious establishment on Terrace Walk had just been described in an updated edition of Defoe's *Tour* as 'one of the finest Bookseller's Shops in *Europe*'.[41]

Leake of Bath then appears as the sole named publisher of *Merryland Display'd*. Only when ample time for any attempt at prosecution had elapsed does Curll identify himself on a title page as the lead or sole publisher of any book in the series, as he finally does in the 'tenth' edition (1742) of the original pamphlet, and in a tired second sequel of 1743, first advertised in December 1742 and entitled *A Short Description of the Roads Which Lead to That Delightful Country Called Merryland*.[42]

There are numerous rats to be smelled here, and more still if one also considers the gloriously inconsistent newspaper advertisements that Curll placed for the *Merryland* pamphlets; these, among other flourishes, add a long and implausible list of fashionable London booksellers involved in the venture, including 'R. Dodsley of Pall-Mall'.[43] Nothing in all this is more implausible, however, than Curll's attempt to implicate James Leake, a senior and distinguished book-trade figure with no other traceable connection to Curll throughout his long career. Yet rather than question Curll's veracity Baines and Rogers conduct a fruitless search for Joneses and Lobbs in the book trade at Bath, express regret that Leake had sullied his prestige by associating with Curll, and even conclude by identifying Leake as Curll's 'spiritual descendant in the trade'.[44] But why assume that any detail on Curll's playful, pragmatic title pages is accurate or true, other than (when belatedly made) the revelation of his own name? Curll was then at the height of his notoriety as a purveyor of false imprints and decoy titles: the 'fair Frontispiece[s] to the World' and 'Certain Title Pages, by Mr. Curl' that Fielding was still joking about in the *Champion* that same year.[45] It is much more likely that Curll chose to attribute these scandalous pamphlets to his fashionable west-country colleague out of malice, mischief, or pure unmotivated fun. Perhaps he was drawn in some unfocused way to the urinary connotations of 'Leake', as in the nasty joke about Pope's allegedly infected penis ('the leaky Condition his Cockboat is in') that was shortly to be cracked in *A Voyage to Lethe*.[46] Perhaps a simple coincidence of names prompted the idea, for Curll seems to have had some of his *Merryland* printing done by a smalltime London printer named John Leake (of Angel Street, St Martin's le Grand), who was not, as Baines and Rogers propose, James Leake's son, and probably had no connection at all with his eminent namesake.[47] This shadowy London Leake was eventually prosecuted in 1745 for printing several other pornographic works, at which point he also asked for *Merryland* to be taken into account, acknowledging that he had printed it and three related pamphlets ('Bettyland, Frutex V[ul]varia & the Flowering Shrub' – presumably the Curll reprints of 1741) 'for Daniel Lynch living in

New Street near Shoe Lane'. Lynch may have been Curll's intermediary with his printer, or a collaborator set up to take the rap if necessary; at any rate, we may be sure from the legal record that if Curll had any co-publisher at all for the *Merryland* pamphlets it was not James Leake but the hapless and struggling Lynch – referred to dismissively elsewhere in the depositions as 'one Lynch, a hawker' – who was duly convicted in 1745 for publishing another pornographic work, *The School of Venus*.[48]

Could it be that Curll was really attacking Leake of Bath as an indirect way of getting at Samuel Richardson, the influential printer and pillar of the Stationers' Company, who was now, with his first novel *Pamela*, also rising to prominence as a major author? Richardson had printed for Curll when starting out in business, but enmity had set in by 1728, when Curll tried to fit Richardson up for seditious libel by fingering him to the authorities as printer of an allegedly treasonable number of a dissident periodical, *Mist's Weekly Journal*. Richardson was certainly involved with Mist and Tory-Jacobite circles at the time, but the evidence suggests that he did not handle the issue involved, and there is unusual malice in the wording of Curll's denunciation of Richardson as a man responsible for 'this unheard of attack upon the Constitution', and an attack alongside which Curll's own 'Past offences ... to This are indeed but Ven[i]al'.[49]

If Richardson was the ultimate target on this later (and, by comparison, much more benign) occasion, several oddities of the *Merryland* pamphlets start to fall into place. It may be mere coincidence that *A New Description of Merryland* came out almost simultaneously with the much-heralded *Pamela*,[50] but if Curll was aiming to mock and discredit the novelist's literary circle and power base in Bath, he could not have done a better job. Leake was Richardson's brother-in-law and regular business partner (he may still have had a stake in the Richardson establishment), and this explains the hyperbole in Defoe's *Tour*, which Richardson by then was editing and printing. Also among Richardson's friends in Bath were Samuel Lobb and his son William; Samuel Lobb had indeed been a Bath bookseller some years earlier, but was now in holy orders as Rector of the nearby village of Farleigh Hungerford, and cannot conceivably have had anything to do with publishing *Merryland*. Nor can his son William, who was five years old at the time.[51] But there is no need to look beyond the evidence of the text itself to establish the facts at this point. In a perverse but utterly characteristic move, Curll then used *Merryland Display'd* to admit, or brag, that he himself had slyly perpetrated the original pamphlet, foisting it falsely on a printer who had never existed and a bookseller who had now retired.

As Stretzer writes, certainly with Curll's approval and probably on his instructions:

> The TITLE PAGE sets out with a barefaced *Falsity*, pretending it was printed at BATH for *William Jones*, and sold by *William Lobb* there. I have already shewn it was printed in *London* for E. CURLL. As for *William Jones*, there is no such Man as I can find at *Bath*; and for *William Lobb*, it is true there was formerly a Bookseller of that Name, but he left the Business many Years ago, and entered into holy Orders, which makes it the more impudent for our Author to mention him as the Publisher of an obscene Pamphlet.

Impudent, for sure, but also fun. It is hard not to feel at a point like this that Curll is now simply playing: enjoying his ruses for their own sake, and asking his reader to relish them as pure outrageous showmanship. His intrigues have lost all instrumental function, and are now held up for admiration in themselves, as deft and brazen performances of the bookseller's deepest arts. In the same passage, Curll even goes on to have the pamphlet accuse him of 'downright CURLISM', this time for the rather innocuous trick of recycling an irrelevant old frontispiece engraving, and he rounds off the display by insouciantly binding *The Dunciad* to himself as a crown. 'This', writes Stretzer with reference to the recycled frontispiece, 'is one Method of puffing peculiar to that *great Artist*, who as Mr *Pope* observes in his DUNCIAD, "has carried the (Bookseller's) Trade many Lengths beyond what it ever before had arrived at; and that he *is* the *Envy* and *Admiration* of all his Profession"'.[52] Curll's implicit claim throughout his career is at its clearest here: bookselling is an art, like everything else; he does it exceptionally well.

Perhaps the funniest part of the original *Merryland* pamphlet comes in its dedication to George Cheyne, the celebrated physician and mystic, which parodies Cheyne's notoriously arcane and unwieldy medical jargon (also a target of Fielding's mockery in the *Champion* at about this time).[53] Richardson was Cheyne's patient, and he printed several of Cheyne's works for publication by Leake. The pair corresponded extensively, and when Cheyne was not urging on Richardson a rigorous daily regime of puking and farting ('Vomits are the best Preservatives from Apoplexies after little Phlebotomies', he advised Richardson in characteristic style[54]), he complained bitterly about Leake's deficiencies as a publisher who had mishandled the promotion and sale of various Cheyne works. Whatever the tensions within this circle, however, it is clear that Leake, Cheyne, and Richardson, with satellites like Lobb, made up a formidable cultural coterie in Bath, and one that was shortly to show its power in a way that Curll would have detested, when no less an authority than Pope himself was persuaded to make his celebrated public endorsement of *Pamela*, probably in the arena of Leake's shop.[55] They offered a tempting target, and a target apparently identified by Curll's imitators in *A Voyage to Lethe*, published soon after *Merryland*, which heaps further mockery on the Richardson circle as complicit, in their enthusiasm for *Pamela*, in something awkwardly close to pornography themselves.[56] As for Cheyne, although he may never have met Curll in person, his strictures on booksellers in general fell especially on him, as the worst of a bad lot. 'All Booksellers I fear are Curls by profession', he told Richardson, resuming his theme in a later letter to dismiss the whole trade as 'specious Curls'.[57]

Eighteenth-century booksellers were not, of course, all specious Curlls. They were more, yet also less. By operating so flamboyantly on or beyond the margins of respectability, Edmund Curll became a convenient point of reference for anyone with a vested interest in tarring the trade as corrupt and corrupting in whatever sense: aesthetic, cultural, financial, moral, or all these things at once. His disreputable energies placed him personally, and bookselling generally, at the heart of the Scriblerian vision of cultural decay, even as the Leakes and Richardsons around him were steadily pursuing, and collectively achieving, that massive eighteenth-century expansion of print and reading that was so necessary a component of Enlightenment progress. Yet Curll's single-minded search for reliable profits and market openings also illustrates the entrepreneurial motivations and commercial techniques that, in more muted form, catalyzed the whole bookselling operation as practised by his enemies and rivals. Even the upright Richardson was suspected of using Curllian techniques to promote dubious wares when a denunciation of *Pamela* as disguised pornography – 'a Piece of *Curlism*', as one witness called the pamphlet in question, *Pamela Censured* (1741)[58] – was rumoured to have been sponsored by the novelist himself. In this context, Cheyne's constant insistence that Curll was entirely, albeit in exaggerated form, representative of his profession – 'I think them all more or less Curls', he tells Richardson on a third occasion[59] – is a useful reminder that the tenuously regulated world of eighteenth-century publishing was marked by differences of degree more than kind, and demanded ingenuity and rewarded bravado, perhaps more than scruple or caution. It was a world in which Curll could operate and flourish, not only as the self-befouled guttersnipe of Scriblerian satire, but also as a virtuoso performer of Curlism as an impudent art.

Notes

1. Samuel Johnson, Preface to *A Dictionary of the English Language* (1755), in *Samuel Johnson: The Major Works*, ed. Donald Greene (Oxford: Oxford University Press, 2000), p. 327.
2. Thomas Chatterton, *Memoirs of a Sad Dog* (1770), in his *Miscellanies in Prose and Verse* (1778), p. 207.
3. 'I have seen many words in Print which are not in *Baily's* Dictionary: *Curlicism* for one', protests John Ozell in his *Defence against the Remarks Publish'd ... on His Translation of the Roman History* (1725), p. 88. Somewhat fussily, Ozell adds that this coinage – which he attributes to the bookseller Thomas Woodward, though Defoe is a better candidate – should have been '*Curlism* not *Curlicism*, unless his name had been *Curly* instead of *Curll*' (p. 88 n.).
4. *General Evening Post*, 12 December 1747, quoted by Paul Baines and Pat Rogers, *Edmund Curll, Bookseller* (Oxford: Clarendon Press, 2007), p. 309.
5. *Some Account of the Life of the Right Reverend Father in God, Dr. Walter Curll* (1712).
6. J. H., *Remarks on 'Squire Ayre's Memoirs of the Life and Writings of Mr. Pope ... With Authentic Memoirs of the Life and Writings of ... E— C—l* (1745), pp. 43, 44.
7. *OED Online*, s.v. Conger, quoting the 1731 edition of Nathan Bailey's *An Universal Etymological English Dictionary*, s.v. Conger, Congre.
8. For Curll's dispute of 1707 with Prior and Tonson, one of his earliest copyright clashes, see Baines and Rogers, *Edmund Curll*, p. 27.
9. The best account of this complicated episode is by James Anderson Winn, *A Window in the Bosom: The Letters of Alexander Pope* (New York: Archon, 1977), pp. 13–41, 203–21.
10. Baines and Rogers, *Edmund Curll*, p. 9.
11. On Bookweight as Curll, see Henry Fielding, *Plays, Volume I, 1728–1731*, ed. Thomas Lockwood (Oxford: Clarendon Press, 2004), pp. 245–6 n.; Laetitia Pilkington instinctively equated the two, congratulating herself 'that Mr. *Curl* had not ... secured me a Prisoner in his poetical Garret, which the ingenious Mr. *Fielding* charmingly ridicules' (*Memoirs of Laetitia Pilkington*, ed. A. C. Elias, Jr, 2 vols [Athens: University of Georgia Press, 1997], I, 194). For the term 'Literatory', see below, n. 21.
12. Henry Fielding, *Contributions to The Champion and Related Writings*, ed. W. B. Coley (Oxford: Clarendon Press, 2004), pp. 213–4 (1 March 1740), 381 (21 June 1740).
13. The appended 'and Other Creatures' is a masterly touch by Curll; the text itself, by the seventeenth-century cleric Nicholas Bernard, is mainly a tract about penitence, though Bernard also has fun with the religious trope of the lost sheep.
14. A rare miss was Curll's failure to produce the treatise on erotic asphyxiation ('a more dangerous and modern Improvement on the Art of *Lewdness*') that he promises in the Preface to *The Use of Flogging*, making typically opportunist reference to the recent death by misadventure of Peter Motteux, the translator of Rabelais, in a brothel near Curll's own house.
15. For Millar's role see Henry Fielding, *The Journal of a Voyage to Lisbon, Shamela, and Occasional Writings*, ed. Martin C. Battestin (Oxford: Clarendon Press,

2008), pp. 355, 359–60; he acknowledged the publication and identified Fielding as author in a *Whitehall Evening Post* advertisement of 25 March 1756, two years earlier than Battestin suggests. For Millar as Maecenas, see Samuel Johnson, *The Lives of the Poets*, ed. Roger Lonsdale, 4 vols (Oxford: Clarendon Press, 2006), IV, 406.

16. *Daily Post*, 27 September 1725.

17. *Mist's Weekly Journal*, 5 April 1718, reprinted in William Lee, *Daniel Defoe: His Life and Recently Discovered Writings*, 3 vols (1869), II, 31; II, 32. For the collusion assumption, and the rebuttal of Baines and Rogers, see Maximillian E. Novak, *Daniel Defoe: Master of Fictions* (Oxford: Oxford University Press, 2001), pp. 491–2; Baines and Rogers, *Edmund Curll*, pp. 119–20.

18. Ralph Straus, *The Unspeakable Curll* (London: Chapman and Hall, 1927), p. 32, quoting John Spinke (the source does not appear to be Spinke's *Quackery Unmask'd* (1709, 1711), and may be a newspaper advertisement); Samuel Wesley, *Neck or Nothing: A Consolatory Letter from Mr. D-nt-n to Mr. C-rll upon His Being Tost in a Blanket* (1716), p. 6.

19. *The Correspondence of Jonathan Swift*, ed. David Woolley, 5 vols (Frankfurt: Peter Lang, 1999–), III, 578 (Arbuthnot to Swift, 13 January 1733), quoted by Baines and Rogers, *Edmund Curll*, p. 229.

20. *Gulliver Decypher'd* (1727), p. 16. This pamphlet is reprinted in *The Miscellaneous Works of the Late Dr. Arbuthnot* (Glasgow, 1751), though without obvious rationale.

21. *Grub-street Journal* 4 (29 January 1730); 17 (30 April 1730); 148 (30 October 1732); Curll announced the opening of 'The LITERATORY: Or, *Universal Library*' on 15 September 1729 (*Daily Journal*; see Baines and Rogers, *Edmund Curll*, p. 208).

22. Alexander Pope, *The Dunciad (1728) & The Dunciad Variorum (1729)*, ed. Valerie Rumbold (Harlow: Pearson Longman, 2007), pp. 218–19 (ii.71–2); see also, on 'Curl's chaste press', p. 180 (i.38).

23. Curll probably made this move during his war with Pope over Pope's correspondence in 1735, and he first uses the 'Pope's Head' address on various title pages of that year (Baines and Rogers, *Edmund Curll*, p. 244).

24. Baines and Rogers, *Edmund Curll*, pp. 135, 312.

25. Edmund Curll, Preface to *The Case of Seduction* (1725), pp. v–vi.

26. Alexander Pettit, '*Rex v.* Curll: Pornography and Punishment in Court and on the Page', *Studies in the Literary Imagination* 34.1 (2001): 67, 63.

27. John Fortescue-Aland, *Reports of Select Cases in All the Courts of Westminster-Hall* (1748), p. 100. In defending Curll's book, Fortescue evidently laid emphasis on the second rather than the first term in 'obscene libel', noting that '*The Nun in Her Smock* ... contained several Bawdy Expressions, but did contain no Libel against any Person whatsoever'.

28. Paul Baines and Pat Rogers, 'The Prosecutions of Edmund Curll, 1725–28', *The Library* 5.2 (2004): 188, quoting the trial judge, Sir John Strange, from Donald Thomas (ed.), *State Trials: Treason and Libel* (London: Routledge, 1972), p. 143.

29. On Curll's imagined ear-cropping, see *Grub-street Journal* 172 (12 April 1733), echoing Pope's joke about 'earless' Defoe in *The Dunciad*, p. 231 (ii.139).

30. Thomas Stretzer, *Merryland Display'd: or, Plagiarism, Ignorance, and Impudence, Detected* (1741), p. 8, referring to Patrick Gordon, *Geography Anatomiz'd: or, The Geographical Grammar* (1704), p. 116; this much-reprinted work reached its sixteenth edition in 1740.

31. BL, Add. MS 38728, fo. 197, partly quoted by Baines and Rogers, *Edmund Curll*, p. 323; see also Straus, *Unspeakable Curll*, p. 314. Baines and Rogers are 'virtually sure that "Stretser" was a pseudonym' (p. 291), but it is not clear why concealment would be needed in Curll's private register of payments to authors, which otherwise uses real names. A clue to Stretzer's identity may lie in David Stevenson's conjecture that members of a libertine club near St Andrew's in Scotland, which in 1739 began calling itself 'The Most Ancient and Puissant Order of the Beggar's Benison and Merryland' and issued documents in the style of Stretzer's pamphlet, may have had pre-publication access to his material; this club also seems to have had a version of Cleland's *Memoirs of a Woman of Pleasure* before publication (David Stevenson, 'Preposterous Pleasures in Merryland: The Early Influence of *Fanny Hill* in Scotland', *Times Literary Supplement*, 15 August 1997; also Stevenson's *The Beggar's Benison: Sex Clubs of Enlightenment Scotland and Their Rituals* (East Linton: Tuckwell Press, 2001), pp. 17–19.

32. Baines and Rogers, *Edmund Curll*, p. 8.

33. All three works were reissued by Curll in 1741 following his *Merryland* success. *The Natural History of the Arbor Vitae; or, The Tree of Life* (1732) and *The Natural History of the Frutex Vulvaria ... by Philogynes Clitorides* (1732) appeared under the false imprint of 'E. Hill', and *Bettyland* as part of a miscellany subtitled *Succours from Merryland* (see below, note 42). *Bettyland* is usually attributed to Charles Cotton, but on uncertain authority; the standard attribution of *Arbor Vitae* and *Frutex Vulvaria* to Stretzer is also uncertain, and may simply be an inference drawn from Curll's appropriation of both pamphlets and the resemblance to *Merryland*. On the subgenre as a whole, and its play on scientific discourse, see Paul-Gabriel Boucé, 'Chthonic and Pelagic Metaphorization in Eighteenth-Century English Erotica', in Robert P. MacCubbin (ed.), *'Tis Nature's Fault: Unauthorized Sexuality During the Enlightenment* (Cambridge: Cambridge University Press, 1987), pp. 202–16.

34. For a good example, see *A Voyage to Lethe; By Capt. Samuel Cock; Sometime Commander of the Good Ship the Charming Sally. Dedicated to the Right Worshipful Adam Cock, Esq; Of Black-Mary's-Hole, Coney-Skin Merchant* (1741).

35. Notably Julie Peakman, *Mighty Lewd Books: The Development of Pornography in Eighteenth-Century England* (Basingstoke: Palgrave Macmillan, 2003), pp. 71–8, 86–102, 188–90; Karen Harvey, *Reading Sex in the Eighteenth Century: Bodies and Gender in English Erotic Culture* (Cambridge: Cambridge University Press, 2004), pp. 50–3, 103–6, 181–4. For an annotated edition of *A New Description of Merryland* (lacking, however, the preliminary matter), see Bradford K. Mudge (ed.), *When Flesh Becomes Word: An Anthology of Early Eighteenth-Century Libertine Literature* (New York: Oxford University Press, 2004), pp. 257–86; the text is also reprinted in Alexander Pettit and Patrick Spedding (eds), *Eighteenth-Century British Erotica*, 5 vols (London: Pickering and Chatto, 2001), III.

36. Baines and Rogers, *Edmund Curll*, p. 291.
37. Thomas Stretzer, *A New Description of Merryland*, 2nd edn (1740), p. ii. Stretzer polishes and intensifies his innuendo at this point, which in the first edition reads simply 'Red-Haired'.
38. *The Natural History of the Arbor Vitae* (1732), p. 4.
39. James Boswell, *London Journal, 1762–1763*, ed. Frederick A. Pottle (New York: McGraw-Hill, 1950), p. 304 n. (15 July 1763).
40. Stretzer, *New Description of Merryland*, p. ii. The right point of reference here is probably Pepys: 'I went up to her and played and talked with her and, God forgive me ... I spent in my breeches' (*OED Online*, s.v. Spend, 15c, quoting Pepys's diary for 7 September 1662).
41. Daniel Defoe, *A Tour thro' the Whole Island of Great Britain*, 2nd edn, 4 vols (1738), II, 241.
42. An earlier spin-off was *The Potent Ally; or, Succours from Merryland* ('Paris', 1741), a hasty compilation brought out by Curll in January 1741 to cash in on the success of *A New Description of Merryland*.
43. *Craftsman*, 8 November 1740. See also the *Craftsman* for 6 December, implausibly announcing a 'fourth' edition within a month of the first, this time with Leake in the role of printer (though he was not a printer); Dodsley again appears as a London distributor, followed, in a neat double bluff, by 'E. Curll, in Rose-Street, Covent-Garden'.
44. Baines and Rogers, *Edmund Curll*, p. 294.
45. Fielding, *Contributions to The Champion*, pp. 381 (21 June 1740) and 381 n. (10 July 1740).
46. *Voyage to Lethe*, p. 30; see the gloss on this joke in Raymond Stephanson, *The Yard of Wit: Male Creativity and Sexuality, 1650–1750* (Philadelphia: University of Pennsylvania Press, 2004), pp. 26–7.
47. Baines and Rogers, *Edmund Curll*, p. 368; see also my *ODNB* entry, 'Leake, James (1686–1764)'.
48. David Foxon, *Libertine Literature in England, 1660–1745* (New York: University Books, 1965), pp. 16–17, 36. John Leake the printer also gave evidence about a later *Merryland* publication that seems not to have involved Curll, and does not survive: this was *A Compleat Set of Charts of the Coasts of Merryland* (1745), a series of erotic engravings 'printed by one Thomas Harper printer near Fleet Market, & published by Thomas Read printer in White Fryars' (p. 17).
49. T. C. Duncan Eaves and Ben D. Kimpel, *Samuel Richardson: A Biography* (Oxford: Clarendon Press, 1971), pp. 31–3; the quotation (p. 32) is from Curll's letter to a ministerial official, John Hutchins, dated 6 September 1728 (National Archives, SP 36/8, 113–14).
50. According to the later *Merryland Display'd* (p. 10), *A New Description of Merryland* was published on 23 October 1740, but I have found no newspaper notice of publication before 8 November (in the *Craftsman*: 'This Day is Publish'd ...'), and Curll paid Stretzer for the copy on 10 November. *Pamela* was published on 6 November.
51. On the eminently respectable Lobbs, see Eaves and Kimpel, *Samuel Richardson*, pp. 196–7. Samuel Lobb assumed the living of Farleigh Hungerford in 1736, probably thanks to patronage from Ralph Allen. He had previously co-published (with Leake and three London booksellers)

Mary Chandler's *Description of Bath* (1733), and was also the publisher or distributor of several religious and medical books between 1730 and 1733, at least one of which Richardson printed (Keith Maslen, *Samuel Richardson of London, Printer* (Dunedin: University of Otago, 2001), p. 99).

52. Stretzer, *Merryland Display'd*, pp. 15, 16, 17.
53. Fielding, *Contributions to The Champion*, p. 329 (17 May 1740). The main text of *Merryland* also directly quotes 'that learned Physician and Philosopher *Doctor Cheyne*', playing obscenely on his account of man as 'an *hydraulic Machine*, filled with a Liquor' (p. 28).
54. *The Letters of Doctor George Cheyne to Samuel Richardson (1733–1743)*, ed. Charles F. Mullett (Columbia: University of Missouri, 1943), p. 58 (26 October 1739).
55. See Thomas Keymer and Peter Sabor, *Pamela in the Marketplace: Literary Controversy and Print Culture in Eighteeenth-Century Britain and Ireland* (Cambridge: Cambridge University Press, 2005), pp. 24–5.
56. *A Voyage to Lethe* (1741) follows Curll's lead by mocking *Pamela*'s most conspicuous clerical patrons, Benjamin Slocock, who preached the famous commendatory sermon at St Saviour's, Southwark, and John Conybeare, Dean of Christ Church, whose enthusiasm for the novel was widely reported from Oxford, and whose felicitous name no doubt added to his appeal as a target. This teasing publication bills itself as 'Printed for *J. Conybeare* in *Smock-Ally* near *Petticoat-Lane*'; its mock subscriber list records 3,000 copies for 'the Rev. Mr. *Slowcock*, for himself and Parishioners, to bind up with ... *Pamela*'.
57. *Letters of Cheyne*, pp. 48 (27 March 1738), 65 (12 February 1741).
58. John Kelly, *Pamela's Conduct in High Life*, 2 vols (1741), I, xiii; see Keymer and Sabor, *Pamela in the Marketplace*, pp. 34–5.
59. *Letters of Cheyne*, p. 53 (1 July 1739).

12
Charlatanism and Resentment in London's Eighteenth-Century Literary Marketplace

Simon During

It is a commonplace that British literary production became increasingly commercialised across the eighteenth century, and that shifts in literary genre, address and mood over the period need to be considered in that light. In this chapter, I want to address two quite specific structures within this process, concentrating on the mid-century period. The first is the close relationship between writing and forms of quackery or charlatanism. The second structure, which I will attend to more briefly, is the slow emergence among writers of what will later come to be called *ressentiment* from out of that old Satanic vice, envy. Setting these very different events side by side may seem perverse, but, by focussing on a cluster of commercial book-trade participants – John Newbery, Oliver Goldsmith and Christopher Smart – I want to make the case that, in the narrow period between about 1750 and 1780, they are in fact linked and in ways that help us make sense of the romanticism to come.

In brief, my argument is that literary production in the period was 'charlatanised' in three related ways: first the book trade was materially connected to the patent medicine trade which was one diluted and rationalised form of quackery; second, the literary world itself was often engaged in practices of charlatanism, and third, the difficulties of escaping the contingencies of commerce and politics led to a widely accepted diagnosis of charlatanism as infecting the society and culture quite broadly. In this environment, I further contend, cultural affects were unstable – a situation that fostered not just sentimentalism but a particular nexus between feeling and print in which certain writers were dominated by resentments that they could not transparently express in their writings – Goldsmith and Smart being my examples.

Definitions

When Hester Piozzi discussed the terms 'charlatans', 'quacks' and 'mountebanks' in her *British Synynomy* (1794) – words which had become familiar in the early modern period and which, with their demystifying force, had helped carry out enlightenment's work – she declared her personal preference for the first, but nonetheless claimed that they shared a single meaning.[1] In fact, however, these terms do seem quite quickly to have acquired somewhat different senses. Who, then, was a quack or a charlatan? Not just mountebanks who earned their bread in the medicine trade by making grandiose claims about nostrums but any self-advertiser pretending to more knowledge or power than they possessed. That extension of reference arrived early, perhaps most famously in the Enlightenment era, in Menke's polemic, *Charlatanerie Eruditorium* (1715). And there is a sense in which, across the eighteenth century, while the craft of the mountebank declines, charlatans of a vaguer and more figurative kind become more prevalent. It is telling that Samuel Butler's *Characters*, written in the late 1670s, describes mountebanks but not charlatans, and that by the time Butler's manuscript was first published in 1759, the old mountebank, the nomadic trader working fairs, public houses and village greens had, on the one hand, been marginalised by nationally distributed patent medicines, and, on the other, been subsumed by charlatans of a very different ilk with prominent cultural profiles – such as John Henley the unorthodox preacher, lecturer and political journalist, or John Hill, the journalist, botanist, novelist, reviewer and patent-medicine proprietor.

Yet these terms, charlatanism and quackery are hedged about by ambiguities. As Roy Porter notes, no one calls themselves a charlatan or quack – and this in itself exposes the terms to dispute.[2] More than that: the fraud or pretension that at one level defines them cannot easily be dismissed as valueless for the simple reason that non-truthful, non-rational marketing claims helped extend commercial activity over the period (and, of course, since). Indeed eighteenth-century charlatanism can be regarded as an avant-garde of the modern consumer marketplace. We can put it like this: charlatanism, thought neutrally or analytically, becomes diffused through the market economy as more and more services and commodities derive their value primarily from the seductive force of their sales pitch rather than from any post-purchase use-value, and also when attracting custom is sufficient justification for production. At the same time, the critique of charlatanism turns away from its enlightenment targets – superstition, credulity and ignorance – towards the empty promises and valorised nullities of a culture organised around the market.

Books, newspapers and patent medicines

And so to turn to the connections between the patent medicine trade and literature which helped underpin the era's charlatanism.[3] What form did they take? To begin with: many booksellers were involved in retailing and in some cases preparing, patent medicines. Given that medicines seem to have been more profitable than books (it was estimated that profits of 25 per cent were possible in the pharmaceutical business), one might suppose that, at least for some booksellers, they subsidised the book trade, although there is little good data on this matter, and according to the booksellers' accounts published by Jan Fergus, patent medicines were marginally less important to total sales than printed material (though not necessarily to profits) which themselves became less important than stationary and other items as the century went on.[4] Newspapers could add complexity to these relations since larger booksellers were also sometimes involved in the production or distribution of newspapers.[5] This tied them to patent medicines since newspaper profits depended on advertising, while patent medicine proprietors required newspaper advertising to achieve a wide distribution. Once newspapers were being circulated across most of Britain, patent-medicine name recognition could become national, indeed they seem to have constituted the first national brands.

This interdependency between print and proprietary medicines was further structured around certain similarities between the two commodities. Both could be more or less mass-produced. Both could be identified by legally-protected proper names. Both were normally retailed at fixed prices which, still rare through retailing as a whole, was a prerequisite of the modern market. Both could be easily transported. Both could be stored without decaying, and easily sold alongside one another.[6] And finally, both had a value largely dependent on commentary, marketing and reputation, but which was not necessarily acknowledged as such.

Patent medicines themselves were so sellable for two main reasons. There were relatively few physicians per head of population, and the non-patent medicines that they prepared were often prohibitively expensive.[7] Furthermore patients routinely self-diagnosed: the modern structure of authority by which doctors provide the sick with binding expertise after physical examination was not yet in place. Patent medicines operated under a different philosophy than that underpinning university-legitimated medicine. In one direction they sometimes claimed that their powers derived from analogical relations that referred back to older 'magical' cosmic ontologies in which the world was bound by esoteric sympathies. In another direction, they worked simply because they worked ('empiric' was another name for a quack after all), which was why testimonials were so important to their profitability (and one mode of modern medical research begins in the testing of quack medicine's claims – such work made the philosopher David Hartley's name for instance). But it was because patent medicines were testimonial and brand name driven that they required massive publicity – which the book trade could provide.

John Newbery

Let me now turn to a particular case within these exchanges between patent medicine and print – John Newbery who stands near the centre of the charlatanised literary world. Newbery began his career in Reading but in 1744, transferred his business to London where he purchased distribution rights to Dr James's Fever Powder which was to become the era's most widely used patent medicine.[8] One of the reasons for the powder's success was that Robert James, its inventor, was a well-known authority on the basis of his *Medicinal Dictionary* whose preface had been written by Samuel Johnson. Dr James's reputation underpinned a sustained sales blitz on behalf of his powder, incorporating not just advertisements, handbills, testimonials from famous figures like Lord Chesterfield, Colley Cibber and the playwright, Richard Cumberland, but mention in fictions mainly published by Newbery and his associates. For example, John Shebbeare's *The Marriage Act* (1754) included a chapter-heading attesting to the medicine's efficacy; Dodsley's *The World* inserted a puff in a widely reprinted essay-fiction; and, most famously, the best-selling children's tale, *Little Goody Two-Shoes* has its heroine's father deposed from his land, dying because he was 'seized with a violent Fever in a place where Dr James's Powder was not to be had'.[9] From a different ideological position, when Christopher Smart recovered from a nervous breakdown in 1756, he published his *Hymn to the Supreme Being* to which he attached a letter to Dr James, which began, 'Having made an humble offering to HIM, without whose blessing your skill, admirable as it is, would have been to no purpose: I think myself bound by all the ties of gratitude, to render my next acknowledgments to you, who, under God, restored me to health from as violent and dangerous a disorder, as perhaps ever man survived. And my many thanks become more particularly your just tribute, since this was the third time, that your judgement and medicines rescued me from the grave, permit me to say, in a manner almost miraculous'.[10] This may have been a response to an anti-powder advertisment inserted into Fielding's *Amelia* but whatever its immediate intent, here Dr James acquires a quasi-magical power deriving from divinity itself, which is all the more ironical since it is possible that his powder was actually causing Smart's mental illness. Certainly there is a body of respectable medical opinion today that believes that George III's madness may have been caused by the arsenic that he absorbed through the powder.[11]

The powder was not without its critics however. In 1748, Dr James wrote another book *A Dissertation on Fevers* in order to support faltering sales, and to shore the product up against sceptical voices, notably the anonymous author of *Quackery Unmask'd* (1748).[12] The powder soon sustained a number of more damaging attacks, including in 1751 a claim by the printer and pharmacist William Baker that its patent had been granted on false grounds since its formula had been first developed in Germany.[13] In the early 1750s, the Admiralty, desperate to find a cure for scurvy, instructed James Lind to undertake trials of supposed therapies against fevers, especially James's powder. His results, remarkably carefully obtained for the time and guided by a suspicion of medicines that claimed effectiveness over a wide range of complaints, were negative. But Lind's work was to have little impact for at least 20 years.

Perhaps most damaging of all was the scandal surrounding Oliver Goldsmith's death in 1774, which produced a minor paper war. Goldsmith turned to the powder when he fell victim to kidney disease, insisting on taking it in large doses against the recommendation of his medical advisor, William Haynes.[14] After Goldsmith's death, Haynes published a pamphlet declaring that James's powder was responsible for the fatality. This was rebutted in a campaign organised by the Newberys, contending that the medicine which Goldsmith had taken had not been produced by the correct formula.

In 1783 new government charges were laid on the patent-medicine trade and this, along with a gradual increase in the availability of medical practitioners, the formal professionalization of medical practice (particularly as implemented in the 1815 Apothecaries Act) and the increasing credibility of critiques of proprietary medicines, very slowly reduced medicines' economic value in Britain, although, despite its formula having been publicised, James's powder remained profitable well into the next century.¹⁵ For a while, none other than Byron's publisher, the gentlemanly John Murray, held a share in it.¹⁶

The book trade's interconnection with the pharmaceutical business was in decline by the 1780s for reasons the scholarship has not persuasively uncovered. Clearly the pressures on the patent medicine trade just outlined were important but perhaps also because the print market became more self-sustaining. That was a consequence of increased affluence and opportunities to buy books, but was also enabled by the 1774 reform of copyright (which led, at least in the short term, to a flood of cheap books) and by the development of more sophisticated business techniques, such as, for instance, wholesaling and warehousing, remaindering, and the prominent display of new books in bookshops. In sum: as books became an increasingly autonomous commodity within the market, their dependence on pharmaceuticals declined.

John Newbery was also a key player in these developments. He was one of the publishers of the era who clearly recognised the opportunities opened up by the print market's extension, reaching into new readerships by multiplying the opportunities for reading in everyday life, developing new consumer-friendly binding formats, investing heavily in the children's and schoolroom markets, publishing books able to be used practically, many in the increasingly popular pocket format – dictionaries, abridgements, bibles and how-to books for instance, as well as periodicals and daily newspapers.

As a result of this commercial activity, he became a widely recognised public figure, famous for his energy, multitasking and, more dubiously, for his benevolence via a suite of representations which carry a whiff of charlatanism, since once more they tended to appear in his own publications. He figures as Jack Whirler in *The Idler* (1758) where he is presented as the archetype of the modern businessman, too active to live life except through substitutes. He also makes an entry in Goldsmith's *The Vicar of Wakefield* (1766) where he is referred to, less obliquely, as the 'philanthropic bookseller in St. Paul's Church-yard'.¹⁷ A more contemptuous sketch was published by George Colman, whose account of an uneducated, boastful, money-grubbing bookseller under the name of Mr Folio was taken to refer to him.¹⁸ And indeed, Newbery was capable of charlatanism on his own account. To help sell his edition of Walter Raleigh's *The Interest of England*, he claimed that a copy of the original MS could be viewed at his shop, although no such manuscript existed—a trick that was later to be tried by another literary figure who was regularly to be described as a charlatan, James Macpherson of Ossian fame.

Literary charlatanism

We are beginning to see that the relations between patent medicines and publishing that I have been describing underpinned a series of looser or more discursive intersections between literature and charlatanism. In turning to examine these relations more closely we should briefly note the old practice of comparing literature positively to a 'pill' (to cure melancholy for instance) or as 'purge' – as if writing could itself be medicinal. But, of course such tropes could not create a functional equivalence between writing and patent medicine, and cannot themselves be aligned to charlatanism. More to the point in thinking about forms of literary charlatanism: books were often over-advertised. Typeface could be surrounded by a sea of white paper in order to fill books out, a charge James Ralph brings against the Warburtonians in *The Case of Authors*.[19] Their titles routinely promised much more than the text finally provided, in a practice which John Nichols called 'titulary puffing'.[20] (Laurence Sterne's *Tristram Shandy*, with its creative use of the white page for much more than print would seem to be simultaneously a joke on, and case of, this kind of puffing – it's no accident that Sterne himself was portrayed in a popular satirical print as a mountebank (and *Tristram Shandy* does claim that enjoying it is of medicinal value.)[21] Publishers also routinely exaggerated edition numbers to hype the popularity of their books. The common practice of advertising for subscription could also lapse into charlatanism, as Henry Fielding remarks at some length in *Joseph Andrews*.[22] Sometimes outright fraud was involved: in the 1760s, a self-ascribed French aristocrat canvassed for subscriptions for a luxury book (a fifteen volume history of England in French) which was probably never intended to appear.[23] Later in life, Christopher Smart turned to subscription publishing as a form of begging, producing one slight book after another so that his friends might support him, although he was ashamed of the practice.[24] Something like charlatanism is at work here, at least to the degree that promise exceeds performance.

Book trade debates could also be tinged with charlatanism. One thinks in particular of what we can call false paper wars in which authors and publishers conspired to create controversies so as to gain publicity. These were quite common in the mid eighteenth-century and John Newbery organised several. No less importantly during this period, writing and entrepreneuralism systematically overlapped. Authors themselves were often entrepreneurs, and drawn into charlatanism in this way. In many cases, books can be regarded as business projects managed by authors – Johnson's *Dictionary* being one example, and Macpherson's collection of the Ossian poems another. Not even Johnson escapes charlatanism, at least to the degree that his project – the authoritative fixing of meanings to words – can be regarded as making overweening claims for commercial gain. Writers were also regularly involved in dubious non- or quasi-literary businesses. For instance, Smollett projected an Academy of Belles Lettres in terms which were at least criticised as quackery. One critic dismissed the project in these terms: 'in the close of the Year 1755, a certain *Caledonian* Quack, by the Curtesy of *England*, call'd a *Doctor of Physick*, whose real, or assum'd Name was FERDINANDO MAC FATHOMLESS, form'd a Project for initiating and perfecting the Male-Inhabitants of this Island, in the Use and Mangaement of the *linguary Weapon*, by the erection of a *Scolding Amphitheatre'*.[25]

Sometimes such projects had a more direct relation to charlatanism. At least one author entered the patent medicine trade on his own account – John Hill, who began his career as an apothecary. And John Shebbeare notoriously touted the theory that, to quote a sarcastic contemporary, 'the primary cause of all diseases proceeds from excess or defect of the electric fire; the novelty and *Verity* of which could not fail to recommend it to his fashionable readers'.[26] Less obviously, Christopher Smart cashed in on the success of the magazine *Mother Midnight* by adapting it as a burlesque musical which he compered, cross-dressed, as an elderly midwife. At the show's centre was its satire of John Henley and his Oratory. Although, as Paula McDowell is making clear in her current (unpublished) scholarship, Henley had a serious pedagogical project, he was also a charlatan by almost any definition, if a self-ironising one. He ran a bizarre advertising campaign to attract a paying audience to his 'chapel' which was part place of instruction and part place of amusement, and had long been cited as the crucial instance of the threat of a charlatanised culture (in *The Dunciad* for instance). Smart's show largely consisted of farcical music performed on vernacular instruments in a complex play with the taste canons from which Henley kept his distance. Did Smart's customers get their money's worth? Horace Walpole at least did not think so.[27] Here Smart's critical, comic parody, in offering so much triviality and cacophony, veered perilously close to charlatanism on its own account.

Given literary entrepreneurship's intimate relationship with fraud and hype, it is unsurprising that this was a period when literature in general was engaged with charlatanism as a topic. As we know, satire and commentary routinely denounced their objects as being involved in, or as instances of, quackery or charlatanism, and, more abstractly, represented the general social and cultural scene as being organised around charlatanism or (what was closely related) conjuring or trickery. Of the thousands upon thousands of instances of this, let me just gesture at one.

In his 1763 satire *The Ghost*, Charles Churchill, the stunningly successful verse satirist, represented contemporary British society, and especially the Scots, as inheritors of a long lineage of quackery reaching back to the ancient Chaldeans, moving past early eighteenth-century charlatans like Duncan Campbell (the astrologer, and patent medicine and magic charm seller) into present media culture, at whose centre, Churchill believes, or pretends to believe, lurks Smollett. In verses about those who belong to this genealogy of charlatanism, Churchill writes:

> Some, with high Titles and Degrees,
> Which wise Men borrow when they please,
> Without or trouble or expence,
> PHYSICIANS instantly commence,
> And proudly boast an equal skill
> With those who claim the *right* to *kill*....
> Some, the more subtle of their race,....
> Came to the *Brother* SMOLLET's aid,
> And carried on the CRITIC trade.
> Attach'd to Letters and the Muse,
> *Some* Verses wrote, and some wrote News.
> *Those*, eve'ry morning, great appear
> In LEDGER, or in GAZETTEER;
> Spreading the falshood of the day,
> By turns for FADEN and for SAY.[28]

Here the world of news and most especially of criticism is pictured as continuous with that of quackery because of the falsity and indifference to cultural and social distinctions that they share. Churchill's is a politically motivated attack – he was about to be aligned with John Wilkes and the radical reform movement while Smollett was a propagandist for George III's ministry. But it is a sign of the power of the discourse of charlatanism that Churchill chooses it to obscure his own political bias: anti-quackery provides him with easy access to the high ground. To accept that provision, however, is to join charlatanism since to denounce one's opposition as a charlatan from a partisan position is to flirt with deceit. And here the full reach of charlatanism's cruel logic becomes apparent: as the preferred name for false promises or overweeningness it is all but inescapable within a structure that places its participants into particular and limited positions within a commercialised and politicised field, at the same time as demanding of them truth and objectivity.

Sentimentalism and objectivity

The drive to help the cause of objectivity was part of what propelled the first media organs of modern criticism, Ralph Griffiths's *Monthly Review* (1749) and Smollett's *Critical Review* (1756), both of which aimed to provide authoritative assessment of books. But, as we might expect, these journals, far from transcending the deceptions and falsities of the literary world, intensified abuse, insecurity, divisions and charlatan discourse. At just this moment – and this is my final topic – literary mood and subjectivity underwent a significant transformation. Most openly this shift in mood manifested itself in the sentimentalism that swept the culture after the success of Richardson's novels and then Sterne's *Tristram Shandy*. Here we have a real break with the old tradition of denunciatory satire (whose last important figure was Churchill) as well as with popular literature-as-instruction (in which Newbery's career was largely made) both of which were entangled in charlatanism and its critico-figurative uses. One can understand the literary fashion for sentimentalism as a means by which literature and drama helped compensate for the slow dissolution of rurally based communitarian connections, as if affective benevolence and philanthropic intent, nourished in fictions, might replace the responsibilities implicit in the hierarchies of the landed estates and indeed the financial burdens of the parochial poor-law system.[29] This interpretation at least has the virtue of helping to explain why sentimentalism, as a product of a loosening of social structures and connections, was accompanied by an increase of alienation and – let me emphasise – resentment among writers, as we are about to see in more detail. It also helps explain why sentimentalism – despite its break with older charlatanised literary forms – is still imbricated with charlatanism, since the transports of tears, benevolence and sympathy it promoted in lieu of practical responsibility were so easy to manipulate and so difficult to authenticate.

It is no accident that key instances of early sentimental writing – the well-known failure in *A Sentimental Journey* of Yorick's intense sensibility and benevolence to end in practical alms-giving (except when disavowed quasi-prostitution is involved) and Mr Harley's tarnished sentimental charity towards an itinerant conman in Henry Mackenzie's *Man of Feeling* – both expose the vulnerability of the new mood to costiveness and fraud, and by the same token, reveal how close to falsity the mood itself could be. In this passage, where Harley is about to give money to the fraudulent supplicant, let the dog's neat trick stand as an allegory of sentimentalism's undermining of virtue and its incorporation of charlatanism:

> Harley had drawn a shilling from his pocket; but Virtue bade him consider on whom he was going to bestow it. Virtue held back his arm; but a milder form, a younger sister of Virtue's, not so severe as Virtue, nor so serious as Pity, smiled upon him; his fingers lost their compression, nor did Virtue offer to catch the money as it fell. It had no sooner reached the ground than the watchful cur (a trick he had been taught) snapped it up, and, contrary to the most approved method of stewardship, delivered it immediately into the hands of his master.[30]

As sympathetic compassion, their 'younger sister', replaces Virtue and Pity, it is exposed to a wholly manipulative environment – even the conman's dog has learnt a trick by which he can protect his master's reputation at the same time as guarding the money. Indeed the cur expresses the sheer empiricism and materiality to which both sentimentalism and charlatanism tend.

Resentment: Smart

In abstract the social structure of the resentment that appeared alongside charlatan-tainted sentimentalism can be analysed quite simply: an urbanised, commercialised, mediatised cultural field encouraged individual competition and, as just noted, undermined oligarchic social dependencies and cultural hierarchies. But the market had not yet found mechanisms by which writers could be adequately rewarded for their work. This meant that they were habitually beset by disjunctions between their own notions of their worth (notions which they inherited from the classically orientated culture of the past) and the financial value of that work. This meant that, as older canons dissolved under a stream of money mainly flowing to booksellers, their energies were often released around what was also a value crisis. For a period, this structure abetted the circulation of the discourse of charlatanism. All the more so since the three means by which market instabilities and the value crisis could be managed were not in place. These were, firstly, institutions and collectivities supportive of social hope and reformism, which by the century's end would nurture both the romantic avant-gardes and political progressivism. Secondly, the extension of reading's powers of cultivation into new class layers, which would only take off from the late 1770s, accelerating through the last decades of the century.[31] And thirdly: the aestheticisation and autonomisation of non-classical literature which was not yet fully under way. In a sense, the mid-eighteenth century marked a hiatus within the processes of modernisation. And many individuals paid a price for working at this moment of relative disorganisation. Among writers in particular, madness, aggression, poverty and imprisonment were commonplace. So too was resentment.

Let us take as instances the two writers most closely associated with John Newbery: Christopher Smart and Oliver Goldsmith.[32] Both, as we have seen, incorporated advertisements for Dr James's Powder in their work and both were supported and, indeed, housed by Newbery for a period. Although two more different kinds of writers can scarcely be imagined, socially Smart and Goldsmith shared a great deal – at least if we ignore Goldsmith's Irishness. Both were born into that sector of the middling classes bordering on the lower gentry. Both were university trained but chose the urban writer's life over established professions, and were drawn into the heart of the booktrade/patent medicine nexus by virtue of their exceptional talent. Both spent time in debtors' prison and experienced difficulty living within their means, spending, in particular, more than they could afford on fine clothes to solicit social recognition. Both won their reputation for their poetry but turned to more entrepreneurial literary projects to make a living. Both were propelled by emotions they could not control, although only Smart was confined in a mad-house. The emotion that Smart experienced was an intense religiosity which expressed itself in a compulsion to adore God in public; the emotion that beset Goldsmith was envy, joined to an irrepressible impulse to put himself forward in social gatherings.

Although nothing seems more oppositional than envy and religious adoration, in fact once we read Smart and Goldsmith's oeuvres and biographies in relation to one another it is possible to regard them as two expressions of a shared experience and social structure – the structure being, of course, the literary economy, described above, within which charlatanism flourished and in which Newbery was a key player.

Smart's adoration was expressed most unguardedly and fully in the text that we know as *Jubilate Agno*, which is often called a poem although it seems more to be a spiritual and prophesising diary.[33] It was written while Smart was confined in a madhouse, in imitation of biblical rhetorics, although Smart, appropriating the newspaper/literature synergy, called himself the 'Lord's News-Writer'.[34] Like much grace- and prayer-based evangelicalism, *Jubilate Agno* has a deep relation to the ontology of quackery: many of its last verses praise quasi-magical remedies: 'Let Usher, house of Usher rejoice with Condurdon an herb with a red flower worn about the neck for scurvy'. Some even combine bookselling and medicine: 'Let Crockett, house of Crockett rejoice with Emboline an Asiatic Shrub with small leaves, an antidote. I pray for the soul of Crockett the bookseller the first to put me upon a version of the Psalms'.[35]

But the primary force that the text conveys is that of an imprisoned man, less than certain of his soteriological status, encyclopaedically journalising his learning and everyday life by reference to a benevolent, if occluded, divine force from out of an overwhelming sense of bitterness and envy. 'For the Tall and the Stately are against me, but humiliation on humiliation is on my side',[36] he writes. Or: 'God consider thou me for the baseness of those I have served very highly'[37] – a verse which may single out Newbery who had stopped supporting Smart and may have been partly responsible for his incarceration. He buoyed himself up by noting 'For the Sin against the Holy Ghost is Ingratitude'[38] and declared, 'I preach the very GOSPEL of CHRIST without comment and with this weapon I shall slay envy'[39] mainly, one assumes, his own envy. Even Smart's benedictions of his associates, for all their investment in God's love, hint at resentment. Why, for instance, does he write, 'God bless Charles Mason and all Trinity College'[40] when, in turning to the surgeon, Middleton he can only declare, 'God be gracious to the immortal soul of Dr Middleton'[41] and pronounce less positively still on Christopher Anstey, 'Lord have mercy on Christopher Anstey and his kinsmen'?[42] Blessing, graciousness, mercy: it's hard to see these diminishing gradations of God's love as free from judgement.

Smart, then, attaches himself to a vitalist ontology in which rationalism and empiricism are marginalised, partly in flight from his everyday troubles, and partly in an attempt to deploy religio-magical forces against his enemies. In this move, he connects to a discourse of the patent medicine retailers. But finally *Jubilate Agno* does not belong to charlatanism. Its intensity and verbal brilliance, its profound sense of language as a material *thing*, along with its eccentricity and obscurity and privateness, locate it where calculation, pretension and deceit cease to operate, that is, where madness and writing meet. Nonetheless it also belongs to a moment where envy – for Smart, a sin – is being repudiated only to be almost mutely replaced, if not quite by resentment as a sociopolitical emotion, at least by a pervasive sense of personal injustice. It will be Edmund Burke in his *Reflections on the Revolution in France* who, in yet another return to charlatanism, will theorise and transparently politicise that mutation in relation to evangelicalism: insisting that religious enthusiasm often masks 'envy and malignity' towards 'distinction, and honours, and revenues' and that therefore it often speaks the 'patois of fraud'.[43] Smart's religion cannot be thought of simply as charlatanised and displaced social resentment, but it's not quite outside of it either.

Resentment: Goldsmith

Goldsmith is a more thoroughly secular writer, whose attempt to escape the culture of charlatanism takes him in the opposite direction to Smart's. As is often noted, he is the only author in the Anglophone canon to achieve lasting success in the novel, the drama and poetry, which he managed by contriving a twist to cultural conservatism. Most notably, he refused the temptations of sentimentalism as well as the kind of celebrity that Sterne pioneered, in which an author's public persona merges into that of his characters. But he did not turn to the satire tradition still maintained by his contemporary Churchill, for instance, and whose anti-charlatanism, as we have seen, was itself infected.

In the epilogue to *The Good Natur'd Man*, Goldsmith invokes quackery conventionally enough:

> As puffing quacks some caitiff wretch procure
> To swear the pill, or drop, has wrought a cure:
> Thus, on the stage, our playwrights still depend
> For Epilogues and Prologues on some friend,
> Who knows each art of coaxing up the town,
> And make full many a bitter pill go down.[44]

This draws Goldsmith into the net of charlatanism in familiar terms. He rejects the 'pill' that he is in the process of administering by demanding that the audience ignore his canvassing and 'blame where you must, be candid where you can' – that is, deploy the kind of hard but fair judgement that he enjoins in the play itself. His epilogue is, in fact, marketing the play by denying its own role as advertisement.

But this is not Goldsmith's habitual move. In his poem, *The Deserted Village*, for instance, he polemically resisted the social extension of market forces by drawing attention to the suffering caused by enclosures and emigration, that is, by capitalism's extension into agriculture. His politics are not, however, those of contemporary 'patriotism' – of the populist resistance to infringements upon English liberties. Rather, like his friend Johnson, if less assertively, he defends 'traditional', quasi-absolutist, rurally-based subordination against sentimentalism. But Goldsmith can also call upon a cross-cultural perspectivalism as a means of acquiring distance from the modern charlatanised, capitalised scene. After all, his first major foray into journalism was his essay-series *Chinese Letters* for Newbery's *Public Ledger*. Here a Chinese visitor to England casts a puzzled eye over the English social scene, revealing it as arbitrary and irrational in many aspects. It's a technique that, for all its problems and limits, allows Goldsmith to write as if he stands outside but not above his society, and to remove himself from the nationalism that was important to Smart for instance. It is as if the cosmopolitanism of a writer who began his career largely by exploiting the experiences of a youthful trip to Europe, enables the degree of detachment and scepticism required not just to avoid charlatanism but to embrace the old rurally-based social institutions and hierarchies.

In *The Vicar of Wakefield*, Goldsmith turns to a sunny objectivity able to contain both farce and melancholy, so as to mount a critique of benevolent sentimentalism. *The Vicar of Wakefield* is a retelling of the Job story: in it, a naïve, open-hearted rural parson with vague aspirations to primitive Christianity from the vantage point of a vulnerable, uxorious gentility, fails to act sufficiently sceptically for his own secular interests. He is beset by tribulation after tribulation, and ultimately finds himself in a debtor's prison, only to be miraculously rescued by the generosity of a member of the local landed gentry. One historical basis of sensibility's emergence, namely its displacement of institutionalised care of the poor, is here staged with exceptional lucidity. Somewhat similarly, in Goldsmith's first comedy, *The Good Natur'd Man*, young Mr Honeywood finds himself facing ruin because, in his benevolence, he falls prey to 'every sharper and coxcomb'.[45] But in this case, benevolence is presented more as a result of a fear of offending others than of innocence of heart. The message in both texts is that modern society is crammed with money-seeking charlatans whom the cult of sentimental good-feeling only encourages. Once again, it is adherence to traditional ways of life and hierarchies, and a rational scepticism, that can resist the tide of fraud, emotion and huckstering.

Goldsmith's reputation was at odds with his public values. It is almost as if he separates his private life and his textual values in resistance to the sentimentalism which, of course, hoped to join these two domains. He became famous for his private insecurity and enviousness. Anecdotes to this end are one of the bass-notes of Boswell's *Life of Johnson* as well as of more contemporaneous accounts. Goldsmith was resentful that, for all his fame and recognition, he was still required to write compilations, popular science books and so on for the booksellers in order to live something like a gentleman. He was especially bitter because, unlike Johnson, he was never granted a government pension. In sum, for all his success, he resented being viewed by many, as an Irish scribbler of little social note and dignity. But again this did not quite add up to *ressentiment* in that his personal envy and bitterness did not take a consciously politicised turn.

In other words, he was responding precisely to the gulf between his literary and social success. Indeed we can interpret his mode of subjectivity as at least in part a consequence of the contradictions involved in his rejection of sentimentalism and his appeal for traditional subordination from within the heart of the charlatanised book trade. Yet it seems as if Goldsmith, in mainly eluding the cultural economy of charlatanism, opened the way for another less nameable situation in which the writer's private affective life begins to exist not so much extrinsically to, or barred from, the work, but in systematic and dynamic contradiction to it. Goldsmith's personality negates his work almost algebraically: he personally possesses no defamiliarising eye; he is incapable of subordinating himself; he knows no tranquillity; charity is difficult for him. Yet he goes on preaching subordination, charity and traditional order.

In more abstract terms still: charlatanism dominated mid-eighteenth-century culture and began to lose its capacity to provide an interpretative grid in the century's last decades (despite the denunciatory rhetoric of a figure like Thomas Carlyle who is still partly organised around it) partly because the book and medicine trades move apart but also because relations between literature, politics and the market are reorganised so that literary writers, decreasingly reliant on patronage, can become primary agents in forming new political, social, cultural and affective structures. This capacity for agency decreases tensions between the commercial and cultural aspects of their work, and enables a new 'romantic' insistence on authenticity and expressiveness based on the requirement that a writer's life and their message cohere in terms which move past those of sentimentalism. That is another story, but it is worth gesturing to here since it helps us see that Goldsmith and Smart – so connected to the patent medicine trade and so unable to harmonise their lives and their works except, in the case of Smart, at the threshold of sanity – stand as exemplars of the disorganised and charlatanised literary scene out of which romanticism and *ressentiment* both emerged.

Notes

1. Hester Lynch Piozzi, *British Synonymy or, an Attempt at Regulating the Choice of Words in Familiar Conversation*, vol. 2 (London: G.G. and J. Robinson, 1794), pp. 174–5.
2. Roy Porter, *Quacks: Fakers & Charlatans in English Medicine* (Stroud: Tempus, 2000), p. 15.
3. I have found the following scholarship useful in relation to this topic: Jeremy Black, *The English Press in the Eighteenth Century* (London: Croom Helm, 1987); F. C. Doherty, *A Study in Eighteenth-Century Advertising Methods: The Anodyne Necklace* (Lewiston, NY: Edwin Mellen Press, 1992); John Feather, *The Provincial Book Trade in Eighteenth-Century England* (Cambridge; New York: Cambridge University Press, 1985); C. Y. Ferdinand, *Benjamin Collins and the Provincial Newspaper Trade in the Eighteenth Century* (Oxford and New York: Oxford University Press, 1997); Jan Fergus, *Provincial Readers in Eighteenth-Century England* (Oxford: Oxford University Press 2006); Peter Isaac, 'Charles Elliot and Spilsbury's Antiscorbuic Drops', *The Reach of Print: Making, Selling and Using Books*. Eds. Peter Isaac and Barry McKay (Delaware: Oak Knoll Press, 1998), pp. 157–74; A.S. Hargreaves, 'Some Later Seventeenth-Century Book Trade Activities', *Quadrat* 6 (1997): 3–6.
4. Jan Fergus and Ruth Portner, 'Provincial Bookselling in Eighteenth-Century England: the case of John Clay Reconsidered', *Studies in Bibliography*, 40 (1987): 157–63. Fergus, however, does not include cash-sales in her account of John Clay's sales, and it is not inconceivable that patent medicines were more often sold in this manner than books.
5. See Michael Harris, 'Periodicals and the Book Trade', *Development of the English Book Trade, 1700–1899* (Oxford: Oxford Polytechnic Press, 1981), p. 71 ff.
6. Hoh-cheung Mui and Lorna H. Mui, *Shops and Shopkeeping in Eighteenth-Century England* (Kingston, Ontario: McGill-Queen's University Press 1988), pp. 229–30.
7. The material in this paragraph is mainly drawn from Roger A. Hambridge, '"Empiricomany, an Infatuation in Favour of Empiricism or Quackery": The Socio-Economics of Eighteenth-Century Quackery', *Literature and Science and Medicine: Papers Read at the Clark Library Summer Seminar 1981* (Los Angeles: William Andrews Clark Memorial Library 1982), pp. 47–102, and Roy Porter's book on quacks cited above.
8. Charles Welsh, *A Bookseller of the Last Century: Being Some Account of the Life of John Newbery, and of the Books He Published : With a Notice of the Later Newberys* (London: Griffith, Farran, Okeden & Welsh 1885), p. 17 ff. See also the introduction to S. Roscoe, *John Newbery and His Successors, 1740–1814: A Bibliography* (Wormley, Hertfordshire: Five Owls Press, 1973). More information on the Powder is to be found in Bruce Dickens, 'Dr James's

Powder', *Life and Letters* 2 (1929): 36–47, and Frederick Pottle, 'James's Powder', Notes and Queries 149 (1925), pp. 11–12.

9. For *The World*, see numbers 24 and 176.
10. Christopher Smart, *The Annotated Letters of Christopher Smart*, eds Betty Rizzo and Robert Mahony (Carbondale: Southern Illinois University Press, 1991), p. 67.
11. See www.rpsgb.org.uk/members/pdfs/pr040426.pdf. Accessed 21 July 2008.
12. See Roger A. Hambridge, '"Empiricomany, an Infatuation in Favour of Empiricism or Quackery": The Socio-Economics of Eighteenth-Century Quackery', in *Literature and Science and Medicine: Papers Read at the Clark Library Summer Seminar 1981* (Los Angeles: William Andrews Clark Memorial Library 1982), pp. 80–2.
13. Walter Baker, *The affidavits and proceedings of Walter Baker, administrator to the late Baron Schwanberg, upon his petition presented to the King in Council, to vacate the patent obtained by Dr. Robert James for Schwanberg's powder, ... with a copy of the report, upon the hearing before the Attorney and Solicitor General, the sixth of December, 1752* (London: Printed, and there published for physicians, surgeons, and apothecaries, and all others whom it may concern, 1754).
14. See E. H. Mikhail (ed.), *Goldsmith: Interviews and Recollections* (Houndmills, Basingstoke and New York: Macmillan 1993), pp. 102–6 for a reprint of Haynes' pamphlet and notes on its context.
15. The formula was published in Donald Monro, *A treatise on medical and pharmaceutical chymistry, and the materia medica*, vol. 1 (London: T. Cadell 1788), p. 366, Monro having obtained it from the Chancery patent. For an interesting account of certain cultural aspects of the Victorian patent medicine trade, see Thomas Richards, *The Commodity Culture of Victorian England: Advertising and Spectacle, 1851–1914* (Stanford, CA: Stanford University Press, 1990), pp. 168–204.
16. William Zachs, *The First John Murray and the Late Eighteenth-Century London Book Trade: With a Checklist of His Publications* (Oxford: Oxford University Press 1998), p. 46.
17. Oliver Goldsmith, *The Vicar of Wakefield: A Tale Supposed to Be Written by Himself*, ed. Arthur Friedman (London: Oxford University Press, 1974), p. 91.
18. See John Rowe Townsend, *John Newbery and His Books: Trade and Plumb-Cake for Ever, Huzza!* (Metuchen, NJ: Scarecrow Press, 1994), pp. 117–27.
19. James Ralph, *The Case of Authors by Profession or Trade, Stated; with Regard to Booksellers, the Stage and the Public* (London: R. Griffiths, 1762), p. 18 ff.
20. John Nichols, *Literary Anecdotes of the Eighteenth Century: Comprizing Biographical Memoirs of William Bowyer, Printer, F. S. A., and Many of His Learned Friends: An Incidental View of the Progress and Advancement of Literature in This Kingdom During the Last Century: And Biographical Anecdotes of a Considerable Number of Eminent Writers and Ingenious Artists; with a Very Copious Index.* Vol. 3 (London: Printed for the author by Nichols, son, and Bentley 1812), p. 508.
21. For a portrait of Sterne as a mountebank, see *The Scheming Triumvirate*, 1760. British Museum Catalogue 3730.
22. Henry Fielding, *Joseph Andrews*, ed. Paul A. Scanlon. Peterborough, Ontario: Broadview Press, 2001), pp. 269–270.

23. Ralph M. Wardle, *Oliver Goldsmith* (Lawrence, Kansas: University of Kansas Press, 1957), p. 168.
24. Arthur Sherbo, *Christopher Smart*, pp. 222–3.
25. Cited in Lewis Mansfield Knapp, *Tobias Smollett, Doctor of Men and Manners* (Princeton: Princeton University Press, 1949), p. 167.
26. James Adair, *Essays on Fashionable Diseases. The dangerous Effects of Hot and Crouded [sic] rooms. The Cloathing of Invalids. Lady and Gentlemen Doctors. And on Quacks and Quackery* (London: T.P. Bateman n.d.), p. 189.
27. Arthur Sherbo, *Christopher Smart*, p. 80.
28. Charles Churchill, *The Poetical Works of Charles Churchill*, ed. Douglas Grant (Oxford: Clarendon Press, 1956), p. 75.
29. The mutuality of exchanges between sentimental benevolence and political-economy's critique of the poor laws is nowhere more clear than in the closing paragraph of Joseph Townsend's influential pamphlet *A Dissertation on the Poor Laws by a Well-wisher to Mankind* (1786).
30. Henry Mackenzie, *The Man of Feeling*, ed. Brian Vickers (Oxford: Oxford University Press, 1967), p. 18.
31. See William St Clair, *The Reading Nation in the Romantic Period* (Cambridge: Cambridge University Press, 2004), pp. 103–22.
32. For an interesting approach to Newbery, Smart and Goldsmith but with different interests than mine here, see Lori Branch, *Rituals of Spotaneity: Sentiment and Secularism from Free Prayer to Wordworth* (Waco, Texas: Baylor University Press 2006), pp. 135–75.
33. See Harriet Guest, *A Form of Sound Words: the Religious Poetry of Christopher Smart* (Oxford: Clarendon Press, 1989) for a pioneering account of this poem and its theopolitical setting.
34. Christopher Smart, 'Jubliate Agno', *Selected Poems*, eds Karina Williamson and Marcus Walsh (London: Penguin, 1990), Fragment B, no. 326. p. 85.
35. Ibid, Fragment D, no. 227, p. 140 and Fragment D, no. 200, p. 138.
36. Fragment B, no. 112, p. 62.
37. Fragment D, no. 223, p. 139.
38. Fragment B, no. 306, p. 83.
39. Fragment B, no. 9, p. 51.
40. Fragment B, no. 283, p. 81.
41. Fragment B, no. 282, p. 81.
42. Fragment D, no. 104, p. 130.
43. Edmund Burke, *Reflections on the Revolution in France*, ed. Leslie Mitchell (Oxford: Oxford University Press, 1993), p. 104.
44. Oliver Goldsmith, *The Miscellaneous Works of Oliver Goldsmith*, ed. David Masson (London: Macmillan, 1904), p. 641.
45. Goldsmith, *The Miscellaneous Works*, p. 610.

Index

Ex Libris

Arthur A. Francis

From a painting by J. B. Marston now in the collection of the Massachusetts Historical Society

STATE STREET, BOSTON, IN 1801

The Royal Exchange Tavern is shown on the right, with a stagecoach departing. The present location of the
State Street Trust Company is on the corner of Congress Street at lower left.